THIS IS
THE FAITH

"And he said to them: Go ye into the whole world, and preach the Gospel to every creature. He that believeth and is baptized shall be saved, but he that believeth not shall be condemned."

—Mark 16:15-16

OTHER WORKS BY THE AUTHOR

TERRIBLE AS AN ARMY
HOLINESS THROUGH MARY
LETTERS TO MURIEL
LETTERS TO MOLLY
A BLUE-PRINT FOR LAY ACTION
CALLING ALL APOSTLES
A PLAN OF CAMPAIGN
A DAILY THOUGHT
MARY, MOTHER OF THE CHURCH
PRIEST OF CHRIST
and, with F. S. Mitchell,
SOULS AT STAKE

THIS IS
THE FAITH

By

Canon Francis J. Ripley

PRIEST OF THE CATHOLIC MISSIONARY SOCIETY

Foreword by

The Most. Rev. Richard Downey, D.D., Ph.D., LL.D.

ARCHBISHOP OF LIVERPOOL

THIRD EDITION

"Wherefore, laying away all malice and all guile and dissimulations and envies, and all detractions, as newborn babes, desire the rational milk, without guile, that thereby you may grow unto salvation."
—1 Peter 2:1-2

TAN Books
An Imprint of Saint Benedict Press, LLC
Charlotte, North Carolina

Imprimatur for the 1951 edition:

Nihil Obstat: J. Canon Morgan, S.T.D.
                  Censor Librorum

Imprimatur: ✠ Richard
                  Archbishop of Liverpool
                  Liverpool, England
                  January 25, 1951

First published by The Birchley Hall Press, Billinge, Lancashire, England. Reprinted in 1952 by The Newman Press, Westminster, Maryland. Compact edition of the 1951 text published in 1960 by Guild Press, Inc. Updated edition copyright 1973 by Print Origination, Liverpool. New edition of the 1951 text, with some revision, expansion and minor updating by the Publisher, published in 2002 as the Third Edition by TAN Books, an Imprint of Saint Benedict Press, LLC.

ISBN 978-0-89555-642-4

Library of Congress Control No.: 98-61395

Cover illustration: "The Sermon on the Mount," 1877, by Carl Bloch (1834–1890). Photo of painting: Det Nationalhistoriske Museum på Frederiksborg, Hillerød, Denmark.

Printed and bound in the United States of America.

TAN Books
An Imprint of Saint Benedict Press, LLC
Charlotte, North Carolina
2013

3) Beatitudes (page 65)

This book is hereby dedicated to the
Virgin Mother of God, Mary Most Holy,
with filial affection and gratitude,
for the enlightenment and salvation
of souls through her intercession.

pages 188
Thru 203 Commandments of the Church

1st) To keep Sundays Holy and
to attend Mass. (Holy day of obligation)

2nd) Keep the days of fasting
and abstinence appointed by
the Church,

3rd) Go to Confession at least once
a year.

4th) Receive the blessed sacrament at
least once a year and that at Easter
time.

5th) Contribute to the support of the
Church.

6th) Obey the laws concerning marriage.
Page (202)

Foreword

For the past several years in Liverpool, principally under the auspices of the Legion of Mary, an opportunity has been given to an increasingly large number of non-Catholic enquirers to hear talks on Catholic faith and practice. Regular assemblies have been held in convents in various parts of the city, and the resulting conversions and the high percentage of attendance have more than justified the scheme. This work is ancillary to the Catholic Evidence Guild and caters for many who could not bring themselves to stand at street-corner meetings.

This Is the Faith is the substance of a series of such talks given in Liverpool by Father Francis J. Ripley over a period of three years. I am happy to commend it because I feel it will be of great use and encouragement to others engaged in similar work, to kindred movements and to enquirers themselves. It seems to me to be singularly propitious that it should be the first work to come from the Birchley Hall Press, thus preserving the spirit of the work done by the secret press at Birchley Hall in less happy times.

✠ Richard
Archbishop of Liverpool

Archbishop's House
Liverpool, England

January 25, 1951
The Conversion of St. Paul

"Ignorance of religion is one of the greatest evils in the modern world!
pg. 68/69
Faith is man's greatest gift.

Publisher's Preface

When Our Lord commissioned the Apostles just before His Ascension into Heaven, He commanded them: **"Go ye into the whole world, and preach the gospel to every creature. He that believeth and is baptized, shall be saved: but he that believeth not shall be condemned."** (*Mark* 16:15-16).*

In our era we daily witness a paradox . . . and many of us moreover are living it. The paradox is this: The vast majority of people today revere Jesus Christ, respect Him more than anyone else who ever lived, honor Him in fact, in many cases, as God-made-man. And yet most people do not know Him; they do not know the many crucial things He has said; they do not know what He expects them to believe or what He expects them to do. Consider for a moment some of His startling statements:

"Without me, you can do nothing." (*John* 15:5). "I am the way, and the truth, and the life." (*John* 14:6). "No man cometh to the Father, but by me." (*John* 14:6). "I am come that they may have life, and may have it more abundantly." (*John* 10:10). "Except you eat the flesh of the Son of man, and drink his blood, you shall not have life in you." (*John* 6:54).

These arresting statements by Our Lord are cited because many people do not know them; or if they have heard them or read them, they have forgotten their import; or further, if they are familiar with them, they misconstrue their meaning by giving them a wrong interpretation. Our Lord was good and gentle, "meek and humble of heart" (*Matt.* 11:29), but He also said some very strong things relative to our salvation, and these words we should know well and heed.

Consider now some of His powerful statements in their larger context: "I am the vine; you the branches: he that abides in me, and I in him, the same beareth much fruit, **for without me you can do**

---

*All bold face in the Scriptural quotes in this preface and throughout the book has been added for emphasis.

nothing. If anyone abide not in me, he shall be cast forth as a branch, and shall wither, and they shall gather him up, and cast him into the fire, and he burneth. If you abide in me, and my words abide in you, you shall ask whatever you will, and it shall be done unto you. In this is my Father glorified; that you bring forth very much fruit, **and become my disciples**. As the Father hath loved me, I also have loved you. Abide in my love. If you keep my commandments, you shall abide in my love; as I also have kept my Father's commandments, and do abide in his love. These things I have spoken to you, that my joy may be in you, and your joy may be filled. This is my commandment, that you love one another, as I have loved you . . . . You are my friends **if you do the things that I command you . . . If I had not done among them the works that no other man hath done, they would not have sin;** but now they have both seen and hated both me and my Father." (*John* 15:5-14, 24). In other words, if we live (abide) in Christ, we will be fruitful in spiritual matters. But if we cut ourselves off from Christ, we wither and die and are lost eternally.

In another place, Our Lord has said: "I am the bread of life. Your fathers did eat manna in the desert, and are dead. This is the bread which cometh down from heaven; that if any man eat of it, he may not die. **I am the living bread which came down from heaven. If any man eat of this bread, he shall live forever;** and the bread that I will give, is my flesh, for the life of the world . . . **Amen, amen I say unto you: Except you eat the flesh of the Son of man, and drink his blood [in Holy Communion], you shall not have life in you. He that eateth my flesh, and drinketh my blood, hath everlasting life:** and I will raise him up in the last day. For my flesh is meat indeed: and my blood is drink indeed. He that eateth my flesh and drinketh my blood abideth in me and I in him. As the living Father hath sent me, and I live by the Father; so he that eateth me, the same shall also live by me. This is the bread that came down from heaven. Not as your fathers did eat manna, and are dead. **He that eateth this bread shall live forever.**" (*John* 6:48-59). What Our Lord refers to here is the Sacrament of Holy Eucharist, or Holy Communion, though for reasons of His own, He did not make this immediately clear to those who heard Him. But we should notice especially the repetition and reiteration Jesus uses, so there is no doubt He means what He said. After these words even some of His disciples ceased to walk with Him, but He did not deter them from leaving. He obviously, therefore, meant literally what He said!

To Nicodemus, "a ruler of the Jews" who "came to Jesus by night," "Jesus answered and said to him: Amen, amen I say to thee, unless a man be born again, he cannot see the kingdom of God . . ." (*John* 3:3). Nicodemus was perplexed and asked: "How can a man be born when he is old? Can he enter a second time into his mother's womb and be born again?" To this Jesus answered: **"Amen, amen I say to thee, unless a man be born again of water and the Holy Spirit [i.e., receive the Sacrament of Baptism], he cannot enter into the kingdom of God."** (*John* 3:4-5). In other words, without receiving the Sacrament of Baptism a person cannot be saved.

Again, Our Lord has said: "As Moses lifted up the [brazen] serpent in the desert, so must the Son of man [Jesus] be lifted up [crucified]: **That whosoever believeth in him, may not perish; but may have life everlasting.** For God so loved the world, as to give his only begotten Son; that **whosoever believeth in him, may not perish,** but may have life everlasting. For God sent not his Son [Jesus] into the world, to judge the world, but that the world may be saved by him. He that believeth in him is not judged. But he that doth not believe, is already judged: because he believeth not in the name of the only begotten Son of God. And this is the judgment: **because the light is come into the world, and men loved darkness rather than the light: for their works were evil.** For everyone that doth evil hateth the light, and cometh not to the light, that his works may not be reproved. But he that doth truth, cometh to the light, that his works may be made manifest, because they are done in God." (*John* 3:14-21). In other words, Jesus is saying that faith in Him and in His teaching is necessary for salvation. And as a proof that what He says is true, He has worked many miracles. Also, His very words are a "testimony to the truth," (*John* 18:37), "the light . . . come into the world," for those who are of the truth to acknowledge, to believe and to follow. If people do not accept His teaching, it is because they are not of the truth, are living in sin, and prefer to continue in the darkness of error.

Again: "Then Jesus said to those Jews who believed him: If you continue in my word [do what I say; obey my commandments], you shall be my disciples indeed. And you shall know the truth, and the truth shall make you free." (*John* 8:31-32). Notice the context of these famous words: If **first** you are good, **then** you will start to know the truth, which will then set you free. In other words, we must **first** believe what He says to be true, **live** by His teachings and **correct our actions,** and then we will really see the truth and we shall be free from the bondage of sin.

At another time He declared: "Amen, amen I say to you: He that entereth not by the door into the sheepfold, but climbeth up another way, the same is a thief and a robber. But he that entereth in by the door is the shepherd of the sheep . . . and the sheep hear his voice: and he calleth his own sheep by name, and leadeth them out. And when he hath let out his own sheep, he goeth before them: and the sheep follow him, because they know his voice. But a stranger they follow not, but fly from him, because they know not the voice of strangers. **Amen, amen I say to you, I am the door of the sheep . . . I am the door. By me, if any man enter in, he shall be saved:** and he shall go in, and go out, and shall find pastures. The thief cometh not but for to steal, and to kill and destroy. **I am come that they may have life, and may have it more abundantly.** I am the good shepherd. The good shepherd gives his life for his sheep . . . I am the good shepherd; and I know mine, and mine know me. As the Father knoweth me, and I know the Father: and I lay down my life for my sheep. **And other sheep I have, that are not of this fold: them also must I bring, and they shall hear my voice, and there shall be one fold and one shepherd.**" (*John* 10:1-5, 7, 9-11, 14-16). Here again is another analogy or comparison, this time of Himself to the door of a sheepfold or corral, which represents Heaven. Through Jesus Christ only shall we enter Heaven, for He is the "door" through which all must pass to get there. His "sheep," or followers, know this. "And other sheep" (people) He has who are not members of His "fold" or Church, whom He intends to bring in, that there may be one fold (one Church) and one shepherd (Christ).

Again: "Pilate therefore said to him: Art thou a king then? Jesus answered: **Thou sayest that I am a king. For this was I born, and for this came I into the world; that I should give testimony to the truth. Everyone that is of the truth, heareth my voice.**"

(*John* 18:37). In other words, if we have heard Our Lord's message and do not follow Him as His disciples, we are not "of the truth," not living correctly.

"He that receiveth you [His disciples], receiveth me; and he that receiveth me, receiveth him that sent me." (*Matt.* 10:40). "He that heareth you [His disciples], heareth me; and he that despiseth you, despiseth me; and he that despiseth me, despiseth him that sent me." (*Luke* 10:16). **"Amen, amen I say unto you, that he who heareth my word, and believeth him that sent me, hath life everlasting; and cometh not into judgment, but is passed from death to life."** (*John* 5:24). Jesus uses His followers (Apostles, Popes, bishops, priests—the official teachers of the Church—but also lay people, and even books) to spread His word. If we do not hear them, we do not hear Him, or His heavenly Father, who sent Him to us; it will be the same for us at the time of Judgment as if we heard Jesus personally and had rejected His teaching.

"Not everyone that saith to me, Lord, Lord, shall enter into the kingdom of heaven: but he that doth the will of my Father who is in heaven, he shall enter into the kingdom of heaven. Many will say to me in that day: Lord, Lord, have we not prophesied in thy name, and cast out devils in thy name, and done many miracles in thy name? **And then will I profess unto them, I never knew you: depart from me, you that work iniquity."** (*Matt.* 7:21-23). In other words, we have to **believe** what He requires us to believe and **do** everything that He wants us to do, not just call ourselves Christians.

"Jesus saith to them: But whom do you say that I am? Simon Peter answered and said: Thou art Christ, the Son of the living God. And Jesus answering, said to him: Blessed art thou, Simon Bar-Jona [son of John]: because flesh and blood hath not revealed it to thee, but my Father who is in heaven. And I say to thee: **That thou art Peter** [Peter means 'rock']; **and upon this rock I will build my church, and the gates of hell shall not prevail against it. And I will give to thee the keys of the kingdom of heaven. And whatsoever thou shalt bind upon earth, it shall be bound also in heaven: and whatsoever thou shalt loose on earth, it shall be loosed also in heaven."** (*Matt.* 16:15-19). It is obvious from these words that Jesus intended to found a Church, to make Peter (and by implication his successors) its visible head, and that the powers of Hell would never be able to overthrow it. Therefore, we should look for that Church which goes back in history to St. Peter. It has to be nearly 2,000 years old! Plus, it has to have suffered persecution and still be suffering persecution from the powers of Hell.

"Everyone therefore that heareth these my words, and doth them, shall be likened to a wise man that built his house [his spiritual life, his soul] upon a rock, and the rain fell, and the floods came, and the winds blew, and they beat upon that house, and it fell not, for it was founded on a rock. And everyone that heareth these my words and doth them not, shall be like a foolish man that built his house [his spiritual life] upon the sand, and the rain fell, and the floods came, and the winds blew, and they beat upon that house, and it fell, and great was the fall thereof." (*Matt.* 7:24-27). If we harken to Jesus' words and do as He says, we are building our spiritual life on a rock-solid foundation. If we do not, we are building our spiritual house, as it were, upon sand. It will not stand the scrutiny of Almighty God on Judgment Day. Further, the implication is that we should build upon "rock," the same Rock (St. Peter) as that on which Christ built His Church.

To repeat the first quotation cited at the beginning of this Preface, when Our Lord commissioned the Apostles just before His Ascension into Heaven, He commanded them: **"Go ye into the whole world, and preach the gospel to every creature. He that believeth and is baptized, shall be saved: but he that believeth not shall be condemned."** (*Mark* 16:15-16). In other words, He gave the Apostles the Gospel ("good news"), which is none other than the "Faith of God" spoken of by St. Paul (*Romans* 3:3), which was delivered by Jesus Christ, the God-man, to be His testimony to the truth (cf. *John* 18:37), and to be the one faith that was to bring all mankind into a single fold (*John* 10:16)—one people of God—a single Church founded on St. Peter as its first head, that is to last till the End of Time, in which His followers can "eat His flesh and drink His blood." (Cf. *John* 6:31-59). Those who believe this "Faith of God," are baptized into Christ's Church, and do what Our Lord teaches, will be saved eternally, and those who do not will be lost eternally. (Cf. *Mark* 16:15-16).

But again herein is the paradox mentioned at the start: Jesus was quite clear about the fact that one's eternal salvation requires belief in His teaching—in "the faith of Our Lord Jesus Christ" (*James* 2:1)—in being baptized into and in adhering to that faith. The faith He was referring to is not any one of a number of faiths that we are "free" to follow, all leading more or less in the same direction toward God—but **one** Faith—as St. Paul says: "I, therefore, a prisoner in the Lord, beseech you that you walk worthy of the vocation in which you are called, with all humility and mildness, with patience, supporting one another in charity, **careful to keep the unity of the Spirit in the bond of peace: One body and one Spirit, as you are called in one hope of your calling; one Lord, one faith, one baptism, one God and Father of all,** who is above all, and through all, and in us all." (*Ephesians* 4:1-6). It is obvious from this passage of Sacred Scripture that there is only one true Church, only one true Faith, only one religion, only one People of God, only one Mystical Body of Christ. In every science and applied technology people all, automatically, recognize the unity of truth—for there is only one truth. It is the same in religion.

However, people in our time still adhere to a variety of religious beliefs. Even within what is called Christianity there is a wide divergence of belief. Yet, from Scripture we can see quite clearly that our faith should be one, the same from person to person, all mankind adhering to the same common set of beliefs, as given to us by Jesus Christ, **and by Our Lord's own command, we should all be officially baptized into this faith** (cf. *Mark* 16:15-16), baptized into His Church, which will last till the End of Time. Yet paradoxically and despite the clarity of this issue in Scripture, division of religious belief continues to exist.

And that is why Canon Ripley has written this present book— to point the way to that Faith which we must all believe in order to be saved: **"THIS IS THE FAITH"** he is saying. **"Here it is for all to see,** and to understand, and to accept, and to adhere to, and to join, that indeed 'there shall be one fold and one shepherd.' (*John* 10:16). It is not hard to see it," the author is implying, "if you look at it seriously from several different perspectives." When examined critically from a number of viewpoints, only the Roman Catholic Faith (including the Eastern Catholic Churches in union with Rome) stands up to the criteria of being the one, true Faith referred to by St. Paul. Only the Roman Catholic Church is historically founded by Christ on St. Peter and the other Apostles; only the Roman Catholic Church has a holy doctrine, from its holy Heavenly Founder, and produces holy people in every age; only the Roman Catholic Church teaches the "entire" faith of Christ (*katholicos* in Greek, from which we get the word "Catholic" or universal), and teaches it universally throughout the world and throughout all time; only the Roman Catholic Church is *one* in its teaching, *one* in its practice, *one* in its government, *one* in its people, and *one* in its head—the Pope in Rome. Only the Roman Catholic Church makes complete common-sense—when viewed from all these perspectives.

"It is not hard to see," Canon Ripley says, "once you view the evidence. All facts point to the truth that **This Is the Faith!**" And he has written this book by that title to show us the way.

The Catholic Faith is enormous; it cannot be comprehended at a single glance. It must be studied with prayerful patience—over time—before the picture of it becomes clear to one's mind. And Canon Ripley has painted in *This Is the Faith* perhaps the best picture in words of the Catholic Faith for popular reading that has ever been done in modern times. Those unfamiliar with Catholicism may think the Catholic Faith is very intellectual, but even St. Peter, in his first Epistle, calls the Catholic Faith "rational," i.e., filled with intellectual content—*easy* intellectual content, to be sure, but intellectual all the same, a content in which we are to grow: **"As newborn babes, desire the rational milk without guile [deceitfulness], that thereby you may grow unto salvation."** (*1 Peter* 2:2). The Faith is like "milk," food for babies, easy to digest, but "rational," intellectual, all the same. And we are to grow in it by imbibing more and more of it. Plus, it is easy to comprehend—if we are free from guile.

No one could possibly learn and understand all the teachings of the Catholic Church at a mere introduction; **time and some effort are required to absorb it sufficiently just to accept it**. And that is why Canon Ripley's book is rather *extensive*. It is by no means *exhaustive* of the Catholic Faith, but it is *thorough*, especially for beginners and those whose Catholic education has been incomplete. A fairly large book is necessary to cover all the essential points which even the beginner needs to know before he can intelligently join the Church. The reader needs to accept this as a given. But the very extensiveness and complexity of the Catholic Faith are only further proofs of its truth.

The layman to every field is usually amazed at how complex the subject under study actually is, once he begins to examine it. For example, though in principle almost identical to its original, simple prototypes, the modern automobile is really quite a complex machine. (Just look under the hood.) Another example is good health, which depends upon only a few basic, simple principles; but just examine the complexity of the body as described in the medical texts which every doctor must master. Likewise and relative to the Faith, as the famous Catholic historian Hilaire Belloc has observed, there is a commonality among all the Christian heresies, namely, that they attempt to simplify the Catholic Faith, which though simple in its essence, is highly wrought and complex—this to make it easier for their adherents to understand. He notes that these many heretical "isms" may seem to work for a while, but they ultimately break down when employed to solve the spiritual problems of actual human beings, for they are missing many elements of True Religion. They just cannot stand up to reality, which concerns itself with a highly complex physical, intellectual and spiritual creature—the human person.

The many Bible quotes cited at the beginning of this preface have been selected purposely to capture the reader's attention and to emphasize that "the good and gentle Jesus" said many very strong things. Yes, His words were also often filled with tenderness and consolation, e.g., "Come to me, all you that labor and are burdened, and I will refresh you." (*Matt.* 11:28). "Where there are two or three gathered together in my name, there am I in the midst of them." (*Matt.* 18:20). Yet the passages cited earlier in this preface are intended to demonstrate that perhaps most of us are not so familiar with Our Lord's entire doctrine as we should be.

Catholic theologians explain, for example, that Heaven (the Beatific Vision of God Himself) is above and beyond what man can ever achieve working through his own nature and by his own efforts—it is not his "natural" destiny. He has no right to Heaven by reason of his nature only. Therefore, to reach Heaven, man needs the help of Almighty God, **to lift him up to that level**—the level called in theology, the "supernatural." Understanding this basic theological principle, however, we can begin to realize the meaning of many of the cryptic, pungent sayings of Our Lord, such as, "Without me you can do nothing." (*John* 15:5). "I am the way, and the truth and the life." (*John* 14:6). "No man cometh to the Father, but by me." (*John* 14:6).

In effect, what Our Lord is saying is this: "Without me, you can do nothing **of supernatural value**." "No man cometh to the Father but by me because I [Christ speaking to us] **have provided the absolutely necessary supernatural means to enable you to get there**." "You must all come via **Me** [Jesus]—**with my help!**" That is why He says, "I am the door," etc.

The present book was first published in 1951, and it went through a number of printings by 1970. But much has happened since 1951: There has been an Ecumenical Council of the Catholic Church (Vatican Council II—1962-1965), and many subsequent changes in the disciplines of the Church have occurred. This book was the first publication of Birchley Hall Press in England, and it bears all the hallmarks of a book that was either never edited by an experienced publisher or was given only a light "copy editing" job. It is for these two reasons that I have presumed the task of actually editing the book of a deceased author. Were it to have been merely reprinted as it was originally written, it would 1) have caused a certain amount of confusion for not mentioning current Church disciplines, and 2) not have reflected the degree of persuasiveness which I believe it now has. Indeed, it was persuasive in its original state, but it lacked the thoroughness it now possesses.

Canon Ripley has written here a fairly large book, but one can detect in his original text an attempt to keep it as brief as possible. However admirable this effort may have been, it thus led to certain defects in the text, namely, that some topics were introduced, but then not sufficiently developed to be perfectly clear to the uninformed reader. I have attempted to rectify this type of problem by fleshing out the subjects wherever they appeared to be inadequately developed.

Overall, **Canon Ripley's entire book is still here**, in exactly the sequence and format in which he originally published it. **It is just that there is *more!*** It has been added to, augmented, clarified, fleshed out, and as mentioned, current Church disciplines have been included. Only in the last chapter—"Some Catholic Social Principles"—were excisions made and nothing much new added. This is due to the fact that much of the author's original chapter discussed economic solutions obviously with the post-World War II British model in mind, which included significant state ownership of basic industries. Much of what was done in Britain economically in the 1940's and 1950's has subsequently been changed, so mention of this was dropped from the present book. And besides, these "solutions" did not pertain to basic Catholic social teaching—which main elements, as Canon Ripley expounded them, are still present in this edition.

In one case, that of the Catholic Church's teaching that "there is no salvation outside the Church," we replaced the explanation with a quotation from Pope Pius XII's encyclical *The Mystical Body of Christ* (1943). And in the chapter on marriage, we expanded the section on birth prevention to express more clearly the Church's traditional teaching. We edited the section on Limbo, also, to express more clearly the Church's position. Moreover, in discussing "General Confession," the author was obviously hurried and overly brief; this section was completely rewritten and amplified. Finally, we added an Afterword.

Throughout the book, I have tried to maintain a sufficient exactness in the wording of the questions and answers at the chapter beginnings to reflect the wording of the original book, plus that of British catechisms. Yet some of these questions and answers have been slightly rephrased—in their expression only—to reflect also a similarity to U.S. catechisms. American spellings have been used throughout the book, except for Our "Saviour" and perhaps a few other words. From beginning to end and at all times I have corrected punctuation and any clumsy or loose phrases. These types of corrections are typical of any competent editing job. Also, some reformatting of the paragraphs has been done, especially where there have been numbered lists of items; usually the various items in a list have been started on a new line.

It bears repeating that **Canon Ripley's original book is still**

basically here in its entirety, save for the changes mentioned above; and it is even in the same format that he created. However, it is my opinion—and that of a priest-theologian who consulted on the book—that the work is now vastly improved. The size of type, the new typography, the expanded topics, all combine to make it a far more persuasive book and a far more user-friendly one than it was originally, so that the present version can truly be called a Third Edition. (In 1973, the author issued a Second Edition, substantially altered, but it did not enjoy anywhere near the circulation or popularity of his First Edition. For this edition, therefore, we have retained the very successful First Edition and have expanded it, as explained.) I would hope that were Canon Ripley alive today and had he co-operated on this Third Edition of *This Is the Faith*, that he would have heartily endorsed all the changes and would have given them his stamp of approval. As it is, I would hope that he is smiling down from Heaven in approval that a new and current edition of his book *This Is the Faith* is now once more available to help people find "the way, and the truth and the life." (*John* 14:6).

Publisher
May 9, 2002
Feast of the Ascension

Contents

With Summaries of the Chapters

THIS IS
THE FAITH

"And other sheep I have, that are not of this fold: them also must I bring, and they shall hear my voice, and there shall be one fold and one shepherd."

—John 10:16

Chapter 1

About God

Who made you? *God made me.*

Who is God? *God is the supreme Being, who alone exists of Himself and is infinite in all perfections.*

Why is God called Almighty? *God is called "Almighty" because He can do all things: "With God all things are possible." (Matt. 19:26)*

Why is God called the Creator of Heaven and Earth? *God is called the "Creator of Heaven and Earth" because He made Heaven and Earth and all things out of nothing, by His word.*

Did God have a beginning? *God had no beginning: He always was, He is, and He always will be.*

Where is God? *God is everywhere.*

Does God know and see all things? *God knows and sees all things, even our most secret thoughts.*

Does God have a body? *God has no body; He is a spirit.*

Is there only one God? *There is only one God.*

How must we love God? *We must love God above all things.*

How must we learn to love God? *We must learn to love God by begging God to teach us to love Him: "O my God, teach me to love Thee."*

What will the love of God lead us to do? *The love of God will lead us often to think how good God is, often to speak to Him in our hearts, and always to seek to please Him.*

ONE of the hardest things for thinking people to understand is the present-day neglect of God. It is not that men have ceased

1

to believe in God, but that they have become completely indifferent to Him. Hence, it is very necessary to review the arguments for His existence and to discuss His nature and His claims.

God's existence can be proved in many ways, but the simplest is that known as the argument from design. Not only must a watch come from a watchmaker, but every part of it must have had a designer who knew how to make it. Or, imagine a man entering one of the great stores in London or New York, Harrod's or Macy's, and on asking for the manager, being asked: "How did you know there is a manager?" Such a counter-question would rightly be taken as evidence of insanity.

The universe is full of design, infinitely more wonderful than the watch or the great store. Obviously, then, it must have had a designer with tremendous intelligence. More than that—even matter itself is designed. Therefore, not only the universe, but even the very matter of which the universe is made must have had a designer. Another word for the Designer of matter is the "Creator."

The whole universe can be compared to a giant "Meccano" outfit, or an Erector set, in which the atoms are the various "meccano" parts. They can be fitted together to make all the countless substances useful to man.

Matter did not exist forever. It was created, and the Creator is called God.

The story is told of a famous astronomer who was being visited by a scientist friend who claimed to be an atheist. The latter was admiring a working-model of the solar-system that stood upon a table; by turning the handle, the planets could be made to revolve in their respective orbits around the sun.

"Very ingenious, indeed," he remarked. "Who made it?"

"Oh, nobody particular."

"Tell me; I want to know—who made it?"

"Nobody made it. It just happened—it made itself."

The scientist realized he was being taught a lesson and became annoyed.

"You are trying to be funny," he said.

"How silly you are!" exclaimed the astronomer. "You can't believe that this little model made itself, and yet you can believe that the real sun and moon and earth, planets and stars, and everything else in the vast universe just came into existence without any Maker!"

What God has told us

God has spoken to us through Holy Scripture. Therein He has revealed much about Himself. For example:

His existence: "The fool hath said in his heart: 'There is no God.'" (*Ps.* 13:1). "For the invisible things of him, from the creation of the world, are clearly seen, being understood by the things that are made; his eternal power also, and divinity: so that they are inexcusable." (*Rom.* 1:20).

His name: At the Burning Bush, God told Moses He was to be the deliverer of the Israelites. Moses said: "If they [the Israelites] should say to me: What is his name? What shall I say to them?" God said to Moses: **I Am Who Am**. He said: Thus shalt thou say to the children of Israel: **He Who Is** hath sent me to you." (*Exodus* 3:13-14). By this God reveals that His essence is subsistent being itself, that He is not dependent on any being for His existence, but subsists in His own right. Everything else has but a borrowed being; that is, all else is dependent on Him for its existence.

His nature: God is a pure spirit, incorruptible. (*John* 4:24; *Rom.* 1:23). There is no composition of any description in God. As St. Augustine put it: "What He has, He is."

He is unchangeable: "For I am the Lord and I change not." (*Mal.* 3:6).

He is eternal: **He had no beginning and will never cease to be**: "Before the mountains were made, or the earth and the world was formed; from eternity and to eternity thou art God." (*Ps.* 89:2). "Before Abraham was made, I am." (*John* 8:58).

He is everywhere; **He knows and sees all things**: "Neither is there any creature invisible in his sight: but all things are naked and open to his eyes . . ." (*Heb.* 4:13). "For in him we live, and move, and are." (*Acts* 17:28). *Psalm* 138 is a good meditation on the omnipresence of God.

He possesses each and every perfection in an infinite, unlimited degree: "They shall speak of the magnificence of the glory of thy holiness." (*Ps.* 144:5); "Neither is he served with men's hands, as though he needed anything; seeing it is he who giveth to all life, and breath, and all things." (*Acts* 17:25).

He is one: Not only is He one in that He is absolutely indivisible, but also He is one in that there can be no other like Himself, no other God. "The Lord, our God, is one Lord." (*Deut.* 6:4). "I alone am, and there is no other God besides Me." (*Deut.* 32:39).

He is holy: For the angels cry out ceaselessly in His honor, "Holy, holy, holy." (*Is.* 6:3).

He is love and Our Father: St. John defines Him as love: "God is charity." (*1 John* 4:16—"charity" is divine love). Our Lord tells us to pray to God as "Our Father" and continually refers to Him by this title. "Is He not thy Father, that hath possessed thee, and made thee, and created thee?" (*Deut.* 32:6). "Can a woman forget her infant, so as not to have pity on the son of her womb? And if she should forget, yet will not I forget thee." (*Is.* 49:15).

He is just and merciful: Thou art just, O Lord: and Thy judgment is right." (*Ps.* 118:137). "The Lord is sweet to all: and his tender mercies are over all his works." (*Ps.* 144:9).

He is all powerful: "For all things are in Thy power and there is none that can resist Thy Will." (*Esther* 13:9).

He cares for all things, even the smallest, by His providence: "He made the little and the great, and He hath equally care of all." (*Wis.* 6:8). "Good things and evil, life and death, poverty and riches, are from God." (*Ecclus.* 11:14, cf. *Matt.* 6:26-32).

He wants all men to be saved: "Who will have all men to be saved, and to come to the knowledge of the truth." (*1 Tim.* 2:4).

"The study of God is the only study which can be called wisdom in the fullest sense of the word." (St. Thomas Aquinas).

Evil: Sometimes it is objected that the presence of evil or disorder in the world proves that the world was not created by God. That is no more true than the fact that one unmade bed in a dormitory containing nineteen beds which have been made proves that there was no bed-maker there. It would be obvious that for some reason known to himself the person who made the nineteen beds left the other one unmade. So it was that, when God made the world, for reasons best known to Himself, He permitted evil to exist in it. Of course, evil is not a *positive* thing, which can be the result of a direct creative act. It is the absence of good, or of due order, just as a shadow is the absence of light. Men always tend to exaggerate the amount of evil present in the world. Death, for instance, is really the beginning of life; suffering is always a grace.

The facts are that God exists and that He is Goodness, Wisdom, Love and Power. He knows everything; our knowledge is very limited. Therefore, it is absurd for us to sit in judgment on God. Reason alone tells us that He is to be trusted by us. Revelation tells us how He died for love of us, embracing the most bitter suffering in the process. We must bow down in faith, trust and love before His Will.

"**God Almighty would in no way permit evil in His works were He not so omnipotent and good that even out of evil He could work good.**" (St. Augustine).

Evolution: It has been suggested that Evolution, as accepted by some modern scientists, rules out the fact of direct creation of the universe by God. That is not so. Evolution refers to the development of matter, not to its making. Before matter could evolve, it must have come into existence. If ever there were nothing in existence, nothing could exist now. Evolution merely describes one of the ways in which God **may** have acted; it deals with the **development** of design, not with the **creation** of the material designed. It is anything but an argument against the existence of God and, if limited to material things, does not appear to contradict Catholic teaching. Obviously spirit cannot evolve from matter—the soul of man, for instance, could not evolve from a beast without a spiritual soul. The Church has always maintained that God creates the human soul. [However, not only is there no proof for Evolution, but the evidence from DNA would indicate that Evolution **cannot** occur. Cf. *Creation Rediscovered*, TAN, 1999. —Publisher 2002.]

We must love God

Man's highest activity is love, and there is no nobler object of his love than God. So the First and Greatest Commandment is: "Thou shalt love the Lord thy God with thy whole heart, and with thy whole soul, and with thy whole mind." (*Matt.* 22:37).

Nothing is more important, then, than that. "**Would that I had as many hearts as there are grains of sand in the depths of the**

seas to love Thee with, O God." (St. Augustine).

"Love alone maketh heavy burdens light and beareth in like balance things pleasant and unpleasant; it beareth a heavy burden and feeleth it not, and maketh bitter things to be savoury and sweet . . . Nothing is sweeter than love, nothing higher, nothing stronger, nothing larger, nothing more joyful, nothing fuller, nor anything better in Heaven or in Earth; for love descendeth from God, and may not rest finally in anything lower than God." (*Imitation of Christ*, Bk. 3, Chap. 5).

So many men today expect God to tolerate from them contempt, insubordination, disobedience and neglect, such as they would never tolerate from their own children. In Scripture God asks: "If then I be a Father, where is My honour? And if I be a Master, where is My fear?" (*Mal.* 1:6).

Failure to love God can only result in tragedy for the individual, either in this world or in the next.

God's claims

"Can't I do what I like with my own life?" What a frequent objection that is! Yet, how silly!

At a beach sand-building competition, a boy and a girl had finished a magnificent castle, when they then wandered around to look at the efforts of other children. On returning, they found that another boy had occupied their castle and was adding what he considered to be improvements.

"What are you doing? That's our castle!" they exclaimed.

"No, it's mine. You left it; I found it."

"But it's *our* castle!"

"What do you mean, yours?"

It's *our* castle—**we made it**, and we can do what we like with it because we made it."

Of course, everybody said the boy and girl were right; the intruder was turned out, and they won the prize.

God made me out of nothing, and so I belong to Him. I am His to do with what He likes.

Thus, life is not our own. God made us; God owns us. We have no rights against God. He has the right to lay down all the conditions as to how we must use the life He has given to us. We are not our own property. We belong to God. He has the right to do just what He likes with us.

Our duty

Our duties to God can be summed up as follows:

1. **Adoration**: We owe him adoration because He is goodness itself and we owe Him our homage and love.

2. **Contrition**: When we have sinned, we have not been good to God, and we must tell Him we are sorry.

3. **Thanksgiving**: For all He has done for us and will continue to do for us we owe Him our profound thanks.

4. **Supplication**: Because we are totally dependent on His graces to be or to do good, we need to pray to Him for these graces and aids.

NOTE: The acronym **ACTS** stands for and reminds us of our four-fold duty toward God: viz., **Adoration, Contrition, Thanksgiving** and **Supplication.**

God wants our loving service. He has made us free in order to love Him or to reject Him. He does not want the service of a human machine. We are able to resist His rights, but of course it is wrong for us to do so. Another name for resistance to God is **sin**. It may appear to give temporary happiness, but in the end sin is what takes us from our Maker, and it can only bring us sorrow.

"Thou hast made us for Thyself, O Lord, and our hearts are restless until they rest in Thee." (St. Augustine).

We must dedicate to God all our being—our **intelligence,** by striving to know Him more and more, especially through prayer, and our **will**, by daily increasing in love for Him, which is proved by our obedience to His Commandments and the other manifestations of His will.

St. John Vianney, the Curé of Ars (1786-1859), was walking through the fields one spring day with a friend. The trees were full of birds and the air was full of their singing. The Curé stopped to listen. "Ah, little birds!" he said. "You were created to sing, and you are singing. Man was created to love God, and he does not love Him."

Chapter 2

What Is Man?

Why did God make you? *God made me to know Him, to love Him and to serve Him in this world, and to be happy with Him forever in the next.*

To whose image and likeness did God make you? *God made me to His own image and likeness.*

Is this likeness to God in your body, or in your soul? *This likeness to God is chiefly in my soul.*

How is your soul like to God? *My soul is like to God because it is a spirit and is immortal.*

What do you mean when you say that your soul is immortal? *When I say my soul is immortal, I mean that my soul can never die.*

Of which must you take most care, of your body or your soul? *I must take most care of my soul, for Christ has said, "What doth it profit a man if he gain the whole world, and suffer the loss of his own soul?" (Matt. 16:26).*

Is there any likeness to the Blessed Trinity in your soul? *There is this likeness to the Blessed Trinity in my soul: that as in one God there are three Persons, so in my one soul there are three powers.*

Which are the three powers of your soul? *The three powers of my soul are my memory, my understanding and my will.*

MAN is a creature of God; he has a body and a soul, the latter made to God's image and likeness, in that it is a spirit, is immortal and is endowed with intelligence and free will.

Soul is not just another word for **Spirit**. Animals have souls, but their souls are not spirits. Only man's soul is a spirit; in man is the only kind of soul that is also a spirit.

Soul is defined as **the principle of life in a living body**. Angels, therefore, are **not** souls; they do not animate a body. But animals have souls, which however are material and not immortal.

The Human Soul is defined as **the ultimate internal principle which animates our bodies and by which we feel, think and will**.

A Human Person is a **union** of soul and body. Although the human soul is a spiritual substance, capable of existing by itself (as we know from Revelation that it does so exist between physical death and Resurrection of the Body), it has a natural aptitude and even need to exist in a body.

In this life, the body cannot perform a single action independently of the soul, nor can the soul do anything independently of the body.

Souls are not inherited. Each is a distinct creation of God and is united with the body at the time of conception.

Man has a spiritual soul

There is an obvious difference between a living human body and a corpse. That difference is the soul. It is the soul which prevents a living body from doing the only thing a corpse can do—return to dust. There must be a **principle of operation** behind every activity. In man there must be a **principle** which thinks and wills. That principle **cannot** be a mere chemical; otherwise, doctors and scientists would be able to discover it. Yet **it is something**—a spiritual soul which is beyond the reach of chemical analysis.

A material principle could not have spiritual operations; man's soul has spiritual operations; therefore, it cannot be only material.

All day long we make statements which show that we have abstract or universal concepts, e.g., the dog is a noble animal. Making such a statement, we do not think of a particular dog of definite shape, color, size or breed, but we have taken, so to speak, the essence "dog" and are thinking of a thing we cannot contact with our senses. The idea in our minds is a spiritual one.

Similar to this is our anticipation of the future, the consideration of possibilities, the logical deduction of conclusions from premises, the notion of spiritual being and so on.

John thinks. He can reflect on his thinking. He can apprehend himself (who is reflecting) to be identical with the being who thinks. There is complete and perfect **reflection of an agent back upon itself**, a process quite impossible to matter, e.g., a piano cannot play itself, an eye cannot see itself, and a scythe cannot cut itself.

The soul is immortal

Therefore, man's soul is spiritual. It is not made up of parts which are distinct and separable. Hence, even though the body dies, the soul cannot undergo corruption (i.e., disintegration) in itself or be killed through the agency of any creature. The only way it could cease to exist would be by annihilation by God, and that would be against His infinite wisdom, goodness and justice.

Again, all men desire perfect happiness. If that desire could only end in frustration, human nature would have been created defective by God, in that it is unable to fulfill the end for which it was created by Him, namely, for happiness. His wisdom and justice demand that a desire springing from human nature itself must be capable of attainment. In other words, perfect happiness is the destiny God has appointed for man; it must, therefore, be attainable by all who act in conformity with the Divine Will. But perfect happiness cannot be attained in this world, and therefore, there must be a future life in which it is to be found.

Another proof that the soul is immortal is to be found in the conviction that God's justice demands a future life in which the obvious inequalities of this life will be redressed. Conscience implies the existence of a Supreme Legislator who will recompense the good and punish the wicked. Yet during this life, the wicked only too often prosper, while the good often suffer. To suggest that death is the end of everything is an affront to the infinite justice of God.

What does Scripture say?

Scripture is full of proof that the soul of man is spiritual and immortal. "The Lord God formed man of the slime of the earth: and breathed into his face the breath of life, and man became a living soul." (*Gen.* 2:7).

"The souls of the just are in the hand of God, and the torment of death shall not touch them. In the sight of the unwise they seemed to die: . . . but they are in peace . . . their hope is full of immortality." (*Wis.* 3:1-4).

The bringing of the dead to life, e.g., by Elias and Eliseus, would be impossible unless the soul had remained in existence, in order to be able to return to the body. Also, it is clear from many texts in the Old Testament that the Jews always believed in the afterlife. They had to be forbidden, for instance, to attempt to contact the spirits of the dead.

There is the famous incident, too, of the prophet Ezechiel's vision: "[The Lord] set me down in the midst of a plain that was full of bones . . . and I prophesied as he had commanded me: and the spirit came into them, and they lived." (*Ezech.* 37:1, 10).

The Book of Proverbs speaks of the afterlife of the good and the wicked: "The wicked man shall be driven out in his wickedness: but the just hath hope in his death." (*Prov.* 14:32).

The classic text is from the second Book of Machabees: "It is therefore a holy and wholesome thought to pray for the dead, that they may be loosed from sins." (*2 Mach.* 12:46).

In the New Testament, the soul is always considered to be distinct from the body and to be destined to live on after the body's death: "And fear ye not them that kill the body, and are not able to kill the soul." (*Matt.* 10:28).

"For what man knoweth the things of a man, but the spirit of a man that is in him?" (*1 Cor.* 2:11).

Many times Our Lord speaks of the afterlife. Here are some examples: "Labor not for the meat which perisheth, but for that which endureth unto life everlasting, which the Son of man will give you." (*John* 6:27). "If any man eat of this bread, he shall live forever." (*John* 6:52). "For God so loved the world, as to give His only begotten Son; that whosoever believeth in Him, may not perish, but may have life everlasting." (*John* 3:16). "This day thou shalt be with Me in paradise." (*Luke* 23:43).

In a word, Our Lord's whole mission, His entire life, His suffering and His death are built upon the belief in eternal life. The latter, He emphasizes, is the real, the true, the strong, the beautiful life.

How magnificently St. Paul writes on the subject: "The trumpet shall sound, and the dead shall rise again, incorruptible: and we shall be changed. This corruptible must put on incorruption; this mortal must put on immortality." (*1 Cor.* 15:52-53).

How right, then, was Voltaire in saying: "Materialism is the most enormous of all absurdities and the greatest folly that has entered the human mind." How right is our simple catechism which bids our little children to repeat: "I must take most care of my soul, for Christ has said, 'What doth it profit a man if he gain the whole world and suffer the loss of his own soul?'"

On one occasion a young man came to visit St. Philip Neri and informed him that he was sitting for an examination.

"And after the exam?" asked the Saint.

"A degree, I hope."

"And after the degree?"

"I want to be a barrister."

"And then?"

"I suppose I shall have to work hard to make some money to settle down in life."

"And then?"

"Oh, I may end up as a judge."

"And then?"

"At any rate, I shall have a pension on which to retire."

"And then?"

"I suppose I shall have to die someday."

"And then?"

Is it any wonder that that young man later gave up his worldly career to devote himself to the service of God in St. Philip's own Congregation of the Oratory?

During life we are engaged in the task of making our souls ready for eternity. We cannot escape from that task—even for a second! Just as a great masterpiece of painting is made up of a multitude of little strokes, so the state of our soul for all eternity will be the result of our every thought, word, deed and omission during life. Everyone needs to keep this fact foremost in mind at all times.

We are free

The very fact that good is to be rewarded and evil punished

implies that men are free to do good and avoid evil. Every man will reap what he sows. He is free during life to identify himself with either good or evil; the choice rests with him.

Before acting, he deliberates; in acting, he chooses; but deliberation and choice testify to man's freedom. It is he who determines which group of motives is to prevail, and he knows that he is not merely passively swayed by those motives. He is conscious, too, that he does not let himself drift in the direction of the predominating enticement, e.g., temptation to sin. When he has chosen, he knows he could have chosen otherwise.

Duty, law, obligation, responsibility, punishment, reward, merit—all these and many other words imply moral liberty. The universal consent of mankind, expressed in the laws, literature and language, of all ages and nations, affirms that real obligations do exist. The lunatic—who is not legally responsible for his actions—is carefully distinguished in the law from the criminal, who *is* responsible for what he does.

The internal feelings of self-approbation after good actions and remorse after evil ones imply profound realization of one's personal responsibility.

Character traits which are influenced by heredity and environment and the circumstances of the moment obviously count tremendously in a person's conduct, but they do not absolutely control the action of any person's will. It is one thing to be influenced, e.g., by a motive; it is quite another thing to be inexorably determined by it.

That man is personally responsible for his thoughts, words and deeds is well expressed by Shakespeare when he puts these words into the mouth of Iago: " 'Tis in ourselves that we are thus or thus. Our bodies are our gardens, to the which our wills are gardeners; so that if we will plant nettles, or sow lettuce, set hyssop and weed up thyme, supply it with one gender of herbs, or distract it with many, either to have it sterile with idleness, or manured with industry, why, the power and corrigible authority of this lies in our wills." (*Othello*, Act I, Scene iii).

What does life mean?

Every man, whether he likes it or not, must live on for eternity after his physical death. His eternal destiny depends on his own choice. It may be an eternity of life in the vision of God, or an eternity of suffering and pain at enmity with God.

"Good Master, what shall I do that I may receive life everlasting?" is a question we all should ask, in one form or another, as did the rich young man of the Gospel. (*Mark* 10:17). For we each have an immortal soul, we are made for life everlasting, and we are able to choose good rather than evil.

In the words of the Catechism: "God made me to know Him, to love Him and to serve Him in this world and to be happy with Him forever in the next." I cannot know God without being moved to love Him; I cannot love Him without serving Him; I cannot faithfully serve Him without receiving the reward of life with Him for all eternity.

Hence, knowledge—especially that supernatural knowledge called "Faith"—is essential to achieving our true eternal destiny of life with God forever.The knowledge of God and what He expects of us is, therefore, the most important thing that can possibly claim the attention of man.

The body is but dust; the things of the world will pass away; but God and the soul are eternal; they will live forever. The soul is made for happiness with God. If it misses that goal, its whole destiny is ruined. What sense is there, then, in treating the things of the world—wealth, ambition, comfort—as if they are more important than God and the soul? Eternal life is worth any sacrifice. "For what doth it profit a man, if he gain the whole world, and suffer the loss of his own soul?" asked Our Lord. (*Matt.* 16:26). And that is a question we can never afford to forget.

Chapter 3

The Necessity of Religion

What must you do to save your soul? *To save my soul I must worship God by Faith, Hope and Charity; that is, I must believe in Him, I must hope in Him, and I must love Him with my whole heart.*

WHAT is **religion**? The word probably comes from a Latin word meaning "to bind." An ancient writer, Lactantius, said: "We are tied to God and bound to Him by the bond of piety, and it is from this that religion has received its name."

Religion implies:

a) **The recognition of a Divine Personality** behind and producing the forces of nature, the Lord and Ruler of the world, God.

b) **The conviction that the mysterious, supernatural Being has control over the lives and destinies of men**, who are, therefore, dependent on Him.

c) **The persuasion on the part of man that he can bring himself into friendly, beneficent communion with the Godhead** on whom he feels he depends.

d) **The performance of certain acts of homage** meant to bring him divine help, peace and happiness.

Religion may be defined as the voluntary subjection of oneself to God, that is, to the free, supernatural Being on whom man is conscious of being dependent, of whose powerful help he feels the need, and in whom he recognizes the source of his perfection and happiness.

St. Thomas Aquinas says **religion is the virtue which prompts man to render to God the worship and reverence that is His by right. Objectively, religion is the voluntary acknowledgment of man's dependence on God through acts of homage.**

The conception of a personal deity is necessary for religion.

Imagination is stirred by the recognition of the unseen world.

The **longing for communion with God** arises from man's need for divine help.

Hope is engendered by the possibility of obtaining communion with God.

Joy is excited by the consciousness of friendship with God.

Thankfulness is prompted by the obtaining of benefits in answer to prayer.

Awe results from knowledge of God's immense power and wisdom.

Fear, sorrow and the desire for reconciliation arise from consciousness of having offended God and having deserved punishment.

Love of God springs from the contemplation of His goodness and excellence.

Religion implies faith or **belief**. *Correct* views concerning the existence of a personal God, divine providence and retribution, the immortality of the soul, free will and moral responsibility are of vital importance to *right* religion. But in **Christianity**, which is a **supernatural** religion, these fundamental beliefs are **supplemented** and **complemented** by a larger knowledge of God and of His purposes in regard to man through divine Revelation. **Christians know** that God has spoken to men, telling them that they are destined for filial communion with Him through the life of grace and that this has been brought within their reach through the Incarnation and Redemption of Jesus Christ. In **Christianity** the things to be believed and the things to be done, in order to obtain salvation, are **guaranteed by divine authority**.

Today men talk of **religion without dogmas**, but any thinking man must recognize that **right belief** is essential to religion and that **right belief implies dogmas**, which are specific truths.

Christian dogmas are not intellectual puzzles. They have the practical purpose of **enlightening man** on the whole range of his religious and ethical duties, on the right fulfillment of which his supernatural perfection and eternal destiny depend.

The practice of religion

The practice of religion comprises acts of homage toward God, by which man acknowledges God's dominion over him and seeks His help and friendship. These acts of homage are of three kinds: 1) direct acts of worship; 2) regulation of conduct *outside* the sphere of moral obligation; and 3) the regulation of conduct *within* the recognized sphere of moral obligation.

a) **Acts of Worship**. Religion demands that God be **adored, thanked, propitiated** [appeased] and **asked** for all that is needful for soul and body. It is by prayer and sacrifice that these forms of worship are carried out.

b) **Regulation of Conduct**.

1) *Outside the sphere of moral obligation*: All religions recognize the practice of self-denial, works of piety, etc., with a view to obtaining a larger share of the divine favor or to secure more than ordinary sanctity or perfection.

2) *Within the sphere of moral obligation*: God is the guardian of the moral law. That law, therefore, is to be regarded as His command. Obedience to it merits God's favor; disobedience to it merits His punishment.

The need for religion

No one can deny truthfully that **the practice of some form of religion by man is universal**. Whether one studies those tribes whose existence is hidden in the dim mists of history or the so-called primitive peoples of the present day, the fact that they all practice religion must be acknowledged. Dogmas are found everywhere—at least belief in the existence of some Supreme Being, superior to man, caring for man, capable of helping or injuring man, and therefore, to be placated, adored and propitiated. Everywhere moral laws exist, always forbidding disrespect toward the deity or parents and injustice toward fellow men. Everywhere the deity (God or gods) is worshipped according to minutely regulated rites.

Therefore, the **history of religion proves that religion is necessary to human nature and entirely natural**, that is, that man by his whole nature is impelled to worship a Supreme Being, whose existence he spontaneously recognizes.

The only valid explanation for the universality of religion is to be found in the fact that, **without religion, man cannot attain the complete satisfaction of the highest aspirations of his nature.** He finds his intellect striving after knowledge of the whole truth in regard to his origin, nature, last end, and the means to attain it; he finds his will seeking out what is good and true; he finds even his senses needing the satisfaction which comes from the acknowledgment of a Supreme Being. It is only religion that can satisfy these yearnings of the intellect and will and senses of man. It is religion which convinces the intellect that man comes from God and must go to Him and that teaches him the means to attain God as the last end; it is only in religion that man's will finds the goodness and truth capable of satisfying its aspirations; it is in religious worship that man's sensible nature finds its greatest satisfaction.

Religion is a duty

Right reason teaches that if God exists as man's Creator and Conserver, on whom man is totally dependent, **His supreme dominion must be recognized by adoration.** The fact that He has freely bestowed existence and many other favors on man requires that **God be thanked.** That man is conscious of having offended God brings the duty of **penance** and **sorrow**, while the knowledge that God is the source of all good and of everything of which man stands in need, dictates the obligation of **asking God to help him.** Hence, the very relationship of man to God places on man the grave obligation of practicing religion, that is, of acknowledging God as the Principle on whom he entirely depends and expressing that acknowledgment in **worship.** Therefore, religion is not merely useful for man; it is absolutely obligatory. **God has a strict right to the worship of man**; to refuse to recognize that right is to **offend against justice**.

Religion, then, is part of the virtue of justice. It is a *VIRTUE*. Now a virtue is a good habit, that which makes a person good; vice is a sinful habit, that which makes a person evil. It is therefore **good** to practice religion and evil to neglect it.

Irreligion is a **vice**, a sinful habit. An irreligious man is a vicious man. Only by accident can a man be moral without believing in God, for God is the only basis of morality. God has, to cite St. Paul, written the obligations of the law in the hearts of men—"Who show the work of the law written in their hearts, their conscience bearing witness to them . . ." (*Rom.* 2:15). He has given men the light of reason to discover the moral law that He has revealed.

Morality needs religion

Liddon, in his *Elements of Religion*, says: "Morality severed from religious motives is like a branch cut from a tree; it may here and there, from accidental causes, retain its greenness for a while, but its chance of vigorous life is a very slender one. Nor is it possible to popularize a real morality, a morality that shall deal with motives as well as acts, without unveiling to the eye of the soul something more personal than an abstract law."

If religion is not the basis of morality, what is?

Not utility—for man is not wholly subject to society, and the good of society is far from being his only and all-embracing end.

Not pleasure—for that would legalize immorality and crime.

Not the fact that virtue is its own reward—for often virtue walks in rags.

Not the inner sanction of conscience—for experience shows how easily indulgence in evil deadens conscience.

Not legal sanctions—for these cannot touch the inner motives and thoughts.

Not public opinion—for it is often corrupt, praising evil men and blaming the good.

God alone can read the inmost secrets of minds and hearts; He alone can estimate every motive; He alone can adequately and justly punish or reward good and evil thoughts, words and deeds.

A morality divorced from God, the Author of the moral law, cannot be sustained. As Cardinal Mercier says: "It is a vain hope to expect the moral law to be observed without recourse to the idea of God. For how is the observance of the moral law to be sufficiently guaranteed, if man has no certitude that a Just and Powerful God will sooner or later establish an eternal harmony between virtue and happiness on the one hand, and between vice and misery on the other?"

It is submission to God that makes a man good, rebellion against God that makes him evil. **No man can be good without religion**. Men who want to be thoroughly evil persecute religion and try to suppress it because it opposes their evil designs.

Religion is a form of *JUSTICE*. This means that it is concerned with what is **right,** and not merely with what is pleasant, useful, fashionable or consoling.

Some false notions

Many people look upon religion as a source of pleasure for themselves; they even derive gentle entertainment from it. For them it is little more than a pastime, a hobby or a luxury. When they feel like it, they practice it; when they do not, they neglect it. Often they flit about from one religion to another to satisfy their peculiar desire for this type or that of fascination and entertainment.

But their motive is the obtaining of pleasure for themselves. **This is a perversion**. There are even Catholics who neglect to attend Mass on Sundays because "they get nothing out of it." These people are not interested in doing their duty to God; they want Him to serve them. For them the center of their universe is self, not God. Somewhat similar are the people whose only concern with religion is that it may be useful for themselves. When things go wrong, they turn to God; when all is well, they ignore Him. This is an abuse of religion akin to that practiced by those who only seek what they can make out of religion by commercializing it and turning it into a racket.

It is perfectly true that religion is often a source of consolation and happiness, **but this is a consequence of it and not the reason for practicing it**! The reason for practicing religion must simply be **the will to be just**.

Non-Catholics have said that Catholics only attend Mass because they are forced to do so. The truth is that Catholic churches are full at Mass time on Sundays because Catholic people have been consistently taught that it is their duty to attend Sunday Mass. It is right for them to be there, wrong for them to be away. Therefore, other things being equal, the person who goes to church is better than the person who stays away, for the one who goes discharges his debt to God according to the laws of his religion.

Public worship

External worship is due to God, for He is the Creator of both body and soul. Both must recognize His dominion. Therefore, by the very posture of his body at prayer, man acknowledges that he must worship God with his whole being, and not merely internally, by acts of the will. If this internal worship is sincere, it will express itself outwardly in words and special ceremonies or rites. In other matters, we express outwardly what we feel inwardly. Our hand-shake expresses friendship, our kiss love, our blows anger. Why, then, should we not give outward expression to our love of God and our friendship with Him? We are not disembodied spirits, but crea-tures composed of body and soul. Our senses are apt to draw us away from God; we need some help in the form of externals to make the senses help awaken spiritual ideas and drive away distractions.

Social worship is due to God. Society—composed of the Fam-ily and the State—is a divine institution, a creature of God, under a debt of gratitude to Him as Creator and Provider. It must discharge that debt through the public practice of religion. Moreover, it is in the interest of the community for the civil authority to promote reli-gion, for without religion there can be no true basis of respect for authority.

Nowadays, religion has become identified with the service, not of God, but of man. Man is the god of the universe. Philanthropy has come to be regarded as better than prayer; it is now often thought that it is better to build homes for men than temples for God. Reli-gion and respectability have generally come to be thought of as the same thing. In fact, religion is now often regarded as little more than sanctified "good form" or decency. Someone has said that if reli-gion does nothing else in England, "it puts a gentleman and a good cricketer into every parish." "Playing the game"—so delightfully vague—has taken the place of the Ten Commandments.

All these tendencies are a reversal of the true order of things. **Religion is right: it is a fundamental need of man. Duty to God**

the Creator is more important than duty to man the creature. But duty to God *implies* **duty to man.** In fact, duty to man will only be properly fulfilled by those who are faithful to their higher duties to God.

Very often the "reasons" alleged by the irreligious and unbelievers are no more than smoke-screens covering up the fact that they have not the courage to practice religion because true religion would come into conflict with the gratification of their human passions. If religion is true, they would have to change their lives or go to Hell. The former is unthinkable to them, the latter unpleasant; hence, they raise a smoke-screen of arguments which it is an insult to ask an intelligent man to consider.

Multitudes of men today are indifferent to the practice of religion. They boast that they are Christians. In fact, they claim to be proud to have fought during the war against Hitler for the survival of Christianity. But how do they differ from the pagans? To the personal practice of religion they are quite indifferent. In other words, they are indifferent to God. Yet they say they believe in Him. Hence, there is no excuse for them.

They do their duty to wife, children and friends, but their main duty—to God—is completely neglected.

Morally speaking, this is criminal. For as long as God is God and we are His creatures, religious duties—definite, private, public, social—will be obligatory and the right thing to do.

The conclusion is obvious. Religion matters more than anything else in life. It is the one supremely important thing. It must occupy the most important place in every person's life—and actually in the life of every nation as well.

Chapter 4

The Sources of Faith

The Church and the Bible

THE modern heckler at the platforms of the Catholic Evidence Guild is ready enough to admit that **recent Popes have encouraged Catholics to read the Bible**. But he contends that in the Middle Ages, the Bible was never given to the laity. On the other hand, Ruskin in *Stones of Venice* wrote that the medieval Church taught Scripture to her children, but that the Catholic Church does not do so today.

The truth is that the Church has **always regarded the Bible as her treasure and has at all times taken the most practical means to make it understood by her children**. During the period of the **Roman Empire**, the people, mostly literate, heard the Bible read aloud at the services by a person specially ordained for the purpose, i.e., a *lector*, or reader. The copies used for this purpose were naturally rare and jealously guarded because they were all copied by hand. Most of the early copies were on papyrus rolls, but when parchment came into use, the Emperor Constantine had fifty copies of the entire Bible made.

After the fall of the Roman Empire, illiteracy grew apace. Priests, monks and nuns continued to copy the Bible, but the Church found that direct reading of it was less useful for the Faithful, and so devised other methods to impart knowledge of the Bible to her children. These were **pictures, statues, mosaics, mystery plays, sermons**, etc.

Since the invention of printing, the Church has done everything to make the Bible known and loved. Translations have been multiplied; cheap editions have been issued; and the Popes have written many great letters urging the people to read the Bible.

Through her **liturgy,** which is daily filled with Scripture passages, the Church still brings knowledge of the Bible to the people, and she urges that the Bible be used as the subject of **private prayer** and **meditation**.

The Catholic Church is today **the greatest defender of the Bible**, not only against **unbelieving rationalists,** but against **Protestant attacks**. Professor G. H. Betts, a Protestant University Professor, sent out 56 questions on religion to **1,309 Protestant ministers** and to **5 Protestant theological seminaries**. In their replies, 2 percent of the Lutheran ministers, 38 percent of the Baptist ministers, 60 percent of the Episcopal ministers, 65 percent of the Methodist ministers, 56 percent of the Presbyterian ministers, 83 percent of the Congregational ministers and 92 percent of the students of the seminaries **denied or doubted** the divine inspiration of the Bible. [The statistics cited here were from 1951. —Publisher 2002.]

Before dealing, however, with the divine **inspiration** of the Bible, it is necessary to show that it is an authentic document, really written by the authors to whom it is ascribed and at the time claimed. It must be shown, too, that when history is being related, the books of the Bible are actually reliable historical documents and that they have come down to us unchanged.

For our present purpose, it is sufficient to confine ourselves to the New Testament, and especially to the Gospels. We ask: "Are they authentic, historical and unchanged?"

The Gospels are authentic

This can be proved from evidence from both Catholic and non-Catholic sources, outside the text of the documents themselves, and this evidence is strongly supported by evidence afforded by the actual text.

From the second century, there exists an unbroken line of Christian writers who state explicitly that there are four Gospels, written by Matthew, Mark, Luke and John. Further, it is possible to put together the greater part of the Gospels merely from quotations found in the early Christian writers from the first century. Again, the Latin version and the Syrian version dating from the second century have Gospels identical in form with what we read today.

Turning to non-Christian writers, the fact has to be admitted that second century heretics, believing the Gospels to be authentic, tried to pervert the text to fit in with their false teachings. They could not deny the Apostolic origin of the Gospels, so they attempted to change the text.

The Jews still observe silence regarding the life of Christ. They cannot discredit the Gospels. If they could, they surely would. Moreover, the Jewish historian, Josephus, mentions Christ and confirms the Gospel account.

At least four famous pagan writers of the first two centuries offer evidence in favor of the authenticity of the Gospels. Pliny the Younger, who was born about 62 A.D., says the divinity of Christ was an essential doctrine of Christianity. In his *Annals,* Tacitus reports Christ's death under Pontius Pilate. Suetonius, who wrote the lives of the first Roman Emperors, testifies to the early spread of Christianity. About the same time, another scribe, Celsus, composed a violent tract against the followers of Christ, showing a knowledge of the Gospel story.

There is much evidence to be gathered also from the Epistles, Christian letters written almost entirely in the first century by St. Paul and others. Three-quarters of them were written before 65 A.D. The authors write of facts as known to and believed by all. How could they have done this if the Gospel accounts were not true? In addition, very many passages from the Gospels are quoted or mentioned in the Epistles.

The above is but a short summary of the external evidence that the Gospels are authentic documents, really written by Matthew, Mark, Luke and John within a few years of the death of Christ.

Add to that evidence the following from the text itself. The language used in the Gospels is the Greek dialect current throughout the Roman Empire at the beginning of the Christian era. At the same time, there is a coloring of the Aramaic, the native language of the Palestinian Jews.

Jerusalem was destroyed in the year 70 A.D. The fact that there is not the slightest mention of this event, except as something foretold, shows that the Gospels must have been composed before it took place.

No conscientious, unprejudiced reader of the Gospels would deny that the vivid description of the words and actions of Jesus, with so much intimate detail, could only have been written by eyewitnesses, or those to whom the events were related by eyewitnesses.

The Gospels are true history

The writers actually say that they are writing history, not fiction. St. Luke, for instance, begins his Gospel like this: "Forasmuch as many have taken in hand to set forth in order a narration of the things that have been accomplished among us; according as they have delivered them unto us, who from the beginning were eyewitnesses and ministers of the word." (*Luke* 1:1-2).

The style of the Evangelists is full of assurance; the facts they relate are confirmed by non-Catholic historians, particularly Josephus. Moreover, the findings of archaeologists entirely support the Gospel story. For example, recent research has proved that St. Luke was perfectly correct in stating that during the mission of John the Baptist, Lysanius was Tetrarch in Abilina.

The Gospel writings breathe sincerity. There is not the slightest evidence of any intention on the part of the writers to deceive. Deception would profit them nothing. They record humiliating as well as glorious events in Christ's life. Even when they have to report themselves as being blameworthy, they do so without excuse or palliation. They depict themselves as lacking in understanding (*Matt.* 13:36; *Mark* 4:13; 6:52; *John* 6:61), as being ambitious and jealous (*Mark* 9:33 ff; *Luke* 9:46; 22:24), as wanting in faith and courage (*Matt.* 26:40; *Mark* 16:13; *Luke* 8:25) and as being rebuked by Christ (*Matt.* 16:23; *Mark* 16:14). Most noteworthy of all, they gave their lives in defense of the truth which they had written.

It is impossible to suppose that the Evangelists were themselves deceived. They were in a position to know the truth. Matthew and John were eyewitnesses of the events they relate; Mark was the secretary to St. Peter and had St. Peter's evidence, and Luke had that of St. Paul and the other Apostles, plus he was a close friend of the Blessed Mother. They were not overly credulous. In the spirit of the times, they did not expect a spiritual Messias, but one who would establish a temporal kingdom and free Israel from the power of Rome. Because of this, they quarreled about who would have the highest places in the new kingdom. Even if they had been too credulous, their evidence would easily have been corrected by the many eyewitnesses who saw the events about which they wrote.

The Gospels are still complete and unchanged

It has already been stated that it would be possible to piece together almost the whole of the Gospels from quotations appearing in the works of the earliest Christian writers. Those quotations are from the Gospels as we know them today. Copies of the originals of these works are still extant and date back to the fourth and fifth centuries; their text is substantially the same as that which we use. Further, the most ancient translations—the Latin and Syriac of the second century, the Coptic of the third and the Gothic and Armenian versions of the fourth and fifth centuries—lead to the same conclusion. It is, too, a matter of history that the Church has always guarded the Sacred Books most carefully and rejected anything save what was inspired.

The Bible is the inspired word of God

The Catholic Church has always regarded the Bible as the inspired word of God, and she demands that all her children accept the Bible as such.

The Scriptures themselves frequently claim to be divine in their origin. In both the Old and the New Testaments there are passages which are described as coming from God. For example: "And the Lord said to Moses: Write this for a memorial in a book." (*Exodus* 17:14). "And the Lord said to Moses: "Write thee these words by which I have made a covenant both with thee and with Israel." (*Exodus* 34:27). In the New Testament, Jesus Christ Himself says that David "himself saith by the Holy Ghost: the Lord said to my Lord," etc. (*Mark* 12:36). In St. Matthew's Gospel we find Him telling the Jews that God was speaking to *them* through what they were accustomed to read in the Scriptures: "Have you not read that which was spoken by God?" (*Matt.* 22:31-32).

Again, Jesus Himself refers to the Old Testament writings as a certain proof that His mission was divine and as a final court of appeal to convince the Jews: "Search the Scriptures, for you think in them to have life everlasting; and the same are they that give testimony of me." (*John* 5:39). "How then shall the Scriptures be fulfilled that so it must be done?" (*Matt.* 26:54). "The words of Scripture cannot be broken." (*John* 10:35). About 150 times the expression, "The Scripture says," or its equivalent, occurs, clearly attributing to the Scriptures divine authority. Nor is this true of only small portions of the Old Testament. Our Lord expressly refers to all that was written of Him in "the law of Moses, and in the Prophets, and in the Psalms."

The clearest statement of the inspiration of the Scriptures, however, is to be found in St. Paul's second Epistle to Timothy: "All scripture, inspired of God, is profitable to teach, to reprove, to correct, to instruct in justice." (*2 Tim.* 3:16).

Nevertheless, even though these texts from Scripture are exceedingly clear, they cannot possibly be our main proof that the Bible is the inspired word of God. To regard them as such would be to argue in a vicious circle.

Consider also the fact that the Bible is infinitely superior to all other sacred books, that the most searching criticism has proved it to be always historically accurate, and that it is obviously supernatural in character. But even these facts are not the principal criteria for determining the inspiration of the Sacred Books.

To prove conclusively that the Bible is inspired, you must first consider the Gospels as historical books only, abstracting from the fact of their inspiration. These historical documents tell us of a certain historical Person who said He was God and, as we shall prove in a later instruction, justified that claim by works which no mere man could have done, and said He would establish an infallible Church—**a Church that is still in this world, after nearly 2,000 years.**

We prove Christ's life and works from **historical documents**. We prove **His divinity** from His life and works. We prove the **infallible Church** from the promise of this **divine Person**, and then we ask what this **infallible Church** says about the Bible. St. Augustine (354-430) wrote: "I would not believe the Gospel unless the authority of the Catholic Church moved me thereto." (*Contra Ep. Fund.* 5).

Here is what the **Church says** in the **First Vatican Council**: "The Church holds these books as sacred and canonical, not because, composed merely by human industry, they were thereupon approved by her authority; nor alone because they contain revelation without error; but because, written under the inspiration of the Holy Ghost, they **have God for their author**, and as such were delivered to the Church herself." [Vatican Council I—1869-1870].

Pope Leo XIII, in his Encyclical on the Bible, wrote: "The Holy Ghost Himself by His supernatural power, stirred up and impelled the Biblical writers to write, and assisted them while writing in such a manner that they conceived in their minds exactly, and determined to commit to writing faithfully, and render in exact language, with infallible truth, all that God commanded and nothing else; without that, God would not be the author of Scripture in its entirety."

When we say that the Bible is the very **Word of God**, we do not mean that He actually wrote it with pen and paper Himself. We mean that **He inspired** different **human authors** to write the different Books contained in the Bible and to write **just what He wished** those Books to contain. He is the **principal author** because He inspired the human writers in all that they wrote. Therefore, **everything in the Bible is infallibly true**.

Minor errors, of course, could and did occur in **later copies and translations**, but these have **not affected the substantial content** of Scripture, when made with the **authority of the Church,** and they are easily corrected by the comparative study of documents.

Facts about the Bible

The Bible is a gift God wished men to have. The human authors of the various Biblical books were **actual living men of a most fascinating variety of character**—Matthew, a civil servant; Mark, Peter's secretary; Peter himself, formerly a fisherman; Paul, a former Pharisee, and his secretary, Luke, a physician; John, the "Son of Thunder," yet the Beloved Disciple; Job, King David, etc.

The Bible contains an account of God's relations with men and tells us much about what we would otherwise be in ignorance of.

The Old Testament explains how men came to need a Saviour and how God prepared the world for His coming.

The New Testament tells us of the Saviour's coming, the completion of His work, and the founding of a Church to make available to men all He had won for them. In the New Testament we have an **intimate picture of Christ,** drawn by those who knew Him and loved Him best. Apart from this, we know little of His life. Therefore, as St. Jerome says, **"ignorance of Scripture is ignorance of Christ."**

Texts and versions

The official text of the Bible used by the Catholic Church is known as the **Latin Vulgate**. The word "Vulgate" merely means the accepted, current or common version.

The Vulgate was translated into Latin by St. Jerome in the 4th century. (He completed his work about 405.) He was the greatest Scripture scholar of his day, and when Pope St. Damasus (366-384) asked him to translate the Bible, he used for the work all the best Hebrew and Greek manuscripts then available—many of which have since been lost to history.

The English Douay-Rheims Version and the new version by **Mgr. Ronald Knox** are **translations** from the Vulgate. The Westminster Version, on the other hand, is translated from the original Hebrew or Greek.

In the Catholic Bible, the **Old Testament** is based on **The Septuagint**, a **Greek Version** made by 70 (*septuaginta*) translators at Alexandria for the Jews who mostly spoke Greek. It was begun about 280 years before Christ and was completed in the next century. All Jews **acknowledged it to be authentic,** and **it was used by Christ and the Apostles**. Three hundred of the 350 quotations from the Old Testament found in the New Testament are taken directly from the Greek Septuagint.

There are 73 Books in the Catholic Bible—46 in the Old Testament and 27 in the New.

Through anti-Catholic prejudice, the early Protestants repudiated the Septuagint and thus omitted from their translation the Books of *Tobias*, *Judith*, *Wisdom*, *Ecclesiasticus* and *Baruch*, and later, *I* and *II Machabees,* plus sections of *Esther* and *Daniel*. That is why these books are not in the Protestant authorized versions.

But the early Christians, with Christ and His Apostles, certainly **accepted** these Books, frequently quoting and alluding to them in their writings.

The Bible is not the only rule of faith

Thus, there **must be some external authority** to decide which books are part of the inspired Bible, and which are not. The Bible itself does not say. **It is only through the infallible authority of the Catholic Church that men today know for certain the contents of the Bible. The Church** provides a **correct and complete** version of the Scriptures and forbids Catholics to use the Protestant Bible.

Christ founded a teaching Church, and He **commanded** all men to believe in it. Yet:

(a) He did **not** tell His Church to teach by writing;

(b) The Church did not for many years use the written word at all. Her standard method of teaching was **by word of mouth**. Hence, the written word **cannot be of the very essence of the constitution of the Church**;

(c) It was only later that **some** of the Apostles wrote down **some** of the teaching of Christ.

St. John concludes his Gospel thus: "There are also many other things which Jesus did; which, if they were written every one, the world itself, I think, would not be able to contain the books that should be written." (*John* 21:25).

St. Paul wrote also: "Therefore, brethren, stand fast; and hold the traditions which you have learned, whether by word, or by our epistle." (*2 Thes.* 2:14).

Insisting that these **traditions** be handed on, he wrote: "And the things which thou hast heard of me by many witnesses, the same commend to faithful men, who shall be fit to teach others also." (*2 Tim.* 2:2).

St. Peter makes another noteworthy point when he writes: "As also our most dear brother Paul, according to the wisdom given him, hath written to you: as also in all his epistles, speaking in them of these things; in which are certain things hard to be understood, which the unlearned and unstable wrest [twist], as they do also the other scriptures, to their own destruction." (*2 Pet.* 3:15-16).

Thus, the writings which now form the New Testament never displaced the teaching Church. It was **in the Church** that they were read; it was **by the Church** that they were treasured as inspired. Moreover, the Church always taught that they **needed explaining**, as St. Peter said so clearly; that they needed synthesizing; that they had to be brought to the knowledge of the great majority of men, who either could not read or could only understand the simplest things (as so many today); that the passage of the years would make them even more difficult to understand.

Again, the Church had to supplement the Bible teaching to supply some of the things which St. John says were never written down. In many parts of the world, the Scriptures could not become available until printing was invented.

Most important is the fact that the Scriptures **needed a guarantee of authenticity**. The Church alone could give that guarantee; without the Church, the Bible cannot exist. It is only through the Catholic Church that Protestants know what the Bible contains. In the early years of Christianity, there were many, many books claiming to give accounts of Christ's life and miracles. Who was to decide which were inspired and which were not? Obviously, only an infallible Church could do this.

Tradition

As we shall see later, the Holy Ghost guides the Church; He, too, inspires the Scriptures. Hence, the one cannot contradict the other. Scripture was written **for the Church**, to be used **by the Church**, but as Scripture itself says explicitly, it is not a complete account of all the teachings of Christ, and so there must be **another source of faith**, namely **Tradition**.

It is through rejecting **Tradition** and leaving every man to interpret the Bible for himself that Protestantism has resulted in such a multiplicity of contradictory sects, and that the Bible is less respected, less used and less understood in the world today than ever before.

The Christian Tradition is contained in early **Church history**, in the **decrees of early Councils**, in primitive **liturgies**, in the **Acts of the Martyrs**, in the books of the **early Fathers** and **Doctors** of the Church and **ecclesiastical writers**, in inscriptions in the **Catacombs** and on **Christian archeological monuments**.

The Catholic Church gives to men **through Scripture and Tradition** the whole of God's teaching, its meaning and a guarantee of its authenticity.

Chapter 5

Prayer

What is prayer? *Prayer is the raising of the mind and heart to God.*

How do we raise our mind and heart to God? *We raise our mind and heart to God by thinking of God; by adoring, praising and thanking Him; and by begging of Him all blessings for soul and body.*

Do those pray well who at their prayers think neither of God nor of what they say? *Those who at their prayers think neither of God nor of what they say do not pray well, but they offend God, if their distractions are willful.*

Which is the best of all prayers? *The best of all prayers is the "Our Father," or "The Lord's Prayer."*

Who composed The Lord's Prayer? *Jesus Christ Himself composed The Lord's Prayer.*

Say The Lord's Prayer. *Our Father, Who art in Heaven, hallowed be Thy name; Thy kingdom come; Thy Will be done, on Earth as it is in Heaven. Give us this day our daily bread, and forgive us our trespasses, as we forgive those who trespass against us; and lead us not into temptation, but deliver us from evil. Amen.*

In The Lord's Prayer, who is called "Our Father"? *In the Lord's Prayer, God is called "Our Father."*

Why is God called "Our Father"? *God is called "Our Father" because He is the Father of all Christians, whom He has made His children by Holy Baptism.*

Is God also the Father of all mankind? *God is also the Father of all mankind because He made them all, and loves and preserves them all.*

Why do we say, "our" Father, and not "my" Father? *We say "our" Father, and not "my" Father, because being all brethren, we are to pray, not for ourselves only, but also for all others.*

When we say, "hallowed be Thy name," what do we pray for? *When we say, "hallowed be Thy name," we pray that God may be known, loved and served by all His creatures.*

When we say, "Thy kingdom come," what do we pray for? *When we say, "Thy kingdom come," we pray that God may come and reign in the hearts of all by His grace in this world, and bring us all hereafter to His Heavenly kingdom.*

When we say, "Thy Will be done on Earth as it is in Heaven," what do we pray for? *When we say, "Thy Will be done on Earth as it is in Heaven," we pray that God may enable us by His grace to do His Will in all things, as the Blessed do in Heaven.*

When we say, "give us this day our daily bread," what do we pray for? *When we say, "give us this day our daily bread," we pray that God may give us daily all that is necessary for soul and body.*

When we say, "forgive us our trespasses, as we forgive those who trespass against us," what do we pray for? *When we say, "forgive us our trespasses, as we forgive those who trespass against us," we pray that God may forgive us our sins, as we forgive others the injuries they do to us.*

When we say, "lead us not into temptation," what do we pray for? *When we say, "lead us not into temptation," we pray that God may give us grace not to yield to temptation.*

When we say, "deliver us from evil," what do we pray for? *When we say, "deliver us from evil," we pray that God may free us from all evil, both of soul and body.*

INTELLIGENT men recognize the sovereignty and absolute dominion of God and their dependence on Him. It is in prayer that this recognition is shown in practice. **To pray** is a universal instinct of the human race. The desire to raise up the mind and heart to God is found even among pagan peoples who have only the vaguest conception of God. Those who ridicule prayer ridicule one of the deepest instincts in human nature.

The **foundation** of prayer is the realization of the omnipotence of God, the nothingness of man, and man's utter dependence on God. It is, therefore, **unintelligent** not to pray. The man who does not pray reduces himself to the level of the beasts.

Early in 1918 when the German offensive was threatening to bring defeat to the Allies in World War I, General Foch was appointed Generalissimo on the Western Front. The time chosen for the great counter-offensive, which was to result in the victorious conclusion of the War, was dawn of July 18th. The previous evening, Foch left Allied General Headquarters, asking to be allowed an undisturbed hour to himself.

He had been absent some time when a dispatch rider came with a message of such importance that the Staff Officers felt that General Foch should be informed. They looked for him in his billet, but he was not there. However, his orderly, knowing the General's habits, led them to the village church. There they found Foch kneeling motionless before the altar.

Imagine two men sharing a ship's cabin on a voyage to Australia. It would be unnatural for them not to speak to one another. But suppose one of the men was completely dependent on the other—for his food, to be dressed and undressed, to be moved about; and suppose the other cared for him with the utmost devotion; what would be said of the invalid if he never so much as spoke to his benefactor? That is exactly our position in regard to God if we do not pray. He is not only always with us on the voyage through life, but we are completely dependent upon Him for our very being and even for every breath we breathe. How unnatural it is not to speak to Him, to ask Him to help us, to express our sorrow if we offend Him, to admire His goodness, to thank Him for His benefits.

The necessity of prayer

Prayer is absolutely necessary for salvation. Man must dispose himself for justification; otherwise, he cannot be saved. He must, therefore, turn to God in some way.

Prayer is just as necessary for our spiritual life as breathing is necessary for our bodily life. Our spiritual life depends on God's grace, and He has, so to speak, given us the power to breathe it in by prayer. Not to pray will have the same results for the life of the soul as not to breathe would have for the life of the body—i.e., sickness and death.

Sometimes it is argued that prayer is not necessary because God knows our needs without our telling them to Him, or that God is so infinitely generous that he could not possibly make the granting of our needs conditional upon our asking Him, or that God is unchangeable and therefore we cannot hope to change Him by our prayers.

Our Lord, who is God, showed that He wished people to lay their requests before Him. He let people ask Him, and then He granted their requests. Moreover, He tells us to ask and keep on asking. Consider, for instance, the parables of the Unjust Judge and the man coming to his friend in the night. "And he spoke also a parable to them, that we ought always to pray, and not to faint . . . will not God revenge his elect who cry to him day and night . . .?" (*Luke* 18:1,7).

Nor would it be more generous on God's part to give us all without making us ask. He has already given us very much without our asking at all. But it is His Will that many other things that we receive should depend on our prayer. By it we are taught our rightful position in relation to God; we are trained in reverence toward Him. It is through regular prayer that the Saints have received so many and so varied gifts of soul. God wants us to pray precisely that He may be even more generous toward us.

We do not change the intentions of an unchanging God by our prayers. **He wills that we shall obtain certain favors if we ask for them and that we shall not obtain them if we do not.** God, who dwells in Eternity, sees all time at once, past, present and future. Simultaneously, He sees our needs and our prayers. He always intended that if we ask certain favors, we get them. He foresees us asking and Himself granting as a result. Hence, God is not changed. But prayer may easily change us and make us fit to receive God's gifts.

Christ's teaching

By example and word, Christ taught the necessity of prayer.

By example: He spent thirty of His thirty-three years in the hidden life of work and prayer. At His Baptism, He prayed. He went to the desert for forty days of prayer, at the beginning of His Public Life. Before his actual work began, He retired to the region of the Jordan. It is said that when He was in Capharnaum, He departed into a desert place and "there He prayed." Before calling the Twelve, He prayed. Feeding the five thousand, He prayed, and then went into a mountain to pray alone. Before curing the deaf and dumb man at Decapolis, He prayed. Before Peter's Confession, He prayed. At His Transfiguration, He prayed. At the tomb of Lazarus, at the Last Supper, in the Garden of Gethsemani and on the Cross, He prayed.

By Word: Again and again, He commands us to pray. "Therefore I say unto you, all things, whatsoever you ask when ye pray, believe that you shall receive; and they shall come unto you." (*Mark* 11:24).

"And all things whatsoever you shall ask in prayer, believing, you shall receive." (*Matt.* 21:22).

"Watch ye, therefore, praying at all times, that you may be accounted worthy to escape all these things that are to come, and to stand before the Son of man." (*Luke* 21:36).

The Saints have all been men and women of prayer, and they have all recommended prayer to their followers. "Prayer is the key of Heaven," says St. Augustine. "Provided you keep firm and persevere in the practice of prayer, you will get to Heaven," is St. Teresa's assurance. Similarly, St. Alphonsus says: "Pray and never give up praying; if you pray, you will certainly be saved; if you do not pray, you will certainly be lost."

From the first, the convert must take up seriously the duty of prayer. It may be hard at first because he may not be used to it. But he will grow into it. We learn to pray by praying, as a child learns to walk by walking. Many a priest devotes hours to instructing prospective converts, but his work will be fruitful just in so far as the convert helps himself by praying.

The conditions of prayer

1. **Sincerity**: We must mean our prayers, never forgetting that we need God's help more than a starving man needs the crust of bread to live.

2. **Attention**: This means the voluntary application of the mind to the object of prayer. Attention should be

    a. **External**: securing circumstances of time, place, position, etc., conducive to recollection;

    b. **Internal**: i. **Spiritual**—to God Himself or Our Lady or the Saint to whom we pray;

        ii. **Literal**—to the meaning of the words and the significance of things. This is to be aimed at;

        iii. **Material**—merely saying the words rightly. This alone is not sufficient. "This people honoureth me with their lips: but their heart is far from me." (*Matt.* 15:8). We must have at least external attention and the sustained purpose of worshipping God.

Note: Distractions are sinful if deliberate. They are not sinful when they are not willful or not through our own fault, or when they arise from weakness or incapacity.

3. **Humility**: "God resisteth the proud, and giveth grace to the humble." (*James* 4:6). This is why we kneel at prayer.

4. **Confidence**: This springs from a lively faith in the truth of God's promises and trust in His fidelity and goodness. Remember the story of the Canaanite woman: "Great is thy faith: be it done to thee as thou wilt." (*Matt.* 15:26).

5. **Perseverance**: It is so much easier to give up prayer than to keep it up. It takes effort. Whether we feel like prayer or not, God is still God and equally deserving of our acknowledgment. Our Lord cured the blind man who, although rebuked, cried out all the more, "Son of David, have mercy on me." (*Luke* 18:39). Recall also the parable of the man who had a friend arrive late from a journey and the host had no food to feed him, so he went to a friend to borrow food, who was already in bed and who refused to get up and open his door; but he did, finally, in order to stop the man from knocking.

(*Luke* 11:5-8). It is not for us to say when God will grant our petition. He may wish to try our earnestness.

6. **Resignation**: We must always be prepared to leave our position in the hands of God, who knows best. Nor must we complain if our request is not granted. It will certainly be rewarded in some way. "Father," he said, "if thou wilt, remove this chalice from me: but yet, not my will, but thine be done." (*Luke* 22:42).

Often our driest prayers are the best. Anyone can pray when he feels like it, enjoying the consolation he finds in it. But to be constant in prayer, on principle, whether one likes it or not, is true service of God and merits His special blessings.

Unanswered Prayers: The reason why our prayers do not seem to be always answered may be because some condition is lacking in us or in our prayer. But Our Lord has supplied another answer. Even a good earthly father, He tells us, will not give his son a stone when he asks for bread, or a serpent instead of a fish, but we often ask God for a stone because we think it is bread. God knows better than we do. He gives us bread instead of the stone we are clamoring for. Thus, many people who are honest with themselves are able, even here below, to thank God as much for the things they prayed for and did not get as for those they received in answer to their prayers.

The practice of prayer

Every convert should learn by heart the **Our Father**, the **Hail Mary**, the **Glory Be**, the **Apostles' Creed**, the **Confiteor**, and the **Acts of Faith, Hope, Charity and Contrition**.

The Catholic Church insists that her children must in some measure combine prayer with daily life, however busy the latter may be. Thus, She teaches them to begin the day with prayer, especially with the Morning Offering, by which every thought, word and deed of the forthcoming day is offered to Jesus through Mary and thus becomes a prayer. In the morning, God's blessing should be asked on the day that is beginning and a promise made to do all well for His sake. If possible, Mass should be heard and Holy Communion received.

During the day, the mind should be raised to God through ejaculatory prayer.

At night, one's conscience should be examined, contrition and amendment expressed, God thanked for His favors, and His blessing asked against temptation.

Suitable forms of morning and night prayers will be found in any Catholic prayer book.

It is surely fitting that we should begin the day by addressing ourselves to God. Later, we shall talk to many of our fellow men. Let us speak to God first. Deliberate omission of morning prayers is rather like telling God we do not need His help, that we can manage quite well without Him, and that He can safely leave us to ourselves. Why should we be surprised, then, if God does leave us to ourselves—with disastrous results?

It is equally fitting that our last thought before retiring to rest should be of Him who is ever watching over us and into whose keeping we entrust ourselves when we sleep.

There is an obligation to pray when interior faith, hope and charity oblige us to do so, on coming to the use of reason, in evident danger of death, and frequently during life. Circumstances may oblige us to pray in time of temptation, which would otherwise be difficult to overcome, as for instance when duty demands that we go into a proximate occasion of sin; also, when some duty is to be fulfilled which requires prayer, such as receiving a Sacrament or hearing Mass, in time of great personal or public necessity, and when charity to others demands it. It is fitting that we should pray morning and evening, before and after meals, plus extra on Sundays and Holydays.

What is prayer?

Prayer is a lifting up of the mind and heart to God. That is the essence of prayer. This simple definition explains much about prayer. For instance: "How, when and why shall I pray?" One might as well ask: "How, when and why shall I converse with my best friend, who is infinitely good and rich and powerful, while I am sinful and poor and powerless?" No one needs elaborate instruction on such points as these. The heart of a man—his natural instinct—tells him how and when and why to speak when dealing with his friend; it is the same when dealing with God.

Prayer is divided into two main categories: **vocal prayer** and **mental prayer**.

Vocal prayer

Vocal prayer expresses in words the thoughts of the mind, the sentiments of the heart, the aspirations of the will. The vocal element is not the chief one. The words are but a vehicle—less important than what is conveyed through them. Each prayer is useful in so far as it lifts up the mind and heart to God. Thus, the value of any particular form of vocal prayer depends on how it works for the individual who uses it. It may have worked for the Saint who composed it centuries ago, but it may not work for a workingman in the twentieth century. The test is this: does it raise the mind and heart to God?

When we come to select our prayers, there is an almost numberless variety of printed prayers. Some have, quite obviously, special power to remind us of stirring things, to awaken fervor, to move the will; e.g., the divinely taught *Our Father*, the *Hail Mary*, *Acts of Faith, Hope* and *Charity,* etc. But these are only a few. The Missal and Breviary are full of prayers; there are even many in the Bible, in both the Old and New Testaments; many well-known prayers have come down to us through centuries of pious usage. Every prayer book contains a multitude of prayers for many occasions and circumstances. But they all possess value to the extent that they help us to "lift up mind and will to God." If it works well for me, it is good for me.

We should not undervalue home-made prayers. Sometimes people who cannot pray have written down what they would really like to say to God in time of prayer. This is really helpful. No one should hesitate about expressing himself to God in his own words. "I cannot pray; I wish I could," says someone. All he needs to do is to tell that to God, and he is praying.

Another way of helping ourselves to pray is to take some favorite prayer and repeat the words slowly, dwelling on each as long as it yields appropriate meanings, comparisons, relish and consolation. Then we pass on to the next word, continuing in like manner. Father C. C. Martindale, S.J. does something like this in his useful book, *Words of the Missal*.

Nor must we forget the value of aspirations. The monks of the desert preferred to make their prayers short and frequent, rather than long. There are hundreds of ejaculations which help to raise the mind and heart to God almost in an instant.

Mental prayer

Mental Prayer means prayer with the mind alone. Sometimes it is called **meditation**, although, strictly speaking, meditation is a preparatory process, and not the prayer itself.

A delightful story tells of an old man so slow of speech in the witness box that the judge ordered him to speed up and cease delaying everybody. Half bewildered and wholly apologetic, he answered: "Mister Judge, I ain't no lawyer. I ain't no judge. I have to think before I speak." In other words, he felt the need of meditating. Meditation is essentially nothing more than a process of collecting one's thoughts, of focusing one's attention, of recalling pertinent facts, principles and circumstances.

Here is a very simple method of meditation:
1. Choose a subject.
2. Focus attention on it, examining it in detail.
3. In view of what then presents itself, say to God whatever it seems fitting to say.

Under the second heading, such simple questions as, Who? What? Where? Why? When? How? etc. may be asked concerning the subject, but the whole purpose of meditation is to raise the mind and heart to God. It is not merely an intellectual exercise. Once this purpose is achieved, cease to meditate; just pray.

Of course, some people do not take kindly to meditation. Prayer may be wordless, for the use of words is certainly not indispensable to the raising of the mind and will to God. One can pray well without saying anything, as with the woman in the Gospel story who suffered from an issue of blood, who said to herself, "If I shall touch only his garment, I shall be healed." (*Matt.* 9:21).

The convert should be recommended some simple booklet on the various methods of prayer and encouraged in the daily practice of mental prayer. The aim of the instructor should be to produce a fervent Catholic, and prayer is one of the best means to attain fervor.

All who pray can live in constant communion with God—with what effects?

1. The soul will receive all the graces necessary for salvation.
2. God's goodness will be realized, sin will be hated, and every effort made to avoid it. God will be asked for help in temptation; love of Him and of other souls because of Him will grow; and a sincere effort will be made, with His help, to practice virtue.
3. God's gifts will be appreciated. It will be realized that we are but stewards of material things, not absolute owners. We must therefore be faithful stewards and try to do good.
4. Prayer will bring a sense of nearness to God, of His friendship, of His interest in each one, of His help in sorrow. This will be a new incentive to virtue.
5. Prayer means growth in concern for the next world and appreciation of the true value of this one. Gradually, the attitude of mind will be developed by which everything is judged from the standpoint of eternity.

"If you would endure with patience all the adversities and miseries of this life, be a man of prayer;

"If you would acquire strength and courage to vanquish the temptations of the enemy, be a man of prayer;

"If you would crush yourself with all your inclinations and desires, be a man of prayer;

"If you would know the wiles of Satan and defend yourself against his snares, be a man of prayer;

"If you would live with a gay heart and pass lightly along the road of penance and sacrifice, be a man of prayer;

"If you would drive away vain thoughts and cares, which worry the soul like flies, be a man of prayer;

"If you would nourish the soul with the sap of devotion and have it always filled with good thoughts and desires, be a man of prayer;

"If you would uproot all vices from your soul and plant virtues in their place, be a man of prayer.

"If you would mount to the summit of contemplation and enjoy the sweet embraces of the spouse, exercise yourself in prayer, for it is the road that leads to contemplation and the taste of what is heavenly." —St. Bonaventure.

> "In prayer
> the soul cleanses itself from sin,
> charity is nourished,
> faith is strengthened,
> hope is made secure,
> the spirit rejoices,
> the soul grows tender,
> the heart is purified,
> truth discovers itself,
> temptation is overcome,
> sadness takes to flight,
> the senses are renewed,
> failing virtue is made good,
> tepidity disappears,
> the rust of sin is rubbed away.

In it are brought forth flashes of heavenly desire, and in these fires the flame of divine love burns up."—St. Laurence Justinian.

Chapter 6

What Is Faith?

What is Faith? *Faith is a supernatural gift of God which enables us to believe without doubting whatever God has revealed.*

Why must you believe whatever God has revealed? *I must believe whatever God has revealed because God is the Very Truth and can neither deceive nor be deceived.*

What are the chief mysteries of Faith which every Christian is bound to know? *The chief mysteries of Faith which every Christian is bound to know are the Unity and Trinity of God, who will render to every man according to his works, and the Incarnation, Death, and Resurrection of our Saviour, Jesus Christ.*

IN the last paragraph of his Gospel, St. Mark reports these words of our Lord: "He that believeth and is baptized, shall be saved: but he that believeth not shall be condemned." (*Mark* 16:16). St. Paul makes this solemn declaration: "Without faith it is impossible to please God." (*Heb.* 11:6). These two texts alone are sufficient to demonstrate the **importance of Faith**.

Supernatural faith includes the following principles:

God is our **First Beginning** and our **Last End**.
God has supreme dominion over us.
We owe God due service, which we express in **religion**.
True religion is the true worship of the true God.
God has told us how He wants to be worshipped.
Man must obey this teaching of God.
Man has no right to practice a religion of his own making against God's Will.
God alone can declare to us in what true religion consists.
This declaration of God contains the body of revealed truths.

We are bound to **believe** them; we must **have Faith** in them.
No one can be indifferent about such vital matters.

Even at the time of the Reformation, the **necessity** of Faith was
never questioned. Those who left the true Church **still believed** in
God and Christ. Nowadays, many **reject Faith itself and are
utterly indifferent about religion.** Faith, they say, is nothing more
than an emotion.

No one can be received into the Catholic Church without a **genuine** and **sincere Faith** in the Catholic religion. Faith is the very
foundation on which the whole religious and spiritual edifice of
Catholicism is erected. It is the root holding the tree against all the
storms and difficulties of life and providing the sap which makes
our religion a living force in our lives.

The solemn teaching of the Church on Faith may be summed up
as follows: **Faith** is a **divine virtue** by which we believe revealed
truth, **not** because it is known to us by the natural light of reason,
but because it is known to us **by the authority of God**, who can neither deceive nor be deceived. The virtue of Faith is **infused** into the
soul with Sanctifying Grace, and it is lost **only by a grave sin of
unbelief**, which a man commits by **deliberately** doubting or denying a truth which **he knows** God has revealed. Further, **without a
gift from God consisting in His enlightening and helping grace,
no man can make an act of faith profitable for salvation.** Still,
Faith does **not** deprive a man of liberty, but it is a help which he
freely accepts and with which he freely cooperates; it is **not** a blind
movement of the mind but **is in conformity with reason**. The fact
of God's existence can be most certainly known by the mind of man,
reasoning from created things; the fact that **God has spoken** to us
can be most certainly known from miracles and prophecies. **The
truths which God has revealed are found in Sacred Scripture
and Tradition**. Among these truths are **mysteries** which can never
be understood by the mind of man in this life, no matter how far it
may advance in knowledge.

Faith defined and explained

Faith is a supernatural gift of God by which one chooses rea-

sonably to believe most firmly all that God has revealed because God must know the truth and is incapable of telling a lie.

1. **A Supernatural Gift**: One can neither deserve nor merit it. All we can do is to pray for it, hope for it and make every effort to fulfill the conditions appointed by God. It is **supernatural**, that is, not essential to our nature, not ours at birth, not given for natural ends. If Faith is God's gift, those who possess it are bound to thank Him for it.

2. **Of God**: Only God can bestow it. No amount of instruction can, of itself, give the Faith. All the instructor can do is to explain it and try to help the convert by his example and his prayers. "No man can come to me, except the Father, who hath sent me, draw him; and I will raise him up in the last day." (*John* 6:44). The fact that God, the Creator, the Supreme Being and the Infinite Good is the bestower of the gift of Faith shows how precious it is. How we would cherish a personal gift from an earthly king! (*Eph.* 2:8). Here we have one from the heavenly King!

3. **By which one chooses**: We are not **compelled** to believe. Christ in fact has promised to reward our loyalty. "He who believeth and is baptized, shall be saved." (*Mark* 16:16). It is possible to **lose** the Faith; many have lost it, although they have been intellectually convinced of the truth. Others have refused to accept the gift of Faith because of vanity, human respect or material difficulties. That is why **Christ condemns unbelief**! "He that believeth not shall be condemned." (*Mark* 16:16).

4. **Reasonably**: Every day of our lives we accept truth on the word of man. It is therefore reasonable for us to accept truth on the word of God. The store of information any man can brand as his own, without having acquired it from others, is very small. He continually accepts truth from his fellow men; in fact, dependence on them is a law of human nature. But the higher the authority for information received, the more reasonable is the act of submission to it. God's is the highest possible authority. He is absolute Infallibility itself! Once it is certain that God has spoken, it would be the height of folly to refuse to accept His word. We have more than sufficient evidence to prove that **God has spoken to men**. The historical facts concerning Christ and the Church can be verified by

reason alone, thus justifying their Divine Authority.

Faith does not ignore reason but presupposes it. Nor does it ever contradict reason. It teaches knowledge which is **beyond**—but **never against**—the powers of reason. It guards reason, controls reason (as the laws of arithmetic control the accountant), but Faith does not degrade reason, any more than belief in lovely flowers degrades the blind man who cannot see them. Faith checks intellectual independence, but no more than a lighthouse checks the movements of a sailor.

5. **To believe**: Not to think, or suppose, or even agree to, because a truth is fully understood and demonstrated, but to assent fully to a truth on the word of another—namely, God. The telescope is sometimes used as an example of the function of Faith. As in the natural order, a powerful telescope will enable us to see heavenly bodies otherwise invisible to the human eye, so Faith is an additional power of spiritual "sight," or rather "insight." It brings an **interior conviction about the reality** and a new **appreciation of the significance** of spiritual truths. One who believes finds that these truths impress him ever more deeply. Faith is not, as Luther said, mere trust in the fidelity of God to keep His promises. St. Paul described it as "evidence" (*Heb.* 11:1) and speaks of Faith as "bringing into captivity every understanding unto the obedience of Christ." (*2 Cor.* 10:5).

6. **Most firmly**: It is to be expected that many of the things which God reveals are beyond reason. Nature is full of mysteries—the seed, for instance, falling to the ground and in a few years growing into a great tree—and it is certainly as reasonable to expect mysteries in religion as it is to expect them in nature or physical science. Indeed, if religion had no mysteries and were perfectly and fully comprehensible, its divine origin would be open to suspicion. **What can be fully proved from reason might well have been discovered by reason.**

Belief in mysteries tends vastly to increase our reverence for God. When a child is afraid to go out in the dark, its father says: "Give me your hand and come with me." The child is satisfied; it does not ask for a scientific explanation of the darkness. So we ought not to wish to understand the impenetrable mysteries of God. He is Love, Wisdom and Goodness; we put our hand in His, knowing He cannot lead us astray.

7. **All that God has revealed**: It is the fashion nowadays outside the Catholic Church to pick and choose one's beliefs. **All of God's revelation must be accepted!** Any other course is unreasonable. The Catholic Church never panders to the fashion of the moment in the beliefs she demands of her children. **She stands always by what reason proves to be Divine Revelation, and from it she will never deviate by one hair's breadth**.

8. **Because God knows the truth and could not tell a lie**: He is **All Truth**, and so we must believe all He has chosen to reveal.

Thus, a Catholic's faith should be:

- **Entire:** It must embrace every article of Faith without exception.
- **Firm:** It is not accepted as one would accept a mere opinion, but as one believing on absolute certainty without hesitation.
- **Steadfast**: Faith is accepted in spite of all difficulties and opposition and at the cost of any sacrifice.
- **Living:** Faith is active and effectual, the basis of life.
- **Supernatural**: Faith has God as its source, its end and its motive.

The convert's first act of Faith

In order to dispose himself for the reception of the gift of Faith, the convert should strive especially after the following:

a) **Prayerfulness**: "But if any of you want wisdom, let him ask of God, who giveth to all men abundantly, and upbraideth not; and it shall be given him." (*James* 1:5). Prayer is necessary in order to obtain the gift of Faith; but Faith is not necessary for prayer. The latter is the act of a rational being who knows by pure reason that he is a creature of a Supreme Being on whom he is entirely dependent. Particularly during the period of instruction, the **convert must pray for the gift of Faith**.

b) **Humility**: "God resisteth the proud and giveth grace to the humble." (*James* 4:6). The convert will try to understand his own infirmity, his incapacity to discover all religious truth by unaided reason, the weakness of his will and his tendency to evil. The humble man seeks God; the proud man expects God to seek him, to allow him to adjudge of God's revelation according to his own arrogance. The humble man is conscious of the great privilege he is receiving in being instructed in the True Faith with a view to reception into the Church; the proud man thinks he is conferring a favor on the Church by entering the fold.

c) **Earnestness and conscientiousness**: He must use all diligence to ascertain the truth and be willing to accept it in spite of former notions, prejudices and the habits of a lifetime, and in spite of the additional—sometimes even irksome—duties it will entail.

d) **Cleanness of heart**: A special effort should be made during the period of instructions to lead a good life and check indulgence of the passions, for unchristian conduct is one of the greatest obstacles to Christian belief.

e) **Sorrow for sin**: One of the greatest obstacles in the way of receiving the gift of Faith from God is dishonesty with oneself, deceiving one's conscience into denying that one has ever done evil. It is important that one who aspires to become a Catholic be trained early in the practice of the ready acknowledgment of his guilt before God and the expression of his sorrow. "For every one that doth evil hateth the light, and cometh not to the light, that his works may not be reproved." (*John* 3:20). God threatens, "Woe to you that call evil good, and good evil." (*Is.* 5:20), that is, to those who deny that sin is sin.

There are people who do wrong, know it is wrong, yet lull themselves into the comfortable feeling that it is not wrong and that they are really virtuous. God will be repelled by such an attitude of mind. Christ said that he came to call sinners to repentance. All are not expected to be Saints when they come to religion, but all are expected to admit, at least before God, that they have known the touch of evil, and need God's forgiveness.

Faith is the gift of God and of God alone, yet God expects us to do our part. "**He who made you without you, will not save you without you**," are the wise words of St. Augustine.

The convert will do well to note that conviction is not necessarily Faith. For instance, he might make an act of conviction as follows: God must be worshipped; He has revealed to us how He wishes to be worshipped; therefore, we must worship Him in that way and in no other. But that way is the way of Jesus Christ, God-made-Man; and the way of Jesus Christ includes the Catholic Church. Therefore, Catholicism is the authentic, divinely revealed way of worshipping God. But such conviction, reached under God's grace, is not necessarily in itself an act of Faith. It is one thing to recognize a duty; another to fulfill it. The act of Faith, as the Church teaches, cannot be made without a further and a higher grace, without a very special help from God, and God will not deny that help to one of good disposition. A person with the disposition to find the truth and live by it will then find himself receiving the grace of a gentle submissiveness, moving him to honor God by freely, piously and reverently submitting his mind to God's word; this grace enables him to **give effect** to his conviction and to say: "I **do** believe that God has given me the Church to be my teacher. I do believe it **on the word of the good God** himself who can neither deceive nor be deceived." And that is a true act of Faith.

Faith rests not on reason, but on the authority of God, who is worthy of all reverence and love. Reason can assuredly help lead to Faith; reason can determine nearly for certain that God has spoken. In other words, it can open a door which leads to a higher and different kind of certainty, that given by the word of God. By Faith, however, one believes not because of any argument or reasoning, but precisely because God says it is true.

To bring about the act of Faith, God so strengthens the will by His grace that it commands the assent of the intellect, which in turn has been so strengthened that it obeys and accepts as true even that which it cannot understand. Of course, **God's grace does not force the soul into submission; indeed, there are those who, to their own grave detriment, have rejected the gift of Faith offered them by God**.

St. Augustine wrote: "Thou hast made us for Thyself, O Lord, and our hearts are restless until they rest in Thee." When a man attains to Faith, his mind slips into the socket God has made for it; there it rests securely, never to be dislodged, except by its own grave fault.

Chapter 7

Sin

What is sin? *Sin is an offense against God—by any thought, word, deed or omission against the law of God.*

How many kinds of sin are there? *There are two kinds of sin, Original Sin and actual sin.*

What is Original Sin? *Original Sin is that guilt and stain of sin which we inherit from Adam, who was the origin and head of all mankind.*

What was the sin committed by Adam? *The sin committed by Adam was the sin of disobedience, when he ate the forbidden fruit.*

Have all mankind contracted the guilt and stain of Original Sin? *All mankind have contracted the guilt and stain of Original Sin, except the Blessed Virgin Mary, who, through the merits of her Divine Son was conceived without the least guilt or stain of Original Sin.*

What is this privilege of the Blessed Virgin Mary called? *This privilege of the Blessed Virgin Mary is called the "Immaculate Conception."*

What is actual sin? *Actual sin is every sin which we ourselves commit.*

How is actual sin divided? *Actual sin is divided into mortal sin and venial sin.*

What is mortal sin? *Mortal sin is a grievous offense against God.*

Why is it called mortal sin? *It is called mortal sin because it kills the supernatural life of the soul and makes the soul deserving of Hell, should the person die in that state without repentance.*

How does mortal sin kill the supernatural life of the soul?

Mortal sin kills the supernatural life of the soul by depriving it of Sanctifying Grace, which is the supernatural life of the soul.

Is it a great evil to fall into mortal sin? *It is the greatest of all evils to fall into mortal sin.*

Where will they go who die in mortal sin? *They who die in mortal sin will go to Hell for all eternity.*

What is venial sin? *Venial sin is an offense against God which does not kill the supernatural life of the soul, yet which displeases God and often leads to mortal sin.*

Why is it called venial sin? *It is called venial sin because it is more easily pardoned than mortal sin.*

How must we hate sin? *We must hate sin above all other evils, in order to be resolved never to commit a willful sin, for the love or fear of anything whatsoever.*

Which are the Seven Capital Sins, or vices, and their contrary virtues? *The seven capital sins, or vices, and their contrary virtues are the following:*

1. *Pride*	1. *Humility*
2. *Covetousness*	2. *Liberality*
3. *Lust*	3. *Chastity*
4. *Anger*	4. *Meekness*
5. *Gluttony*	5. *Temperance*
6. *Envy*	6. *Brotherly Love*
7. *Sloth*	7. *Diligence*

Why are they called Capital Sins? *They are called Capital Sins because they are the **sources** from which all other sins take their rise.*

Which are the six sins against the Holy Ghost? *The six sins against the Holy Ghost are:*

1. *Presumption*	4. *Envy of another's spiritual good*
2. *Despair*	5. *Obstinacy in sin*
3. *Resisting the known truth*	6. *Final impenitence*

Which are the four sins "crying to Heaven for vengeance"? *The four sins "crying to Heaven for vengeance" are:*

1. *Willful murder*   3. *Oppression of the poor (widows, etc.)*
2. *Homosexual acts* 4. *Defrauding laborers of their wages*

When are we answerable for the sins of others? *We are answerable for the sins of others whenever we either cause them or share in them, through our own fault.*

In how many ways may we either cause or share the guilt of another's sin? *We may either cause or share the guilt of another's sin in nine ways:*

1. *By counsel.*
2. *By command.*
3. *By consent.*
4. *By provocation.*
5. *By praise or flattery.*
6. *By concealment.*
7. *By being a partner in the sin.*
8. *By silence.*
9. *By defending the ill done.*

Which are the enemies we must fight against all the days of our life? *The enemies which we must fight against all the days of our life are the world, the flesh and the devil.*

What do you mean by the world? *By the world I mean the false maxims of the world and the society of those who love the vanities, riches and pleasures of this world better than God.*

What do you mean by the devil? *By the devil I mean Satan and all his wicked angels, who are ever seeking to draw us into sin, that we may be damned with them.*

Why do you number the world and the devil among the enemies of the soul? *I number the world and the devil among the enemies of the soul because they are always seeking, by temptation and by word or example, to carry us along with them on the broad road that leads to damnation.*

What do you mean by the flesh? *By the flesh I mean our own corrupt inclinations and passions, which are the most dangerous of all our enemies.*

**What must we do to hinder the enemies of our soul from draw-

ing us into sin? *To hinder the enemies of our soul from drawing us into sin, we must watch, pray and fight against all their suggestions and temptations.*

In the warfare against the world, the flesh and the devil, on whom must we depend? *In the warfare against the world, the flesh and the devil, we must depend, not on ourselves, but on God only: "I can do all things in Him who strengtheneth me." (Phil. 4:13).*

"IF we say that we have no sin, we deceive ourselves, and the truth is not in us." (*1 John* 1:8). These words of St. John serve to introduce the subject of sin, now a fact of universal experience.

The Catholic catechism teaches that **sin is an offense against God, by any thought, word, deed or omission against the law of God**.

When a man violates the law of his country, he is a criminal in the sight of that law, and usually he is punished.

Sin is a crime, not against the law of any land, but against the law of God; hence, the sinner is a criminal in the sight of God, his Maker, his infinitely good and loving Father, his Judge.

Sometimes sinners try to justify themselves by explaining that in doing wrong they "did not go against their conscience." But it is the duty of everyone to make sure that his conscience is reliable and in conformity with the true law of God. He has to have a "correct conscience," in the terms of the moralist. It is not enough just to have a "certain conscience," which could obviously deceive him. One's conscience must be "correct." A watch is no use to anyone unless it is regulated according to the true time. The conscience is like a watch; it must be regulated according to the true norm of morality, the law of God. Conscience is the interior judgment we make as to the rightness or wrongness of our actions, and such judgment can only be reliable in so far as it does not contradict the only real norm of right and wrong. People sometimes warp their consciences, or stretch them. In fact, they are rather like "sweet Molly Malone," who followed her barrow wherever she pushed it around the streets of "Dublin's fair city"—except that, instead of a barrow, they have what they like to call their conscience, which they push wherever they want it to go.

Conscience is only "correct" when its verdict is in harmony with the Ten Commandments of God, the Six Commandments of the Church and the demands of the Christian virtues. These we shall learn in due course in order to educate our conscience.

Sin in Scripture

Sin is disastrous for both the soul and the body: "He that soweth iniquity shall reap evils, and with the rod of his anger he shall be consumed." (*Prov.* 22:8). "Do no evils, and no evils shall lay hold of thee. Depart from the unjust, and evils shall depart from thee. My son, sow not evils in the furrows of injustice, and thou shalt not reap them sevenfold." (*Eccles.* 7:1-3). "For a wicked soul shall destroy him that hath it, and maketh him to be a joy to his enemies, and shall lead him into the lot of the wicked." (*Eccles.* 6:4).

Mortal sin deprives our words and undertakings of merit: "If the just man turn himself away from his justice . . . all his justices which he hath done, shall not be remembered." (*Ezech.* 18:24).

Mortal sin brings with it both temporal and eternal punishment: "But transgressors shall all of them be plucked up as thorns." (*2 Kings.* 23:6). "But the fearful, the unbelieving, and the abominable, and murderers, and whoremongers, and sorcerers, and idolaters, and all liars, they shall have their portion in the pool burning with fire and brimstone, which is the second death." (*Apoc.* 21:8). "Then he shall say to them also that shall be on his left hand: Depart from me, you cursed, into everlasting fire which was prepared for the devil and his angels." (*Matt.* 25:41).

Sin causes blindness and ignorance in the understanding: "They shall walk like blind men because they have sinned against the Lord." (*Soph.* 1:17). "These things they thought, and were deceived: for their own malice blinded them." (*Wis.* 2:21).

Sin turns away the will from the Supreme Good and hardens it in evil: "Therefore pride hath held them fast: they are covered with their iniquity and their wickedness." (*Ps.* 72:6).

Sin begets fear and perplexity: "For whereas wickedness is fearful, it beareth witness of its condemnation: for a troubled conscience always forecasteth grievous things." (*Wis.* 17:10).

Sin brings with it shame and shamelessness: "What fruit

therefore had you then in those things, of which you are now ashamed? For the end of them is death." (*Rom.* 6:21). "The wicked man impudently hardeneth his face." (*Prov.* 21:29).

Sadness and despair are the end of sin: "Into how much tribulation am I come, and into what floods of sorrow, wherein now I am: I that was pleasant and beloved in my power! But now I remember the evils that I have done . . ." (*1 Mach.* 6:11-12).

Sin robs body and soul of strength: "There is no health in my flesh, because of thy wrath: there is no peace for my bones, because of my sins." (*Ps.* 37:4).

Sin shortens life and hastens death: "Humble thy spirit very much: for the vengeance on the flesh of the ungodly is fire and worms." (*Ecclus.* 7:19).

Sin destroys reputation, honor and fame: "The memory of the just is with praises: and the name of the wicked shall rot." (*Prov.* 10:7). "Who will justify him that sinneth against his own soul? And who will honor him that dishonoureth his own soul?" (*Ecclus.* 10:32).

Sin ruins prosperity: "Justice exalteth a nation: but sin maketh nations miserable." (*Prov.* 14:34). "Woe to them, for they have departed from me: they shall be wasted because they have transgressed against me." (*Osee* 7:13).

Sin makes a man hated by God: "To God the wicked and his wickedness are hateful alike." (*Wis.* 14:9). "For the Lord thy God abhorreth him that doth these things, and he hateth all injustice." (*Deut.* 25:16).

The horror of sin

Just how terrible mortal sin is can be judged from the following:

1. Mortal sin is a supreme contempt for the infinite majesty of God. The creature despises the laws the Creator has made for him and laughs Him to scorn. The grievous sinner would kill God if he could; for God and sin cannot exist close together. Those who live in grave sin act as if God did not exist. Infinite Love, Power, Goodness, Wisdom and Mercy could be dead, as far as the grave sinner is concerned. He is not interested. Yet God has already shown how He

hates sin by subjecting all the children of Adam to the evils of life and to death, by permitting the Deluge, by destroying Sodom and Gomorrha, by slaying 23,000 idolatrous Israelites (*Exod.* 32:28) and by suffering so much Himself after the Incarnation.

2. It was sin which caused the sufferings of Christ—the Agony, the Scourging, the Crowning with Thorns and the Crucifixion. Sinners crucify Him all over again, mocking Him and His love. Mortal sin is the deepest, blackest ingratitude to the loving Heart of Christ.

3. Mortal sin deforms the souls of men, destroying all the spiritual beauty that is in them. It makes the soul bankrupt, by robbing it of all past merit; it paralyzes the soul, because the soul is then unable to gain supernatural merit from any good works done while in the state of mortal sin. In fact, mortal sin kills the soul by taking away from it all supernatural or spiritual life. A man in grievous sin ceases to be the temple of the Holy Trinity, a sharer in the Divine Nature and a spiritual brother of Christ. If a man has committed mortal sin, his body is but a living coffin for a supernaturally dead soul, and if he dies unrepentant, he will be condemned to the living death of Hell for all eternity. In a word, **mortal sin is the greatest of all evils**. When St. Louis of France was a boy, his mother, Blanche of Castile, once said: "You are as dear to me as any son could be to any mother, yet I would rather see you lying dead at my feet than that you should ever commit a mortal sin." Later in life, the King himself remarked on one occasion to a friend who said he would prefer to commit a serious sin if by it he could avoid leprosy: "You are wrong. Nothing is more to be dreaded than to displease God."

When Leonardo da Vinci was painting his famous picture of the Last Supper, he took as his model for Our Lord a young choir boy of Milan Cathedral—Pietro Bandinelli. Years later, da Vinci was looking for a model for the face of Judas. In the streets of Rome he came across a man whose hardened eyes and vice-lined countenance struck him as being ideal for his purpose. On being asked to sit in the studio, this new model said: "Of course, you have already painted me once before—I am Pietro Bandinelli." Whether the story be true or not, it certainly brings out the fact that whereas the state of grace makes one like to Christ, that of mortal sin makes him like to Judas.

The divisions of sin

Sin may be **Original** or **actual**; and **actual** sin may be **mortal** or **venial**.

Original Sin: This is the sinful condition in which men are born and which we inherit from our first parents, Adam and Eve. When Adam fell, by deliberately sinning against God, he plunged the whole human race into a state of guilt. In fact, he **was** the human race; his was not only a personal sin, but a racial, a family sin. The **effects** of the sin of Adam for his descendants were as follows:

1. **In the soul** there was the loss of divine grace, privation from Heaven, ignorance in the intellect, weakness and malice in the will, concupiscence in the heart;
2. **In body** there was the loss of man's extraordinary natural gifts; plus, the new conditions of work, sickness, death and corruption;
3. **On earth** there was unfruitful soil, which had to be tilled; some of the animals were now ferocious and beyond control.

The sin committed by Adam was the sin of disobedience when he ate the forbidden fruit. His story can be read in the Book of *Genesis*.

To a man who denied he was born in Original Sin, G. K. Chesterton replied: "The only thing you know about original innocence is that you never had it."

The Church has declared that Catholics may not call into doubt the literal meaning of the Book of *Genesis* with regard to "the original happiness of our first parents, the command given by God to test their obedience, their disobedience of this command at the instigation of the devil, and the loss of their primitive state of innocence."

St. Paul, in his Epistle to the Romans, clearly teaches the doctrine of Original Sin: "Wherefore as by one man sin entered into this world, and by sin death; and so death passed upon all men, in whom all have sinned. For as by the disobedience of one man [Adam], many were made sinners; so also by the obedience of one [Christ], many shall be made just." (*Rom.* 5:12, 19).

Original Sin does not imply any injustice on the part of God, for it does not injure man in anything that is natural to him. Adam, it is true, lost all his supernatural and preternatural gifts, not only for himself, but for us, his descendants, as well. But those gifts were neither his nor ours by right of our nature; God only gave them to him gratuitously, on the one condition that Adam was to obey His commandment. As Fr. C. C. Martindale, S.J. says so well: "Original Sin is **not** an evil bias, a tendency to wrong, a taint in spirit or in flesh, a corruption of any part of human nature as such. Concupiscence, the natural activity of instincts or passions not subordinate to reason, is not Original Sin, but a consequence of it, even though it may lead, often enough, to actual sin." All men, except Our Lady, come into this world deprived of that sanctity and justice God intended them to have; it is precisely in this deprivation that Original Sin exists. It is a true sin, one which we inherit, but do not ourselves commit. It is voluntary in us only because, physically, we were included in Adam, in that he and we form one family. He could represent us, and God appointed him to represent us. Adam held the special gifts God gave him in trust for himself and all his descendants, just as a peer [a lord in the English government] may hold his title and emoluments for himself and his descendants. Hence, our whole race stood or fell with Adam. He, in fact, failed, and all mankind were thus involved in his loss.

Actual sin: These are the sins we ourselves commit. They may be thoughts, desires, words, deeds or omissions.

Actual sin is divided into **mortal sin** and **venial sin**.

Mortal sin: This type of sin is so grave that through it God's love and friendship are lost, together with the life of grace in the soul—God's life that is given to us and which is called Sanctifying Grace. "Mortal" comes from the Latin word, *mors,* which means "death." It is so called because it kills the soul by depriving it of Sanctifying Grace, or supernatural life. As the soul is the life of the body, and without a soul, a body is dead in the sight of men, so grace is the life of the soul, and without grace, the soul is dead in the sight of God.

For a sin to be mortal, the following conditions must be fulfilled:

1. **Grave matter:**
   a) The nature of the sin in itself is grave: e.g., murder, a large theft, willful impurity.

  b) The nature of the sin in the purpose of the law is grave: e.g.,
     receiving Holy Communion after breaking one's fast.
  c) The nature of the sin in its circumstances is grave: e.g., steal-
     ing a small sum from a very poor person.

2. **Knowledge and advertence**: There must be knowledge that the matter is grave; willful ignorance will not excuse a person from the gravity of a mortal sin (or of the seriousness of a venial sin).

3. **Full consent**: There must be full consent by the sinner to do the sin, or to enter into the occasion of it.

If one of the above conditions is absent, or if the act be done under compulsion or grave fear, what would otherwise be a mortal sin may become only a venial sin at most.

Venial sin is an offense which does not kill the soul, yet which displeases God and often leads to mortal sin. Examples of venial sin are sins of infirmity, surprise, impetuosity, indeliberation or habit, in a small matter. "For in many things we all offend." (*James* 3:2).

Instead of killing the soul, venial sin, as it were, bruises it. It displeases the infinitely holy God, dims the soul's beauty, diminishes its fervor, weakens faith and the hatred of sin, reduces the reception of grace and deserves temporal punishment here and/or hereafter.

No number of venial sins, as such, ever constitutes a mortal sin, but as wounds in the body, if unheeded, may lead to sickness and death, so also, frequent venial sin often gradually leads one to commit mortal sin. The greatest things usually take their rise from small beginnings—the river from the spring, the tree from the seed, the conflagration from a spark, death from a germ, etc.—and mortal sin gets its start from venial sin.

Hence, venial sin is not something to be taken lightly. After mortal sin, it is the greatest evil before God, and we may not commit it for any good or gain whatsoever, not even to convert the world.

We must try to obtain **a true estimate of sin**. We can do this by meditating seriously and frequently on the consequences of sin—of the sin of Lucifer, of the sin of Adam, on the Passion and death of Christ, and on the fact of the eternity of punishment which awaits those who die in the state of mortal sin.

The time of instruction in the Catholic faith is a time of preparation for the reception of great graces. It should therefore be a period of repentance and contrition for past sins—mortal or venial.

The absence of penance is an obstacle to the reception of grace. Therefore, the habit should be formed of reciting daily **an act of contrition**, such as the following:

An Act of Contrition: O my God, I am heartily sorry for having offended Thee, and I detest all my sins because I dread the loss of Heaven and the pains of Hell, but most of all because they offend Thee, my God, Who art all good and deserving of all my love. I firmly resolve, with the help of Thy grace, to confess my sins, to do penance and to amend my life. Amen.

Chapter 8

The Commandments of God (1)

What is Charity? *Charity is a Supernatural Virtue—a supernatural gift of God by which we love God above all things and our neighbor as ourselves for God's sake.*

Why must we love God? *We must love God because He is infinitely good in Himself and infinitely good to us.*

How do we show that we love God? *We show that we love God by keeping His commandments: for Christ says, "If you love Me, keep My commandments." (John 14:15).*

Which are the two great precepts of Charity? *The two great precepts of Charity are:*

1. *"Thou shalt love the Lord thy God with thy whole heart, and with thy whole soul, and with thy whole mind, and with thy whole strength." (Mark 12:30).*
2. *"Thou shalt love thy neighbor as thyself." (Mark 12:31).*

Which are the seven Corporal Works of Mercy? *The seven Corporal Works of Mercy are:*

1. *To feed the hungry.*
2. *To give drink to the thirsty.*
3. *To clothe the naked.*
4. *To visit the imprisoned.*
5. *To shelter the homeless.*
6. *To visit the sick.*
7. *To bury the dead.*

Which are the seven Spiritual Works of Mercy? *The seven Spiritual Works of Mercy are:*

1. *To admonish the sinner.*
2. *To instruct the ignorant.*
3. *To counsel the doubtful.*
4. *To comfort the sorrowful.*
5. *To bear wrongs patiently.*
6. *To forgive all injuries.*
7. *To pray for the living and the dead.*

Which are the Eight Beatitudes? *The eight Beatitudes are:*

1. *Blessed are the poor in spirit, for theirs is the Kingdom of Heaven.*
2. *Blessed are the meek, for they shall possess the land.*
3. *Blessed are they that mourn, for they shall be comforted.*
4. *Blessed are they that hunger and thirst after justice, for they shall have their fill.*
5. *Blessed are the merciful, for they shall obtain mercy.*
6. *Blessed are the clean of heart, for they shall see God.*
7. *Blessed are the peacemakers, for they shall be called the children of God.*
8. *Blessed are they that suffer persecution for justice' sake, for theirs is the Kingdom of Heaven. (Matt. 5:3-10).*

Does Jesus Christ also command us to love one another? *Jesus Christ also commands us to love one another—that is, all persons without exception—for His sake.*

How are we to love one another? *We are to love one another by wishing well to one another and praying for one another, and by never allowing ourselves any thought, word or deed to the injury of anyone.*

Are we also bound to love our enemies? *We are also bound to love our enemies, not only by forgiving them from our hearts, but also by wishing them well and praying for them.*

THE FIRST COMMANDMENT

What is the First Commandment? *The First Commandment is, "I am the Lord thy God, who brought thee out of the land of Egypt, and out of the house of bondage. Thou shalt not have strange gods before Me. Thou shalt not make to thyself a graven thing, nor the likeness of anything that is in heaven above, or in the earth beneath, nor of those things that are in the waters under the earth. Thou shalt not adore them nor serve them." (Exodus 20:2-5).*

What are we commanded to do by the First Commandment? *By the First Commandment we are commanded to worship the one, true and living God, by Faith, Hope, Charity and True Religion.*

What are the sins against Faith? *The sins against Faith are believing in a false religion, willful doubt, disbelief or denial of any article of the Faith, and also culpable ignorance of the doctrines of the Church.*

How do we expose ourselves to the danger of losing our Faith? *We expose ourselves to the danger of losing our Faith by sinning, failing to pray, failing to study our faith, neglecting our spiritual duties, reading bad books, going to non-Catholic schools and taking part in the services or prayers of a false religion.*

What are the sins against Hope? *The sins against Hope are presumption and despair.*

What are the chief sins against Religion? *The chief sins against Religion are the worship of false gods or idols and the giving to any creature whatsoever that honor which belongs to God alone.*

Does the First Commandment forbid the making of images? *The First Commandment does not forbid the making of images, but the making of idols; that is, it forbids us to make images to be adored or honored as gods.*

Does the First Commandment forbid dealing with the devil and superstitious practices? *The First Commandment forbids all dealing with the devil and superstitious practices, such as consulting spiritualists and fortune-tellers, and trusting to charms, omens, dreams and similar fooleries.*

Are all sins of sacrilege and simony also forbidden by the First Commandment? *All sins of sacrilege and simony [selling religious services] are also forbidden by the First Commandment.*

Is it forbidden to give divine honor or worship to the Angels and Saints? *It is forbidden to give divine honor or worship to the Angels and Saints, for this belongs to God alone.*

What kind of honor or reverence should we pay to the Angels and Saints? *We should pay to the Angels and Saints an inferior honor or reverence, for this is due to them as the servants and special friends of God.*

What honor should we give to relics, crucifixes and holy pictures? *We should give to relics, crucifixes and holy pictures a relative honor, as they relate to Christ and His Saints, and are memorials of them.*

Do we pray to relics or images? *We do not pray to relics or images, for they can neither see nor hear nor help us, but we do pray to those Saints or holy people whom they represent, for their intercession with God for us.*

"IF you love me, keep my commandments." So says Our Lord. (*John* 14:15).

Just as the Creed is a compendium of faith, so the Ten Commandments of God are a compendium of morals. They are an explicit statement of the natural laws of truth, order and justice. Because God made them for all men and for all time, they must be holy, just, true and unchangeable. They are a light on the pilgrimage of men through the dark valley of this life of trial, and if they are observed, they will bring happiness, even on this side of the grave. It is not sufficient to believe God's revelation; we must also **do what He tells us**. If men would only do this, most of the troubles with which they find themselves afflicted would be at an end.

The Ten Commandments in their briefest form are as follows:

1. I am the Lord thy God. Thou shalt not have strange gods before Me.
2. Thou shalt not take the name of the Lord thy God in vain.
3. Remember that thou keep holy the Sabbath day.
4. Honor thy father and thy mother.
5. Thou shalt not kill.
6. Thou shalt not commit adultery.
7. Thou shalt not steal.
8. Thou shalt not bear false witness against thy neighbor.
9. Thou shalt not covet thy neighbor's wife.
10. Thou shalt not covet thy neighbor's goods.

Protestants divide the First Commandment into two and join the ninth and tenth into one.

Since the Ten Commandments represent God's law for all men, **they are possible for all men** to observe successfully. God would not make laws that it is impossible to observe. Moreover, God always gives those graces necessary to observe the Commandments. Not only is it possible for all men to observe them; **it is necessary and obligatory for them to do so. Therefore, everyone has the obligation to know them**.

The story of God's giving the Ten Commandments to Moses can be read in the Book of Exodus, Chapter 19. It was fifty days after the passage of the Red Sea, on 7,000-foot-high Mt. Sinai in Arabia, after three days' preparation by the people and amid thunder and lightning. The Commandments given to Moses were ratified by Jesus Christ, God made Man, who said: "Do not think that I am come to destroy the law, or the prophets. I am not come to destroy, but to fulfill." (*Matt.* 5:17).

The First Commandment

The First Commandment enjoins the worship of God by Faith, Hope, Charity and True Religion. It commands us to believe firmly in God and in His word, to learn what He has taught and to profess our belief. It bids us also to trust or hope in God, to love Him, and to adore Him by prayer and sacrifice.

Sins against Faith

Therefore, all forms of false religion—all those not established by God Himself—are forbidden. It is obviously wrong to maintain that religions established by men, with no divine authority or mission, are equal to that which was established by God. **One religion is not as good as another**. When it is certain that God has revealed something to us, it is sinful to willfully doubt it or to disbelieve it. The latter is rebellion against God, arising from pride. Nor may one pick and choose his beliefs: **everything** revealed by God must be accepted by **everyone**. Moreover, men have the duty to find out God's revelations. **Ignorance of religion is one of the greatest evils**

in the modern world; even many Catholics are not innocent in this matter. All have the duty of knowing their religion. If ignorance is due to one's own fault or neglect, it is sinful; and if it is a serious fault or neglect, it would be mortally sinful.

Faith is man's greatest gift. If he loses it, he loses his greatest treasure, and experience proves that, once a person loses the gift of Faith, it is very difficult to get it back.

Willfully to expose oneself to the danger of losing the Faith would be a grievous sin. We expose ourselves to the danger of losing our Faith by:

a) **Committing sin, especially mortal sin:** When a person sins, he has to lie to himself and say that what he is doing is **not** a sin, or that the sin is not so bad as the Church maintains, or that "God will understand." To live habitually in sin, especially mortal sin, is to live with these rationalizations in one's mind, which, being lies, will eventually subvert one's belief in the truth revealed by God.

b) **Failing to pray:** It is a teaching of the Faith that a person will only save his soul through the grace of God, and that God will only give this grace if a person asks for it. **Therefore, we must pray in order to save our souls;** we must ask God for His help to achieve this goal. "According to the ordinary course of Divine Providence man cannot be saved without prayer."—Fr. Michael Mueller, C.SS.R. (Cf. also St. Alphonsus Liguori on the necessity of prayer.)

c) **Failing to study our faith:** True religion is a subject of study, just like any other subject; we cannot really know the Faith unless we continue to learn about it. The knowledge of our Holy Religion acquired when we were children, or when we first heard of the Faith, will not be sufficient to serve us as adults. After all, no one in his right mind would allow a physician to remove his appendix who had not studied medicine beyond twelfth grade in high school, and who had never consulted a medical book since! Since we are the primary doctors of our own souls; so must we continue to study the True Religion to keep ever in mind what is required to be saved. Our faith must grow as we grow and as we become more worldly wise and more learned in our various secular professions. Our knowledge of the

Faith needs to grow within us and also be refreshed and augmented as we advance in other knowledge. Otherwise, we risk losing our faith through lack of adequate knowledge of it.

d) **Neglecting our spiritual duties:** A machine left idle will rust and become useless. The Sacraments are the sources of grace. Confession will enable a person in mortal sin to regain the life of Sanctifying Grace in his soul, or help him to achieve an increase of grace if he has committed only venial sins; it will also help him overcome his sins and resist temptations. Holy Communion is the food of the soul, giving the strength necessary to grow in virtue. Neglect of the Sacraments, especially of Holy Communion, means that the soul is spiritually starved.

e) **Reading bad books:** Bad books include those against religion and morality. Bad literature is very common nowadays, especially novels describing immorality in either a veiled or open way. Parents should be particularly careful to safeguard their children against bad reading. Magazines and newspapers are also a danger in this regard.

f) **Going to non-Catholic schools:** This does not mean only Protestant schools, but also those in which no religion is taught. In such places there is no Catholic atmosphere, and an essential element—the most important element—in education is lacking, i.e., the teaching of one's proper duty toward the Creator.

g) **Taking part in the services or prayers of a false religion**: Protestants usually believe that all Christian religions are as good as one another, that the denominations are merely various branches of Christ's Church. Hence, they usually have no objection to attending Catholic services. But Catholics believe that their own Church is the **only** one founded by God Himself and that all others are false. Hence, it is illogical of Catholics to attend services held by ministers of false religions. If for a sufficient reason anyone wishes to attend a service in a Protestant church, e.g., the marriage of a close friend or relative, he must take no part in the service. If there is doubt as to the sufficiency of the reason or the possibility of scandal, a priest should be consulted beforehand.

Sins against Hope

It is possible to sin against **Hope** both by excess and by defect, that is, by **presumption** or by **despair**. The sin of **Presumption** means having a rash expectation of salvation without taking the means to achieve it; e.g., those who continue to live in mortal sin, hoping for a deathbed repentance, or those who trust in their own efforts to save their souls without the grace of God. **Despair** means distrust of obtaining salvation and the means to it. Both presumption and despair are grievous sins against the Holy Ghost. The great example of *presumption* was St. Peter, whom it led to denying Our Lord; the great example of *despair* was Judas, whom it led to commit suicide.

Sins against Religion

The chief sins against **religion** are the worship of false gods or idols and the giving to any creature whatsoever the honor that belongs to God alone. Complete idolatry is not common in civilized countries nowadays, but one of the most frequent sins is **interpretative** idolatry, or an inordinate love of creatures and created things, which prevents perfect love of God.

The First Commandment does not forbid the making of statues. There are several examples from Scripture of the lawful use of images, e.g., the images of angels in the Jewish Tabernacle, the Brazen Serpent, the adornments of the walls of the Temple (cf. *Exod.* 25:18; *Num.* 21:8 and *3 Kings* 6:29). The early Christians had their images and holy pictures in the Catacombs. Statues and holy pictures teach or recall important truths or the example of holy men and women; they catch and fix our attention and are an aid to devotion. *and teaching.*

All dealings with the devil are, of course, clearly against the First Commandment. So are spiritualism, consulting fortune-tellers, trusting to charms, omens, dreams and all other superstitious practices.

Spiritualism

Spiritualism is condemned in Scripture: "Neither let there be found among you any one that shall expiate his son or daughter, making them to pass through the fire: or that consulteth soothsayers, or observeth dreams and omens; neither let there be any wizard, nor charmer, nor any one that consulteth pythonic spirits, or fortune tellers, or that seeketh the truth from the dead." (*Deut.* 18:10-11). Those who practice spiritualism are most often animated by motives that are far from supernatural and find the practice a lucrative profession. It gives great scope for trickery and for deceit by the devil. Physical evils—even insanity—sometimes follow indulgence in necromancy, or consulting the dead.

God alone knows the future; mercifully, He has hidden it from us. To consult fortune-tellers is wrong. Even if it is done only for amusement, it is sinful amusement, may give scandal, and can lead one to consult spiritualists and to sin seriously.

Sacrilege

Sacrilege means the violent or irreverent treatment of what is consecrated to God. It is of three kinds, depending on whether it is the violation of a sacred person, place or thing. Of its nature, sacrilege is a mortal sin, although it may be only venial through the smallness of matter, lack of deliberation or some other cause. **We ought always to practice reverence for and obedience to God's specially chosen and anointed ministers**, as also for all those consecrated to God and for everything which pertains especially to His service. Our conduct in church should always be worthy of the House of God; there we should always be on our most formal, best behavior, including proper posture at all times that is worthy of our being in the presence of Almighty God.

Simony

Simony, called after Simon Magus, who tried to buy spiritual power from St. Peter (*Acts* 8:18), means the buying or selling of spiritual things for a temporal price or reward. Offerings made **on**

the occasion of spiritual favors—and not in payment for them—are not simony, e.g., Mass stipends, offerings on the occasion of baptisms, marriages, etc. These are meant to be contributions toward the upkeep of the clergy, who are dependent on the offerings of the people, and also to provide for the necessities of the public worship of God. It is customary for Catholics to support their priests in this way, for thereby they merit special blessings for themselves. In order to guide people and to prevent abuses in regard to Mass stipends and stole fees, many dioceses have standardized the amount which it is usual to offer, although, of course, there is no question of the performance of a spiritual work being conditional on a certain offering being forthcoming. **Priests do not sell Masses nor do people pay for Masses**. The Mass **cannot be sold**, but its offering supposes the outward necessities: bread, wine, altar, vestments and a person specially authorized to offer the Mass in the name of Christ and the Church. The Mass offering is a contribution toward these external necessities, and especially toward the upkeep of the priest, who stands at the altar on behalf of the people. When a Catholic gives a Mass stipend, the Mass is applied according to his intention.

Catholics honor the Angels and Saints, but not with divine honor. As the special friends of God, they are worthy of special honor, but only of an inferior honor, one befitting them as creatures, infinitely below the Creator. The practice of thus honoring them is very ancient. It is not forbidden by any Commandment, and it is a useful practice, for the Saints are our friends and God's friends, filled with charity toward us and toward God. The best way to honor the Saints is to imitate their virtues.

Relics, crucifixes and **holy pictures** are honored, not for their own sakes, nor for their intrinsic value, but because they relate to those who are worthy of honor. Even in worldly affairs, men honor the memorials of the great and prize their possessions. Of course, we do not pray to relics or images, for they can neither see, hear, nor help us.

Chapter 9

The Commandments of God (2)

THE SECOND COMMANDMENT

What is the Second Commandment? *The Second Commandment is "Thou shalt not take the name of the Lord thy God in vain."*

What are we commanded by the Second Commandment? *By the Second Commandment we are commanded to speak with reverence of God and all holy persons and things, and to keep our lawful oaths and vows.*

What does the Second Commandment forbid? *The Second Commandment forbids all false, rash, unjust and unnecessary oaths; as also blaspheming, cursing and profane words.*

Is it ever lawful to swear or to take an oath? *It is lawful to swear, or to take an oath only when God's honor or our own or our neighbor's good requires it.*

THE THIRD COMMANDMENT

What is the Third Commandment? *The Third Commandment is "Remember that thou keep holy the Sabbath day."*

What are we commanded by the Third Commandment? *By the Third Commandment we are commanded to keep Sundays holy.*

How are we to keep Sundays holy? *We are to keep Sundays holy by hearing Mass and resting from servile work on that day.*

Why are we commanded to rest from servile work? *We are commanded to rest from servile work, that we may have time and opportunity for prayer, for going to the Sacraments, for hearing instruction, for reading good books, and for gaining rest and refreshment for the coming week.*

THE FOURTH COMMANDMENT

What is the Fourth Commandment? *The Fourth Commandment is "Honor thy father and thy mother."*

What are we commanded by the Fourth Commandment? *By the Fourth Commandment we are commanded to love, reverence and obey our parents in all that is not a sin.*

Are we commanded to obey our parents only? *We are commanded to obey, not only our parents, but also our bishops and pastors, the civil authorities and all our lawful superiors.*

Are we bound to assist our parents in their needs? *We are bound to assist our parents in their needs, both spiritual and temporal.*

Are we bound in justice to contribute to the support of our pastors? *We are bound in justice to contribute to the support of our pastors; for St. Paul says, "The Lord ordained that they who preach the Gospel should live by the Gospel." (1 Cor. 9:14).*

What is the duty of parents toward their children? *The duty of parents toward their children is to provide for them, to instruct and correct them, and to give them a good Catholic education.*

What is the duty of masters, mistresses and other superiors? *The duty of masters, mistresses and other superiors is to take proper care of those under their charge and to enable them to practice their religious duties.*

What does the Fourth Commandment forbid? *The Fourth Commandment forbids all contempt, stubbornness and disobedience to our parents and lawful superiors.*

Is it sinful to belong to a Secret Society? *It is sinful to belong to any Secret Society that plots against the Church or the State, or to any Society that by reason of its secrecy is condemned by the Church; for St. Paul says, "Let every soul be subject to higher powers . . . he that resisteth the power resisteth the ordinance of God. And they that resist purchase to themselves damnation." (Rom. 13:1-2).*

THE FIFTH COMMANDMENT

What is the Fifth Commandment? *The Fifth Commandment is "Thou shalt not kill."*

What does the Fifth Commandment forbid? *The Fifth Commandment forbids all willful murder, fighting, quarreling and injurious words, and also scandal and bad example.*

Does the Fifth Commandment forbid anger? *The Fifth Commandment forbids unjust anger, and still more, hatred and revenge.*

Why are scandal and bad example forbidden by the Fifth Commandment? *Scandal and bad example are forbidden by the Fifth Commandment because they lead to the injury and spiritual death of our neighbor's soul.*

The Second Commandment

THE **Second Commandment** is the natural sequel of the First. Scripture enjoins reverence for the name of God in other places also: "O Lord, our Lord, how admirable is thy name in the whole earth!" "Holy and terrible is his name." (*Ps.* 8:1, *Ps.* 110:9).

It is clearly implied that due reverence must always be used in speaking of God and all holy persons and things. The mere thought of the relationship existing between the Creator and the creature should be a sufficient reminder of this.

Oaths and **vows** are forms of speech having special reference to God.

An **oath** is calling God to witness the truth of what we say. We **swear** only when we take an oath. "And thou shalt swear: As the Lord liveth, in truth, and in judgement, and in justice." (*Jer.* 4:2). It is lawful to take an oath only when God's honor, or our own, or our neighbor's good requires it. We must believe that what we swear is true; we should only swear when there is a good reason for doing so, and after careful reflection and with discretion. The thing sworn to and our intention in swearing must be honest. False, rash and unnecessary oaths are, of course, forbidden.

A **vow** is a promise to God, binding oneself to do some good. For a vow to be lawful, it must be a **true promise** (not just a resolution) and it must be made to **God** with full **knowledge, freedom** and **deliberation** to do something more perfect than what we are already doing, and it must also be morally possible. Persons who enter the **religious orders** in the Catholic Church usually take the three vows of **poverty, chastity** and **obedience**. Those who wish to be released from vows must apply for a dispensation to the competent authority over them.

Blaspheming, cursing and **profane words** are forbidden by the Second Commandment.

Blasphemy is any thought, word, desire or act that insults God. In itself it is gravely wrong, and history gives many examples of how God has punished it.

Cursing means praying for evil on ourselves or on any of God's creatures. It is directly opposed to the love of God and the object of the Incarnation—the salvation of all men. When the evil prayed for is grievous and adverted to (i.e., fully intended), or when the habit is continued, cursing is a mortal sin.

We use **profane words** when we speak in a light or jocose way of God or holy things. Much language of today comes under this heading, e.g., the frequent use of the word "Hell."

Catholics would do well to remember that they very easily give scandal by the careless use of bad language. It is one of the things most noticed by non-Catholics, who are far less particular about other and more serious matters than they are about the language they use. We should, therefore, always be particularly careful in this matter and in our speech practice the virtue of reverence for God and all sacred persons, places or things.

The Third Commandment

The Third Commandment, the only one emphasized by the word "Remember," refers to the "Sabbath." When Moses received this Commandment from God, he was bid to keep holy "the Sabbath," that is, the "rest-day," not necessarily Saturday, or any particular day. The Jews decided it should be Saturday, the last day of the week, but the Apostles of Christ chose the first day because several events of crucial importance for Christianity happened on Sunday, the first day of the week—the Resurrection, the Descent of the Holy

Spirit, the conferring by Christ of the power to forgive sins.

We are to keep Sunday holy by hearing Mass and resting from servile work. Later, the reader will learn how the Mass is the greatest act of the Catholic Faith and that therefore the Church has decreed that this command of God can only be fulfilled by those who worship Him by attending the Holy Sacrifice of the Mass on Sunday. That point will be dealt with under the first Commandment of the Church, for it is the Church which interprets the commands of God and gives us the details of how they are to be observed.

At present, we must remember that God's command is to keep Sunday holy. Attendance at Mass and abstinence from servile work are only two ways of doing this. One who merely goes to Mass and forgets about God for the rest of the day can scarcely be said to keep Sunday holy, although he may, thereby, avoid **mortal** sin. So it is that the Church urges all to attend the other services which she provides for them—such as the Rosary, Vespers, Instruction, Benediction—and also to devote some time to pious or religious reading or other exercises for the sanctification of the soul. Every Catholic should, for example, maintain his interest in the Church through reading Catholic newspapers, periodicals, books and magazines. To do this on Sunday is a help toward keeping the day holy.

The Fourth Commandment

The Fourth Commandment bids us to love, reverence and obey our parents and other lawful superiors in all that is not sinful.

If we are commanded to love all men, how much more should we love our parents, to whom we owe so much. Such love corresponds to the most natural feeling of the heart. In practice, parents should receive from their children affection, thanks, good wishes, consideration, prayer, kindness in thought, word and deed, material help in their needs, continual reverence and hearty, prompt and exact obedience.

We are commanded to obey, not only our parents, but also our bishops and pastors, the civil authorities and our lawful superiors.

Bishops and pastors are spiritual parents, since they beget the life of grace in the soul; they hold the place of God, who speaks through them. "Fear the Lord," says God, "and reverence his priests." (*Ecclus.* 7:31). St. Paul is referring to priests when he urges the Hebrews: "Obey your prelates, and be subject to them. For they watch as being to render an account of your souls; that they may do this with joy, and not with grief. For this is not expedient for you." (*Heb.* 13:17).

Writing to the Romans, St. Paul also enjoins obedience to the civil authorities. "Let every soul be subject to higher powers: for there is no power but from God: and those that are, are ordained of God. Therefore, he that resisteth the power, resisteth the ordinance of God . . . Wherefore be subject of necessity, not only for wrath, but also for conscience' sake. For therefore also you pay tribute . . . Render therefore to all men their dues. Tribute, to whom tribute is due: custom, to whom custom: fear, to whom fear: honour, to whom honour. (*Rom.* 13:1-2, 6-7).

Servants are bound to be just, obedient and respectful to their masters. (The same is true of employees toward their employers.) "Exhort servants to be obedient to their masters, in all things pleasing, not gainsaying: Not defrauding, but in all things showing good fidelity, that they may adorn the doctrine of God our Saviour in all things." (*Titus* 2:9-10).

We are bound to assist our parents in their spiritual and temporal needs—respectfully advising them, bringing the priest to them, warning them in case of sickness or death, praying for them after death. In poverty we should, if possible, procure for them the necessities of life; in sickness we should visit them; in old age we should remember how they supported us in infancy, and after death we should faithfully carry out their last wishes.

According to the Fourth Commandment, we are also bound in justice to support our pastors. "Know you not, that they who work in the holy place," says St. Paul, "eat the things that are of the holy place; and they that serve the altar, partake with the altar? So also the Lord ordained that they who preach the gospel, should live by the gospel." (*1 Cor.* 9:13-14). In the early Church the faithful were always most generous to their priests; later, the custom grew of everyone offering to the Church one tenth of his income (tithes).

From the duties of inferiors to superiors, we turn to the duties of superiors to inferiors.

The duty of parents toward their children is to provide for them, to instruct and correct them, to give them good example and to give them a good Catholic education.

The family is the basic unit of society: parents are heads of the family. Therefore, the welfare of society depends on how parents acquit themselves of their duties.

Parents are strictly bound to provide for their children:

1. Life. Mothers must take due care of their children before birth as well as afterwards.

2. Food and clothing according to their rank and position.

3. Home. To make them happy, according to their means—which includes shelter and care in sickness and misfortune.

4. A state of life by giving their children due training and by fostering a religious vocation if it is present.

5. Adequate provision for the future by making a will.

Parents are strictly bound to instruct their children: They are the first and principal educators of the little ones. Efforts of priests and teachers will be of little avail without the help of the parents. School is intended to provide a supplement to the education received in the home, not to be a substitute for that education.

The most important instruction is in a child's duty to God. This is a parent's sacred privilege and responsibility. Words, threats and punishment will be quite useless without the example of parents. The home must be the child's first school of fervor. There he must be taught to love God and hate sin, to say his prayers and to practice his faith by regular attendance at Mass and frequent reception of the Sacraments. He must be safeguarded from all evil influence from outside the home—books, films, companions, amusements, etc. "But he that shall scandalize one of these little ones that believe in me, it were better for him that a millstone should be hanged about his neck, and that he should be drowned in the depth of the sea." (*Matt.* 18:6).

Parents are strictly bound to correct their children in justice and in prudence. "He that loveth his son frequently chastiseth him." (*Ecclus.* 30:1). "Give thy son his way, and he shall make thee afraid." (*Ecclus.* 30:9).

Parents are strictly bound to give their children a good Catholic education. To educate their children is a most serious obligation on parents. Not only should they see that they attend as good a school as possible, but they must assist the teachers in every way.

It is a natural duty—fulfilled even by the brutes—for parents to love their children; and they cannot be said to do this if they neglect to pray for their children.

Under this Commandment also comes the prohibition against joining secret societies which plot against Church or State and also those which by reason of their secrecy are condemned by the Church. Among these would be the Freemasons, the Oddfellows and the Communist party (although this last may not be necessarily a secret society).

The Freemasons are really a body professing a false religion. The *Universal Manual of Freemasonry* defines Freemasonry as "the activity of closely united men who, employing symbolical forms borrowed principally from the mason's trade and from architecture, work for the welfare of mankind, striving morally to ennoble themselves and others and thereby to bring about a universal league of mankind, which they aspire to exhibit even now on a small scale." It is essentially Naturalism and is therefore absolutely opposed to Christianity, which is essentially Supernaturalism. Its ultimate purpose is "the utter overthrow of that whole religious and political order of the world which the Christian teaching has produced, and the substitution of a new state of things in accordance with their ideas, of which the foundations and laws shall be drawn from mere 'Naturalism'." (*Humanum Genus*—"On Freemasonry," Leo XIII, Par. 10, April 20, 1884).

Masonry is

(a) A Secret Society of a character opposed to right moral principles.

(b) An organization demanding from its members an oath which is unjust and too sweeping.

(c) Proved guilty of much social injustice.

(d) Essentially anti-Catholic.

(e) A false religion.

The Church does not condemn any society merely because it is secret, but she condemns secret societies when she knows that the obligation of secrecy is being misused.

A Catholic may not join the **Oddfellows**, [a type of secret society similar to the Freemasons, formed in England in 1812—but with some lodges begun as early as 1745—and introduced into America in 1819], although that society does not fall under so strict a condemnation as Freemasonry.

The Church forbids her children to be Communists because Communism is fundamentally materialistic, atheistic, anti-Christian, anti-God and opposed to the fundamental rights of man and the basic principles of society. It restricts, for instance, the right to private property, sanctioned by the Natural Law and the positive law of God; it takes away every true incentive to self-development and progress; it destroys liberty; it breaks up the family; it is unjustly totalitarian; etc.

The Fifth Commandment

The Fifth Commandment is "Thou shalt not kill." Without this Commandment, there would be no security for the life of man, either for his physical life or his spiritual life.

Life is man's greatest good, so God wishes to safeguard it against attack. God alone is the author of life; He alone may take life—apart from the circumstances of a just war, the execution of a criminal, and legitimate self-defense.

The Fifth Commandment forbids:

a) **Willful murder**, which is one of the sins crying to Heaven for vengeance because it usurps God's right over life, destroys one whom God has made to His own image and likeness, robs him of his most precious possession, and sends a soul into eternity unprepared.

b) **Abortion**, which is willful murder committed before a child's birth. Often disguised as "termination of pregnancy," it deprives a child of Heaven forever. It is punished by the Church with excommunication.

c) **Suicide**, which is willful self-murder—a crime against God, against society, against one's family and against oneself.

d) **Exposing one's life or health to unnecessary danger without sufficient cause**.

e) **Fighting**, which is opposed to the law of charity and which can lead to physical harm to self or others, and which can lead to murder.

f) **Quarreling**, which tends toward fighting and even murder;

g) **Injurious words**, which lead to quarrels and their consequences. "Whosoever shall say, Thou Fool, shall be in danger of hell fire." (*Matt.* 5:22).

h) **Scandal**, which is any word, deed or omission, wrong or seeming to be wrong, and leading others to sin. Those who give bad example to those under them, such as parents who curse and quarrel before their children, those who by their behavior teach or suggest evil, those who ridicule piety in others, those who counsel others to do evil, and those who provoke others to sin are guilty of malicious scandal. Another name for it is "soul murder." What a terrible sin! Even murder of the body is one of the sins mentioned in the Bible as "crying to Heaven for vengeance." Scandal is undoing the work of Christ, who came to save all men, and doing the work of the devil. "Woe to the world because of scandals," said Our Lord, and "he that shall scandalize one of these little ones that believe in me, it were better for him that a millstone should be hanged about his neck, and that he should be drowned in the depth of the sea." (*Matt.* 18:7, 6). Often ill-instructed people take scandal from even lawful things; hence, particular care is necessary when this danger is present.

i) **Bad example**, which is really scandal of a milder form. Evil, like fever, is contagious, especially with the young;

j) **Anger**, which leads to quarrels and many other evils. "Whosoever is angry with his brother, shall be in danger of the judgment." (*Matt.* 5:22). It is sinful, especially when shown for a merely accidental injury, when it is directed against the offender rather than the offense, when it causes one to inflict excessive punishment, when it becomes a passion beyond the control of reason. But anger may sometimes be lawful, as was that of Jesus Christ when he drove from the Temple those who were carrying on worldly business there. St. Paul makes the distinction when he writes: "Be angry, and sin not. Let not the sun go down upon your anger." (*Eph.* 4:26). Therefore, when there is displeasure only, or when restrained indignation is directed against the fault or wrong disposition, rather than against a person, or when it brings about just redress and reasonable punishment for wrongdoing, anger may be lawful.

k) **Hatred**, which is enmity, directly opposed to the love of God and of our neighbor. Hatred must be distinguished from mere dislike. "If any man say, I love God, and hateth his brother, he is a liar," says St. John. (*1 Jn.* 4:20). In fact, the Beloved Disciple makes hatred appear equal to murder: "Whosoever hateth his brother is a murderer." (*1 Jn.* 3:15).

l) **Revenge**, which is returning evil for evil. It is directly opposed to God's Law. "Revenge is mine, and I will repay them in due time." (*Deut.* 32:35). "He that seeketh to revenge himself, shall find vengeance from the Lord." (*Ecclus.* 28:1). "Be not overcome by evil, but overcome evil by good." (*Rom.* 12:21). How can a man who is seeking revenge sincerely say in the "Our Father"—"Forgive us our trespasses as we forgive those who trespass against us?"

It is important to remember that injuries caused to others must be repaired. If, for instance, we have led others to sin through scandal, everything possible must be done to bring them back to God.

Chapter 10

The Commandments of God (3)

THE SIXTH COMMANDMENT

What is the Sixth Commandment? *The Sixth Commandment is, "Thou shalt not commit adultery."*

What does the Sixth Commandment forbid? *The Sixth Commandment **in general** forbids all sins of impurity—including adultery, fornication, masturbation, birth control, homosexual acts and beastiality—and **specifically** those sins of impurity committed with another's wife or husband.*

Does the Sixth Commandment also forbid whatever is contrary to holy purity? *The Sixth Commandment also forbids whatever is contrary to holy purity in words, thoughts, looks or actions.*

Are immodest plays and dances forbidden by the Sixth Commandment? *Immodest plays and dances are forbidden by the Sixth Commandment, and it is sinful to look at them.*

Does the Sixth Commandment forbid immodest songs, books, pictures, movies, TV shows, and websites? *The Sixth Commandment also forbids immodest songs, books, pictures, movies, TV shows, and websites, because they are most dangerous to the soul and lead to mortal sin.*

THE NINTH COMMANDMENT

What is the Ninth Commandment? *The Ninth Commandment is, "Thou shalt not covet thy neighbor's wife."*

What does the Ninth Commandment forbid? *The Ninth Commandment specifically forbids **wanting** someone else's spouse in a married way, and by extension, for a married person to **want** a sin-*

gle person in this manner. It also forbids all willful consent to impure thoughts and desires, and all willful pleasure in irregular (sinful) sexual promptings or motions of the flesh.

What sins commonly lead to the breaking of the Sixth and Ninth Commandments? *The sins that commonly lead to the breaking of the Sixth and Ninth Commandments are gluttony, drunkenness and intemperance, and also idleness, bad company and the neglect of prayer.*

Catholic attitude toward sex

WHATEVER God made is good and, in itself, knowledge of it is good. The Sixth and Ninth Commandments have reference to man's instinct for self- or race-propagation, an instinct which has been implanted in man by God. "Have ye not read, that he who made man from the beginning, *Made them male and female?* And he said: *For this cause shall a man leave father and mother, and shall cleave to his wife, and they two shall be in one flesh?"* (*Matt.* 19:4-5). Therefore, sex and knowledge of sex are in themselves good and noble. Knowledge can and ought to co-exist with perfect innocence.

Man is made in the image and likeness of God. Just as God is Intellect, Freedom and Love, so man is an intellectual being endowed with free will and the power to love. In God, love is a mighty, life-producing love. (He is Love Itself.) Throughout eternity, the Holy Spirit is begotten through the love of the Father and the Son. Man is so much the image of God that he too has the power to love with a life-producing love. By endowing man with the sex faculty, God has made it possible for him to co-operate in the very act by which the future citizens of Heaven come into being. He wills that they, His own companions for eternity, should be the result of the love of husband and wife.

Therefore, marriage is God's plan. The use of sex in marriage is God's plan. By it parents are privileged to share in that plan. Obviously, being parents means making a good deal of sacrifice. For the mother, the very act of child-bearing is painful and sometimes dangerous; the subsequent education of the children is a task which calls for constant effort. For the father, the task of providing all the necessities of life for his children entails hard work and often much mental anxiety. To offset these and other hardships, God has attached intense pleasure to the use of sex.

There is a good parallel between the sexual instinct and that other important instinct of man, the instinct of self-preservation. To preserve his life, a man must eat. Therefore, God has attached to eating considerable pleasure. Otherwise what woman would spend so many hours in cooking food and making it attractive? Who would waste so much time at meals? Now, just as men and women would not readily eat if it were a painful activity, so they would with difficulty have intercourse unless there were the inducement of sexual pleasure.

Obviously, this sexual pleasure is not so much for the individual as for the race, and hence to use it simply and solely for the purpose of self-indulgence and self-gratification is contrary to the Will and designs of God and stultifies His purpose. It makes for the ruin and destruction of society. The virtue which checks, controls and *chastens* the sexual instinct is called chastity.

Why be pure?

Leaving aside the analysis of our unaided reason regarding the role of sex in man's life, the revelation of Christ offers us other compelling motives for preserving holy purity. For example, the ultimate purpose of this life is to reach life eternal with God. Men are made for God, to live with God forever. Impurity means tampering with life at its very source; often, as in birth-prevention, impurity leads to the frustration of life and is responsible for empty places in Heaven throughout eternity.

Catholics regard the body as the dwelling place of the soul—of an unspeakably precious, immortal soul—and the happy companion of that soul throughout eternity. It is also the special dwelling place of the most Holy Trinity on earth. Just as the Catholic Church is holy because it is the special dwelling place of God, so also is the human body holy for precisely the same reason. Moreover, St. Paul tells us that our bodies "are the members of Christ," that "we are members of his body, of his flesh and of his bones." (*1 Cor.* 6:15;

Eph. 5:30). Impurity is the defiling of God's temple and of a member of Christ.

Perhaps you remember the story of Attila, who swore to stable his horses on the altar steps of St. Peter's at Rome. This he intended to be the greatest possible insult to Almighty God. During the French Revolution, crowds of lewd women danced on the altars of the churches of Paris; devout people turned sick at the sight.

The modern world looks upon sex as cheap, maudlin sentimentality; the modern romance portrays it as merely the selfish outlet for passion; the movie screen depicts it as pagan, pleasurable beastliness; supposedly learned men write to prove that sins against sex are not wrong at all; men and women in the street treat sex as a joke and waste, squander, spoil and soil this great and precious power God has given them. Countries which claim to be Christian are often content today to witness without protest the pagan parade of the human body, the shrine of immortal life, the dwelling place of God, the temple of the soul for the rest of eternity, as a bait on stage, screen or billboard to attract people. Such practices are revolting to one who fully understands God's purpose in putting the sexual instinct in man and who ponders the supernatural truths connected with it. "Know you not that your bodies are the members of Christ? Shall I then take the members of Christ, and make them the members of a harlot? God forbid. Or know you not, that he who is joined to a harlot, is made one body? For they shall be, saith he, two in one flesh. But he who is joined to the Lord, is one spirit. Fly fornication. Every sin that a man doth, is without the body; but he that committeth fornication, sinneth against his own body. Or know you not, that your members are the temple of the Holy Ghost, who is in you, whom you have from God; and you are not your own? For you are bought with a great price. Glorify and bear God in your body." (*1 Cor.* 6:15-20). "Blessed are the clean of heart; for they shall see God." (*Matt.* 5:8).

Sins of impurity

Adultery, which is specifically forbidden by the Sixth Commandment, means sexual sin with another's wife or husband, or of a single person with a married person. It is an offense against the sanctity of married life and a crying injustice against a fellow human being. It violates the fidelity which man and wife pledge to each other. It is also a crime against society, often bringing in its wake dishonor, disgrace, dissensions, murder, poverty and the neglect of children.

In addition to adultery, the Sixth Commandment forbids all sins of impurity. St. Paul wrote: "For know you this and understand, that no fornicator, or unclean, or covetous person (which is a serving of idols), hath inheritance in the kingdom of Christ and of God." (*Eph.* 5:5). "Ambition was the sin of the Angels, avarice the sin of men, impurity the sin of the beast," St. Bernard used to say. The great Saints of God went to extraordinary lengths to preserve their purity. St. Benedict rolled in the briars; St. Francis of Assisi rolled in the snow; St. Bernard plunged into a pond.

Thus, the Sixth Commandment forbids immodesty in:

a) **Looks**: The eyes are the windows of the soul, and immodest looks, e.g., at pictures, scantily clothed people, etc., are danger-ous and therefore are forbidden.

b) **Words**: "But now put you also all away: anger, indignation, mal-ice, blasphemy, filthy speech out of your mouth." (*Col.* 3:8). An immodest tongue is the devil's carriage because it carries souls to Hell for him. With our lips we are meant to praise God for-ever, for all eternity. How wrong it is, therefore, to defile them now by impure talk, which often involves the souls of others in sin!

c) **Actions**: Alone or with others.

It is obvious from what has been said that immodest dances, songs, books, pictures, plays, movies, TV shows and websites are all forbidden by the Sixth Commandment. The question is often asked about the morality of viewing **nudity in art museums**, or even in the Sistine Chapel in the Vatican. True art is never sugges-tive to impurity, objectively speaking. Hence, viewing true art is justified and edifying, so long as the viewer is spiritually mature enough to do so without turning such viewing into an occasion of sin.

Causes of impurity

The following are some of the causes of impurity, against which we must be on our guard at all times:

1. **Pride**. "Pride goeth before destruction: and the spirit is lifted up before a fall." (*Proverbs* 16:18).
2. **Idleness**. "Idleness hath taught much evil." (*Ecclus*. 33:29).
3. **Bad books, bad entertainment, and bad company**. "Evil communications corrupt good manners." (*1 Cor.* 15:33).
4. **Immodesty of dress**—a very common cause of impurity in these times of mixed swimming and sun-bathing, as well as the movies.
5. **Excess in eating and drinking**.
6. **Failure of watchfulness over the senses**. "Gaze not upon a maiden, lest her beauty be a stumbling block to thee." (*Ecclus*. 9:5). "Many have perished by the beauty of woman; and hereby lust is enkindled as a fire." (*Ecclus*. 9:9).

Remedies

The remedies for impurity are principally: 1) frequent Confession and Holy Communion; 2) prayer, especially to Our Lady, and especially her Rosary; 3) mortification; 4) innocent occupation of the mind and body; 5) **promptness in resisting the first attacks of temptation by turning away to something else**; and also 6) the steadfast avoiding of any kind of danger to the virtue of purity, especially persons, places and literature that easily lead one into these sins.

Impure thoughts

The Ninth Commandment forbids all willful consent to impure thoughts and desires and all willful pleasure in the irregular sexual promptings or motions of the flesh. That is, it forbids interior sins of thought and desire against the Sixth Commandment.

Many people find themselves tempted by bad thoughts. But **temptation is not a sin**. The sin occurs when the thoughts *are deliberately encouraged*. You may feel that the thought was in your mind for a long time, that you were taking pleasure in it, that you welcomed it and wanted it to go on. But did you recognize the thought as sinful and then, *knowing it to be sinful,* let it go on? Unless you did, there is no sin. No one commits a sin against purity in thought until he **wants** to enjoy bad thoughts.

Bad thoughts must almost be expected—until a person has taken himself firmly in hand and gained considerable virtue in this area. To dilly-dally with them may possibly, in some cases, be only a venial sin of nasty curiosity—depending on whether the will fully consents to entertain them further in the mind, in which case they would be mortally sinful. But definitely, deliberately to accept the thought and take pleasure in it is a mortal sin against purity.

Is every fully deliberate sin of impurity mortal? The answer is, "Yes, most definitely!" Here are the principles which help us to answer this:

1. **To seek of set purpose and of full deliberation to arouse or excite or produce within ourselves sexual pleasure, whether complete or incomplete, outside the lawful use of marriage, is always a mortal sin**. Or, should the pleasure come to us unsought in time of temptation, and then for us to seek to continue to prolong or gratify it is, again, always a mortal sin. In this sense, and only in this sense, is it true to say that every willful sin of impurity is mortal. It does not matter *what* you do, but if you do it for the above purpose, then it is a mortal sin. We say "complete or incomplete" because this pleasure within us is so powerful, vehement and impetuous in its operation—owing to our strong instinct and to our fallen nature—that we cannot promise to be able to check any fully deliberate act to produce or prolong even the *incomplete* pleasure; hence, it is a grave (i.e., mortal) sin, because we are putting ourselves in the proximate danger of sin when we say, foolishly, "I intend to go this far and no farther."

a) The guilty person must have as his **direct and immediate purpose** to produce or prolong sexual pleasure;

b) There must be full deliberation (i.e., advertence of the mind and consent of the will). A person could not commit a mortal sin when asleep or half-asleep, half-adverting or half-consenting.

2. To do something deliberately, of set purpose, to produce or prolong sexual pleasure, even for some reason other than for plea-

sure, yet something which the person foresees or knows from experience will or may produce it . . . such an action, when fully deliberate, **is always a mortal sin**.

There is mortal sin when what a person does is something which of its very nature is apt to excite sexual pleasure, and at the same time the person has no serious reason for so acting. And the same is true if, even granted he has such a reason, there is a real danger of his **accepting** (not merely **feeling**) the pleasure. For example, to look *closely* and for a time at one's own or another's nakedness, to let one's thoughts **dwell** on impure matters, to handle (not as a passing act) oneself or another indecently, to look **fixedly** at **obscene** pictures or to read **obscene** literature would be mortal sins.

There is venial sin when what we do is something which of its nature is **not likely** to produce sexual pleasure, even if at the same time we act out of no good motive, but merely, e.g., out of levity, imprudence, curiosity, bravado, vanity or the like. For example, deliberate but only passing glances at a naked body, a passing glance at immodest pictures, reading unsavory paragraphs in a newspaper out of curiosity, touching oneself deliberately but only lightly or in a passing way, deliberately entertaining *for a moment* an immodest (not an impure) thought—these would be venial sins.

There is no sin at all when what we do is quite innocent or decent in itself, or even if it is something which of its very nature is very likely to arouse sexual pleasure, provided that we have an adequate and just reason for doing it and there is no real danger of our consenting to the pleasure aroused.

The following stages in temptation should be distinguished; we can compare them to someone at a door:

1) **Temptation to sexual pleasure**—the knock at the door;
2) **Feeling the pleasure**—the mind goes out to see who is there;
3) **Taking the pleasure**—"I want you; come in."

Chapter 11

The Commandments of God (4)

THE SEVENTH COMMANDMENT

What is the Seventh Commandment? *The Seventh Commandment is, "Thou shalt not steal."*

What does the Seventh Commandment forbid? *The Seventh Commandment forbids all unjust taking away or keeping what belongs to another.*

Is all manner of cheating in buying and selling forbidden by the Seventh Commandment? *All manner of cheating in buying and selling is forbidden by the Seventh Commandment, and also every other way of wronging our neighbor.*

Are we bound to restore ill-gotten goods? *We are bound to restore ill-gotten goods if we are able, or else the sin will not be forgiven; we must also pay our just debts.*

Is it dishonest for employees to waste their employer's time or property? *It is dishonest for employees to waste their employer's time or property, because it is wasting what is not their own.*

THE EIGHTH COMMANDMENT

What is the Eighth Commandment? *The Eighth Commandment is, "Thou shalt not bear false witness against thy neighbor."*

What does the Eighth Commandment forbid? *The Eighth Commandment forbids all false testimony, rash judgment and lies.*

Are calumny and detraction forbidden by the Eighth Commandment? *Calumny and detraction are forbidden by the Eighth Commandment, and also talebearing, and any words which defame our neighbor's character or injure his reputation.*

If you have injured your neighbor by speaking ill of him, what are you bound to do? *If I have injured my neighbor by speaking ill of him, I am bound to make him satisfaction by restoring his good name, as far as I can.*

THE TENTH COMMANDMENT

What is the Tenth Commandment? *The Tenth Commandment is, "Thou shalt not covet thy neighbor's goods."*

What does the Tenth Commandment forbid? *The Tenth Commandment forbids all envious and covetous thoughts of and unjust desires for our neighbor's goods and profits.*

THE **Seventh and Tenth Commandments:** The Seventh Commandment is, "Thou shalt not steal," and the Tenth is, "Thou shalt not covet thy neighbor's goods."

In the Fifth and Sixth Commandments, God protects our life and honor; in the Seventh He places our property and wealth in security.

The right to private property is the right which a human being has whereby he may possess, use and dispose of material things for his own benefit without interference from others; it arises from the Natural Law and is sanctioned by God in this Commandment. Nature imposes on man a duty to maintain his life. To do this, he must use his intellect and will. He is endowed with foresight and can foresee his future needs and take steps to provide for them. To satisfy those needs, man requires material things of the kind which can be used over again as the need arises. His intelligence urges him to seek after and to acquire those goods and to safeguard them against loss or deprivation. Moreover, a man has a right to marry and have a family. He has the duty of maintaining that family. For this, private ownership is a necessity.

Of course, this right to own is limited by the nature and purpose of things and by the fact that man is a social being, with duties to his fellow men. The State can limit private ownership when the common good requires it, and only with regard to what the public interest demands should be controlled or owned publicly. The State has no authority to abolish all private ownership, because that would be to abolish what is natural to man. Real Socialists and Communists want to abolish private ownership of things which are productive. That is wrong. The Church says that in any given case the system of private ownership may need to be reformed, but that it is neither lawful nor necessary to abolish it.

If a man has a right to own, it is certain that that right must be respected. Therefore, the Seventh Commandment forbids all unjust taking away or keeping what belongs to another—and any other way of wronging our neighbor in regard to his property.

Theft is a mortal sin of its nature, but it may be only venial, by reason of the smallness of what is stolen.

The following are some ways of sinning against the Seventh Commandment:

1. Theft and robbery.
2. Assisting in theft and robbery.
3. Borrowing without hope or intention of repaying.
4. Rash speculation, without being able to bear possible loss.
5. Unfair interference with another's success.
6. Extravagance, especially when others are hurt by it.
7. Accepting bribes.
8. Receiving stolen goods while knowing them to be stolen.
9. Not restoring what has been unjustly taken or what has been lent to us.
10. Not paying just wages within a reasonable time.
11. Not taking reasonable pains to seek the owner of things found.
12. Passing bad money in payment.
13. Forging signatures to checks, etc.
14. Using false weights and measures.
15. Adulteration of goods and any other form of cheating in business.
16. Dishonest statements in insurance contracts.
17. Usury or exorbitant interest.
18. Willfully damaging property.
19. Wasting time at work.
20. Unlawful strikes.
21. Refusal to pay rent.
22. Not paying debts.
23. Gambling away family savings.

24. Cheating on exams in school.
25. Plagiarism.
26. Violation of copyright laws in the reproduction of maga-
    zines articles, books, videos, audio cassettes, movies, com-
    puter software, etc.

Restitution

We are bound to restore ill-gotten goods if we are able, or else
our sin will not be forgiven. When the theft was a mortal sin, neglect
of restitution is also a mortal sin. The obligation is binding until it
is fulfilled, and the greater the willful delay, the greater is the sin.
Restitution must be made to the owner, if possible, or to his heirs, if
he be dead. If neither is possible, it should be given in alms in the
name of the owner. Not only must the stolen property be returned,
but also the loss resulting from the thief's actual injustice must be
made good.

If it is physically or morally impossible for us to make restitution, the obligation ceases to bind us. But apart from such cases, the
sin of theft is not really repented of until restitution has been made,
and so it cannot be forgiven.

The Tenth Commandment forbids all envious and covetous
thoughts about and unjust desires for our neighbor's goods and profits. By this commandment, God wants to protect us against the evil
inclinations of our own hearts and to blunt the sting of the unlawful
desires which make us yearn for things that belong to others.

The gravity of theft

Is theft a grievous sin? This depends on three things:
1. The value of the thing stolen;
2. The person or corporate body (e.g., a business) suffering the
   injustice;
3. The time over which the theft is spread.

The value of the property stolen may be *absolutely grave* or
relatively grave.

a) By *absolutely grave value*, we understand an amount sufficient **in itself** to constitute matter for a mortal sin, regardless of the

relatively great wealth of the person from whom the goods are stolen. There is obviously an objectively grave degree of injustice which (when committed) involves a grave violation of public order. The amount of property necessary to commit such an objectively grave injustice is the *absolutely grave value* which makes theft a mortal sin. Moral theologians are united in fixing this sum as the **equivalent of the weekly wages earned by a person of the middle class of society.** Thus, if that amount is stolen from, say, a large store, it would still be a grave sin, unless there is some other mitigating factor.

(b) By *relatively grave value* we understand an amount so great that its theft would prove a notable loss to the particular owner in question. We think now, not of society at large, but of the individual victim. Theologians fix this amount as **the average day's pay of the victim of the injustice.**

The person (or corporate entity) against whom the theft is committed: If the victim is a business or a very wealthy person, the gravity of the theft would be measured according to the *absolutely grave sum*. If the victim is an individual and is not very wealthy, then the gravity is measured by the *relatively grave sum* of the victim's average day's pay. To steal from one's parents is ordinarily not so grave as unjustly to take the same amount from a total stranger.

The time over which the theft is spread: If the money is stolen at intervals, it does not usually harm the victim so much as if the same amount were taken all at once. Hence, in order to constitute grave matter, thefts performed at intervals would have to fulfill the following conditions: a) **If the thief has the intention to accumulate a large sum by such thefts**; in this case even the first theft is a grave sin. b) **If frequently repeated, thefts automatically add up to make the sum the matter of a mortal sin**—either because restitution is not being made or because the intervals between the thefts are short. The greater the amount taken, the greater must be the interval required to prevent coalescence into a sum which is the matter of a mortal sin. c) **If several people conspire to a theft**, even if the individual thief obtains only a small amount, but the aggregate sum taken is large. Each one would commit a mortal sin. (Cf. Jone's *Moral Theology*, No. 329.)

The Eighth Commandment

This Commandment, "Thou shalt not bear false witness against thy neighbor," safeguards the Natural Law, which demands that the reputation of individuals be protected and faith in human communications be preserved. The right use of the power of speech is necessary for the welfare of society. Untold evils are caused by its abuse in lying propaganda, defamations of character, libel, calumnies and so forth.

1) Hence, the Eighth Commandment forbids:

a) **False testimony:** i.e., giving evidence we know to be untrue. If false testimony is given under oath, it involves a three-fold guilt—falsehood, perjury and injustice.

b) **Rash judgment:** i.e., the assent of the will to suspicions about others, without sufficient grounds. It is obviously opposed to charity and justice. We may be guilty of it by conceiving dislikes at first sight, by imputing unworthy motives to others, by judging a person to have a habit of sin because we know him to have committed it once, and by pronouncing one guilty without having heard his defense.

"Judge not, that you may not be judged," said Our Lord. (*Matt.* 7:1).

c) **Lies**, or words against the truth. A lie is wrong in itself because it involves using a natural faculty in a manner directly opposite to its purpose. The intention to deceive is not necessary for a lie. Merely to employ our God-given faculty of speech in order to manifest as the thought of one's mind what is not the thought of one's mind is contrary to the primary object of speech.

In itself, a lie is never more than a venial sin, but the act of telling a lie may be *gravely sinful* because of some other factor, for example, injury to a person's character. A jocose lie (one told merely to amuse) or an officious lie (a lie of excuse) are venial sins; but a malicious lie, by which someone is injured, would be a mortal sin, if the injury is sufficiently grave.

Holy Scripture speaks very strongly about lies: "Lying lips are an abomination to the Lord." (*Prov.* 12:22). "The mouth that belieth, killeth the soul." (*Wis.* 1:11).

It is never lawful to tell a lie, no matter what the object. However, mental reservations and equivocations are not sinful, so long as they are not unlawfully deceptive. Here we must distinguish between **strict** and **broad mental reservations**:

Strict mental reservations are always a lie and therefore sinful. The reason is that there is no clue given in the person's answer as to the true meaning the speaker is intending, because the mental reservation is kept *strictly* in the speaker's mind, and there is no outward indication as to the limited meaning. For example: You ask a person, "Did you leave town yesterday," and he answers, "No," meaning, "I did not leave town yesterday *in a car.*"

Broad mental reservations are not sinful so long as the broad mental reservation is used only as a refuge to guard a secret from prying questioners who have no right to the information they seek," (Austin Fagothey, S.J., *Right and Reason*. Page 319). In a **broad mental reservation**, there is a clue to the correct meaning of the answer, e.g., when a child under instruction from his mother tells a salesman, "My mother is not at home." The meaning is, "Not at home to you." The saleman did not have a right to know. Our Lord Himself used the broad mental reservation for a serious reason. (Cf. *John* 7:8-10).

d) **Calumny or slander:** Whereas sin destroys the life of grace in the soul, and whereas murder destroys the physical life of the body, **calumny** destroys or injures the civil or social life of a neighbor. Calumny means imputing crimes or faults to others unduly, exaggerating real faults and defects, or denying their good qualities or actions.

Calumny is a sin against truth, charity, justice, manly courage and religion. "If any man think himself to be religious, not bridling his tongue, but deceiving his own heart, this man's religion is vain." (*James* 1:26). Calumny is always sinful because it is always a lie, but its guilt varies according to the nature of the imputation made, the injury intended or effected, and the number of persons who hear it.

e) **Detraction, or libel**, means making known the secret faults of another without just cause. It is commonly done by imparting uncharitable gossip, especially as a secret, hinting at things others do not know of a person, praising a person coldly so as to insinuate that he does not deserve that praise, seeking to lessen the merit of another's good acts, and so on. It is a sin against charity and justice.

"Thou shalt not be a detractor nor a whisperer among the people." (*Lev.* 19:16). "Hast thou heard a word against thy neighbor? Let it die within thee." (*Ecclus.* 19:10). "Detract not one another . . . if thou judge the law, thou are not a doer of the law, but a judge." (*James* 4:11).

The guilt of detraction depends on the character and position of the person who speaks, on the quality and position of the person spoken of, on the nature of the fault revealed, on the number of persons to whom it is made known, and on the injury done or foreseen.

Sometimes, of course, it is lawful to reveal the faults of others when it is for their good, when it is necessary in order to prevent greater evil, when one's motive is pure, when there is no exaggeration, and when the revelation is made only to those who can remedy the evil.

f) **Talebearing** is repeating to anyone what others have said about him. "The talebearer shall defile his own soul." (*Ecclus.* 21:31). Because it is the source of quarrels and animosities, the cause of misunderstandings and the loss of friendship, talebearing is against charity and its guilt will depend on the intention of the speaker and the injury done or foreseen.

g) **Backbiting** is speaking of a person's faults, even though they be known to all. It is opposed to Christian charity. "If a serpent bite in silence, he is nothing better that backbiteth secretly." (*Eccles.* 10:11). Honest criticism may be perfectly lawful, but only too often it degenerates into backbiting and uncharitableness.

h) **Contumely:** i.e., insults, raillery and words of reproach offered a person in his presence. It may be a grievous sin. "But I say to you, that whosoever is angry with his brother, shall be in danger of the judgment. And whosoever shall say to his brother, Raca [a word expressing great indignation or contempt], shall be in danger of the council [the Sanhedrin, the supreme council and highest court of the Jews]. And whosoever shall say, Thou fool, shall be in danger of hell fire." (*Matt.* 5:22).

i) **Betraying secrets:** The guilt of this depends upon the importance of the secret and the injury likely to follow its revelation. It may sometimes be lawful when the matter is trifling and no injury is feared, or when the consent of the person possessing the secret may be reasonably presumed, or when there is good and reasonable cause, e.g., to protect the common good.

It could be grievously sinful to invade the privacy of another by reading his secret documents or letters or e-mail without the consent of either the recipient or the sender, or without legitimate authority to do so, or without just cause, because in so doing, a person is deprived of secrets which he has a perfect right to preserve. (Cf. Prümmer, *Handbook of Moral Theology*, Mercier Press, 1956, par. 296).

2) Restitution of another's good name is obligatory for sins of the tongue:

a) One who has injured another by misuse of speech is strictly bound to make satisfaction as far as possible and without delay. This is a positive obligation which binds gravely if the injury done has been grave. This satisfaction usually entails speaking highly of a person's good qualities.

b) Listening to all the above sinful uses of the power of speech is also forbidden, unless there is a just cause for doing so.

Chapter 12

The Doctrine of the Holy Trinity

Are there three Persons in God? *There are three Persons in God: God the Father, God the Son and God the Holy Ghost.*

Are these three Persons three Gods? *These three Persons are not three Gods: the Father, the Son and the Holy Ghost are all one and the same God.*

What is the mystery of the three Persons in one God called? *The mystery of the three Persons in one God is called the Mystery of the Blessed Trinity.*

What do you mean by a mystery? *By a mystery, we mean a truth which is above reason, but revealed by God.*

Who is the Holy Ghost? *The Holy Ghost is the Third Person of the Blessed Trinity.*

From whom does the Holy Ghost proceed? *The Holy Ghost proceeds from the Father and the Son.*

Is the Holy Ghost equal to the Father and to the Son? *The Holy Ghost is equal to the Father and to the Son, for He is the same Lord and God as They are.*

When did the Holy Ghost come down on the Apostles? *The Holy Ghost came down on the Apostles on Pentecost or Whit Sunday, in the form of "parted tongues, as it were, of fire."*

Why did the Holy Ghost come down on the Apostles? *The Holy Ghost came down on the Apostles to confirm their faith, to sanctify them and to enable them to found the Church.*

W E have already proved that God exists, that He is one and that He has complete dominion over us. All that we can know by reason alone. But it is obvious that in dealing with the Infinite, the finite mind must eventually come to the end of its reasoning powers. It has no right to expect to know the answer to everything connected with God; it ought logically to expect to come up against many questions which it will never be able to resolve without Divine Revelation. In regard to this, it is well to remember that comparisons from material things, while they help to elucidate certain points of Revelation, may actually be misleading when applied to others. For example, the shamrock is a far from perfect illustration of the mystery of the Trinity, which we are going to discuss now.

Mysteries

A mystery of religion is not a truth about which we can know nothing; rather, it is a truth about which we cannot know everything. It is not so much an unscalable wall as an endless gallery into which the mind can progress further and further without ever coming to an end. No matter how much the mind concentrates on a mystery, there will always remain a mass of truth it has not made its own.

All true believers in God must be prepared to accept mysteries as true on His divine authority. That is Faith. Reason tells them that God can and has made revelations to men and that, because He is God, He must be believed.

Thus, Faith does not mean intellectual suicide. The object of the intellect is Truth. Sometimes the intellect arrives at Truth for itself, and that is **reason.** It **knows something.** But sometimes the intellect accepts the Truth on the authority of another, and that is **Faith.** It **believes something.** If the informant is human, we have human faith, if the informant be God, we have divine Faith. But there can obviously be no real conflict between Faith and reason because both give Truth to the intellect.

If there appears to be conflict, it is due to one of the following causes:

    a) The contradiction *appears* to exist in that part of the object of Faith which is outside the sphere of reason, and in this

case, reason must recognize its own limitations and accept
the truth on the authority of God revealing;

b) a misunderstanding of the truth in question;

c) bad reasoning;

d) the reason failing to realize its own limitations, or the depth
of the truth involved.

The truly reasonable believer in God **will accept mysteries**
without hesitation, and he will be pleased that God has deigned by
His Revelation to extend the range of man's intellectual vision. Why
should everything in this world—and the next—be forced to meet
the measure of the human mind? The divine mysteries reveal to us
something of the great immensity which lies beyond the scope and
power of human reason; they bring us into touch with the Absolute.

The Trinity revealed

The principal fact about Himself which God has told us that is
beyond what we can discover about Him by the use of our unaided
reason is that in His one Divine Nature there are three Divine Persons. Thus, He has admitted us into greater intimacy with Himself
by revealing to us something of His own intimate life.

Jesus Christ, who came to teach us about God, revealed the doctrine of the Trinity to us. On the occasion of His Baptism in the Jordan by His Precursor, St. John the Baptist, the voice of *the Father*
was heard speaking from Heaven, proclaiming *His Son* who was
being baptized, and the *Holy Spirit* appeared in the form of a dove
over Jesus. "Jesus being baptized, forthwith came out of the water:
and lo, the heavens were opened to him, and he saw the Spirit of
God descending as a dove, and coming upon him. And behold, a
voice from heaven, saying: 'This is my beloved Son, in whom I am
well pleased.'" (*Matt.* 3:16-17). When Christ gave the Apostles
their mission to baptize, He bade them do so "in the name of the
Father, and of the Son, and of the Holy Ghost." (*Matt.* 28:19).

Explanation

It is not that we say that the same thing is under the same aspect
one and three at the same time. That would be a contradiction. In the

Trinity the term "one" applies to nature; the term "three" applies to person. Contradiction could only exist if person and nature were the same.

In everyday language we continually use the distinction between person and nature. When we ask the question, "Who are you?" the answer is, say, "Frank," a person; when we ask, "What are you?" the answer is, say, "a man," a nature. The word "who" refers to person; the word "what" refers to nature. It is the person, not the nature, who does things, but he does them in virtue of his nature. He is the actor; his nature is the principle of his activity.

In God there is but one single mind, one single will, which is, so to speak, focused three times. Say to God, "What are you?" and He will answer, "God." Say to God "Who are you?" and the answer would be a triple "I."

Imagine three men—White, Brown and Black. They are made in such a way that, although each thinks for himself, wills for himself, decides for himself, loves for himself, yet they use only one soul among them. White can think with Black's intellect, because it is also his own; Black can love with Brown's will, because it is also his will. Now say to White: "Are you a man?" and he would answer, "Of course I am a man." Brown and Black would reply in the same way. Each has everything it takes to make up a man. Yet, who would say there are three men there? Clearly, there are not three distinct human beings, each with his own individual human nature; yet each claims that he is a person. So it is in God. There are not three Gods, but there is only one Divine Nature wholly possessed by each person.

In all things the three Divine Persons are equal, yet they are really distinct from one another. Each is God, each is infinitely perfect. Yet the Son comes from the Father and the Holy Ghost from the Father and the Son. If we think only of the relationship between them, we can say of each Person what we cannot say of either of the other Two. Thus we can say of the Father: "He has begotten the Son"; of the Son, "He is begotten of the Father"; and of the Holy Ghost, "He proceeds from the Father and the Son."

The Trinity and ourselves

Some may be tempted to think that the study of the Holy Trinity is of no practical value to them. That cannot be true. No knowledge of God can be useless, least of all knowledge of this, the principal mystery of our Faith and of the interior life of the Godhead. Moreover, the doctrine is essential for the Christian religion, **which turns on the fact** that the Second Person of the Blessed Trinity took on human nature and died to redeem the human race. That we shall consider later. For the moment, let us ponder the more personal relationship of the soul to the Trinity in the supernatural life.

Sharing in the Divine Nature

In his second epistle, the Prince of the Apostles tells us this astounding truth: "That by these you may be made partakers of the divine nature." (*2 Peter* 1:4). Now, the divine nature is that essential, necessary principle in God by which the Son proceeds from the Father and the Holy Ghost from the Father and the Son.

Cardinal Newman in one of his sermons has a superb description of the life of God throughout eternity. "God," he says, "has lived in an eternity before He began to create anything. . . . There was a state of things in which God was by Himself and nothing else but He. There was no earth, no sky, no sun, no stars, no space, no time, no beings of any kind; no men, no Angels, no Seraphim. His throne was without ministers; He was not waited on by any; all was silence; all was repose, there was nothing but God; and this state continued, not for a while only, but for a measureless duration; it was a state which had ever been; it was the rule of things, and creation was an innovation upon it. Creation is, comparatively speaking, of yesterday; it has lasted a poor six thousand years, say sixty thousand, if you will, or six million, or sixty million million; what is this to eternity? Nothing at all; not so much as a drop compared to the whole ocean, or a grain of sand to the whole earth. I say through a whole eternity God was by Himself, with no other being but Himself; with nothing external to Himself, not working, but at rest, not speaking nor receiving homage from any, not glorified in creatures, but blessed in Himself and by Himself and wanting nothing."

But do not think that God was idle in that eternity, for He was not. Rather, **He was infinite in His activity.** For endless ages God rejoiced in the knowledge of Himself and in knowing Himself; He Thought—just one single, continuous Thought—and that Thought was Himself all over again, in all His Being. That Thought was His Son, the Infinite Word—His only-begotten Son, the Second Person of the Blessed Trinity, to whom He communicates His nature, His life and His perfections. These two Persons then look upon Each Other and love Each Other—so perfectly and so completely that their Act of Love is a perfect, infinite reproduction of the Divine Being: From their "mutual embrace," so to speak, bursts forth the Holy Spirit, the Third Person of the adorable Trinity. That is what we understand by the Divine Processions. God is eternally, essentially active within Himself. It is His nature to be active. It is this perfection of activity that transcends all the perfections of the Almighty which are made visible to us in the created universe. It is only through Revelation that we can even be aware of the existence of His inner activity. It is the expression of the inner life of God. If we penetrate to the very source of this activity, to the principle from which it springs, we have, after our inadequate way of conceiving things, penetrated to the Divine Nature Itself.

Now, St. Peter says that **we are to share the Divine Nature,** that is, in the very source of the Divine Processions by which God is Three Persons in one nature. We are to share in the source of that infinite activity which we have been considering in God as He existed alone for an eternity. We are to share in that by which God knows Himself and in knowing Himself begets a Person, equal in all respects to Himself, and in that by which an eternal, infinite mutual Love springs up between these two Persons, which Love is the Holy Spirit. In other words, we are to share in that by which God knows and loves Himself.

Supernatural life

All this happens in virtue of the new life we receive into our souls when we are baptized, as we shall see later. That life is given to us, so to speak, as a seed. If it is nourished during our time on earth, it will burst forth after death into the perfect flower of the vision of God. By that seed, called Sanctifying Grace, the soul is given aptitudes which do not belong to it in virtue of its nature, but which really belong to God. Through those aptitudes, the soul is enabled to share in the very intimacy which exists between the Divine Persons themselves. It possesses, therefore, a supernature, a new life born of water and the Holy Ghost; it is a new creature, re-generated.

St. Paul refers to this contrast between nature and supernature in the following sublime passage: "Therefore, brethren, we are debtors, not to the flesh, to live according to the flesh. For if you live according to the flesh, you shall die: but if by the Spirit you mortify the deeds of the flesh, you shall live. For whosoever are led by the Spirit of God, they are the sons of God. For you have not received the spirit of bondage again in fear: but you have received the spirit of adoption of sons, whereby we cry: Abba (Father). For the Spirit himself giveth testimony to our spirit, that we are the sons of God. And if sons, heirs also; heirs indeed of God, and joint heirs with Christ: yet so, if we suffer with him, that we may be also glorified with him." (*Rom.* 8:12-17).

Sons of God

Here we are told that we are adopted sons of God, because God has taken us to Himself as sons and given us a right to the divine inheritance. Adopted sons! There is a world of difference between this divine adoption and the ordinary legal adoption with which we are familiar. The latter makes one legally a member of a certain family, but it can never bestow upon anyone a share in the physical life of the father and mother. Yet divine adoption makes us in some way sharers in the very life of God. St. John says, "Whosoever is born of God, committeth not sin: for his seed abideth in him, and he cannot sin, because he is born of God." (*1 John* 3:9). Literally, this last phrase means "the seed of God persists in him." Thus by grace we are empowered to live in a manner resembling the life of God. Moreover, this "seed of God" gives us a sort of inborn right to the divine inheritance. That is the constant doctrine of the New Testament, repeated in dozens of places. "As many as received him, he gave them power to be made the sons of God." (*John* 1:12).

Temples of God

Even these sublime considerations are inadequate to make us understand the closeness of the relationship existing between the baptized soul and the eternal Trinity. "Know you not that you are the temple of God, and that the Spirit of God dwelleth in you?" St. Paul asked the Corinthians. (*1 Cor.* 3:16). Our Lord Himself, in that wonderful discourse after the Last Supper, told His Apostles: "If any one love me, he will keep my word, and my Father will love him, and we will come to him, and will make our abode with him." (*John* 14:23). Here Christ is revealing yet another aspect of the Trinity's relationship to us. God dwells within the soul that is in the state of grace as in a temple. By the gift of Sanctifying Grace, our souls are given a power of reaction, which makes them capable of holding God vitally—of possessing Him—of having Him as their own. Think of the Blessed who have passed to their reward in Heaven. They *possess* God. They have Him in their souls; they have taken hold of Him. They have not merely an idea of God; they have God Himself. The souls of the Blessed are enabled to know God, and knowing Him, to love Him in a way entirely beyond the powers of their nature.

Grace

Without the aid of grace, we can have an idea of God, but we cannot possess God. By grace, we can know and love God in such a way that He is within us, just as an idea is within us when we know an ordinary creature. Note, I say, "*He* is within us," not only an idea of Him. He is within us as the object of our knowledge and love, that is, through Faith and Charity. *He* takes the place of any idea we have formed of Him. For note well what happens through this new seed of life, this elevation to the supernatural order (whereby we become "participators in the Divine Nature"), which is Sanctifying Grace. With it there are *infused* into the soul (cf. *Rom.* 5:5) the Theological Virtues of Faith, Hope and Charity, which proceed from Sanctifying Grace, are intimately linked with it and derive from it as warmth and light come from the sun. In virtue, then, of this supernatural life to which it has been raised, through the elevation of its natural faculties by the infusion of the Theological Virtues, the sanctified soul can now know God and love God, though not in the same manner and degree (*1 Cor.* 14:42), with the same knowledge and love with which it will know Him and love Him eternally in Heaven. The seed will then have fructified in full maturity! That is what we mean by the mysterious dwelling of the Holy Trinity within the soul, on which St. Paul is so insistent.

Therefore, from the contemplation of the mystery of the Holy Trinity we have arrived at some conception of our own supernatural dignity. We are indeed temples of God, children of God, sharers in the nature of God. Then, should not our first care be to love that God to whom we are so closely related?

Chapter 13

Belief in Jesus Christ

What is the second article of the Apostles' Creed? *The second article of the Apostles' Creed is, "And in Jesus Christ, His only Son, our Lord."*

Who is Jesus Christ? *Jesus Christ is God the Son, made man for us.*

Is Jesus Christ truly God? *Jesus Christ is truly God.*

Why is Jesus Christ truly God? *Jesus Christ is truly God because He has one and the same nature with God the Father.*

Was Jesus Christ always God? *Jesus Christ was always God, born of the Father from all eternity.*

Which Person of the Blessed Trinity is Jesus Christ? *Jesus Christ is the Second Person of the Blessed Trinity.*

Is Jesus Christ truly man? *Jesus Christ is truly man.*

Why is Jesus Christ truly man? *Jesus Christ is truly man because He has the nature of man, having a body and soul like ours.*

Was Jesus Christ always man? *Jesus Christ was not always man. He has been man only from the time of His Incarnation.*

What do you mean by the Incarnation? *By the Incarnation I mean that God the Son took to Himself the nature of man: "the Word was made Flesh."*

How many natures are there in Jesus Christ? *There are two natures in Jesus Christ, the nature of God and the nature of man.*

Is there only one person in Jesus Christ? *There is only one Person in Jesus Christ, which is the Person of God the Son.*

Why was God the Son made man? *God the Son was made man to redeem us from sin and Hell and to teach us the way to Heaven.*

What does the holy name "Jesus" mean? *The holy name "Jesus" means Saviour.*

What does the name "Christ" mean? *The name "Christ" means Anointed.*

Where is Jesus Christ? *As God, Jesus Christ is everywhere. As God made man, He is in Heaven and in the Blessed Sacrament of the Altar.*

What rule of life must we follow if we are to be saved? *If we hope to be saved, we must follow the rule of life taught by Jesus Christ.*

What are we bound to do by the rule of life taught by Jesus Christ? *By the rule of life taught by Jesus Christ, we are bound always to hate sin and to love God.*

How are we to follow Our Blessed Lord? *We are to follow Our Blessed Lord by walking in His footsteps and imitating His virtues.*

What are the principal virtues we are to learn of Our Blessed Lord? *The principal virtues we are to learn of Our Blessed Lord are meekness, humility and obedience.*

Summary of the doctrine

"I BELIEVE in Jesus Christ, His [God's] only Son, Our Lord, who was conceived by the Holy Ghost, born of the Virgin Mary, suffered under Pontius Pilate, was crucified, died and was buried; He descended into Hell; the third day, He rose again from the dead; He ascended into Heaven, sitteth at the right hand of God the Father Almighty; from thence He shall come to judge the living and the dead." —The Apostle's Creed, first part.

It is the doctrine of the Church that God the Son, the Second Person of the Blessed Trinity, became Man; that He was born of the Virgin Mary; that He is true God and true Man. Let us prove this last doctrine now.

Jesus Christ is true God

Recall a scene which took place almost 2,000 years ago near the small town of Bethany, just a few miles from Jerusalem. It is hard, dry, barren country, with hillsides littered with millions of limestone chips, or else it is bare and volcanic. A small number of people are seen coming out of the town, walking very slowly toward the northeast. Their leader is a man, tall, handsome, impressive, but obviously filled with grief. Close behind Him are two women, walking silently with bowed heads and clad in the attire of mourners. Following is a straggling procession of men and women, some alone, others in groups. As we watch in silence, the leader begins to weep and those nearest Him in the procession remark softly one to another, "See how He loved him."

Across the road to the slopes of the Mount of Olives they proceed, to a place where the hollows in the rocks have been shaped into square chambers to serve as tombs. It is the cemetery of Bethany. Now one of those in the procession moves forward to lead the way to a tomb only recently closed. Before the entrance they halt. It is scaled like all the others with a large stone. Still the leader is weeping softly as all eyes are fixed upon Him. Quietly He turns to one of the women beside Him, saying, "Take away the stone." Immediately she replies: "Lord, the air is foul by now; he has been four days dead." He turns slightly and looks at her. His gaze pierces her soul. "Have I not told thee," He says, "that if thou hast faith, thou wilt see God glorified?" That is sufficient. With a gesture, she bids the men remove the stone.

The silence of amazement and expectation has fallen on the gathering. With the aid of crowbars the stone is slowly rolled back. Now they watch His every gesture and motion. Standing a few feet from the entrance to the cave, He slowly raises His eyes upwards; He seems to forget His surroundings; He begins to pray. "Father," He says, "I give thee thanks that thou hast heard me." (*Jn.* 11:41). Now He seems to peer into the darkness of the tomb. There is a pause. Then, raising His voice so that all can hear, He cries: "Lazarus, come forth." (*Jn.* 11:43).

What a terrifying moment! The tomb—a man dead for four days—the fixed eyes, the bated breath, the straining necks. Then, suddenly, at the entrance of the tomb, the dead man himself appears—covered with bandages, clothes and wrappings. It is an apparition, a corpse walking! After a moment that seems like an eternity, the man who has caused this strange scene turns to those nearest Him and says quietly, as if nothing out of the ordinary has happened: "Loose him, and let him go." And He begins to move away. (*Jn.* 11:44).

Immediately a babble of conversation and expressions of astonishment burst forth. Lazarus, the man raised from the dead, is surrounded by an excited throng. They must convince themselves that he is really alive, that this is the same man whom they buried less than a week ago. Naturally, they begin to ask one another: "Who is this man that works such wonders? Who is he that brings the dead back to life?" "He is the carpenter of Nazareth," says one. "He has cured lepers," says another. "He raised a poor boy to life in Naim," says a third. "He quelled a storm on the sea of Galilee," contributes a fourth.

Christ foretold

The story of Jesus is told in certain important history books known as the Gospels that were written by His contemporaries. Not only that, this unique Person had been prepared for during thousands of years. His life had been prophetically written in advance in amazing detail. Not one, but many Prophets, had foretold numerous things concerning Him. All these prophecies converged upon and met in Christ. He was to be a real man, of the seed of Adam, of Abraham and of David; He was to be, nevertheless, a pre-existing supernatural Being. (*Dan.* 7:9-14). Although He was the only "Just One," He was to suffer for the sins of His people, thereby redeeming them, and He was to establish an everlasting kingdom and to rule over the whole earth (*Is.* 49:1-7; 43:1-7; 50:4-10; 52:13-15; 53:12). Further, it was through the Saviour that the non-Jewish peoples were to know and worship the God of the Jews; through Jesus Christ that happened. Therefore, prophecy culminated in Christ, and with Him the Old Testament Jewish revelation stopped.

The character of Christ

Examine well the life and character of Christ. See in Him a man who is without sin; a man who is acknowledged to be sinless even by His enemies; a man who is filled with every virtue—truth, fortitude, humility, gentleness, compassion, love; a man who is religious and prayerful, selfless and mortified. The people of His own day were in admiration at His doctrine; no age, no sex, no grade, no class-distinction could stand between Christ and His people. Little children run to Him from their mothers' arms, attracted by His gentleness and charm; public sinners, the dregs of humanity, find at His feet compassion and forgiveness; even His enemies, who would have cast Him from the brow of a cliff, are repulsed from doing so merely by the majesty of His presence, and He goes His way. In Him see the vigor of perfect manhood combined with the tenderness of a mother's heart, authority with sympathy, the power to command with perfect accessibility.

In Him you cannot find a fault. Compare Him with the greatest men who have ever lived—with the philosophers of Greece, with the Emperors of Rome, with the Saints and the holy men who have dwelt and died on this earth; compare Him with whomsoever you please, and you will find in Him something that excels the virtue of them all. No character has ever been admitted to be so universally perfect and so absolutely harmonious in all its parts. Even the Rationalist must admit that the portrait of Christ remains the most sublime that the artist called "world-history" has ever painted.

The power of Christ

Add to the charm of His character His power. See Him walking on the waves of the sea; see Him raise aloft His hand to still the raging gale; present yourself at the funeral procession when He halts the little company of mourners and restores the young man to his widowed mother; stand by while He heals the sick, the blind, the lame, the dumb, by a mere word, and even at a distance. Then listen to Him appealing to His miracles as proof that He is sent by God: "For the works which the Father hath given me to perfect; the works themselves, which I do, give testimony of me, that the Father hath sent me." (*John* 5:36).

So, even if for the moment you do not admit that Jesus Christ is God, you must at least concede that God is with Him, that at least He uses the power of God, that at least what He says and does is guaranteed by God. In other words, if He has any message for the world, if He has any claims to make, that message and those claims must be true, sealed with a divine guarantee of truth.

The claims of Christ

What, then, are the claims of Christ? He certainly claimed to be the **Messias:** "I am he." (*John* 4:26).

He claimed to be God, the **Judge of all men:** "When the Son of Man comes in his glory, and all the Angels with him, he will sit down upon the throne of his glory and all nations shall be gathered into his presence . . ." (*Matt.* 25:31-46).

He claimed to be the **Lord of the Sabbath:** "The Son of man is Lord even of the Sabbath." (*Matt.* 12:8).

Making Himself equal to God, the Lawgiver of the Old Law, He claims the right to enlarge and interpret the Ten Commandments on His own personal authority: "You have heard that it was said to the men of old . . . For I tell you . . ." (*Matt.* 5:20 ff).

He claimed to be all-powerful, a Divine Person, equal to the Father in power, and to be in fact God the Son: "All power is given to me in heaven and in earth" (*Matt.* 28:18). All things are delivered to me by my Father; and no one knoweth who the Son is, but the Father; and who the Father is, but the Son, and to whom the Son will reveal him." (*Luke* 10:22).

Moreover, He praised St. Peter when that Apostle proclaimed Him to be God the Son: "Thou art Christ, the Son of the living God. And Jesus answering, said to him: Blessed art thou, Simon Bar-Jona: because flesh and blood hath not revealed it to thee, but my Father who is in heaven." (*Matt.* 16:16-17).

On the occasion of His trial before the High Priest, Jesus was asked: "Art thou the Christ, the Son of the blessed God? Jesus said to him: I am." The High Priest understood this as blasphemy: "He has blasphemed." (*Mark* 14:61-64; *Matt.* 26:63-66). What was the blasphemy if not that Jesus claimed to be the true Son of God, one in nature with the Father?

St. John tells us of several instances in which Jesus made similar claims: "Before Abraham was made, I am." (*John* 8:58). "For as the Father raiseth up the dead, and giveth life: so the Son also giveth life to whomsoever He will." (*John* 5:22-23). "Now glorify thou me, O Father, with thyself . . . all my things are thine, and thine are mine." (*John* 17:5, 10).

It is clear, too, that **the Jews understood Jesus to be claiming to be God:** "For a good work we stone thee not," answered the Jews; "But for blasphemy; and because that thou, being a man, makest thyself God." (*John* 10:33). "Hereupon therefore the Jews sought the more to kill him, because he said God was his Father, making himself equal to God. Then Jesus answered, "As the Father raiseth up the dead, and giveth life: so the Son also giveth life to whom he will." (*John* 5:18, 21). Before Pilate: "The Jews answered him: We have a law; and according to the law, he ought to die, because he made himself the Son of God." (*John* 19:7).

Again, Jesus did or allowed certain acts which are in themselves an implicit claim to the Divinity. For example, he forgave sins as of His own independent power: "Son, thy sins are forgiven thee." But the Scribes who were present thought to themselves, "Who can forgive sins, but God only?" . . . "But that you may know that the Son of man hath power on earth to forgive sins . . ." (*Mark* 2:5-12). To Mary Magdalen: "Thy sins are forgiven." (*Luke* 8:48).

He accepted adoration: "Dost thou believe in the Son of God? . . . I believe, Lord. And falling down, he adored him." (*John* 9:38).

It is abundantly clear that **the Apostles and Disciples knew that Christ claimed to be God:** "But these are written, that you may believe that Jesus is the Christ, the Son of God." (*John* 20:31). "The author of life you killed," St. Peter told the Jews. (*Acts* 3:15). "I believe that Jesus Christ is the Son of God." (*Acts* 8:37).

Christ foretold the future

There are two other proofs of the Divinity of Christ, which we summarize for the sake of completeness. The first is from His prophecies. He showed by them that He had knowledge of the future, which could not have been possessed by any mere man. In astonishing detail, He foretold His Passion, Resurrection and Ascension into Heaven; He foretold His betrayal by Judas, His denial by Peter and His desertion by all the disciples; He foretold the growth of His Church, its persecution and its triumphs over the powers of Hell. Again, in extraordinary detail, He described the destruction of Jerusalem and the dispersion of the Jewish people. By His prophecies, therefore, Jesus Christ proved Himself to be God.

The Resurrection

The second argument is from the fact of Christ's Resurrection from the dead. The Gospels, contemporary history books, describe what took place:

"Joseph taking the body . . . laid it in his own new monument . . . and he rolled a great stone to the door of the monument . . . And when the sabbath was past, Mary Magdalen, and Mary the mother of James, and Salome brought sweet spices, that coming they might anoint Jesus. Very early in the morning, the first day of the week, they come to the sepulchre, the sun being now risen. . . And looking, they saw the stone rolled back. For it was very great. And entering into the sepulchre, they saw a young man sitting on the right side, clothed with a white robe: and they were astonished. Who saith to them: Be not affrighted; you seek Jesus of Nazareth, who was crucified: he is risen, he is not here" . . . Some of the guards reached the city, and told the chief priests of all that befell. These gathered with the elders to take counsel, and offered a rich bribe to the soldiers, "saying: Say you, His disciples came by night, and stole him away when we were asleep." The soldiers took the bribe, and did as they were instructed; and this is the tale which has gone abroad among the Jews, to this day. (*Matt.* 27:59-60; *Mark* 16:1-6; *Matt.* 28:13).

Therefore, it cannot be denied that Christ's body was put into the tomb on the Friday night of His death; nor can it be denied that it was not there on the next Sunday morning. Similarly, it cannot be denied that Christ appeared to many after His death: "The Lord is risen indeed, and hath appeared to Simon . . . The other disciples therefore said to him [Thomas]: We have seen the Lord." (*Luke* 24:34; *John* 20:25, etc.).

St. Paul, writing thirty years later, mentions it as an undoubted fact, known to all and witnessed by numbers of people **who were still alive:** "For I delivered unto you first of all, which I also received: How that Christ, according to the Scriptures, died . . . was buried, and then . . . rose again on the third day: That He was seen by Cephas [Peter]; and after that by the eleven, then he was seen by more than five hundred brethren at once: of whom many remain until this present." (*1 Cor.* 15:3-6).

Within a few months, in the very city in which it took place, **Peter was preaching the Resurrection**: "Ye men of Judea, and all you that dwell in Jerusalem . . . hear these words: Jesus of Nazareth, a man approved of God among you . . . being delivered up . . . you by the hands of wicked men have crucified and slain. Whom God hath raised up, having loosed the sorrows of hell, as it was impossible that he should be holden by it." (*Acts* 2:14-32). He was preaching, too, to those who could have found out the truth. Did they deny it? Did Christ's enemies come forward to disprove Peter's assertion? No. It was believed: For St. Luke says, "And there were added in that day about three thousand souls." (*Acts* 2:41).

We can be sure that **if the Jews could convincingly have denied the fact of Christ's Resurrection, they would have done so, because they knew it was the chief point of the doctrine of His followers:** For St. Paul says, "If Christ be not risen again, then our preaching is vain, and your faith is also vain." (*1 Cor.* 14:14).

Miracles

Modern thinkers who claim not to accept the Resurrection simply discount the whole story, **not from legitimate historical criticism,** but because they are antecedently prejudiced against miracles. "Miracles do not happen," they say. "The Resurrection was a miracle; therefore, it did not happen." But, **on the evidence of history, the Resurrection of Christ from the dead must be accepted as a fact. It did happen; it was a miracle.** Deny it, and you must logically deny a host of facts which everyone accepts today on evidence not nearly so strong.

It follows from all this that **Christ is God.** When challenged for a sign in proof of His divinity, the sign He gave was **His Resurrection:** "What sign dost thou show unto us, seeing thou dost these things? Jesus answered them, Destroy this temple, and in three days I will raise it up. . . . But he spoke of the temple of his body." (*John* 2:18-21). "A sign shall not be given it, but the sign of Jonas the prophet. For as Jonas was in the whale's belly three days and three nights: so shall the Son of man be in the heart of the earth three days and three nights." (*Matt.* 12:39-40).

The Jews understood this sign to mean that He would rise from the dead, and for that reason they said to Pilate after the Crucifixion: "Sir, we have remembered that that seducer said, while he was yet alive: After three days I will rise again." (*Matt.* 27:63).

Here is the conclusion. Either Christ rose from the dead by His own power, or God, distinct from Him, raised Him to life. If the former, He is God. If the latter, He is certainly supported by God, Who works a stupendous miracle in His favor. This could not be if He were an impostor. Hence, His claim is true. **Christ is God.**

Chapter 14

Redemption

What is the third article of the Creed? *The third article of the Creed is, "Who was conceived by the Holy Ghost, born of the Virgin Mary."*

What does the third article mean? *The third article means that God the Son took a body and soul like ours, in the womb of the Blessed Virgin Mary, by the power of the Holy Ghost.*

Did Jesus Christ have a Father on earth? *Jesus Christ had no Father on earth. St. Joseph was only His guardian or foster-father.*

Where was our Saviour born? *Our Saviour was born in a stable at Bethlehem.*

On what day was our Saviour born? *Our Saviour was born on Christmas Day.*

What is the fourth article of the Creed? *The fourth article of the Creed is, "Suffered under Pontius Pilate, was crucified, died and was buried."*

What were the chief sufferings of Christ? *The chief sufferings of Christ were: first, His agony and His sweat of blood in the Garden; secondly, His being scourged at the pillar and crowned with thorns; and thirdly, His carrying His Cross, His crucifixion and His death between two thieves.*

What are the chief sufferings of Our Lord called? *The chief sufferings of Our Lord are called the Passion of Jesus Christ.*

Why did our Saviour suffer? *Our Saviour suffered to atone for our sins and to purchase for us eternal life.*

Why is Jesus Christ called our Redeemer? *Jesus Christ is called our Redeemer because His precious Blood is the price by which we were ransomed.*

On what day did our Saviour die? *Our Saviour died on Good Friday.*

Where did our Saviour die? *Our Saviour died on Mount Calvary.*

Why do we make the Sign of the Cross? *We make the Sign of the Cross, first, to put us in mind of the Blessed Trinity, and secondly, to remind us that God the Son died for us on the Cross.*

In making the Sign of the Cross, how are we reminded of the Blessed Trinity? *In making the Sign of the Cross, we are reminded of the Blessed Trinity by the words, "In the name of the Father, and of the Son, and of the Holy Ghost."*

In making the Sign of the Cross how are we reminded that Christ died for us on the Cross? *In making the Sign of the Cross we are reminded that Christ died for us on the Cross by the very form of the Cross which we make upon ourselves.*

B ECAUSE Christ is God, Christianity is true. It is God's revelation to mankind. Hence, the proper understanding of it is of vital importance. For example, **one must be absolutely certain that the form of Christianity one professes is that revealed by Christ, that it is authentic and complete.** In succeeding instructions we shall learn more on this point. For the present we must learn a little more about the God-Man, Christ, and the purpose for which He assumed our human nature.

One Person, two Natures

In Christ, the nature of God and the nature of man are united in one **Divine Person.** God really **became** man: "The Word was made flesh." (*John* 1:14). St. John does not say, "The Word was changed into flesh," but his language implies that to His own unchanging, eternal Person, God the Son assumed a human nature in the very act of its creation. That Human Nature, although it possessed every human perfection and every human faculty, **was not a human person.** There is only **one Person in Christ,** and that is the **Person of God the Son.** He is the second Person of the Blessed Trinity.

A person is defined as a rational being, existing as a complete individual entity. It does not exist as part of another. The Human Nature of Christ **never** existed as a complete individual entity; it never had an independent created existence.

The Hypostatic Union

This union of the two natures in the one Person of Christ is called **The Hypostatic Union,** the word "hypostatic" being the adjective derived from "hypostasis," which means an existing, independent, complete thing. Thus a cabbage, a robin, a man or an angel would be an hypostasis; but a leaf of the cabbage, a wing of the bird, the soul of a man or the thought of an angel could not be described as such.

We have already discussed the meaning of the terms "person" and "nature" while learning about the Blessed Trinity, in which we saw there are three **Persons in one Nature.** In Christ there are two **Natures** in one **Person.**

Since this is so, it is perfectly allowable for us to attribute to the One Divine Person of Christ both the attributes and actions of His Divine Nature and the actions, qualities and passions of His Human Nature. So we say, "God was born," or "God died," or "God wept," and so on.

Nevertheless, the Human Nature in Christ is not mixed or fused with His Divine Nature. The latter *is* Infinite Perfection; the former has its own finite faculties and perfections. Christ has a true human body, a true human soul—therefore human feelings, a human intellect and a free, human will.

Thus, in Christ there are two Wills—the Divine and Human; there are both the Divine Omniscience and true human knowledge. This latter embraces the highest perfection of every kind of knowledge possible to the human mind.

Christ could, and did, perform human acts in virtue of His Human Nature. They were finite, since they were acts of a created nature, **but in merit and dignity they were infinite because they are the acts of an Infinite Person.**

Atonement

One of the reasons—maybe the principal reason—why God became man, why He became **incarnate,** was to buy us back—to **redeem** us from the power of the devil: "For there is one God, and one mediator of God and men, the man Christ Jesus: Who gave himself a redemption for all." (*1 Tim.* 2:5-6).

In our instruction on Original Sin, we saw how Adam sinned officially, as head of the human race, and how that sin of his meant for all of us the loss of supernatural life and of the added gifts of immortality in the body, integrity and the great knowledge possessed by Adam and Eve. It created a breach in the union between God and the human race. Through the Incarnation, that breach was healed. Supernatural life, but not the added gifts, was won back. In a word, an "at-one-ment" took place.

By His Passion and death, suffered through obedience and love, Christ really and truly bought us back from the power of Satan. That is why He became man: "For the Son of man is come to seek and save that which was lost." (*Luke* 19:10). Again and again throughout His public life, Christ made this perfectly clear, especially in the parables of the Good Shepherd, the Lost Drachma and the Prodigal Son. Several times, too, He said that His death, predicted by the prophets, was necessary that the purpose of His coming might be attained: "Jesus began to show to his disciples, that he must go up to Jerusalem and . . . be put to death, and on the third day rise again." (*Matt.* 16:21). This death is to be the cause of our Redemption: "For the Son of man also is not come to be ministered unto, but to minister, and to give his life a redemption for many." (*Mark* 10:45).

The Apostles have some very pertinent things to say about the death of Christ and its purpose. St. Peter teaches: "For unto this are you called: because Christ also suffered for us, leaving you an example that you should follow his steps. Who did no sin, neither was guile found in his mouth . . . Who his own self bore our sins in his body upon the tree: that we, being dead to sins, should live to justice: by whose stripes you were healed." (*1 Peter.* 2:21-24). St. Paul makes this his chief message, a fundamental of his teaching, handed on to him by Jesus: "For I delivered unto you *first of all,* which I also received: how that Christ died for our sins, according to the scriptures." (*1 Cor.* 15:3, emphasis added). "When we were enemies, we were reconciled to God by the death of his Son." (*Rom.* 5:10). And St. John: "The blood of Jesus Christ, his Son, cleanses us from all sin . . . And he is the propitiation for our sins: and not only for ours only, but also for those of the whole world . . ." (*1 John* 1:7; 2:2). "He hath loved us, and washed us from our sins in his own blood." (*Apoc.* 1:5). In his Gospel, St. John teaches how, through His death, Christ freed us from slavery to sin and brought us into His kingdom of light and life; how He laid down His life for all men, whom He attracted to Himself, the Good Shepherd, who was willing to sacrifice all for His flock.

The explanation of all these Scriptural references is easier when we recall that since Christ was God and Man at the same time and in His single divine Person, every act of His, whether in His Divine or in His Human Nature, was an act of God, and as such, of infinite value. Thus, when He made an act of satisfaction to God in His manhood, this act (His death on the Cross) was of infinite value (because Jesus is a divine Person) and therefore satisfied the justice of His infinite Father, who had been offended by the sin of Adam (Original Sin). Humanity, therefore, really made satisfaction for Original Sin, for the act of satisfaction was infinite in value because it was the act of a Divine Person who was at the same time also man. **What a marvelous plan! How far beyond the sphere of even the most advanced human imagination! It is certainly without parallel in any other religion!**

How all these considerations show the great love of God for us! One single act of Christ's will would have been the act of a Divine Person and thus would have redeemed a million worlds—but Christ chose to suffer and die on the Cross to show His love for us, to give us an unforgettable example of the renunciation of self as reparation for a sin in which Adam had placed self before God, and to show us what the gravity of sin really means.

The Sacrifice of Christ

The Redemption of the human race was accomplished through a real sacrifice. Christ, the eternal High Priest, offered Himself on the Cross as a victim to His Father.

St. Paul devoted the fifth chapter of his Epistle to the Hebrews to a discussion of the priesthood of Christ. Long before, David had foretold that Christ was to be a priest according to the order of Melchisedech. Now St. Paul enlarges on that point:

"For every high priest taken from among men, is ordained for men in the things that appertain to God, that he may offer up gifts and sacrifices for sins: Who can have compassion on them that are ignorant and that err: because he himself also is compassed with infirmity. And therefore he ought, as for the people, so also for himself, to offer for sins. Neither doth any man take the honor to himself, but he that is called by God, as Aaron was. So Christ also did not glorify himself, that he might be made a high priest: but he that said unto him: 'Thou art my Son, this day have I begotten thee.' As he saith also in another place: 'Thou art a priest for ever, according to the order of Melchisedech.' Who in the days of his flesh, with a strong cry and tears, offering up prayers and supplications to him that was able to save him from death, was heard for his reverence. And whereas indeed he was the Son of God, he learned obedience by the things which he suffered: And being consummated, he became, to all that obey him, the cause of eternal salvation. Called by God a high priest according to the order of Melchisedech." (*Heb.* 5:1-10).

Later on the Apostle asks: "How much more shall the blood of Christ, who by the Holy Ghost offered himself unspotted unto God, cleanse our conscience from dead works, to serve the living God? So also Christ was offered once to exhaust the sins of many; the second time he shall appear without sin to them that expect him unto salvation." (*Heb.* 9:14, 28).

So it was that Christ substituted Himself for us, taking our punishment on Himself. He did not **assume** our guilt; He suffered for us, but not **as** us.

Of course, the value of Christ's act of satisfaction infinitely exceeds all sin, but it is not true to say, as Luther did, that, without change in ourselves, we are saved by reminding God of His Son. Rather, we have been endowed with a free will, and God has appointed certain definite channels by which the merits of Christ's death are applied to our souls. Those channels are called **Sacraments,** and we shall consider them in detail later.

The sufferings of Christ are called His Passion. The story of them can be read in any of the Gospels, and Catholics love to meditate on them as the great example of God's abounding love for men. The thought of the greatness of His sufferings arouses feelings of compassion for the Sufferer, of contrition for the sin which caused Him such torment, of gratitude for the benefits we have received through the Cross, of admiration for the wonders of the mystery of Redemption, of yearning to imitate the virtues of the Redeemer, and of love to repay Him for the love He thus manifested for us. There is indeed no subject of contemplation more fruitful than the blessed Passion of our Redeemer.

Chapter 15

Why Organized Religion? (1)

What is the ninth article of the Creed? *The ninth article of the Creed is "The Holy Catholic Church; the Communion of Saints."*

What is the Catholic Church? *The Catholic Church is the union of all the truly Christian Faithful under one head.*

Does the Church of Christ have any marks by which we may know her? *The Church of Christ has four marks by which we may know her: she is One; she is Holy; she is Catholic; she is Apostolic.*

How is the Church one? *The Church is One because all her members agree in one Faith, have all the same Sacrifice and Sacraments, and are all united under one Head.*

How is the Church holy? *The Church is Holy because she teaches a holy doctrine, offers to all her members the means of holiness, and is distinguished by the eminent holiness of so many thousands of her children.*

What does the word Catholic mean? *The word Catholic means whole, Universal, all.*

How is the Church Catholic or Universal? *The Church is Catholic or Universal because she subsists in all ages, teaches all nations, and is the one Ark of Salvation for all.*

How is the Church Apostolic? *The Church is Apostolic because she holds the doctrines and Traditions of the Apostles and because, through the unbroken succession of her Pastors, she derives her priestly Orders and her Mission from them.*

B ELIEF in God excludes atheism. Acceptance of the divinity of Christ excludes all non-Christian religions. So far have our instructions progressed. Christianity is true. But many problems still remain.

Imagine a perfect stranger arriving on this earth in the full maturity of manhood from, let us say, Mars. He would obviously set himself to learn our language, our ways, our customs, our lives. Many things would bewilder him, but probably few would puzzle him more than the extraordinary multiplicity of religious beliefs and loyalties he would find among Christian peoples. In every town and village he visited, he would find churches, chapels and religious assemblies in great numbers, all belonging to different Christian denominations.

If he were a sensible man, he would begin to ask himself some questions. He would not rest until he had sifted the mystery to the bottom. Unlike ourselves, he would be far from taking the existence of so many diverse views of Christianity for granted. "If, as you say, God has made a revelation," he would tell us, "**all men have an obligation to find out exactly what that revelation is**, and then to live up to its teaching. If God revealed how He wants to be worshipped, it is the duty of men to accept that revelation and not to persist in worshipping Him in ways contrary to it."

Different ideas of "church"

No doubt such a visitor from space would receive the reply that "It does not matter much to which of the denominations you belong—Anglican, Methodist or Roman Catholic—for Christ founded but one Church, a spiritual body with no earthly organization, and of that Church one becomes a member through christening, or Baptism. The important thing is to acquire a certain outlook from Christ and to mold our characters according to it. He is the great example of a good life. At most, it is necessary to believe certain things He told us about His Father, the forgiveness of sins and the world to come. Of course, groups of members of the spiritual Church Christ founded are perfectly free to form among themselves individual churches, if they so wish and find it spiritually helpful; but these are not essential. They are like clubs within a city. You may or may not belong to them, as you wish."

The Catholic Church does not accept the above view of

Christianity! It teaches that Christ founded His Church just as immediately and directly as General Booth founded the Salvation Army. Before He ascended into Heaven, He set up on earth a **visible** organization, with a central authority and properly constituted officials, each with definite functions to perform. It is not just that Catholics differ from Protestants on one or two additional points of doctrine, which Catholics believe and Protestants do not, such as, indulgences and the infallibility of the Pope. The difference is much more fundamental. **Every Catholic believes that the first requisite for the true following of Christ is to belong to the visible, external organization which Christ founded.**

Christ founded a visible, organized Church

That He did actually found an organization is perfectly clear from the Gospels. There we see Christ regarding the Church as a society which can be approached by and which can excommunicate its members: "If he will not hear them, tell the church, and if he will not hear the church, let him be to thee as the heathen and publican." (*Matt.* 18:17).

The injunction, "tell the church," would be impossible of fulfillment if the Church were merely the spiritual society, which so many today apparently believe it is.

Moreover, we actually see Christ at work founding a definite, organized, clearly visible religious society. After spending the night in prayer, He chose His twelve Apostles, and it is clear from His words to them that He was intent upon establishing an organization having officials with clearly defined functions to perform, a central authority and a unity of doctrine.

a) **Demarcation of Function:** The Apostles are definitely set apart as officials: "And he said to them: To you it is given to know the mystery of the kingdom of God: but to them that are without, all things are done in parables." (*Mark* 4:11).

They are to **teach:** "Going therefore, teach ye all nations; baptizing them in the name of the Father, and of the Son, and of the Holy Ghost, teaching them to observe all things whatsoever I have commanded you: and behold, I am with you all days, even to the consummation of the world." (*Matt.* 28:19-20).

They are to **govern:** "Amen I say to you, whatsoever you shall bind upon earth, shall be bound also in heaven; and whatsoever you shall loose upon earth, shall be loosed also in heaven." (*Matt.* 18:18).

They are to **sanctify:** "And Jesus coming, spoke to them, saying: All power is given to me in heaven and in earth. Going therefore, teach ye all nations, baptizing them in the name of the Father, and of the Son, and of the Holy Ghost . . . Whose sins you shall forgive, they are forgiven them; and whose sins you shall retain, they are retained." (*Matt.* 28:18-19; *John* 20:23).

b) **A Central Authority.** In the next instruction we shall discuss at length the position of St. Peter in the Church as depicted by the Gospels. For the moment, we are content with making this point— that however you interpret the Petrine texts (*Matt.* 16:18 and *John* 21:15-17), you cannot escape the conclusion that some special authority is being conferred on Peter—especially when this is considered in the light of all the other references to St. Peter, from his first calling and the change of his name to his life story after the Crucifixion. Nobody can logically deny that Peter did occupy a position of authority in the infant Church.

c) **Oneness of Doctrine:** The Apostles are to teach only what Christ has commanded them. In fact, Christ prayed to the Father to "keep them in thy name whom thou has given me; that they may be one, as we also are." *(John* 17:11). He prayed too for all those who would be converted by the Apostles, "that they all may be one, as thou, Father, in me, and I in thee; that they also may be one in us; that the world may believe that thou hast sent me." (*John* 17:21).

Perhaps it is not altogether superfluous to add that **Christ also compared His Church to a number of very visible objects—a Body, a Kingdom, a Sheepfold, a Net, a City, a Field.**

Unless this contention of ours is true, Christ did an extraordinarily foolish thing in founding a Church with the definite task of converting the world, and yet giving it no organization with which to accomplish the task. He would have founded a rabble rather than an organized force, and surely He who was Infinite Wisdom did not expect a rabble to do what He commanded—nothing less than to preach the Gospel to the whole of creation! Moreover, Christ left for mankind authoritative teaching on many vital issues. Reason demands that He would leave some central authority to interpret that teaching according to the concrete circumstances of each succeeding age. Not to have done so would have been to leave the way open to disunity of every kind—the very thing against which He prayed so fervently after the Last Supper.

All must belong to Christ's Church

We Catholics believe that Christ founded a visible Church and placed on all men a grave obligation to belong to that Church. "He that heareth you, heareth me, and he that despiseth you, despiseth me; and he that despiseth me, despiseth him that sent me." (*Luke* 10:16). "He that believeth and is baptized, shall be saved: but he that believeth not shall be condemned." (*Mark* 16:16). We reject as false the view that Christ founded an invisible society, the view that the hierarchy is a merely human institution, with no power to teach, govern or sacrifice. We cannot accept the opinion that all the various Christian denominations are branches of the one Church of Christ, because all these denominations disagree on many essentials, from the words and books of Holy Scripture, to the very meaning of articles of belief, to the difference between right and wrong in observing the Ten Commandments. We also feel bound to reject all attempts at *corporate* reunion (i.e., false ecumenism). When people ask why all the branches of Christ's Church cannot be reunited, we reply simply that we do not believe there are any branches of Christ's Church. The only form of reunion we could accept would be within the one visible organization founded by Christ—which is still in the world today, the One, Holy, Catholic, Apostolic Church, governed by the Pope, reigning in Rome as the successor of St. Peter.

This idea of the "invisible Church" is one which has been forced upon Protestants because it is the least indefensible of the series of theories about the Church they have tried to elaborate since the Protestant "Reformation" (begun in 1517). It was certainly not held by any of the Protestant "Reformers," and it was certainly unheard of before the Protestant "Reformation." On the contrary, the history of the Church at the time of the Apostles shows that the true Catholic idea was in undisputed possession. Then the Church was clearly regarded as a clear-cut, easily discernable society, of which the Apostles were the chief officers. They appointed deacons as subsidiary officers and "Episkopoi" (priests) to rule the Church of God. At the Council of the Apostles held at Jerusalem in the year 50 A.D., Peter makes a solemn juridical statement that the Gentiles are not to be excluded from the Church. St. Paul is more than clear in his conception of what kind of a Church Christ founded. For instance, he asks Timothy: "But if a man know not how to rule his own house, how shall he take care of the Church of God? . . . which is the Church of the living God, the pillar and ground of the truth." (*1 Tim.* 3:5, 15). In the succeeding chapter, he refers to Timothy's own ordination as a bishop. Writing to Titus, he told him: "For this cause I left thee in Crete, that thou shouldst set in order the things that are wanting, and shouldst ordain priests in every city, as I also appointed thee: for a bishop must be without crime, as the steward of God." (*Titus* 1:5, 7). In the letter to the Ephesians, there is that well-known passage depicting the organization of the Church: "And he gave some apostles, and some prophets, and other some evangelists, and other some pastors and doctors, for the perfecting of the saints, for the work of the ministry, for the edifying of the body of Christ." (*Eph.* 4:11-12). The invisible-Church theory does violence to all these and many more passages of Holy Writ. As St. John Chrysostom so truly said: "It is easier for the sun to be quenched than for the Church to be made invisible."

I believe in the Holy Catholic Church

Thus, when Protestants say in the Creed, "I believe in the Holy Catholic Church," they mean something entirely different from what the Catholic means when he uses the same words. For Catholics, the visible, organized Church founded immediately by Christ is part of the true Faith. Belief in it is required to avoid the condemnation Christ promised to unbelievers. Yet, non-Catholics make no such act of divine faith in regard to their own churches. Most of them, in fact, say that one can be as good a Christian outside a church as within one. Yet Christ put the whole of His religion into His Church, which He identifies with Himself. Of all the Christian denominations, the Catholic Church is the only one which claims to be immediately founded in its organized form by God-made-man, and so far no one has succeeded in disproving that claim.

The marks of the Church

But there are other credentials which the Catholic Church shows to prove that it alone represents authentic, undiluted Christianity in the world today. These credentials are **Four Marks**, four outwardly visible signs, which belong to the Church as essential characteristics. They are **Unity, Catholicity, Holiness and Apostolicity**— things which can be seen by any man who will look, and things absolutely necessary to the constitution of the True Church.

Unity

Consider the history of mankind: Someone has very truly called it a study of difference. It is the story of almost continual war, of the supplanting of one dynasty by another, of the slavery of a nation by its neighbors, of revolt, assassination, invasion, aggression, persecution, oppression. The record of our own times is simply a cross-section from the history of our race; it cannot be so vastly different from any other age.

Is it not a picture of irreconcilable differences—of differences of nation, of tongue, of color, of ideals, of customs, of points of view? World unity seems further away than ever; indeed, true national unity does not appear to have been achieved in any single country. Class-warfare, educational differences, opposition of commercial and economical interests, the jealousy of the sexes, party politics—these are some of the obstacles to unity. Every small town, every village, exemplifies the same fact by the multitude of activities and interests and ideals and practices represented among even its small population.

Such is the world today; such has been the world at any day. History is indeed the study of difference—of political, cultural, moral, ethnological, artistic, geographical, religious difference. The social life of man seems to have been concentrated upon the liquidation of these many differences. Yet, history proves that men cannot agree.

They aim at unity of faith or philosophy, of government, of ethical conduct, of political ideals—at every kind of unity—but they ever fail to achieve it.

World unity is not in nature. It is not natural for man to agree all the world over at all times on questions of religion, of government, of morals. Therefore, if there is in the world a society which can prove that it has existed throughout the Christian era in practically all places and has satisfied the needs of every type and class of man, and yet possesses in itself unity of teaching, of government, of life—then such a society is more than natural. **It is a miracle in itself.** And that is precisely what we claim for the Catholic Church. Its unity and its universality existing together are more than merely natural characteristics; **they are marks of a society possessing a constitution that is divine!**

Universality

Examine the universality of the Catholic Church. Think first of universality in doctrine—of how there has never been on this earth a man who could not satisfy all his legitimate aspirations and desires in the Catholic Church. Its doctrine is meant for the millionaire, as well as for the pauper; for the university professor, as well as the street sweeper; for the king, as well as the slave. All these can, and have, professed the same identical creed, have been sanctified by the same seven Sacraments and have been bound by exactly the same laws.

Pass on to the constitution of the Church. The Church is the subject of no Caesar and of no King, nor is it bound exclusively to any one nation. There is no legitimate form of government to which it cannot adapt itself, and the subjects of any State whatever are invited to enter the Fold.

And in actual fact, the Catholic Church is universal. In Europe she is without doubt the predominant religious society; in Central and South America, she stands unchallenged; in the United States, she counts her sixty millions; in Asia she is the only form of Christianity that is widely known and respected; her conquest in Africa is one of the greatest epics of modern times. **Within her fold she numbers more souls than all other Christians together! And she**

is three times the size of all Protestant Christianity combined.

Nor is that all. Now, as always, she is proud to number among the hundreds of millions of her children members of every stratum of society. There are the poor and the workers, white men and black, yellow men and brown; there are the sound of body and the lepers; there are the lettered and the ignorant; there are specialists in every department of art and science, men whose names are household words in their own professions; and there are all the millions of just ordinary men and women in every country of the world.

A miracle

The important fact is that this wonderful universality co-exists with a miraculous unity. We know in advance that the Church of Christ must possess such unity, if only because she is, as we shall see, the Mystical Body of Christ, carrying on His own life in the world, teaching what He taught, sacrificing as He sacrificed, praying as He prayed, suffering as He suffered, and acknowledging the one hierarchy which, as we have seen, He established. That divine unity is present only in the Catholic Church—today as in all ages.

Is it not food for thought that throughout all the changes of history referred to above, the Catholic Church has remained absolutely unchanged? In every age, in every civilization, in every country, she has remained just what she was when she first stepped out into the lanes of Jerusalem on that first Pentecost morning. Is there any **natural** explanation as to how this Church has succeeded in uniting within herself millions upon millions of people, all differing in race, in culture, in education, in interests? Is there any **natural** explanation of how one society can impose upon men in every age and clime, one faith and one ethic? These are precisely the things on which men differ the most.

Consider these facts in the concrete. Every Catholic priest, anywhere in the world today, celebrates daily, the same holy Mass as that celebrated by St. John in the presence of the Virgin Mary almost 2,000 years ago. More than one billion Catholics today believe what the persecuted Romans believed as they sheltered in the catacombs a couple of hundred years after the coming of Christ. The Catholic who today travels to any part of the world and there meets other Catholics knows that he will find that they all believe exactly what he believes, that they all worship just as he worships, and that they all acknowledge the same spiritual head—the successor of St. Peter. And more—if by some wonderful invention it were possible for a present-day Catholic to visit Catholics in every century of the Christian era and in every country of the world, he would always find the same marvellous unity of belief, of worship and of government. St. Augustine, for instance, accepted a faith exactly the same in every essential as that professed 800 years later by St. Francis of Assisi; and the Emperor Charlemagne in the year 800 believed the same faith as that which Columbus took to America in 1492.

No one who has studied history sincerely and with an open mind can deny that the Catholic Church possesses, and has always possessed, a marvellous and unconquerable unity of faith, of worship and of government, a unity which transcends all ages and all nations and which embraces every level of the social scale. In face of the fashionable vice of each succeeding age—such as, slavery, divorce or birth-prevention—the Church has always succeeded in imposing her moral code, her one divine ethic.

The Church Christ founded was certainly to be One in faith, worship and government. He prayed for this unity: "That they may all be one, as thou, Father, in me, and I in thee; that they may also be one in us." (*John* 17:21). He told the Apostles to teach only what He had commanded them: "Teaching them to observe all things whatsoever I have commanded you." (*Matt.* 28:20). He spoke of only one Church, one fold and one shepherd: "And other sheep I have that are not of this fold: them also I must bring, and they shall hear my voice, and there shall be one fold and one shepherd." (*John* 10:16). He promised to be with this one Church always, even till the End of the World: "And behold I am with you all days, even to the consummation of the world." (*Matt.* 28:20).

The Church Christ founded was certainly to be Universal, in the sense that it would gradually spread over all the earth, and among all the nations, in such a way as to stand out conspicuously among all the other religious bodies. "Go ye into the whole world, and preach the gospel to every creature." (*Mark* 16:15; cf. also *Luke* 2:30-32; *Matt.* 26:13; 8:11; *Luke* 24:47; *Matt.* 28:19-20).

The **Catholic Church** and the Catholic Church **alone** possesses these marks. **It alone is One, Holy, Catholic (Universal) and Apostolic**.

But even if Christ had not referred emphatically to these marks, even if we did not know at all that His Church must possess them, an examination of the history of the Church over the nearly 2,000 years of her existence reveals the most wonderful unity coexisting within her, along with the most astounding universality. This is a supernatural phenomenon, one defying a natural explanation. It is a miracle. It proves that the Catholic Church is indeed divinely guaranteed.

Chapter 16

Why Organized Religion? (2)

H OLINESS as a mark of the Church is that conspicuous and eminent sanctity which is always to be found in the Catholic Church and which is the result of her holy doctrine, of her holy Founder (Jesus Christ), and of her holy Sacraments, which are the means of holiness she offers to her children. Of course, not all the holiness in the Church is outwardly visible, any more than all of an iceberg can be seen above the water. But here we are concerned with holiness precisely as a visible mark of the Church, and therefore with **visible** holiness. The English Catholic Catechism is accurate when it says **"the Church is Holy because**

a) she teaches a holy doctrine;

b) offers to all the means of holiness, and

c) is distinguished by the eminent holiness of so many thousands of her children."

Holiness of doctrine

We are not concerned for the moment with the *truth* of her doctrine. That is proved in other instructions, and the fact that it needs proving shows that it is not part of the mark of holiness. Our immediate concern is with the evident *high morality* of Catholic doctrine. We say "evident" because it is unchallenged. Many wicked things have been said against the Church; many accusations have been made against her; but even her enemies admit that through nearly 2,000 years, amidst the widest possible variety of circumstances, her teaching has never swerved from the highest moral standard. On occasions—as in the case of Henry VIII—she has preferred to lose everything rather than compromise in regard to the high morality of her doctrines. Nor has she been content merely to enunciate a few moral principles: she has always applied her principles to every detail of human life. In fact, the Catholic Church makes this challenge: **Compare my doctrine, she says, on any particular point with the doctrine of any of the denominations on the same point, and you will certainly find that, unless the denomination's doctrine agrees with mine, mine is always the holier and more likely to produce holiness in those who adopt it.** For instance, compare the Catholic doctrine on justification with that of the Lutherans, or the Catholic doctrine of predestination with that of the Calvinists, or the Catholic doctrine on divorce with the uncertain teaching of the Protestant bodies today. There is no article of the Catholic Creed which conflicts with any other article; there are no 'High' or 'Low' divisions in the Catholic Church, and there is no point of Catholic belief which, if logically carried out, will fail to make a person holy, in proportion to his fidelity to the doctrine in question.

Means of holiness

Sometimes people say that the doctrine of the Catholic Church is *too* holy—that it is impossible to live up to it. Such might be so if the Church did not help us so much. (For the moment we are not concerned with the fact that, if God demands anything of men, He always gives them the grace to comply with His Will.) We are concerned here with the visible means to achieve holiness that are available for all members of the Catholic Church. Think, for example, of her Seven Sacraments. These are "outward signs, instituted by Christ, to confer grace" on the soul of the recipient of these Sacraments. If received worthily by a person, the Sacraments always—automatically, so to speak—confer that grace. The Seven Sacraments are Baptism, Confirmation, Holy Eucharist (Holy Communion), Penance (Confession, popularly called the Rite of Reconciliation), Extreme Unction (Last Rites, Anointing of the Sick and Dying), Holy Orders (confers the priesthood), and Matrimony. They were instituted by Christ to help in all important areas of man's life. (Cf. Chapter 22, where the Sacraments are discussed in detail.) Frequent reception of the Sacraments of Penance (Confession) and the Holy Eucharist (Communion) helps a person to grow in holiness and steadily become a better, more virtuous individual. But think also of her method of teaching: It is teaching done with the absolute assurance that she possesses the truth. This assurance derives from the knowledge that it is God Himself who has revealed the truth to the Church; and we see that everywhere in the world, throughout all the centuries since Christ, the Catholic Church has always taught exactly the same things, and that these teachings are for the most part contained in the New Testament, but also in the Old Testament—though there in a more subtle, vestigial form. By itself, the Church's absolute assurance of possessing the truth greatly strengthens our weak human nature and removes all doubt about the possibility of self-deception. Think, too, of the great help and encouragement the individual Catholic gets from his close union with the other members of his Church, all of whom believe exactly as he does. Also note how the whole world is pleased to use the spiritual literature produced by members of the Catholic Church. See too how the Church always keeps before her children the thought of the good example of the Saints, by dedicating each day in the year to the memory of one or more of them. Therefore, we are able to show that the Church offers to each of her children perfectly obvious means of holiness—that she not only teaches them the true ideal, but she provides the Sacraments to help them achieve this ideal and does everything else possible to help them to that goal.

The holiness of members of the Church

"By their fruits you shall know them." (*Matt.* 7:16). The real fruits of the Church are those people—namely, the Saints—who have used most fully the means that the Church offers. No other religious society, non-Catholic Christian or non-Christian, can show to the world such a variety of men and women who have attained heroic holiness through using the means the Catholic Church has offered to them. Among the Saints of the Catholic Church are people from every walk and condition of life, as universal, indeed, as the Church herself. Look through the following list of popular Saints:

St. Agnes—a virgin martyred at the age of 12 about the year 300 A.D.
St. Aloysius—a Jesuit seminary student who died at age 23, tending

victims of a plague in 1591. Patron of Youth.

St. Alphonsus—founder of the great Redemptorist Order. Bishop and Doctor of the Church. Died in 1787 at age 91. Author of 111 books. Thought to be the most published writer in the world.

St. Ambrose—son of a prefect of Gaul and Archbishop of Milan. Father and Doctor of the Church. Died in 397. Converted St. Augustine.

St. Anselm—Archbishop of Canterbury, Doctor of the Church. Father of Scholasticism. Died in 1109.

St. Anthony of Padua—the wonderworker, Doctor of the Church. Patron of Lost Objects. Died in 1231.

St. Augustine of Canterbury—Apostle of England. Died in 604.

St. Augustine of Hippo—possibly the greatest intellectual genius of all time. Wrote on virtually every theological subject. Died in 430.

St. Bede, the Venerable—Father of English History. Doctor of the Church. Died in 735.

St. Benedict—Patriarch of the Western Monks. Founder of the Benedictines. Died in 543.

St. Benedict Joseph Labré—the Holy Tramp. A former nobleman; gave up his possessions. Died in 1783.

St. Bernadette—to whom Our Lady appeared at Lourdes. Died at 35 in 1879. Her body is incorrupt.

St. Bernard—second founder of the Cistercians, preacher of the Second Crusade. "Oracle of the 12th Century." Doctor of the Church. Miracle-worker. Died in 1153. Considered the most influential man on his century of anyone in history.

St. Boniface—the Devonshire man who converted Germany. Martyred in 754.

St. Brigid—the Mary of the Gael. Died in 525.

St. Catherine Labouré—Sister of Charity. Receptor of the Miraculous Medal. Died in 1876. Her body is incorrupt.

St. Edward the Confessor—King of England. Died in 1066.

St. Elizabeth—daughter of the King of Hungary. Died in 1231.

St. Frances Cabrini—Missionary nun. Died in Chicago in 1917.

St. Francis of Assisi—marked with the Wounds of Christ. Founder of the Franciscans. Died in 1226.

St. Francis Xavier—Apostle of India, Malacca and Japan. Died in

1552. His body is incorrupt.

St. Gabriel—an Italian student. A Passionist seminarian. Died young, in 1862.

St. Gerard—a Redemptorist lay-brother and wonder-worker. Died in 1755 at age 29. Patron of Expectant Mothers.

St. Ignatius Loyola—a professional soldier who founded the Jesuits. Probably the world's greatest educator. Died in 1556.

St. Isaac Jogues—Apostle of the North American Indians. Mutilated and martyred in New York State in 1646.

St. Joan of Arc—"The Maid of Orleans," saviour of her country and Patroness of France. Falsely executed in 1431 at only 19.

St. John Baptist de la Salle—great educator. Founder of the Christian Brothers. Died in 1719. Patron of Teachers.

St. John Bosco—Apostle of homeless boys and girls. Founder of the Salesians, one of the largest Church orders. Died in 1888.

St. John Capistran—a lawyer who led an army against the Turks. Died in 1456.

St. John Fisher—A bishop and Chancellor of Cambridge University. Martyred in 1535. The only English bishop to resist Henry VIII.

St. John Vianney—parish priest of Ars in France. Patron of Parish Priests. Died in 1859. His body is incorrupt.

St. Laurence—a deacon in Rome, roasted on a gridiron in 258. After his martyrdom, Roman conversions occurred in vast numbers.

St. Louis IX—King of France. Almsgiver, Patron of the Church, Crusader. Died in 1270.

St. Madeleine Sophie Barat—educator. Died in 1856.

St. Margaret of Cortona—a penitent. Died in 1247.

St. Nicholas—a bishop, known as Santa Claus. Died in 342.

St. Patrick—Apostle of Ireland. Died in 493.

St. Peter Canisius—the second Apostle of Germany. Died in 1597, after the Reformation. Authored Germany's basic catechisms. Doctor of the Church.

St. Peter Claver—Apostle of the Negroes, of whom he baptized over 300,000. Died in 1654.

St. Philip Neri—Apostle of Rome. Founder of the Oratory and Confraternity of the Most Holy Trinity. Died in 1595.

St. Rita—widow, mother of two sons, Augustinian nun. Died in

1457. Patroness of Impossible Cases.

St. Roch—nurse of victims of plague. Died in 1327.

St. Sebastian—captain in the Praetorian Guard at Rome. Martyred in 288.

St. Simon Stock—the Kent man who became General of the Carmelites. Died in 1264.

St. Stanislaus Kostka—a boy of eighteen. Died in 1568.

St. Stephen—deacon, the first martyr. Stoned to death about 36 A.D.

St. Teresa of Avila—Carmelite reformer, foundress, mystic, author, Doctor of the Church. Died in 1582.

St. Thérèse of Lisieux—the "Little Flower." Carmelite. Patroness of Missionaries. Died at 24 in 1897. "The Greatest Saint of Modern Times."—St. Pius X.

St. Thomas Aquinas—poet, philosopher, theologian. "The Angelic Doctor." Greatest of the Doctors of the Church. Died in 1274.

St. Thomas More—Lord Chancellor of England. Martyred in 1535.

St. Vincent de Paul—Founder of the Vincentians. Apostle of the Poor. Died in 1660. "The Father of his Country" (France).

Those mentioned here are but a very few of that glorious company of the heroes of Christianity. Can you name any other group of men and women to whom the world owes so much? Even our enemies have to acknowledge that the Catholic Church alone is capable of producing such people, and they realize also that the Church has never proclaimed anyone a Saint who has not been absolutely worthy of the honor. Not one of our Saints has ever had his character attacked by even the bitterest enemies of the Church. Yet all of them without exception are Saints, only because they **used the means of sanctity offered them by the Church.** As the fruits are holy, so the tree must be holy. Therefore, the Catholic Church must be specially blessed by God to be able to produce these Saints in every era of her existence.

Christ intended holiness to be a mark of His Church. "Christ also loved the Church, and delivered himself up for it: That he might sanctify it, cleansing it by the laver of water in the word of life: That he might present it to himself a glorious church, not having spot or wrinkle, or any such thing; but that it should be holy, and without blemish." (*Eph.* 5:25-27). Therefore, that Christian society which claims to be Christ's Church must be holy. The Catholic Church is pre-eminently and outstandingly holy. Therefore, she is the true Church of Christ.

Miracles

It might be good for the sake of completeness to add just a word about the miracles which throughout the centuries have been witnesses to the holiness of the Church. Christ foretold that this would be so: "Amen, amen I say to you, he that believeth in me, the works that I do, he also shall do; **and greater than these shall he do.**" (*John* 14:12, emphasis added). It is a certain historical fact that holy people within the Catholic Church have, even until the present day, worked miracles of many different kinds. In fact, proof that miracles have been obtained through the intercession of a candidate for Sainthood is a necessary condition of canonization. That these miracles do occur so regularly within the Catholic Church, and only within the Church, is surely a clear proof that the Holy Spirit is within the Catholic Church in a very special way. It is also noteworthy that the Church appears to have a monopoly when the special intervention of Heaven by visions and revelations is in question, such as at Lourdes (1858) and Fatima (1917).

Apostolicity

Apostolicity is the remaining Mark of the Church. By this we mean that essentially, outwardly and visibly the Church is **Apostolic in mission, Apostolic in character and outlook, Apostolic in teaching and Apostolic in descent.**

Apostolic in mission

For centuries, the Catholic Church has fulfilled the mission given to the Apostles by Christ: "Go ye into the whole world, and preach the Gospel to every creature." (*Mark* 16:15). She has never ceased to spread herself. Any nation which is now Christian owes its Christianity to the Catholic Church. The propagation of the Faith has always been one of her first interests. History proves this. Beginning with the Apostles themselves, the Church has in every century numbered among her children missionary pioneers who have carried the Gospel teaching even to the apparently impossible places of the earth. If you are in search of thrilling reading, obtain the lives of some of the great Catholic missionaries—of Fr. Claude Allouez, Apostle of the Ottawas; of Fr. Luis de Azevedo, Apostle of the Agaus, in Ethiopia; of Fr. Felix Barbelin, Apostle of Philadelphia; of Fr. Alonzo de Barcena, Apostle of Peru; of Bishop Augustine Blanchet, Apostle of the State of Washington, U.S.A.; of Fr. Luis Cancer de Barbastro, Apostle of the Indians of Vera Paz; of Fr. Elisha John Durbin, Apostle of Kentucky; of Bishop Edward Fenwick, Apostle of Ohio; of Fr. Philip Jeningen, Apostle of the Ries district in Southern Germany; of Fr. Bartolomé Las Casas, Apostle of the West Indies—**to mention only a few of those who are less well-known than the great missionary Saints of the Church**. Even a superficial knowledge of the spread of Christianity reveals the fact that the Church has always been Apostolic in her Mission.

Apostolic in character

More than that, **the Church is Apostolic in Character.** Her organization is essentially the same as that of the Church described for us in the *Acts of the Apostles*. She still has her bishops, priests and deacons. She still speaks with that certain voice with which she sent out Barnabas and Paul from the Council of Jerusalem. Her missionaries still use the words of St. Paul to the Galatians: "If any one preach to you a gospel, besides that which you have received, let him be anathema." (*Gal.* 1:9).

Any unprejudiced student of the Church depicted in the *Acts of the Apostles* and the Epistles must conclude that the character and outlook depicted there will fit only the Catholic Church, among the many Christian bodies today.

Apostolic in teaching

The Catholic Church is Apostolic in Teaching. It is not necessary to prove here that, doctrine by doctrine, the Church today teaches exactly what the Apostles taught. **That is being done throughout these instructions**. But what is evident is that the Catholic Church teaches today many of the truths taught by the other Christian societies. These latter groups themselves never claim that they teach anything which the Catholic Church has given up. Therefore, at least that much of her teaching is visibly Apostolic. With regard to the rest of her teaching, it has always been her claim that she refuses to yield on a single point of her doctrine precisely because her entire teaching represents the Tradition she has inherited from the Apostles, and therefore from Christ. That was the great stand-by of the Apostles themselves. They stood for Christ; they preached Christ. "For let this mind be in you, which was also in Christ Jesus," was St. Paul's instruction to the Philippians (*Phil.* 2:5), and it is still the instruction of the Catholic Church to all her children. Therefore, she teaches not only the same doctrines as the Apostles themselves taught, but she teaches exactly **as** they taught. An examination of the non-Catholic Christian denominations today reveals a pathetic indifference to this keynote of the Church of the Apostles. Witness, for example, the Church of England's sorry vacillations on the vital question of divorce; note the Methodists' emphasis on the Bible, rather than on Christ. How utterly they are out of harmony with the content and manner of the teaching of the Apostles!

Apostolic in descent

Yet, the most important element in the mark of Apostolicity is **Apostolicity in descent.** As we shall see in the next instruction, Christ established His Church under the supreme government of St. Peter. He said to St. Peter and his brother bishops that He would be with them always, even unto the End of the World, thus implying that they would in some way continue to rule the Church. The only possible way for them to do that is through their legitimate successors. The Catholic Church is the only Christian society in the world today which claims that she is ruled by the successor of St. Peter.

Moreover, Christ willed that all men should be saved and "to come to the knowledge of the truth" (*1 Tim.* 2:4), and that His

Church should "preach the gospel to every creature." (*Mark* 16:15).
This would obviously have been completely impossible if the Apostles had not "ordained to them priests in every church." (*Acts* 14:22). It is perfectly clear that these ordained ministers derived all their authority from the Apostles. "How shall they preach unless they be sent?" asked St. Paul. (*Rom.* 10:15). Thus, until modern times, it was always conceded that no man could set up as an official teacher of Christianity until he had been duly commissioned, appointed and ordained. Is not that true of any society? Can a shareholder of a firm appoint himself chairman of the board of directors? Can a private individual walk into Parliament unelected and take a seat? The whole idea is absurd. Officials in any society need some form of appointment. Why not, then, in the Church? Already we have proved that Christ established a visible, organized Church. By what authority, then, did, say, John Nelson Darby set up his Plymouth Brethren in 1829, or Mrs. Eddy her Christian Scientists in 1879? Who commissioned the Wesleys and Whitfield to establish the Methodists in 1739, or John Knox the Presbyterians in 1560? Whence did Martin Luther derive his authority in 1517, or "General" Booth his in 1865? All these are intruders to Apostolic Christianity; they stand outside the legitimate line of Apostolic succession; they could claim no source of derivation for their presumed jurisdiction. There is only one Christian society in the world today which cannot be dated as starting long after the time of Christ, and that is the Catholic Church. No man, living, dead or yet to come, can point to any founder of the Catholic Church except Jesus Christ Himself, who is God. From Him, and from Him alone, the founding came, as St. Clement wrote in the very first century: **"Christ was sent by God, the Apostles by Christ; they appointed bishops and deacons . . . and they made order that when they died, other men of tried virtue should succeed in their ministry.** We may add, that since the Catholic Church is Apostolic in descent, **it must be Apostolic in doctrine,** for Christ, Eternal Truth, said of it: "The gates of hell shall not prevail against it," and "I am with you all days, even to the consummation of the world." (*Matt.* 16:18, 28:20).

The Reformation

Incidentally, all fair-minded people now acknowledge that the so-called **"Reformation" was nothing short of a complete revolution** against ideas which had been accepted by the whole Christian world for fifteen hundred years. Doctrines which had throughout the centuries been regarded as essential to Christianity were declared false and blasphemous by the so-called "Reformers." According to the Reformers, then, the **whole Church had been in error for fifteen hundred years.** Was Christ wrong in His promises? Was God mistaken? Either the Reformation was a huge error, or Jesus Christ, the God-made-Man, was wrong or untrustworthy. The latter alternative is impossible. Therefore, the first must therefore be accepted, namely that **the Reformation was a huge error.**

Conclusion

The plain fact is that if we go back through history, looking for the Church **personally established by Christ**, we find that all the non-Catholic bodies disappear at various times subsequent to the death of Christ. Only the Catholic Church endures in a search back through history. The others claim Christ as their head, but they admit some man as their founder; **the Catholic Church alone claims Christ as both its Founder and its Head.** And not only does she *claim* divine foundation, she clearly proves that claim.

The only valid conclusion you can draw from this instruction is that

> **Christ, Who was God, founded a visible, organized Church and promised that it would last until the End of Time. Therefore, that visible, organized Church is in the world today. It can be identified by its four marks, imprinted on it by Christ: 1) miraculous unity, 2) universality, 3) outstanding holiness, and 4) unbroken Apostolic descent. No denomination can be Christ's Church unless it possesses those four marks. The Catholic Church alone possesses them; it is in addition the only one of the Christian societies claiming**

direct and immediate foundation by Christ in its present organized form. Therefore, the Catholic Church is the one and only true Church of Christ.

For the Catholic this knowledge carries with it a special obligation. Divine authority demands absolute obedience. "He that heareth you, heareth me; and he that despiseth you, despiseth me; and he that despiseth me, despiseth him that sent me," said Our Lord Jesus Christ. (*Luke* 10:16). As Adam fell away from God and dragged with him the whole human race by a sin of disobedience, so man must return to God through absolute obedience to the divine authority vested in the Church. That authority has one purpose only—the good of souls, which is secured through universal observance of the two Great Commandments: love of God and love of men in God.

It is not surprising that the thousands of converts who annually join the Catholic Church find within that One True Fold certainty for the mind, guidance for the will, consolation for the heart, new graces for the soul, an immediate and personal access to Christ, joy in life and death, and a gratitude extending throughout life into eternity.

Chapter 17

The Supremacy of the Pope (1)

Who is the Head of the Catholic Church? *The Head of the Catholic Church is Jesus Christ Our Lord.*

Has the Church a Visible Head on earth? *The Church has a Visible Head on earth—the Bishop of Rome, who is the Vicar of Christ.*

Why is the Bishop of Rome the Head of the Church? *The Bishop of Rome is the Head of the Church because he is the successor of St. Peter, whom Christ appointed to be the Head of the Church.*

How do you know that Christ appointed St. Peter to be the Head of the Church? *I know that Christ appointed St. Peter to be the Head of the Church because Christ said to him: "Thou art Peter, and upon this rock I will build My Church, and the gates of hell shall not prevail against it. And I will give to thee the keys of the kingdom of heaven." (Matt. 16:18-19).*

What is the Bishop of Rome called? *The Bishop of Rome is called the Pope, which word signifies "Father."*

Is the Pope the spiritual Father of all Christians? *The Pope is the spiritual Father of all Christians.*

Is the Pope the Shepherd and Teacher of all Christians? *The Pope is the Shepherd and Teacher of all Christians, because Christ made St. Peter the Shepherd of the whole flock when He said, "Feed My lambs . . . feed My sheep." (John 21:15-17). He also prayed that his "faith" might never fail, and commanded him to "confirm" his brethren.*

WE saw in the last instruction that the Church Christ founded was certainly a **visible, organized society,** and that it was endowed with the four marks: **unity, universality, holiness and apostolicity.**

The need for authority

It ought to be obvious, therefore, without any further reasoning that there must be in a society of this kind an authority whose word is final. We have already referred briefly to our belief that Christ conferred supreme authority on St. Peter. Now we must go into the matter more fully. First of all, though, we must insist that the position we are about to establish for the Pope as supreme Head of the Universal Church is absolutely in accordance with what we would expect. Ordinary experience shows that in any society there is need for a central authority. "No authority, no society" is equally true of a football team, a family, a trade union, a nation. Sometimes authorities make mistakes; even so, for authority to exist and make mistakes is better than that it not exist at all. Order and security are the result of authority. In obtaining order and security, authority may err, but it is certain that order and security cannot exist in any society in which authority does not exist. An example of that is the state of the world today. Despite the existence of and the intent for the United Nations, it actually lacks the authority to back up its policy decisions, save against the smallest and weakest of nations. The absence of any recognized and accepted international authority has resulted in a state of disorder and chaos among the nations and in the feeling of insecurity, which is giving rise to so much international suspicion. Again, the prevalent immorality in the world is due to the abolition of a central authority at the beginning of the Protestant Reformation (1517).

The teaching of the Church

The Vatican Council of 1870 defined:

1) that St. Peter was appointed by Christ to be visible **Head** of the Church;
2) that he received from Christ a **primacy**, not only of honor, but of jurisdiction, i.e., that he received from Christ supreme

authority to teach and govern the whole Church;

3) that he has, in virtue of the same divine institution, **a per-petual line of successors** in the Primacy;

4) that his successors are the Roman Pontiffs, the **Popes**.

Non-Catholic writers have asserted that the Catholic teaching on the Primacy rests on one text (*Matt.* 16:15-19), "Thou art Peter, etc."

This is completely untrue, as will be clear from the rest of this instruction. Our teaching is derived from a clear and unbiased consideration of the relation of Christ with St. Peter throughout the whole Gospel story. In order to disprove Catholic teaching, certain writers have claimed that the Petrine text in *Matthew* 16 is a later interpolation, not part of the original Bible at all. That is just nonsense. If the text were an interpolation, when was it introduced? Why is there throughout the centuries no sign of opposition to it? The whole style of it is Aramaic, and there is nothing in the history of the manuscripts to suggest that it is not part of the original text.

St. Peter in the Gospels — his name is changed

Let us consider now the position of St. Peter as depicted in the Gospels. He is introduced first by St. John as follows:

"And he [Andrew] brought him to Jesus. And Jesus looking upon him, said: Thou art Simon the son of Jona: thou shalt be called Cephas, which is interpreted Peter." (*John* 1:42).

Note how St. John stresses the fact that Jesus looked at him closely, signifying that Jesus recognized in him the one who was destined for a special office in the Church.

Then God changes Simon's name. In Scripture this was done only as a sign of some special mission to be undertaken. For example, God changed the name of Abram: "Neither shall thy name be called any more Abram: but thou shalt be called Abraham: because I have made thee a father of many nations." (*Gen.* 17:5). Similarly, through an angel God said to Jacob: "Thy name shall not be called Jacob, but Israel: for if thou hast been strong against God, how much more shalt thou prevail against men?" (*Gen.* 32:28). Abraham, Isaac and Jacob were the fathers of God's people in the Old Testament; is it rash to suppose that Cephas is to be the father of

God's people in the New Testament? God does not act without reason. Just as He changed the names of the two Patriarchs to signify the position they were to occupy, so did He change the name of Simon to that of Cephas (or Peter), which means "Rock," to signify that Peter would be the solid foundation, the rock upon which His Church was to be built.

Peter and Christ

The Gospels depict Peter as being the individual companion and special friend of Christ. He is one of the three who witnessed the Transfiguration on the Mount and the Agony in the Garden of Gethsemane, and on each occasion he is named first. "And after six days Jesus taketh with him Peter and James and John, and leadeth them up into a high mountain apart by themselves and was transfigured before them." (*Mark* 9:1). And taking with him Peter and the two sons of Zebedee, he began to grow sorrowful and to be sad." (*Matt.* 26:37).

When Christ wanted to preach to the crowds which pressed around Him on the seashore, He took Peter's boat and preached from it. "And going into one of the ships that was Simon's, he desired him to draw back a little from the land. And sitting, he taught the multitudes out of the ship." (*Luke* 5:3). After the sermon, he put out to sea with Peter and took a miraculous haul of fish. Then "Jesus saith to Simon: Fear not: from henceforth thou shalt catch men." (*Luke* 5:10). Why did Our Lord address these words to St. Peter? Surely, all the Apostles were to save souls? The whole event is symbolical. Peter is to be the leader in the great work of "fishing for men." Note, too, that the story is told by St. Luke, the companion and interpreter of St. Paul. Hence, there cannot have been any difference between St. Luke and St. Paul over such a fundamental point as this. Note, too, that when there is mention in the Gospel of "the ship" alone, or in opposition to others, the ship indicated is St. Peter's. In fact, Christ made Peter's ship His own.

Consider also the position of Peter's house in the Gospel story. "And immediately going out of the synagogue, they came into the house of Simon and Andrew, with James and John." (*Mark* 1:29). St. Matthew describes Capharnaum as Christ's own city. "And entering into a boat, he passed over the water and came into his own city." (*Matt.* 9:1). And it is clear that Peter's house was regarded as Christ's house. The Greek word used in *Matthew* 17:24 means "home." It is referred to as **the** house, and it was here that Christ paid the Temple pence for Peter and Himself. "Take that, and give it to them for me and thee." (*Matt.* 17:26). It was significantly also in **the** house in Capharnaum that Jesus spoke to the Twelve on humility, after they had been disputing about "which of them should be the greatest." (*Mark* 9:33). From all of this it is clear that Peter was the special companion and designate of Our Lord.

We often find Christ explaining things to Peter. It was Peter He told to walk on the water; it was Peter He sent with John to prepare the Pasch; it was Peter he singled out during His agony. On the other hand, Peter often speaks for the other Apostles, giving the appearance of being their acknowledged head:

"Then Peter answering, said to him: Behold we have left all things, and have followed thee: what therefore shall we have?" (*Matt.* 19:27).

"And Simon Peter answered him: Lord, to whom shall we go? Thou hast the words of eternal life." (*John* 6:69).

"And Peter answering, said to him: Expound to us this parable." (*Matt.* 15:15).

The Apostles are referred to by St. Luke as "Peter and they that were with him." (*Luke* 8:46; 9:32).

The Angel at the empty tomb on Easter morning said to the women: "But go, tell his disciples and Peter." (*Mark* 16:7).

It is important to note also that whenever a list of the Apostles is given in the New Testament, although the same order is not maintained amongst the others, Peter's name always comes first. In fact, St. Matthew explicitly acknowledges him as the first.

"And the names of the twelve Apostles are these: The first, Simon, who is called Peter. . ." (*Matt.* 10:2).

The use of the word 'first' here is important, because it clearly does not only refer to Peter's being numerically first. Otherwise the use of numbers would have been continued, "second . . . third . . ." and so on. **The reference is to Peter's pre-eminence and dignity.**

Again, why did Jesus pray specially for Peter? "And the Lord said: Simon, Simon, behold Satan hath desired to have you, that he may sift you as wheat: But I have prayed for thee, that thy faith fail not: and thou, being once converted, confirm thy brethren." (*Luke* 10:31-32). That Peter's denial made no difference regarding his position is clear from the words of St. Paul about the appearances of Christ *after* the Resurrection: "He was seen by Cephas [Peter]; and after that by the eleven." (*1 Cor.* 15:5).

The cumulative value of all these texts must be considered: From them the mind of the Evangelists is perfectly clear. Peter was the acknowledged head of the Apostolic college, and that headship was recognized by Christ. There can be no other grounds for the Apostles' obvious recognition of Peter's supremacy, except their knowledge that it was the positive Will of the Incarnate God.

Promise of primacy

The actual **promise of the primacy** is related by St. Matthew: "And Jesus came into the quarters of Cesarea Philippi: and he asked his disciples, saying: Whom do men say that the Son of man is? But they said: Some John the Baptist, and other some Elias, and others Jeremias, or one of the prophets. Jesus saith to them: But whom do you say that I am? Simon Peter answered and said: Thou art Christ, the Son of the living God. And Jesus answering, said to him: Blessed art thou, Simon Bar-Jona: because flesh and blood hath not revealed it to thee, but my Father who is in heaven. And I say to thee: That thou art Peter; and upon this rock I will build my church, and the gates of hell shall not prevail against it. And I will give to thee the keys of the kingdom of heaven. And whatsoever thou shalt bind upon earth, it shall be bound also in heaven: and whatsoever thou shalt loose upon earth, it shall be loosed also in heaven." (*Matt.* 16:13-19).

The text makes it clear that Christ is speaking to Peter alone. He changes to the singular; He gave Peter the new name He had promised him from the time of their first meeting. As St. Jerome puts it: "Because you said to Me, 'Thou art Christ,' I say to you: 'Thou art Peter.'" Moreover, the words "upon this rock" indicate that the whole passage is addressed to Peter; otherwise, the changing of his name would be completely pointless and stupid.

In interpreting this, as other texts, it must be remembered that

Our Lord was using a dialect of Aramaic when He spoke to the Jews; secondly, that these events happened over nineteen hundred years ago. Anyone who has tried to read Chaucer's *Canterbury Tales* in their original form knows how extremely difficult a task it is—and they are English, and only about 600 years old. To understand these texts, we have to try to find out just what they would have meant to the Jewish audience almost 2,000 years ago. The Catholic Church has studied this question from every angle for hundreds of years and, apart altogether from the fact that she has divine guidance, she is best qualified to explain the meaning of Scripture to us.

"Upon this rock": Jesus is promising Peter that he is to be to the Church as a rock is to a building. But a rock gives durability to a building. As a firm foundation, it holds all the different components together; it makes them cohere and last. The metaphor of the "house built on a rock and the house built on sand" was perfectly familiar to the Jews. What is it that makes any society cohere and last? Surely, authority. If there is no proper authority, there is no proper social existence. Hence, St. Peter is here promised the authority necessary to keep the Church together and to make it endure. Unless this is so, Christ's words are meaningless.

Incidentally, it is worth noting that to find the true Church of Christ, you must find the Rock upon which it stands. To find the Church, find Peter. "Where Peter is, there is the Church." The only man in the world who claims to be the successor of St. Peter through a direct line of descent until the present day is the Pope in Rome.

"The gates of Hell": To His audience, these words of Christ undoubtedly meant "the power of Hell." In the East, the gates corresponded to the Western word "forum." The official title of the government of the old Ottoman Empire, for example, was "Sublime Porte" or "High Gate." In *Genesis* we see the use of "gates" in the sense of "power": "May thy seed possess the gates of their enemies." (*Gen.* 24:60). Alexander Cruden, a staunch Protestant, writes in his *Concordance:* "The word *gate* is sometimes put to signify power or dominion . . . The gates of Hell shall not prevail against the Church, that is, neither the power nor the policy of the Devil and his instruments. For the gates of cities were the places both of jurisdiction or judicature, and of fortification and of chief strength in

war." In the book of *Kings*, for instance, we read: "The king arose
and sat in the gate: and it was told to all the people that the king sat
in the gate: and all the people came before the king." (*2 Kings* 19:8).
Hence, it is clear that Our Lord was referring to the opposition which
would always exist between the authority of Peter and his successors
on the one hand and the authority of the powers of evil, of darkness
and of death on the other. It has also been suggested that "Hell"
could possibly mean "death," but the sense is obviously the same.

"The keys of the Kingdom of Heaven": Even today in Arab
towns men go about the streets with a set of large keys fastened
together with a little cord and dangling prominently on either side
of the shoulder. They are the landlords parading their authority in
that way. But everywhere, the key is a symbol of authority. One who
gives the keys to another gives his own authority. One who has the
keys has supreme dominion over a house or city and can admit or
refuse to admit anyone he wishes.

The Scriptural and Eastern idea of the symbolism of keys is
found in *Isaias* 22:22, where God declares that Eliacim, the Son of
Helcias, shall be invested with office in place of the worthless
Sobna: "And I will lay the key of the house of David upon his
shoulder: and he shall open, and none shall shut: and he shall shut,
and none shall open." St. John in the *Apocalypse* makes it clear that
Eliacim is a figure of Christ (*Apoc.* 3:7).

Thus, Christ is here confirming His promise that Peter is to
exercise complete authority over those who would enter the Kingdom of Heaven, the Church.

The power of Binding and Loosing: The words "Whatsoever
thou shalt bind" are so obvious as to require little comment. They
confer on Peter in a special and unique way the power which was
conferred on the Apostles as a body on another occasion. (*Matt.*
18:18). In contemporary terminology, the idea of binding and loosing was in common usage. The rabbis "bound" when they forbade
something; they "loosed" when they permitted it. For example,
there lived about the year 70 A.D. a rabbi called Nechonya, and he
always prefaced his lessons with the following prayer: "May it
please thee, O Yahweh, my God and God of my fathers, that . . . we
may not declare impure what is pure and pure what is impure; that
we may not bind what is loosed nor loose what is bound."

Protestants of every hue have tried for centuries to escape from the obvious meaning of this text in *Matthew* 16. They used to assert that when Our Lord spoke the words "Upon this rock," He pointed to Himself. But such a statement is completely out of harmony with the whole context and makes nonsense of the phrases which follow. So, non-Catholics of the Modernist school have had to find another device, and what could be simpler than to decide that this text is not part of the original New Testament? Without the slightest shred of genuine evidence, they assert that this incident is sheer invention, that Christ never spoke these words at all. Not a single ancient codex, not a single version or quotation is brought forward to give even the vaguest support to this view.

How significant it is that in their efforts to discard a text which gives such irrefutable support to the Catholic doctrine of Papal supremacy, Protestants and Modernists cancel one another out. While the Protestants certainly regarded it as part of the New Testament, the Modernists say it is not; and while the Protestants deny that it is rightly interpreted as containing a promise of the Primacy to be conferred upon Peter, the Modernists insist that this Catholic interpretation is the only reasonable one. "It is not without reason that Catholic tradition has founded on this (text) the dogma of the Roman primacy." (Loisy, one of the architects of Modernism).

The primacy conferred

The primacy was actually conferred on St. Peter by Our Lord *after* His Resurrection, as related by St. John.

"When therefore they had dined, Jesus saith to Simon Peter: Simon son of John, lovest thou me more than these? He saith to him: Yea, Lord, thou knowest that I love thee. He saith to him: Feed my lambs. He saith to him again: Simon, son of John, lovest thou me? He saith to him: Yea, Lord, thou knowest that I love thee. He saith to him: Feed my lambs. He said to him the third time: Simon, son of John, lovest thou me? Peter was grieved, because he had said to him the third time: Lovest thou me? And he said to him: Lord, thou knowest all things: thou knowest that I love thee. He said to him: Feed my sheep." (*John* 21:15-17).

It is perfectly clear that here Jesus Christ is speaking to Peter alone. He is giving to him complete jurisdiction over the universal Church. For He, the Good Shepherd, is delegating His authority to Peter.

The metaphor of the shepherd

In profane and sacred usage this metaphor of the shepherd is used to indicate the functions of teaching and governing. Homer, for instance, refers to kings as "shepherds of the people." Hesychius [5th c. A.D. Greek lexicographer (dictionary writer)] says shepherd means the same as king.

In Scripture there are abundant examples. God said to David: "Thou shalt feed my people Israel, and thou shalt be prince over Israel" (*2 Kings* 5:2), an example of what is known as Hebrew parallelism, when the second phrase repeats the meaning of the first phrase in a different metaphor. Again: "Behold the Lord God shall come with strength, and his arm shall rule: Behold his reward is with him, and his work is before him. He shall feed his flock like a shepherd: he shall gather together the lambs with his arm, and shall take them up in his bosom, and he himself shall carry them that are with young." (*Is.* 40:10-11).

"For the Lamb, which is in the midst of the throne, shall rule them." (*Apoc.* 7:17).

Throughout the 34th Chapter of the prophecy of Ezechiel, the term "shepherd" is used in reference to the rulers of Israel. "And I will set up one shepherd over them, and he shall feed them, even my servant David: he shall feed them, and he shall be their shepherd. And I the Lord will be their God: and my servant David the prince in the midst of them: I the Lord have spoken it." (*Ezech.* 34:23-24).

"And I will give you pastors according to my own heart, and they shall feed you with knowledge and doctrine." (*Jer.* 3:15). Again in his 23rd chapter, Jeremias attacks the rulers of Israel, referring to them as pastors.

"AND THOU, BETHLEHEM Ephrata, art a little one among the thousands of Juda: out of thee shall come forth unto me that is to be the ruler [shepherd] in Israel." (*Micheas* 5:2, quoted in *Matthew* 2:6). The Douay-Rheims version has "the captain that shall rule my people Israel." (*Matt.* 2:6).

"I will give him power over the nations. And he shall rule them with a rod of iron . . . as I also have received of my Father." (*Apoc.* 2:26-27; cf. also *Apoc.* 19:15 and 12:5).

In *Psalm* 2 the same juxtaposition of ruling and shepherding occurs. The Douay version has: "Thou shalt rule them with a rod of iron," but the Greek could also be rendered by Mgr. Knox's version as: "Thou shalt herd them like sheep with a crook of iron," the "crook" being the shepherd's long hooked staff. The Pope and all other Catholic bishops to this day carry a golden crosier, a hooked staff like a shepherd's crook, during religious ceremonies, and sit on a throne chair, symbolic of rule, in the sanctuary of their cathedral churches. Even the word cathedral comes from the Latin and Greek *cathedra*, meaning a "chair." The bishop's throne seat is still called a cathedra in English. One can see from this that when the Pope in Rome teaches the Universal Church *ex cathedra*—"from the chair," it means "officially" and when the subject is a point of faith or morals, he thereby speaks infallibly.

Thus, when Christ is called the "Good Shepherd," He is really invoked as Christ "the King." Throughout Scripture, the significance of the two metaphors is the same. The Shepherd *is* the King. Therefore, when Christ bestows on Peter the office of shepherd of His flock, He is giving him kingly powers, or a supremacy, not only of honor, but also of jurisdiction. St. Peter himself later referred to Christ when he said: "For you were as sheep going astray; but you are now converted to the shepherd and bishop of your souls." (*1 Peter* 2:25).

Throughout His life, Jesus had referred to Himself as the Good Shepherd. Before His death, He quoted Zacharias: "I will strike the shepherd, and the sheep of his flock shall be dispersed." (*Matt.* 26:31).

The well-known passage in the 10th chapter of St. John is interesting because there Christ refers to Himself not only as the shepherd, but also as the door. "I am the door of the sheep . . . By me, if any man enter in, he shall be saved: and he shall go in, and go out, and shall find pastures." (*John* 10:7,9). In *John* 21, Christ confers on Peter the office of shepherd, which implies the power of the keys promised in *Matthew* 16, by which Christ, the door, is opened to men through sound explanation of His doctrine and jurisdiction over His mystical Body, the Church. "When therefore they had dined, Jesus saith to Simon Peter: Simon, son of John, lovest thou me more than these? He saith to him: Yea, Lord, thou knowest that I love thee. He saith to him: Feed my lambs. He saith to him again: Simon, son of John, lovest thou me? He saith to him: Yea, Lord, thou knowest that I love thee. He saith to him: Feed my lambs. He saith to him a third time: Simon, son of John, lovest thou me? Peter was grieved, because he said to him the third time: Lovest thou me? And said to him: Lord, thou knowest all things: thou knowest that I love thee. He said to him: Feed my sheep." (*John* 21:15-17).

St. John Chrysostom remarks on this passage: "He saith to him, 'Feed my sheep.' Why does He pass over the others and speak of the sheep to Peter? He was the chosen one of the Apostles, the mouth of the disciples, the head of the choir. For this reason, Paul went up to see him rather than the others. And also to show him that he must have confidence now that his denial had been purged away. He entrusts him with the rule over the brethren . . . If anyone should say 'Why then was it James who received the See of Jerusalem?' I should reply that He made Peter the teacher not of that See but of the whole world." (P.G., lix, 478).

Even some Protestant commentators have been forced to admit that Christ certainly intended to confer the primacy on Peter on this occasion (e.g., Hengstenberg and Wiezsacker). The significance of this incident is even more apparent when it is remembered that this commission was given to the man who only a short time before had denied with an oath that he even knew his Master. (Cf. *Luke* 22:32, where Jesus says, "But I have prayed for thee, that thy faith fail not: and thou, being once converted, confirm thy brethren.")

Chapter 18

The Supremacy of
the Pope (2)

Peter in the Acts of the Apostles

IF Christ did make Peter primate, he should be seen acting in that capacity in the Infant Church. An examination of the *Acts of the Apostles* shows that Peter always appears in that position of primacy which Christ assigned to him. He takes charge of the election of St. Matthias to fill the vacancy caused by the suicide of Judas (*Acts* 1:15-22); he receives into the Church the first converts from both the Jews and the heathens (2:14-41; 10:5); he works the first miracle (3:1-8); he inflicts the first ecclesiastical punishment (5:1-10); he excommunicates the first heretic, Simon Magus (8:9-24); he makes the first apostolic visitation of the Churches (9:32); he pronounces the first dogmatic decision (15:5-11). His position was so indisputable that when St. Paul was about to begin his mission to the heathens, he thought it necessary to obtain recognition from Peter (*Gal.* 1:18). Nothing more than that was necessary; Peter's approbation alone was definitive.

Thus, the Holy Ghost in the *Acts of the Apostles* shows us Peter himself at work as primate and recognized as such by all, including St. Paul.

Peter at Rome

It only remains to establish the facts that St. Peter was actually the Bishop of Rome and that not only he, but his successors also in that office, were recognized as supreme head of the Church.

That St. Peter actually visited Rome and was martyred there is no longer denied by any writer of authority. In 1915 his tomb was discovered there—right under St. Peter's Basilica. But there are still some who deny that he was the Bishop of Rome.

An examination of writers of the third century proves that at that time it was believed with absolute certainty that Peter was actually the Bishop of Rome. For instance, St. Cyprian wrote that Cornelius had succeeded to "the place of Fabian, **which is the place of Peter**." (*Ep.* 40:8).

Firmilian of Caesarea remarks that Pope St. Stephen (254-257) claimed the right to decide the controversy about Baptism on the ground that he was the successor of St. Peter (Cyprian, *Ep.* 75:17). If Firmilian could have denied this claim, he would certainly have done so.

Tertullian, who had lived in Rome and would have seized any opportunity to deny the claims of its Bishops, admitted that Pope St. Callistus (217-222) claimed that Peter's power to forgive sins had descended to him in a special manner.

A poem entitled *Against Marcion,* dating from this period, states that Peter passed on to Linus, the second Pope, "the chair on which he himself had sat." (*P.L.,* II, 1077).

In the second century, St. Irenaeus, who was a disciple of St. Polycarp, who was himself a disciple of the Apostle St. John, twice speaks of St. Hyginus (136-140) as being the **ninth** Bishop of Rome, thus using an enumeration which involves the inclusion of St. Peter as first Bishop (cf. *Adv. Haer.* I, xxvii, 1 and III, iv, 3).

Hence, there is no doubt that Peter not only visited Rome but was actually Bishop of the Roman See. **Nor can it be doubted that from the very earliest times the Roman See has always claimed supreme headship of the universal Church and that that claim has been freely acknowledged by the Church.**

The Bishops of Rome recognized as Vicars of Christ—Letter of St. Clement

About the year 95 A.D., St. Clement, the third successor of St. Peter in the See of Rome, found it necessary to write to the Catholics of Corinth, telling them to receive back the bishops whom a troublesome faction among them had expelled. Throughout the letter he uses a tone of authority, which even such a staunch Protestant as Lightfoot acknowledges to be "the first step towards Papal domination." "If any man," says St. Clement, "should be disobedient unto the words spoken by God through us, let them [*sic*] understand that they will entangle themselves in no slight transgression and danger . . . Render obedience to the things written by us through the Holy Spirit." (*Ep.* 59:70). The following facts should be considered in regard to this Epistle of Clement:

1. Reference is made to "the good Apostles," Peter and Paul, those pillars of the Church, martyrs, who gave such good example to the Romans.
2. The whole Epistle is an implicit manifestation of Rome's consciousness of possession of the Primacy in the Church, for
   a) instead of offering excuses for interfering in the affairs of the Corinthian Church, Clement begins by apologizing for his delay in writing. Unless it was his duty to write, there would be no reason for apologizing.
   b) Clement *threatens,* as we have quoted above, and demands obedience.
3. St. John was actually alive at Ephesus at the time. If the Corinthians appealed to Rome, which was far less accessible than Ephesus, it proves that they recognized the authority of Clement over even an Apostle; if Clement's action were spontaneous, it shows that the Church at Rome was already conscious of a superior and exceptional authority.
4. The letter was *welcomed* by the Catholics of Corinth, which proves that they did not think that Rome had interfered unlawfully or exceeded her power. In fact, the Corinthians put this Epistle of St. Clement on almost the same level as the Scriptures, and for a century it was read in the churches.

The Cambridge Ancient History, commenting on the Epistle of St. Clement, says: "The Roman community's sense of its own importance is nevertheless unmistakable, and it finds expression in the whole tenor of the letter. Rome imparts profitable instruction to the Corinthian community and regards this as her right and her duty: but one gets the impression that the Romans would have been greatly surprised had Corinth, let us say, in similar circumstances, dispatched such a letter of admonition to Rome." (XII, 530).

Even Bishop Lightfoot [1828-1889, bishop of Durham] had to admit that three points concerning the early Roman See are clear:

1. Our Lord certainly conferred a primacy among the Apostles on St. Peter;
2. St. Peter visited Rome and was martyred there;
3. At the end of the first century, the Roman Church held a primacy over all other churches—a primacy which ever grew and developed as the ages ran on. (Cf. Abbot Butler, *Religions of Authority,* pp. 113-117).

Ignatius and Abercius

A few years later, about 107 A.D., St. Ignatius, Bishop of Antioch, wrote to the Roman Church a letter in which he clearly indicates her supremacy: "She presides in the country of the Romans . . . she presides at the love feasts [*ágapes*—the prayer meetings with dinner *before* Mass in the early Church, in remembrance of the Last Supper; discontinued by the 8th century], or the charities." He adds, addressing the Church in Rome: "You have never led anyone astray; you have taught others."

St. Ignatius was St. Peter's own successor in the See of Antioch. From the Greek text it is very evident that he is referring to a true supremacy of authority possessed by the Church of Rome over the "Catholic" Church. **In fact, St. Ignatius was the first writer to employ the term "Catholic Church" in his letter to the Christians of Smyrna.**

In 1882 and 1883 an English traveller, Mr. W. Ramsey, discovered at Kalendres in Phrygia, partly built into the masonry of the public baths, a Christian-inscribed slab, a *stele* dating from before A.D. 216, which has been proved to be the epitaph, written by himself, of Abercius, Bishop of Hierapolis. In a mystical and metaphorical style he describes a journey to Rome: "For he (the shepherd) [the Pope] sent me to Rome to contemplate majesty [Papal authority], and to see a queen [Holy Mother Church] golden-robed and golden-sandalled; there also I saw people bearing a shining mark [i.e., in the state of Sanctifying Grace, they having received Baptism and Confirmation]." Archeologists of renown—De Rossi, Duchesne, Cumont and others—are agreed that the Epitaph of Abercius provides clear evidence of Roman supremacy at the end of the second century.

The Easter controversy

About the same time, Pope St. Victor (189-198) most explicitly asserted the authority of the Roman See in regard to other Churches. There was a difference of practice between the Churches of Asia Minor and the remainder of the Christian world about the day on which Easter was to be celebrated. Pope Victor rightly bade the Asiatic Churches keep the feast on the same day as the rest of the Church, but Bishop Polycrates of Ephesus resisted on the grounds that his custom was derived from St. John the beloved Apostle. For this, Pope Victor excommunicated him. Then, at the urging of St. Irenaeus, Bishop of Lyons, he withdrew the excommunication because he felt that it would do more harm than good. But the facts to be noted are that Victor took for granted his right to punish by excommunication and that that right was never questioned either by the victims of its use, the Christians of Asia Minor, or by St. Irenaeus, who disagreed with the advisability of using it on this occasion.

St. Irenaeus

St. Irenaeus, Bishop of Lyons, who was martyred in the year 202, is one of the most powerful witnesses to Papal Supremacy. During his life the Gnostic heresy was flourishing, but he wrote against it and succeeded eventually in killing it. He points out that the true teaching of the Church is that given by the actual pastors, who have received it from the Apostles by way of uninterrupted Tradition. It is that of the Mother Churches who can produce a list of their bishops going back to the beginnings of Christianity. The rule of faith is to be found in the authoritative teaching of the Church.

But since it is difficult to inquire into the teaching of all the Churches, there is a last criterion of truth within reach of all and sufficient for all: it is the teaching of the Church of Rome. Here are his words:

"Because it would be too long in such a volume as this to enumerate the successions of all the Churches, we point to the tradition of that very great and very ancient and universally known Church which was founded and established at Rome by the two glorious Apostles, Peter and Paul: we point, I say, to the tradition which this Church has from the Apostles and to her faith proclaimed to men, which comes down to our time through the succession of her bishops, and so we put to shame . . . all who assemble in unauthorized meetings. **For with this Church, because of its superior authority, every church must agree—that is, the faithful everywhere— in communion with which Church the tradition of the Apostles has been always preserved by those who are everywhere.**" *(Adv. Haer.* iii, 3).

Where could one find a clearer statement of the doctrinal unity of the universal Church, or the unique and sovereign importance of the Roman Church as the witness, guardian and organ of the tradition of the Apostles and of its superior pre-eminence in the whole of Christendom?

Other writers

Another valuable witness is Tertullian, especially because of the fact that he fell into the heresy of Montanism. About 220 A.D. he wrote a work called *De Pudicitia* in which he vehemently attacked an edict of Pope Callistus against his sect. In doing so, he refers to the Pope as "the supreme Pontiff, the bishop of bishops."

St. Cyprian, Bishop of Carthage, who died in 258 A.D., is another who, although he opposed the Popes on other matters, nevertheless attributes to them an effective primacy as the successors of St. Peter. He refers to the See of Rome as "the principal Church, whence episcopal unity had its rise." *(Ep.* 59). This sentiment agrees perfectly with his teaching in his work *De Unitate Ecclesiae.* There he sees the Church torn by schism and says the cause of it is forgetfulness of the firm constitution given to the Church by Christ. The Church is founded on Peter, and since Peter is one, the Church is one. The Roman Church is "the root," "the mother" and "the parent stem" of Catholic unity. It is only when he speaks of the Bishop of Rome that St. Cyprian employs the word "primacy." He holds, too, that the Pope has the right to depose an heretical Bishop. In regard to one such, he wrote to Pope St. Stephen, urging him "to send letters by which, Marcian having been excommunicated, another may be substituted in his place."

We know, too, how St. Denis of Alexandria wrote to Pope St. Xystus II (257-258), asking his advice on a matter concerning Baptism by heretics and begging for his decision, that he may not fall into heresy. Later, the same Bishop—and Alexandria was then the second see [bishopric] in ranking of Christendom—was accused to Pope St. Denis (259-268) of heretical tendencies. The Pope replied by laying down authoritatively the true doctrine on the subject. These two events prove to us that even the Second See of the Catholic Church, Alexandria, recognized that Rome had the right to speak authoritatively on matters of doctrine.

But not only was it recognized by the rulers of Catholic dioceses, even the pagans had come to recognize Rome as the head see of the Church, before the end of the third century. Paul of Samosata, Bishop of Antioch, was deposed for heresy, but refused to leave his residence. The case was brought before the pagan Emperor Aurelian (270-275). Eusebius tells us that "he decided most fairly, ordering the building to be given to those whom the Bishops of Italy and the city of Rome should adjudge it." (*H.E.* vii, 30).

It is unnecessary to pursue this historical argument further than the end of the third century, for after that time, evidence for the supremacy of the See of Rome is to be found on every page of history. The facts related above ought to be sufficient to prove to any unbiased person that papal supremacy was in fact exercised from the time of the Apostles. Of course, the Church of the first three centuries was in her infancy; the system of government and organization was not fully developed. The conservative spirit of those days made frequent intervention by the Bishops of Rome unnecessary, yet it is perfectly clear that when the good of souls demanded it, Rome intervened. Such were the cases discussed above, and in not one of them was the right to exercise supreme jurisdiction by the occupant of the Roman See challenged.

Papal supremacy is reasonable

So we have proved that Christ established a society ruled by a single supreme head. We have seen also that that society was to endure until the End of Time. Therefore, the headship must also endure until the End of Time. The divinely established constitution of the Church cannot be changed; otherwise, the Church would cease to be Christ's Church. Moreover, Christ made it clear that He was going to give the Church strength to resist her foes ("the gates of hell") until the End of Time. The contest was to go on long after the Apostolic Age; it was to be a permanent feature of the Church's life. The means by which the Church was to endure was undoubtedly the supremacy conferred on Peter and inherited by his legitimately elected successors in the Roman See. If a visible authority was needed so close to Christ's own lifetime, it was surely necessary when the Church had grown with the passage of time. Any society without a central authority tends to disintegrate. The larger and more varied the membership of the society, the more necessary that central authority becomes. Therefore, Christ willed the central authority of His Church to reside in the papacy. That is surely clear from the cumulative evidence of all the facts quoted above. Peter was promised the primacy by Christ; it was conferred on him after the Resurrection; it was exercised by him during his lifetime; it was claimed and used by the Bishops of Rome who succeeded him; it was acknowledged by the early Church from the end of the Apostolic Age. Therefore, just as the Bishops of Christendom assembled at the Council of Chalcedon in the year 451 cried out with united voice, "Peter has spoken by the mouth of Leo," so do Catholics today throughout the world rejoice in a miraculous unity which proclaims that Peter still speaks by the mouth of him who reigns in Peter's See, the Supreme Pontiff, the Pope.

Chapter 19

Infallibility

Can the Church err in what she teaches? *The Church cannot err in what she teaches as to faith or morals, for she is our infallible guide in both.*

How do you know that the Church cannot err in what she teaches? *I know that the Church cannot err in what she teaches because Christ promised that the gates of Hell shall never prevail against His Church, that the Holy Ghost shall teach her all things, and that He Himself will be with her all days, even to the consummation of the world.*

Is the Pope infallible? *The Pope is infallible.*

What do you mean when you say that the Pope is infallible? *When I say that the Pope is infallible, I mean that the Pope cannot err when, as Shepherd and Teacher of all Christians, he defines a doctrine concerning faith or morals, to be held by the whole Church.*

CATHOLIC Doctrine: Cardinal Gasparri sums up the Catholic position in his *Catechism* as follows:

1. The Church is infallible in her office of teaching, owing to the perpetual assistance of the Holy Ghost promised to her by Christ, when, either in the exercise of her ordinary and universal governance or by a solemn pronouncement of the supreme authority, she proposes, for the acceptance of all, truths of faith or morals that are either revealed in themselves or connected with Revelation.

2. To pronounce a solemn judgment of this kind is the peculiar function of the Roman Pontiff, and of the Bishops **together with the Roman Pontiff**, especially when assembled in an Ecumenical Council.

3. An Ecumenical or General Council is an assembly of the

Bishops of the entire Catholic Church called together by the Roman Pontiff; over such an assembly he himself presides, either personally or by his legates, and it belongs to him authoritatively to confirm the Decrees of such a Council.

4. The Roman Pontiff exercises his prerogative of personal infallibility when he speaks *ex cathedra*—that is, when, in the exercise of his office as Shepherd and Teacher of all Christians, he defines a doctrine concerning faith or morals to be held by the whole Church.

5. We are bound to believe with divine and Catholic faith truths concerning faith or morals that the Church proposes for acceptance by all the Faithful, whether by her ordinary and universal authority or by some solemn pronouncement.

6. A truth thus defined is called a "Dogma of the Faith"; denial of it is called "heresy."

A divine Church needs a divine guarantee

The present age is one in which reason has been exalted beyond reason. We have already studied some examples of this. For instance, the modern rationalist simply says, "Miracles cannot happen." Armed with that self-made dogma, he continues to assert that Christ never worked miracles and that therefore He cannot be proved to be God. No matter how strong the historical evidence that miracles have actually happened, and are continually happening even today, the disciple of reason sticks to his principle: "Miracles cannot happen. Therefore, they do not happen."

Yet, human reason is so limited that without assistance it cannot even know what is in the mind of another; it cannot know what happens or has happened in some distant place or remote time. To find out these things, one has to be told by another, by someone who knows; otherwise, he must remain ignorant.

There are many things on which a man just cannot remain ignorant—for example, the law of the land. It is his duty to inform himself about the law, and if he does not do so, he will be punished.

Yet there are many far more vital matters about which men ought not to be in ignorance. Consider, for instance, the following questions: "What is the purpose of our existence? Why did God make man? What is the nature of the after-life?" It is obviously essential that men know the answers to these questions; otherwise, they simply cannot shape and orient their lives based on man's final end and destiny.

"What was in the mind of God when He made man?" We cannot know this, unless God Himself tells us. We cannot even know exactly what is in the mind of another man, unless that other man tells us.

"What is the nature of the next world?" We cannot know unless God Himself tells us. We cannot even know exactly what kind of place Australia is, unless we have been there or unless someone who has been there has told us.

So we stand in need of Revelation, or something told to us by God about the object and end of our lives. Otherwise, our existence is ultimately aimless and for no known purpose.

We have shown already in the instruction on the divinity of Christ that God has, in fact, made a revelation to us, that He has given us a great mass of teaching on many vital questions.

We have shown, too, how, in order that men might possess His teaching until the End of Time, Christ founded a Church. That Church is God's own representative, His sole channel of communication with men, apart from special private revelations.

We now assert that God prevents this Church from giving men wrong teaching. He wants them to have certainty about the vital things He has revealed. Therefore:

a) He prevents the bishops as a body from teaching error, i.e., where there is a moral universality of teaching by the bishops throughout the world, that teaching is guaranteed by God. **This is known as the infallibility of the Church.**

b) He prevents the Pope from teaching error when, acting as head of the Church, he teaches the whole Church on some point of faith or morals revealed by Christ. This is known as the **infallibility of the Pope.**

Therefore, **infallibility** does not mean that the Pope cannot sin or that he knows everything or that he is inspired or receives or makes a new revelation. **The function of infallibility is to ensure that we shall be able to know with certainty truths which are vital to us and which we cannot find out for ourselves.** Therefore, the personal character of the Pope as a human teacher is quite beside the point. For God prevents him from falling into error only when he officially teaches the entire Church on matters of faith or morals.

The Infallibility of the Church is reasonable

Mallock, a non-Catholic writer, in his *Is Life Worth Living?* says:

"Any supernatural religion that renounces its claim to infallibility, it is clear, can profess to be a semi-revelation only. It is a hybrid thing, partly natural and partly supernatural, and it thus practically has all the qualities of a religion that is wholly natural. In so far as it professes to be revealed, it of course professes to be infallible; but if the revealed part be in the first place hard to distinguish, and in the second place hard to understand; if it may mean many things, and many of these things [are] contradictory, it might as well never have been made at all. To make it in any sense an infallible revelation, or in other words a revelation at all *to us*, we need a power to interpret the testament that shall have equal authority with that testament itself."

Christ came on earth, as we have seen, to teach a true doctrine which should last for all time. "For this I was born, and for this I came into the world; that I should give testimony to the truth," He told Pilate. (*John* 18:37). One would expect that, being all-wise, all-foreseeing and all-powerful, He would have taken the means to prevent the society to which He committed the continuation of His work from ever falling into error, and therefore corrupting His doctrine. In view of His plainly expressed purpose, one can only suppose that, if He had not established some means for safeguarding His Truth, He would have been neither all-wise, nor all foreseeing, nor all-powerful.

Again, if there is no infallible teaching body on the earth, it means that when Christ ascended into Heaven, His office as teacher ceased. For centuries God had been preparing the hearts of men for the coming of His Son; the whole of the Old Testament is concerned with the story of this elaborate process of preparation. **Is it not inconceivable that, after all this preparation, the Redeemer should teach infallibly only for a period of some three years, to**

a mere handful of people in a small corner of the world? Common sense rejects such obvious disproportion in God's way of acting. Especially when it is remembered that the Redeemer **did found a Church as a teaching body**, it must be conceded that God would enable it to carry on His teaching office. This that Church could not do unless it were endowed with infallibility.

Infallibility of the Church in Scripture

The scriptural proofs of the Church's infallibility are so numerous that it is hard to see how anyone can deny them. Remember that we appeal here to Scripture as a reliable historical source, taking no account of its divine inspiration.

A) "And Jesus coming, spoke to them, saying: All power is given to me in heaven and in earth. Going therefore, teach ye all nations; baptizing them in the name of the Father, and of the Son, and of the Holy Ghost. Teaching them to observe all things whatsoever I have commanded you: and behold I am with you all days, even to the consummation of the world . . . He that believeth and is baptized, shall be saved: but he that believeth not shall be condemned." (*Matt.* 28:18-20; *Mark* 16:16).

Notice:
1) That Christ prefaced His commission with an appeal to His own fullness of power, thus evidently intending to stress the extraordinary nature and extent of the authority being communicated to His Church. The implication is that the authority being conferred is so great that its communication would be impossible were He not omnipotent.
2) That it is doctrinal authority which is principally in question here. The Apostles are to teach in His name and with His authority; those who receive their teaching are to do so as coming from Him and therefore as infallible. There is no other convincing explanation of the phrase "I am with you all days, even to the consummation of the world." (*Matt.* 18:20).
3) That it is clear that Christ here committed to His Church the task of communicating His teaching to all men of all ages,

without corruption. This would be utterly impossible unless the Church could speak infallibly in every generation on any question affecting the substance of Christ's teaching.

4) That without infallibility there could be no absolute certainty or finality in regard to any of the truths which are of the very essence of Christianity. The fact, for instance, that the Church condemned Arius at the Council of Nicæa in 325 for denying the divinity of Christ would have absolutely no weight unless the condemnation could be regarded as certainly free from error.

5) That it has been proved in an earlier instruction that Christ certainly meant unity of faith to be a distinguishing mark of His Church. Having regard to the ease with which differences on religious questions arise, it will be agreed that unity would be impossible without an infallible public authority capable of acting with decision and of pronouncing an absolutely final and irreformable judgment. If Christ were really the Son of God, to whom the whole future history of the Church was present; if He meant His promise to be always with His Church to be taken seriously; and if He were omnipotent; then the Church is certainly right in seeing in His commissioning words a guarantee of her own infallibility.

6) That, moreover, Christ threatens with eternal damnation those who refuse to accept the Church's teaching. How could He make such a threat, if He had left us at the mercy of every false prophet, with no certain, unerring teaching authority?

B) "The gates of hell shall not prevail against it." (*Matt.* 16:18). These words of Christ would be utter nonsense, if it could happen that the Church could be wrong in that teaching which she gives so authoritatively that she threatens with damnation those who refuse to accept it. The "gates of hell" would certainly have prevailed against it, if for 2,000 years the Church had been demanding the assent of men to her essential teaching under penalty of eternal damnation and because she regarded that teaching as certainly true, if, all the time, her teaching could be false.

C) "And I will ask the Father, and he shall give you another Paraclete, that he may abide with you for ever. The spirit of truth, whom the world cannot receive, because it seeth him not, nor knoweth him: but you shall know him; because he shall abide with you, and shall be in you. I will not leave you orphans, I will come to you. . . These things have I spoken to you, abiding with you. But the Paraclete, the Holy Ghost, whom the Father will send in my name, he will teach you all things, and bring all things to your mind, whatsoever I shall have said to you." (*John* 14:6-18, 25-26). "But you shall receive the power of the Holy Ghost coming upon you, and you shall be witnesses unto me in Jerusalem, and in all Judea, and Samaria, and even to the uttermost part of the earth." (*Acts* 1:8). Such words are meaningless if they do not signify that the Holy Spirit is to be responsible for what the Apostles and their successors may define to be part of Christ's teaching. If the Holy Spirit is responsible for such definitions, they are surely infallible. What is guaranteed by the Spirit of Truth cannot be false.

D) "Know how thou ought to behave thyself in the house of God, which is the church of the living God, the pillar and ground of the truth." (*1 Tim.* 3:15). Unless the Church were infallible, this would be an untruth. Elsewhere, St. Paul vindicates the divine authority of the Gospel being taught by the Church: "Therefore, we also give thanks to God without ceasing: because, that when you had received of us the word of the hearing of God, you received it not as the word of men, but (as it is indeed) the word of God, who worketh in you that have believed." (*1 Thess.* 2:13). "For the weapons of our warfare are not carnal, but mighty to God unto the pulling down of fortifications, destroying counsels, and every height that exalteth itself against the knowledge of God, and bringing into captivity every understanding unto the obedience of Christ." (*2 Cor.* 10:45). "But though we, or an angel from heaven, preach a gospel to you besides that which we have preached to you, let him be anathema." (*Gal.* 1:8).

In these quotations St. Paul certainly demands obedience from everyone to the teaching of the Apostles. In the second chapter of his letter to the Galatians he says clearly that his teaching has the sanction of the other Apostles. In a word, the truth emerges that he believed the Apostolic College to be infallible. Otherwise, he could never have spoken in such strong terms.

E) St. Peter devotes a large portion of his second Epistle to the condemnation of false teachers and uses very strong language about those who, "flying from the pollutions of the world, through the knowledge of our Lord and Saviour Jesus Christ, they be again entangled in them and overcome: their latter state is become unto them worse than the former. For it had been better for them not to have known the way of justice, than after they have known it, to turn back from that holy commandment which was delivered to them. For, that of the true proverb has happened to them: The dog is returned to his vomit: and, The sow that was washed, to her wallowing in the mire." (*2 Peter* 2:20-22). St. John makes a similar point: "Dearly beloved, believe not every spirit, but try the spirits if they be of God: because many false prophets are gone out into the world." (*1 John* 4:1).

This condemnation of the false carries with it the implication that the Apostles believe their teaching to be certainly true. This they clearly state when—assembled together at the Council of Jerusalem—they issue a decree in the name of the Spirit of Truth: "For it hath seemed good to the Holy Ghost and to us, to lay no further burden upon you than these necessary things. . ." (*Acts* 15:28). Here the Apostles claim, in the name of the Holy Spirit, to decide a dogmatic question of first importance, namely, whether the Christians were bound to observe the Old Law in its entirety. They would certainly never have spoken in this way unless they were convinced that Christ's promises had assured them of infallible guidance in their solemn utterances in the name of the Church.

Tradition

A study of the history of the Church will certainly convince the unbiased enquirer that throughout her existence she has always regarded herself, and has been regarded by her members, as infallible. (Cf. *Church History* by Fr. John Laux, TAN, 1989.)

St. Ignatius of Antioch, who lived at the end of the first century, has these striking things to say about the authority of bishops: "The bishop is in the place of God; the priests are the senate of the Apostles, and the deacons are the ministers of Jesus Christ. The faithful are to obey the bishops as they would Jesus Christ." (*Magn.* vi; *Trall.* ii, 1, 2).

There is a story, too, that St. Polycarp, who was a disciple of St. John the Evangelist, met the heretic Marcion on the streets in Rome and did not hesitate to denounce him then and there as the "first-born of Satan." That was the spirit of the age, and it is plainly out of keeping with belief in a fallible Church.

St. Irenaeus, one of St. Polycarp's disciples, writing against the Gnostic heretics, practically bases his teaching on the assumption of the Church's infallibility: "Where the Church is, there also is the Spirit of God, and where the Spirit of God is, there is the Church and every grace." (*Adv. Haer.*, III, xxiv, 1). Writing of the successors of the Apostles, he says: "It is they who are the guardians of our faith . . . and securely expound the Scripture to us . . . There must we seek the truth." (*Op. Cit.* IV, xxvi, 5).

About the beginning of the fourth century, there appeared a remarkable work called *Concerning Right Faith in God*. The writer was a certain Adamantius. He bears striking testimony to current belief in the Church's infallibility: "She . . . the Catholic Church, by the truth alone lives righteously, devoutly and in holiness; those who have turned aside from her and gone astray are far from the truth; they proclaim indeed that to them the truth is known, but in reality they are far removed from it." (v. 28).

St. Cyprian, writing to St. Cornelius, said: "Heretics have the audacity to take ship and present letters from profane and schismatical folk to the See of Peter and to the principal Church, whence sprang the unity of the priesthood. They never seem to realize that these latter are the Romans whose faith the Apostle proclaimed and praised; to them infidelity can have no access." (*Ep.* xii, 14).

So we could go on—but little purpose will be served by multiplying quotations. The fact is simply that those nearest to the time of Christ took for granted the infallibility of His Church. Even heretics recognized that, once a doctrine had been defined by a General Council, it was certain and true. They may have refused to obey, but that was on the grounds that the council was not really ecumenical (i.e., convened by the Pope, with all Catholic bishops invited and representing the entire Church). In general, they did not dispute the fact that the decisions of the councils were final and irreformable.

Infallibility of the Pope—Meaning and extent

Papal Infallibility does not mean that the Pope cannot make a mistake or commit a sin, or that he can teach without error on any subject which strikes his fancy, or that he is inspired by God.

It does mean that, **under certain, very specific conditions**, the Pope is preserved from error, namely:

1. When he speaks *ex cathedra* (literally, "from the chair" or throne of St. Peter), as supreme shepherd and teacher of all Christians, and as the successor of St. Peter;

2. When he defines a doctrine, i.e., when he makes it clear that the doctrine must be believed with a firm, interior assent of faith;

3. When the doctrine defined concerns faith or morals, i.e., when it belongs to the doctrinal teachings or the moral principles of the Catholic religion, as found in Scripture or Tradition;

4. When he speaks thus to the whole Church, intending to bind all its members throughout the world.

The Pope does not claim to speak infallibly unless all of these conditions are simultaneously present.

Papal infallibility in Scripture

The Scriptural proofs of Papal infallibility are, if anything, stronger than those for the infallibility of the Church.

a) The Petrine text, already quoted in the instruction on Papal supremacy, page 156. Many good non-Catholic commentators acknowledge that Christ here made St. Peter the foundation of His Church. But the Church is to be infallible. That has already been proved. Therefore, Peter must also be infallible. His authority is to be the sure foundation of the Church's inerrancy. It is the foundation that gives stability to a building; not the building that stabilizes the foundation.

Moreover, communion with the Pope is, as we have seen, a condition of membership in the true Church. If he could err when teaching officially, acceptance of error would be necessary for communion with him, and so with the Church—and that would be an altogether absurd position, in view of the fact of the Church's infallibility.

b) "And the Lord said: Simon, Simon, behold Satan hath desired to have you, that he may sift you as wheat: But I have prayed for thee, that thy faith fail not: and thou, being once converted, confirm thy brethren." (*Luke* 22:31-32).

Christ here prays for Peter alone in his capacity as head of the Church. His prayer is certainly efficacious. Therefore, Peter and his successors until the End of Time will be preserved from error in matters of faith and morals.

c) We have already considered the words of Christ to Peter in St. John's Gospel, last chapter, "Feed my lambs, etc." (cf. pages 159-160). The complete and supreme pastoral charge, with jurisdiction, given to St. Peter, clearly implies supreme doctrinal authority. But unless this is infallible, it cannot effectively secure that unity of faith intended by Christ.

Evidence of Tradition

There can be no doubt that, from earliest times, the whole Church accepted the fact of the Pope's inerrancy. On pages 164 to 169 we have considered at length some of the more important texts from early writers bearing testimony to their acceptance of Papal supremacy. That this supremacy extended also to doctrinal matters is perfectly clear from a study of the same texts. The letter of St. Clement to Corinth, the words of St. Ignatius, the conduct of St. Victor in the Easter controversy and the strong admiration of St. Irenaeus all bear witness to the current belief that the True Faith, handed down from the Apostles, was always to be found through appeal to the Bishop of Rome. When heretics were condemned by local or provincial synods, they appealed to Rome, hoping for a reversal of the decision.

From the time of the Council of Nicaea, A.D. 325, there is abundant explicit evidence of the belief of the whole Church in papal infallibility.

St. Augustine, preaching at Carthage on September 23rd, 417, tells how two African Councils, Mileve and Carthage, had sent reports to Rome about the heresy of Pelagius. "Rome has sent back," he tells us, "her rescripts" (a word borrowed from the Imperial chancery, i.e., her interpretations or decisions about the heresy), "the case is finished; would that the error also were done away with."

The Council of Ephesus (431) calls Pope Celestine the "Guardian of the Faith," who teaches right doctrine because he is the successor of "Blessed Peter the Apostle, the head of the whole faith, and the head of the Apostles."

The Third Council of Constantinople approved the letter of Pope Agatho (680), which declared "that Peter's Apostolic Church has never departed from the way of truth into any error whatsoever."

The doctrine of papal infallibility was solemnly defined by the First Vatican Council in 1870. This does not mean to say it is a new doctrine; it was merely formally stated at that time to be officially part of the Catholic Faith, which all Catholics must believe in order to be Catholic. In the same way, the Council defined as a dogma the existence of a personal God. These truths had always been believed, but an authoritative reassertion of them was felt to be necessary.

How infallibility is exercised

We said already that the Pope uses his infallibility when the conditions requisite for its exercise are present. He is **personally** infallible; no other bishop is. But, as a body, united to their head, the Pope, the bishops are infallible when they teach peremptorily [precluding debate or question]. This they can do in two ways:

a) By their ordinary day-to-day united teaching by means of catechisms, ceremonies, traditional liturgical rites, pastoral letters, general condemnations, provincial or plenary councils, the tacit approval of the unanimous teaching of theologians, etc. When the bishops are morally unanimous in teaching a doctrine as of faith or morals, or in reprobating one as heretical they are infallible in their ordinary teaching;

b) By assembling in General or Ecumenical Councils. A General Council is a gathering of the bishops of the whole world, or of so many of them that they represent the whole world.

To be ecumenical a council must be

    i)   convoked by the Pope;

ii) Presided over by the Pope, either in person or through his Legates;

iii) Ratified by the Pope.

An assembly of bishops without the Pope would not be ecumenical or infallible.

The first General Council of the Church was held at Nicaea in Asia Minor, about 90 miles from Constantinople (modern Istanbul), in what is now Turkey, in the year 325 A.D.; 318 bishops were present; the Pope, Sylvester I, was represented by Hosius, Bishop of Cordova, his Legate; and the Roman Emperor Constantine was also there.

The 20th General Council was held at the Vatican between December 8th, 1869, and July 18th, 1870, when it was adjourned indefinitely.

The 19th General Council was the famous Council of Trent (in the Tyrol) held between 1545 and 1563. It affirmed many Catholic doctrines against the heresies of the so-called "Reformers"—the inspiration of Scripture, the nature and value of Tradition, the doctrines of Original Sin, Justification and the Seven Sacraments. Abuses were corrected and disciplinary reforms introduced.

What a privilege it is to belong to an infallible Church with an infallible Head!

"In the Catholic religion," says Professor R. E. Rogers of the Massachusetts Institute of Technology, a non-Catholic, "there is a certain kind of inner assuredness, an inner conviction of psychological strength," such as is not found in the Jewish or Protestant religions. Thus, "the Catholic Church has been able to maintain a consistent and non-changing cultural belief for more than 1,500 years; whereas the Protestant Church has divided itself into many sects, differing among themselves, not only in superficial things, but in situations of great importance."

Every man desires certitude in regard to the important fundamental questions to which religion alone can supply the answers. In the Catholic Church, and in the Catholic Church alone, will we find certitude in matters of faith and morals. Where there is no certitude, there is no good sense, no barrier against extravagance and no shield against heresy or infidelity. Where there is certitude, there will be unity in truth and truth in unity.

Chapter 20

The Commandments of the Church

Are we bound to obey the Church? *We are bound to obey the Church, because Christ has said to the pastors of the Church, "He that heareth you, heareth Me: and he that despiseth you, despiseth Me." (Luke 10:16).*

What are the chief Commandments of the Church? *The chief Commandments of the Church are: 1. To keep Sundays and Holy Days of Obligation holy, by attending Mass and resting from servile works. 2. To observe the days of fasting and abstinence appointed by the Church. 3. To go to Confession at least once a year. 4. To receive the Blessed Sacrament at least once a year, and that at Easter-time. 5. To contribute to the support of the Church. 6. To obey the laws of the Church concerning marriage, especially not to marry within certain degrees of kindred.*

THE FIRST COMMANDMENT OF THE CHURCH

What is the First Commandment of the Church? *The first Commandment of the Church is, "To keep Sundays and Holy Days of Obligation holy, principally by attending Mass and resting from servile works."*

Which are the Holy Days of Obligation observed in the United States? *The Holy Days of Obligation observed in the United States are: Christmas Day (December 25), the Circumcision (also called the Solemnity of Mary, Mother of God, January 1), the Ascension (the Thursday which falls 40 days after Easter), the Assumption of Our Lady (August 15), All Saints' Day (November 1), and the Immaculate Conception (December 8).*

Is it a mortal sin to neglect to attend Mass on Sundays and Holy Days of Obligation? *It is a mortal sin to neglect to attend Mass on*

Sundays and Holy Days of Obligation.

Are parents bound to provide that their children attend Mass on Sundays and Holy Days of Obligation? *Parents are bound to provide that their children shall attend Mass on Sundays and Holy Days of Obligation.*

THE SECOND COMMANDMENT OF THE CHURCH

What is the Second Commandment of the Church? *The Second Commandment of the Church is "To observe the days of fasting and abstinence appointed by the Church."*

What are fasting days? *Fasting days are days on which we are allowed to take only one full meal.*

Which are the fasting days? *The fasting days according to the new norms (as of the 1983 Code of Canon Law) are Ash Wednesday and Good Friday. (See pp. 197-198 for information on the Former, Traditional fasting days.)*

What are the days of abstinence? *Days of abstinence are days on which we are forbidden to take flesh-meat and soups made from meat.*

Which are the days of abstinence? *(See page 196ff.)*

Why does the Church command us to fast and abstain? *The Church commands us to fast and abstain so that we may mortify the flesh and satisfy God for our sins.*

Has Jesus Christ given us another great rule? *Jesus Christ has given us another great rule in these words: "If any man will come after Me, let him deny himself, and take up his cross daily, and follow Me." (Luke 9:23).*

How are we to deny ourselves? *We are to deny ourselves by giving up our own will and by going against our own dispositions, inclinations and passions.*

Why are we bound to deny ourselves? *We are bound to deny ourselves because our natural inclinations are prone to evil from our very childhood, and if not corrected by self-denial, they will certainly carry us to Hell.*

How are we to "take up our cross daily?" *We are to "take up our cross daily" by submitting daily with patience to the labors and sufferings of this short life and by bearing them willingly for the love of God.*

THE THIRD COMMANDMENT OF THE CHURCH

What is the Third Commandment of the Church? *The Third Commandment of the Church is, "To go to Confession at least once a year."*

How soon are children bound to go to Confession? *Children are bound to go to Confession as soon as they have attained the use of reason and thus are capable of mortal sin.*

When are children generally presumed to have attained the use of reason? *Children are generally presumed to have attained the use of reason by the age of seven years.*

THE FOURTH COMMANDMENT OF THE CHURCH

What is the Fourth Commandment of the Church? *The Fourth Commandment of the Church is, "To receive the Blessed Sacrament at least once a year, and that at Easter-time."*

How soon are Christians bound to receive the Blessed Sacrament? *Christians are bound to receive the Blessed Sacrament as soon as they are capable of distinguishing the Body of Christ from ordinary bread and are judged to be sufficiently instructed—as with Confession, by the age of seven years.*

THE FIFTH COMMANDMENT OF THE CHURCH

What is the Fifth Commandment of the Church? *The Fifth Commandment of the Church is, "To contribute to the support of the Church."*

Is it a duty to contribute to the support of the Church? *It is a duty to contribute to the support of the Church according to our means, so that God may be duly honored and worshiped, and the kingdom of His Church extended.*

THE SIXTH COMMANDMENT OF THE CHURCH

What is the Sixth Commandment of the Church? *The Sixth Com-*

mandment of the Church is *"To obey the laws of the Church con-cerning Marriage, especially not to marry within certain degrees of kindred."*

Which are the times in which it is forbidden to marry with solemnity? *The times in which it was traditionally forbidden to marry with solemnity, without special leave, were Lent and Advent.*

The Church's right to command

THE Church wishes to be a spiritual mother to all the Faithful. Therefore, she does everything possible for their spiritual wel-fare. This entails the making of laws which Catholics in conscience must observe.

Indeed, *every* society has the right to make laws for its own preservation and prosperity. The Church is the most perfect society, because she is divine. Hence, she has power to make laws concern-ing everything connected with religion and worship.

If the Church has the right to make laws, then those for whom the laws are made, the members of the Church, have the duty to obey them. Those who deny this are condemned by the Council of Trent (S. vi, c. xx).

Moreover, Jesus Christ declares that He makes His will known through the Church: "He that heareth you, heareth me; and he that despiseth you, despiseth me; and he that despiseth me, despiseth him that sent me." (*Luke* 10:16).

He also declares how extensive the powers of the Church are: "Amen I say to you, whatsoever you shall bind upon earth, shall be bound also in heaven; and whatsoever you shall loose upon earth, shall be loosed also in heaven." (*Matt.* 18:18).

The Apostles claimed that their right to legislate came from God: "For it hath seemed good to the Holy Ghost and to us . . ." (*Acts* 15:28). "For you know what precepts I have given to you by the Lord Jesus." (*1 Thess.* 4:2).

It is also clear from the New Testament that the Church has the power to punish those who disobey her: "And if he will not hear the church, let him be to thee as the heathen and publican." (*Matt.* 18:17).

There are, of course, many commandments of the Church—to be found in the 1,752 Canons of the Code of Canon Law (1983)—but those usually called the "Six Commandments of the Church" more particularly concern the ordinary spiritual life of the Faithful in general.

The First Commandment of the Church

The First Commandment of the Church is to keep the Sundays and Holy Days of Obligation holy principally by attending Mass and resting from unnecessary servile work.

The very law of nature demands that a man should devote a certain amount of time to the service of God. God Himself has commanded us to keep the Sabbath holy. Now the Church tells us how we must observe these precepts of the law of nature and the positive law of God.

It is a **mortal sin** to neglect to attend Mass on Sundays and Holy Days of Obligation. The reason is that to miss Mass on these days is a transgression of the law in a grave matter and is disobedience to the highest spiritual authority on earth. To miss Mass is to deprive God of the honor due to Him, and it is to deprive our souls of many of the graces we need for our own salvation.*

But why Mass? Cannot the Sabbath be kept holy without attending Mass? When we come to consider Holy Mass in a later instruction, we shall see that it is the official act of sacrifice of the Catholic Church, replacing under the New Law the sacrifice of the Jews under the Old Law. It is, indeed, Calvary re-enacted in our midst. The Church, speaking with divine authority, says that all her members must honor God at least weekly by the offering of sacrifice, and naturally this should be done on the day set apart by God for that purpose. Incidentally, there is no proof in Scripture that God willed the Sabbath to be changed from Saturday to Sunday, so that those non-Catholics who do not accept the value of Tradition as a source of Faith should logically still observe Saturday as the Sabbath.

---

*To realize the importance of the Mass, read *The Incredible Catholic Mass*, by Fr. Martin von Cochem. TAN. 1996. —*Publisher* 2002.

Extent of the obligation to attend Mass

All Catholics who enjoy the habitual use of reason and who are seven years old or older are under a grave obligation to attend Mass on Sundays and Holy Days. There is no upper age limit.

To fulfill the Church law for Mass attendance, four things are required:

a) **One must be BODILY PRESENT** at the Mass, i.e., present in such a way as to be considered as belonging to the group assisting at the Mass. **One cannot fulfill his Mass attendance obligation by radio or over TV.**

b) **One must attend a WHOLE MASS.** If a notable part is omitted—for example, the Offertory, the Consecration, or the Priest's Communion—the obligation is not fulfilled. A part may be notable either in virtue of its importance or in virtue of its length. In the words of Fr. Dominic Prümmer, O.P., "What constitutes a *notable* part is not easily determined. Two points are agreed: *a)* what constitutes a notable part is to be decided not merely from the length of time but more especially from the dignity of the omitted parts; thus a person who is absent for the Consecration and the [Priest's] Communion, even though he may be present for the rest of the Mass, does not fulfill the precept." (Prümmer, *Handbook of Moral Theology*, Mercier Press, 1959, par. 422b). Fr. Heribert Jone in his standard, *Moral Theology*, adds this: "The obligation to hear Mass *is not fulfilled* by him who is not present at the Consecration . . ." (Jone, *Moral Theology*, Newman Press, 1962, par. 196). **Any deliberate omission would be a venial sin.**

Note, too, that under all circumstances **one must be present at the Consecration and Priest's Communion of the SAME MASS.** If one has missed an essential part of the Mass, the missing of which might prevent him from fulfilling his obligation, he must make up for the omission by hearing another Mass. To make up slight omissions is praiseworthy, but not obligatory.

c) **One must assist at Mass with SUFFICIENT ATTENTION** so that he realizes, at least in a confused way, what is going on at the altar, and that he refrain from any action which is incompatible with this attention, e.g., sleeping.

d) **One must have a PROPER INTENTION**, i.e., of worshipping God by hearing Mass. As long as one goes to Church like other Catholics, this requirement is presumed to be present.

According to the 1917 Code of Canon Law, there were certain places (e.g., some private oratories) in which one was not able to fulfill the Sunday obligation, but normally the obligation was fulfilled by hearing Mass in any church, chapel (semi-public oratory) or even in the open air. According to the 1983 Code of Canon Law, the Faithful may fulfill their Sunday Mass obligation . . . "by assistance at a Mass which is celebrated anywhere in a Catholic rite, either on the holy days (Sunday being the principal holy day, per Canon 1246) or on the evening of the preceeding day." (Canon 1248, par. 1). Also, "The Christian faithful may take part in the Eucharistic Sacrifice and receive Communion in any Catholic rite. . . ." (Canon 923).

Excuses for missing Mass

In regard to missing Mass, there is a magnificent tradition of strictness in the English-speaking world, a tradition which must be maintained. But the principle is **that if going to Mass would cause a person a moderately grave inconvenience, he is excused from the obligation of attending**. Therefore, the following would be excused:

1. The sick, or those who must remain at home to care for the sick, little children, etc.

2. Those who would be obliged to travel over an hour (one way) to church. If one is walking, a shorter journey would excuse in bad weather or if one were weak.

3. House servants who are forbidden by their employers to go. (Although they should try to change their position in order to be able to fulfill their obligation.)

4. Those who cannot give up their work without relatively grave loss.

5. Workmen who by going to Mass would deprive themselves of reasonably necessary sleep.

It is far better to err on the side of strictness than to be too

lax in estimating that which constitutes an inconvenience sufficiently grave to excuse attendance at Mass.

It is always preferable to attend Mass in spite of all difficulties. One will certainly never be holy if one accepts every opportunity of escaping obligations. **The fact that one is in the state of mortal sin does not excuse him from attendance at Mass.**

Servile work

The Church commands all Catholics to keep Sunday holy—not merely to attend Mass. To enable them to keep Sunday holy, she orders them to abstain from "those labors and business concerns which impede the worship to be rendered to God, the joy which is proper to the Lord's Day, or the proper relaxation of mind and body." (Can. 1247) This would include the traditional prohibition against "unnecessary servile work" on Sundays and Holy Days of Obligation.

By servile work we mean in general that which requires more of the body than of the mind. Nevertheless, not only the nature of the work must be taken into account, but also the way it is done and how it is commonly regarded. The motive (e.g., to make money) is not the main factor in determining whether a particular work is servile or not.

The following are generally considered to be servile works: plowing, sowing, harvesting, etc.; sewing, laundering, lawn mowing, cobbling, tailoring, printing, masonry work, etc.; all work in mines and factories, etc.

In some places custom justifies knitting, crocheting, etc.

It is also permitted to go walking, riding, driving, rowing, journeying, even though these be very fatiguing.

Literary and artistic works—studying, teaching, drawing, architectural designing, playing music, writing, typing, painting, delicate sculpturing, embroidering, taking photographs—are lawful, even if done for remuneration.

Servile works are forbidden, even though they are done as a form of recreation or for some pious purpose. Two-and-a-half to three hours of such work, according to its arduousness, would be a mortal sin.

The following causes would excuse from the observance of the law forbidding servile work: serious inconvenience, works of charity toward those in need; or necessity, public or private.

Holy Days of Obligation

The modern word "holiday" is derived from "holy day." When the Western world was Catholic, during the centuries before it was disrupted by the Protestant Revolution, holy days were feast days, and they were observed like Sundays, by going to Mass and abstaining from servile work. When Protestantism came on the scene (1517) and the unity of Christendom was broken, all the people no longer went to Mass on the established holy days, and thus, holy days were either no longer observed, or they became holidays. But the Catholic Church still insists on celebrating some holy days every year, to bring to our minds, in a special and emphatic way, the great mysteries of our religion.

In the Universal Church there are **ten** such Holy Days of Obligation. Those **six** with an asterisk are Holy Days of Obligation in the United States. (In earlier times there were many more holy days of obligation when certain countries were entirely Catholic.):

* January 1st—The Circumcision of Our Lord (also called the Solemnity of Mary, Mother of God).
   January 6th—The Epiphany.
   March 19th—The Feast of St. Joseph.
* Ascension Thursday—i.e., the Thursday occurring 40 days after Easter and 10 days before Pentecost Sunday.
   Corpus Christi—i.e., the Second Thursday after Pentecost Sunday.
   June 29th—The Feast of Saints Peter and Paul.
* August 15th—The Assumption of Our Lady into Heaven.
* November 1st—The Feast of All Saints.
* December 8th—The Immaculate Conception of the Blessed Virgin Mary.
* December 25th—Christmas Day.

December 8th and March 19th are not observed as Holy Days of

Obligation in England. In the United States of America, January 6th, March 19th, June 29th and *Corpus Christi* are not observed as Holy Days of Obligation. In Canada, January 6th is a Holy Day of Obligation but August 15th is not; otherwise, the Holy Days of Obligation are the same in Canada and the United States.

The Church considers the Holy Days of Obligation the same as Sundays, with the same prescribed observance of Mass and abstinence from servile work (unless it would involve serious inconvenience or relatively grave loss).

It must be remembered that the purpose of the Church in making this commandment is positive—to help her children to do their duty toward God. Sunday is not meant to be merely a day of rest or pleasure; it is first and foremost **God's day**. Only when we have done our principal duty to Him, are we justified in taking Christian leisure.

"As a man keeps Sunday, so a man dies," someone has strikingly said. While it is perfectly true that the only action we are bound to perform each Sunday is to attend Mass, it is equally certain that the mere attending of Mass does not completely sanctify the day. One should also hear sermons, thus keeping himself informed about the things that matter; attend Benediction, to receive Our Lord's blessing; spend part of the day in the reading of things Catholic; visit the sick and the poor; and in a word, make Sunday really the Lord's day. One special feature of Sunday should be that it gives the family an opportunity to meet together. It should be especially a "home day." **Nowadays, it is neither God's day nor home day for perhaps a majority of people**, and that is a sad thing. Catholics should set the example by falling in completely with, not only the letter, but the spirit of this First Commandment of the Church.

The Second Commandment of the Church

The Second Commandment of the Church is to keep the days of fasting and abstinence appointed by the Church.

This Commandment is important not only for the positive law it embodies but also for the principle it implies—the necessity of mortification. The word "mortification" means literally "put to death," and it is to be found in the Epistle of St. Paul to the Romans: "For if you live according to the flesh, you shall die: but if by the Spirit you mortify the deeds of the flesh, you shall live." (*Rom.* 8:13). Again he wrote: "Mortify therefore your members which are upon the earth; fornication, uncleanness, lust, evil concupiscence, and covetousness, which is the service of idols. . . . now put you also all away . . ." (*Col.* 3:5, 8). "And they that are Christ's, have crucified their flesh, with the vices and concupiscences." (*Gal.* 5:24).

These sentences reveal to us the important fact that mortification is principally directed to life, not death. It is not meant to destroy nature, but to elevate it. The diseases of the soul are to be slain only so that its true life may be restored and strengthened.

To some extent, mortification is obligatory on all—in so far as it is necessary to overcome mortal sin. Resistance to temptation often implies denial of self, but since sin **must** be resisted, self **must** be denied.

Those who wish to serve Christ more thoroughly try to subdue in themselves that "rebellion" of the flesh against the spirit which is the perennial incentive to sin. Hence, by prudent repression, the passions and sensual desires are trained to conform to the rule of faith and reason. In order to achieve this objective, it is not sufficient merely to restrain the unlawful desires of the flesh; real training demands self-denial in matters which are certainly lawful.

The English Catechism tells us that "the Church commands us to fast and abstain so that we may mortify the flesh and satisfy God for our sins." Cardinal Gasparri says, "The Church prescribes fasting and abstinence so that the faithful may do penance for the sins they have committed, may be shielded from future sins, and may give themselves more effectively to prayer."

After prayer, penance is the most effective means of cleansing the soul of past faults and guarding it against future falls.

The continual insistence by Our Lord on the practice of penance is very obvious. When He was about to begin His public life, He had His Precursor proclaim: "Do penance: for the kingdom of heaven is at hand." (*Matt.* 3:2). His mission is "not to call the just, but sinners to penance." (*Luke* 5:32). He demands it from all: "No, I say to you; but except you do penance, you shall all likewise perish." (*Luke* 13:5). The Apostles understood this so well that they insisted on it from the first: "Peter said to them: Do penance, and be baptized every one of you in the name of Jesus Christ, for the remission of your sins." (*Acts* 2:38).

Therefore, penance is:

a) A duty of justice toward God to make up for the injustice of sin. Unless due reparation is made in this life, it will have to be made after death in Purgatory.

b) A duty to Christ, whom we are bound to obey and imitate. We must offer our expiations for sin in union with His. As we shall see in the next instruction, we are members of His mystical Body. He, the Head, has been immolated; we, too, must unite our sufferings with His.

c) A duty to ourselves, to rid ourselves of the baneful effects of past sins and to rectify any disorderly affections within us that will lead us to sin in the future.

d) A duty to our fellow men, for we are all members of the same Body of Christ, the Church. Our works of satisfaction can contribute to the welfare of others.

Fasting and abstinence

There is a difference between **fasting** and **abstinence** from flesh meat. The law of **fasting** commands that there should be only one full meal in the day, but it does not forbid us to take some food in the morning and evening, if we keep the approved local custom regarding its quantity and quality. Meat may be eaten at the principal or main meal on a **fast** day, unless it is also an **abstinence** day. What is allowed by custom in the morning and evening is made known in each diocese when the regulations are published, usually at the beginning of Lent each year. In the United States, the following is generally the approved local custom: In addition to the one full meal, two smaller meals or snacks may also be eaten, sufficient to maintain one's strength, but together they should not equal one's normal full meal. No food may be taken between meals, but liquids, including milk and juice, may be taken between meals.

The law of **abstinence** from flesh meat forbids us to eat meat or soup made from meat, but it does not forbid the use of fish, seafood, the flesh of cold-blooded animals (e.g., turtles, frogs, etc.) eggs, milk or foods made from milk, or any condiments made from animal fats.

Who are bound to fast and abstain? Unless lawfully excused or dispensed, all who are of sane mind and have completed their fourteenth year are bound to abstain, while all who have completed their eighteenth year, but have not begun their sixtieth year (that is, those who have not reached age 59) are bound to fast.

Thus, the obligation to **abstain** continues until the time of death. The sick who need meat for their recovery are excused from this obligation. Others who need meat in order to maintain their strength for really hard work, e.g., miners and construction workers, are excused. If one doubts whether he is excused from the law, but thinks he may have reason to be dispensed from it, he should see a priest from his parish.

Those **excused from fasting** are:
1. Those who have not completed their eighteenth year or who have completed their fifty-ninth year,
2. The sick and convalescent,
3. Those whose health fasting would notably impair,
4. Nursing and expectant mothers,
5. Those who do hard manual work,
6. Those engaged in useful occupations, if fasting would **interfere with the proper performance of their duty**.

A sufficient reason for a dispensation may exist in other cases, e.g., of students. In case of doubt, one should consult a priest.

When are we bound to fast and abstain? The Church's current regulations in the U.S. require fasting and abstinence from meat on Ash Wednesday and Good Friday, and abstinence from meat on the Fridays of Lent.

The New Code of Canon Law (1983) states that "All Fridays through the year and the time of Lent are penitential days and times throughout the universal Church" (Canon 1250). A Pastoral Statement by the U.S. National Council of Catholic Bishops (November 18, 1966) stated that abstinence is "especially recommended" on all Fridays of the year, and that "self-imposed observance of fasting on all weekdays of Lent is strongly recommended." According to the *Modern Catholic Dictionary*, by Fr. John A. Hardon, S.J. (Imprimatur 1979): "The abolition of Friday abstinence is a common misapprehension. Friday abstinence was not abolished; rather the faithful now have a choice either to abstain from meat or perform some other kind of penance on Fridays. According to the Church's law, the 'substantial observance' of Fridays as days of penance, whether by abstinence or in other ways, 'is a grave obligation.'" (Pope Paul VI, *Paenitemini*, 1966, Norm II, 2). Abstinence from meat is not required on any Holy Day of Obligation which falls on a day of abstinence. In the new regulations, abstinence is also not required on any Solemnity which falls on a Friday of Lent. (This would mean the Feast of St. Joseph—March 19, and the Feast of the Annunciation—March 25.)

As these laws sometimes differ in different places, it is important to find out the diocesan regulations in the matter. Careful attention to the notices read out at church on Sundays will remove most difficulties.

Violations of this Commandment:

No food is allowed outside the three meals of breakfast, dinner and supper that are permitted on a fast day. Liquids which are not generally estimated to be foods do not break the fast, for example, tea, coffee, soft drinks, fruit drinks, milk, etc. are permitted.

A substantial violation of **fasting** would occur if the amount of food allowed were exceeded by about four ounces.

To eat about two ounces of meat on an **abstinence** day would be a grave violation of the law, unless local diocesan regulations for commuting abstinence to some other penance were being followed.

Note: Abstinence from meat was formerly (traditionally) binding from age 7, and it is excellent for parents to maintain this practice in their families. Moreover, the new Code of Canon Law (1983) states that "pastors and parents are to see to it that minors who are not bound by the law of fast and abstinence are educated in an authentic sense of penance." (Canon 1252). Fasting was formerly (traditionally) binding from age 21.

Former (Traditional) Penitential Days

A prominent feature of the Church's former discipline (before relaxations of the 1966 and 1983 legislation) was the "Ember Days," that is, the Wednesday, Friday and Saturday of the weeks that occur

at the beginning of each of the four seasons. Ember Fridays were formerly days of fast and abstinence; Ember Wednesdays and Saturdays
were formerly days of fast and partial abstinence (meat permitted
only at the main meal). The Ember days, of ancient origin, were days
of fasting for the special sanctification of the four seasons and for
obtaining God's blessing on the clergy. They occur during the weeks
following: The First Sunday in Lent, Pentecost (Whitsunday), Holy
Cross Day (September 14) and St. Lucy's Day (December 13). Fasting and partial abstinence were formerly required also on the weekdays of Lent and on the vigil of (day before) Pentecost. In addition
to Ash Wednesday, the vigils of the Feast of the Immaculate Conception (December 8) and of Christmas (December 25) were formerly days of fasting and complete abstinence from meat (although
December 23 could be substituted for December 24). It is praiseworthy to continue the former (traditional) penitential observances,
even though they are no longer obligatory. Penance serves to rectify
our self-centeredness, to make up for sins (our own and those of others), and to strengthen our wills. It can be a very pure form of love
for God and can be offered up for the conversion of sinners and the
relief of the souls in Purgatory.

The Third Commandment of the Church

**The Third Commandment of the Church is to go to Confes-
sion at least once a year**.

Later, we shall have a special instruction on the subject of Confession. For the present we must content ourselves with the statement of the law which was enacted by the Fourth Lateran Council
in the year 1215 A.D.

This Confession need not be made during Easter time, but
because of the next Commandment of the Church, it is the custom
to make the annual Confession before receiving one's Easter Holy
Communion. **All children who have attained the use of reason
and have made their First Confession are bound by this law**,
even though they are not yet seven years old.

The year counts from the date of one's last Confession, but if the
year has passed, the obligation still remains. Strictly speaking, this
law binds only if one has committed a mortal sin within the year.

(However, to avoid mortal sin for a whole year without Confession would require extraordinary practice of prayer and virtue!)

The Fourth Commandment of the Church

The Fourth Commandment of the Church is to receive the Blessed Sacrament at least once a year, and that at Easter-time.

This Commandment was also laid down at the Fourth Lateran Council in 1215. We shall explain what we mean by the Blessed Sacrament or Holy Communion in a future instruction. The command to go to Holy Communion during the Easter season is a grave one, and neglect of it for a number of years would be punished by deprivation of Christian burial. The Easter season is determined by the law of each nation or each diocese. It usually begins on the first day of Lent, Ash Wednesday, and extends beyond Easter to Trinity Sunday, a week after Pentecost Sunday.

It is not obligatory to receive one's Easter Communion in one's own parish church, but it is preferable to do so.

Note that both the Third and Fourth Commandments of the Church contain the words "at least," to indicate that it is the Church's wish that we should go to Confession and receive Holy Communion frequently, even daily. Once a year for these Sacraments is the bare minimum.

The Commandment does not limit the **duty**, but the **time**, for fulfilling it. Even so, **the grave obligation still exists, even after the prescribed time has elapsed**. It extends also to children who have reached the use of reason and have made their First Confession and Communion, even though they are not yet seven years of age, so long as they are capable of distinguishing the Body of Christ from ordinary bread and are sufficiently instructed.

The Fifth Commandment of the Church

The Fifth Commandment of the Church is to contribute to the support of the Church. Just as we are bound by the Fourth Commandment of God to support our parents in their needs, so are we bound to help in the support of the Church and of our spiritual fathers in theirs.

The priest is a representative of men in their dealings with God (*Heb.* 5:1). His official calling precludes his following a trade or business. His only means of support is the alms of the Faithful.

"Have we not power to eat and to drink? Have we not power to carry about a woman, a sister, as well as the rest of the apostles, and the brethren of the Lord, and Cephas? Or I only and Barnabas, have not we power to do this? Who serveth as a soldier at any time, at his own charges? Who planteth a vineyard, and eateth not of the fruit thereof? Who feedeth the flock, and eateth not of the milk of the flock? Speak I these things according to man? Or doth not the law also say these things? For it is written in the law of Moses: Thou shalt not muzzle the mouth of the ox that treadeth out the corn. Doth God take care for oxen? Or doth he say this indeed for our sakes? For these things are written for our sakes: that he that plougheth, should plough in hope; and he that thrasheth, in hope to receive fruit. If we have sown unto you spiritual things, is it a great matter if we reap your carnal things? If others be partakers of this power over you, why not we rather? Nevertheless, we have not used this power: but we bear all things, lest we should give any hindrance to the gospel of Christ. Know you not, that they who work in the holy place, eat the things that are of the holy place; and they that serve the altar, partake with the altar? So also the Lord ordained that they who preach the gospel, should live by the gospel." (*1 Cor.* 9:4-14).

Hence, by both the Natural Law and the Divine Law, it is ordained that the Faithful have a duty to support their priests. In the words of the *Catechism of the Council of Trent*: "It is a duty to contribute to the support of religion according to our means, so that God may be duly honored and worshiped and the kingdom of His Church extended."

The Church and money

Unfortunately, the Church in modern times is dependent on money. She could not exist in the world without it. The clergy have to be housed, fed and clothed; mission property has to be preserved and repaired; worship has to be carried out in a becoming way, with vestments, lights and other necessities; the young have to be educated; many of the poor depend on their priests for support; new churches have to be erected to keep pace both with the spread of the Church and the movement of the population; priests have to be educated; seminaries have to be built and schools provided; the vast schemes of charitable works sponsored by the Church—hospitals, orphanages, homes, clubs and institutions of every kind—depend largely on voluntary contributions.

Sometimes one hears it said that the Church is always asking for money. That is usually an exaggeration, but often the clergy are in desperate need of money to carry out their work as efficiently as their sublime vocation demands. One thing is certain—that anything given to the Church is always used to the best advantage. There is no other society in the world which claims so little for the personal salaries of its officials. Everywhere the salaries of bishops and priests are fixed at the rock-bottom level; the religious—monks, friars and nuns—are under the **vow** of poverty, which prevents their receiving any salary. **When Catholics are asked for money, they should remember that good priests and religious repay their generosity with nothing less than the gift of their lives to the service of God and men**. The actual money that Catholics contribute would make a very poor showing in the world of architecture, of education, of social services, of hospitals and of charity, if every shilling and every dollar had not been given to men and women who give it all back to God and who administer it with such canny shrewdness and supernatural devotion that one coin is made to do the work of five.

Throughout the great network of charitable undertakings organized by the Catholic Church everywhere in the world, it is only the fact that heavy overhead expenses are cut, that the cost of high-priced executives is eliminated, and that staffs are composed largely of volunteers who are usually vowed to poverty, that makes it possible for us to match our achievements against those of any other group in modern life. Out of all the money contributed to the Church, the priests and religious get practically nothing for themselves. When they ask for money, it is only that they may be able to supplement the services to which they are devoting their lives in charity.

After all, devout Catholic people want their churches to be more beautiful than the local cinema, and better cared for; they want their hospitals and orphanages to be a credit to the Divine Society, the Catholic Church; they want to extend the Church at home and abroad, that the precious gift of faith may be shared with others. Therefore, they rejoice to give generously, knowing that nearly two thousand years' experience has proved that in general their contributions have been used wisely and well, and that money has never been better or more frugally spent than it is in the Catholic Church. No other administrators have ever asked less for their work than priests and religious—both men and women. In the end, every contribution benefits the giver, because it is for him that the Church and all that she has exists.

Moral theologians are united in teaching that this Commandment of the Church binds under grave sin. The faithful have a duty to contribute according to their means. Yet, while the obligation is a grave one, they would not convict anyone of grave sin unless through his omission the clergy would suffer want or other people be overburdened.

The Sixth Commandment of the Church

The Sixth Commandment of the Church is "To obey the laws of the Church concerning marriage." This especially includes the prohibition to marry within certain degrees of kindred.

Marriage between those who are closely related has often been punished by nature itself. Even in the Old Law, God restricted it; nowhere has it been generally permitted among civilized nations. The Church's Commandment merely determines the limit of these restrictions. The civil law usually has similar precepts.

People related to one another by blood (i.e., **consanguinity**), by marriage (i.e., **affinity**) and through Baptism (i.e., **spiritual relationship**) are forbidden to marry within certain degrees.

In the direct line—which embraces all blood relatives originating from each other by procreation—marriage is invalid between all ascendants [ancestors] or descendants. In the collateral line, marriage is invalid between blood relations to the third degree (second cousins) inclusive. (The 1983 *Code of Canon Law* eliminated the impediment to marrying one's second cousin.)

Affinity exists between a husband and the blood relations of his wife and between a wife and the blood relations of her husband. Affinity invalidates marriages in all degrees in the direct line (i.e., between, say, a woman and her stepfather or stepson), and in the collateral line to the second degree inclusive (e.g., a husband may not marry his late wife's sister or her first cousin).

Spiritual relationship invalidates marriages between the person baptizing and the baptized, and between the baptized person and the sponsors [godparents].

In practice, those who are contemplating marriage should see the priest in good time to make all necessary arrangements.

The times in which it was formerly (traditionally) forbidden to marry with solemnity without special leave were from the First Sunday of Advent till after Christmas Day, and from Ash Wednesday until after Easter Sunday.

Nobody was forbidden to marry during these times; what was forbidden was marriage with solemnity, i.e., with all the festal rites of the Church, e.g., with a Nuptial Mass, bells, organ, etc. Owing to the penitential nature of Advent and Lent, these normal festive accompaniments were forbidden.

(Note: Even though this prohibition is no longer in force, it is praiseworthy for Catholics who are planning marriage to schedule their Nuptial Mass outside of these formerly forbidden times, in order to be more in harmony with the spirit of the Church.)

Chapter 21

The Mystical Body of Christ

What do you mean by the Communion of Saints? *By the Communion of Saints, we mean that all the members of the Church—in Heaven, on earth and in Purgatory—are in communion with each other, as being one body in Jesus Christ.*

How are the Faithful on earth in communion with each other? *The Faithful on earth are in communion with each other by professing the same faith, obeying the same authority, and assisting each other with their prayers and good works.*

W E have spent several instructions in dealing with the Church as the visible **organization** established by Christ to continue His work upon earth. Now we go further. We maintain that the Church is not only an **organization** but an **organic society, a living body, an organism** with its own life-secret and its own life-stream.

The Vine and the branches

You will remember how Our Lord told St. Peter that He would be with His Church at all times, even to the End of the World. Here He hints at the union that is to exist between Him and the members of His Church. Later, He becomes much more explicit. After the Last Supper, in that beautiful discourse so carefully recorded for us by St. John, Christ gives us two comparisons:

a) "I am the vine; you the branches: he that abideth in me, and I in him, the same beareth much fruit: for without me you can do nothing. If any one abide not in me, he shall be cast forth as a branch, and shall wither, and they shall gather him up, and cast him into the fire, and he burneth. If you abide in me, and my words abide in you, you shall ask whatever you will, and it shall be done unto you." (*John* 15:5-7).

b) "And not for them only do I pray, but for them also who through their word shall believe in me; that they all may be one, as thou, Father, in me, and I in thee; that they also may be one in us." (*John* 17:20-21).

In these two extracts one finds the full explanation of those other words of Christ in which He gives us the criterion on which men will be judged: "Amen I say to you, as long as you did it to one of these my least brethren, you did it to me." (*Matt.* 25:40).

The Head and the members

St. Paul received a special revelation of this same truth. When going to Damascus to persecute the Christians, he was stricken, "and falling on the ground, he heard a voice saying to him: Saul, Saul, why persecutest thou me? Who said: Who art thou, Lord? And he: I am Jesus whom thou persecutest." (*Acts* 9:4-5).

This identification between Christ and the members of His Church is taken up by St. Paul in many places throughout those great letters, called Epistles, which he wrote to his converts. Thus:

"For as the body is one, and hath many members; and all the members of the body, whereas they are many, yet are one body, so also is Christ. For in one Spirit were we all baptized into one body, whether Jews or Gentiles, whether bond or free; and in one Spirit we have all been made to drink. For the body also is not one member, but many . . . But now God hath set the members every one of them in the body as it hath pleased him. And if they all were one member, where would be the body? But now there are many members indeed, yet one body . . . but God hath tempered the body together, giving to that which wanted the more abundant honor, that there might be no schism in the body; but the members might be mutually careful one for another. And if one member suffer any thing, all the members suffer with it; or if one member glory, all the members rejoice with it. Now you are the body of Christ . . ." (*1 Cor.* 12:12-14; 18-20; 24-27). "One body and one Spirit; as you are called in one hope of your calling. One Lord, one faith, one baptism. One God and Father of all, who is above all, and through all, and in us all. But to every one of us is given grace, according to the measure of the giving of Christ . . . And he gave some apostles, and some prophets, and other some evangelists, and other some pastors and doctors, for the perfecting of the saints, for the work of the ministry, for the edifying of the body of Christ." (*Eph.* 4:4-7; 11-12).

Meaning of the metaphors

Think for a moment about these three comparisons—the two given by Christ (the unity of the Blessed Trinity and the vine with its branches) and the one elaborated by St. Paul (the human body).

In the instruction on the Blessed Trinity, we saw how we are enabled to share in the very life of God, to know and love Him in the way He knows and loves Himself. We can do this only through Christ. Just as the branches live by the life of the vine, just as the different members all live by the life of the body, so do those who are united with Christ through grace share in the supernatural life of Christ. By this sharing we receive powers that far exceed those which are natural to us; we share in Christ's own divine life and powers. The vine is rooted in the earth; it draws its life out of the earth. Christ is, so to speak, rooted in the Blessed Trinity; from the Blessed Trinity supernatural life flows through Christ to those who are united with Him. Therefore, just as the branches share the life of the vine, so we who are united with the God-Man share the life of the God-Man. That life is divine. Through it we know God in this life by faith, hope and charity; after death, these blossom forth into the flower of the direct vision of God.

Now, turning to St. Paul's metaphor, we notice that the head is the center of man's life. It determines the quality of his life. If his head is clever, his life is clever; if his head is stupid, his life is stupid. His head is the center of all his most important functions—seeing, hearing, speaking and, through the brain, thinking and willing. Thus, all the operations of life flow through a man from the head.

St. Paul tells us that we form one person with Christ; that He is the Head, we the members of that one person. But just as the head is the source and center of life in the human body, determining the quality of its life, so Christ's headship determines the quality of the life of all who are joined to Him in that one spiritual personality, the Church. That is why St. Augustine calls the Church "the whole Christ." "The Church becomes, as it were, the filling out and complement of the Redeemer," wrote Pope Pius XII in his Encyclical letter on this subject, "while Christ in a sense attains through the Church a fullness in all things." And he goes on: "Here we touch the reason why, to the mind of Augustine, the Mystical Head, which is Christ, and the Church, which on this earth as another Christ bears His person, constitute one new man, in whom Heaven and earth are yoked together in perpetuating the Cross's work of salvation; by Christ we mean the Head and the Body, the whole Christ."

Dangers and illustrations

We will find much spiritual help and enlightenment from the contemplation of this union between Christ and His members, but we must, of course, be careful to reject "every kind of mystic union, by which the Faithful would in any way pass beyond the sphere of creatures and rashly enter the divine, even to the extent of one single attribute of the eternal Godhead being predicated of them as their own." Further, we must never fall into the error of uniting Christ and the Church in one **physical** personality; the clear distinction between the physical and social Body of Christ must always be maintained.

Some writers use the analogy of the business corporation to describe the nature of the Church as the Body of Christ, though it must be noted that the resulting unity of the corporation is moral and not physical. Mr. Smith, the owner of a great manufacturing plant, floats a company to take over the ownership and control of the enterprise. Mr. Smith is still head of the firm, but the firm is now completed by the addition of a body of shareholders. A new entity has come into existence, a new moral person, consisting of the head, Mr. Smith, and those incorporated—making one body—with him, the shareholders. Many people will still refer to the products of the

firm as being the work of Mr. Smith, but "Mr. Smith" has now a
new significance. Not only does it mean the physical person, Mr.
Smith, but also the moral or social person, the Smith Manufacturing Company.

So it is with St. Paul. He speaks of the Head of a concern
founded to save and sanctify souls, the physical Person, Jesus
Christ. But He also speaks of that other personality, the moral one,
which consists of Christ as Head and all those incorporated with
Him, making one body, the Catholic Church. Thus it was the physical Christ who died for us and redeemed us, but it is the moral or
Mystical Christ—Head plus members—who actually puts us in possession of the graces won by the Redemption.

The meaning of 'mystical'

Yet, the Church is more than merely a moral body; it is referred
to as the *Mystical* Body of Christ. Unfortunately, that word *mystical*
has other associations, and is liable to give false ideas. It does **not**
mean that the Church is something intangible and mysterious. It
simply implies that the Church is distinct from the physical Christ
and that the Church is the mystery of God's bounty and wisdom and
omnipotence, born in mystery, filled with mysteries, dispensing
mysteries. But further, the term *mystical* distinguishes the Church
from a mere moral body, such as the business corporation we have
been thinking about. It is true that the head and members of such a
company form a moral unity, a moral person, but in the Church
there is a unity of a higher order, compared by Christ to that unity
between the vine and its branches, and it has been traditionally
described by the term *mystical*.

Cells of Christ

We are cells in the Body of Christ—not in such a way that we
lose our own personality in His—but in the sense that we can live in
Him and He in us. All the cells together form the Church, which is
therefore joined to Christ in true organic union. Through the Church
He continues to act in the world as He once acted in His natural
body. In the Church He lives.

Therefore, we can elaborate on the comparison of St. Paul. The Church is the Body of Christ—not the physical body of Christ, yet more closely united to Christ than the members of any society or moral body are united to their head. The unity of the Body comes from the life of grace, which is its "life blood," coursing through its veins. By the life of grace, all baptized Christians, the "cells" of this Body, are united with the Head, the second Person of the Blessed Trinity; they are "partakers of the divine nature." (*2 Peter* 1:4). The "veins" are the channels of grace, the Sacraments, which we shall discuss in future instructions. The soul of the Body is the Holy Spirit, who, as we saw in the instruction on the Blessed Trinity, dwells in each of the cells (individual members).

We see how closely we are related to Christ in the Mystical Body—more closely than we are related to our natural mothers, fathers, sisters or brothers. We are not merely members of the same family or society, but members of the same Body. We are related to Christ more closely than His own Mother Mary was related to Him, simply as His mother in the natural order. Further, we are related to one another in the same intimate way, as fellow cells in the same body. Our relationship with our own mothers in the natural order is less close than our relationship with one another in the Church.

Christ's other Self

It is well that one who is interested in the Catholic Church should, right from the start, appreciate this important doctrine which reveals the nature of the Church's inner constitution. To regard the Church as merely an organization like, say, British Railways is to miss the whole point of her significance in the world. The Church has taken the place of Christ, not only in the way that a company may be said to take the place of its founder, but in the sense that it is an organism living by the supernatural life of Christ. In a very real sense, the Church is Christ's other Self, Christ Himself in very truth and fullness, as by a new incarnation after His Ascension He traverses all the ages, teaching and comforting mankind, shedding mercy and benediction on every side, giving glory to God, His heavenly Father, and redemption and grace to man.

Those who say they are devoted to Christ, lovers of Christ, followers of Christ, yet haters of the Church, simply sever the Head from the Body. A little reflection would soon show them that throughout the centuries Christ and His Church have preserved an amazing identity of spirit and outlook.

During His Public Life, Jesus was noticeably preoccupied with His Church. His work had to go on after His Ascension and until the End of the World. Therefore, to His infant Church He said that its members would be one with Him. Their voice was His voice: "He that heareth you, heareth me; and he that despiseth you; despiseth me; and he that despiseth me, despiseth him that sent me." (*Luke* 10:16). And we have already seen how completely Christ transferred His own power to St. Peter, and to a lesser extent, to the Apostles. He completely identified the Church with Himself. He was indeed the Bridegroom, She the bride, but they were to be "two in one flesh." (Cf. *Matt.* 19:5-6). Every important section of His life, every significant interest of His heart, He transferred to His Church. The early Christians were so full of that notion that they would call their bishops and priests "other Christs," for they were the living and walking continuance of the mission of Christ to the world. As He spoke, they spoke; what He did, they did; whom He loved, they loved; as He prayed, they prayed; as He offered sacrifice, they offered sacrifice; as He forgave sins, they also forgave. When time passed and they died, others carried on their work, confident that until the great work was done, until the very End of the World, Christ was with them—their strength, their inspiration, their source of power, their influence and their unity.

We have already seen how the Catholic Church has gone on throughout the centuries in spite of treachery from within and attack from without. If She had been merely an organization, that would have been impossible; She would have shared the fate of all other organizations. Primarily, the Church is not an organization; She is the continuance of the work of a divine Person; She will never fail simply because Christ can never fail. Her every Calvary will be followed by a fresh Resurrection.

Christ in the Church today

Therefore, in the world today the Catholic Church alone stands out as having the fullness of the mind of Christ. Her thoughts are Christ's thoughts, her interest, her ideals, her objectives are simply the thoughts, interests, ideals and objectives of Christ. In all essentials She uses the very words of Christ and does only the things He started and gave her to carry on. That is why her priests speak with such power and authority. They may be less educated than those who listen to them; they may not have the gifts of eloquence and oratory; they may stumble and stammer as they speak; but they know, and their hearers know, that they have behind them the tremendous authority of God-made-Man.

What they teach, what the Catholic Church teaches today, does not differ in "one jot or one tittle" (cf. *Matt.* 5:18) from what Christ Himself taught in the lanes of Palestine long ago. The so-called difficult mysteries and dogmas of the Church are simply repetitions of the teaching of Christ—the Blessed Trinity, the Holy Eucharist, the relational importance of soul and body and time and eternity, the impossibility of winning Heaven without the continual help of God, the fact of Hell, the supremacy of the successors of St. Peter, the necessity of prayer and penance, the enduring character of marriage, the value of personal purity and poverty of spirit—**these and all other doctrines of Christ are taught today by the Catholic Church, simply because She still speaks to men with the infallible voice of Christ Himself.**

There are still, of course, persons of the type who complained of Christ's words: "This saying is hard, and who can hear it?" (*John* 6:61). When they hedge and quibble about Catholic doctrines—about the so-called hard teaching on divorce, the unwavering attitude of no compromise in the matter of birth-prevention, the demand for Catholic Schools where Catholic children can be taught their Faith by Catholic teachers in a Catholic atmosphere—they are simply referred back to Christ, who would today have taught the self-same things.

In one very outstanding way the Catholic Church proves to the modern world that She has the full outlook of Christ, and that is in her insistence on the observance of the First Great Commandment, the love and worship of God. Whereas for many people humanitarianism, philanthropy and patronizing charity are the sum total of religion, the first concern of the Catholic Church is that which was always the first concern of Christ, God's greater honor and glory. That is why She commands all members of the Church to hear Mass on Sunday under pain of mortal sin; that is why the Holy Sacrifice is continued without interruption in her churches; that is why all her priests are strictly bound to spend such a large part of their day in reciting the praises of God.

Nevertheless, there is not another society in the world, religious or lay, that can show such a thorough observance of the Second Great Commandment, which is like the first, "Thou shalt love thy neighbor as thyself." (*Mark* 12:31). Watching Christ intently, the Catholic Church loves instantly those for whom He showed the most tender compassion—the poor and the afflicted, the little children, the feeble, outcasts from society, the repentant sinner. For them, in truly Christlike fashion, She has built her institutions of charity, opened the doors of her refuge and founded her hospitals.

As the Church thinks and speaks, so does She act. Endlessly, tirelessly, She repeats the actions of Christ. The Seven Sacraments She administers because He gave Her seven—neither more nor less. Her worship is centered around the Mass, because Christ willed His own life to be centered around the prototype Mass, Calvary. As Christ worked miracles, so miracles are worked today, only in the Catholic Church—at Lourdes, for example, and by the Catholic Saints in all ages, for whose canonizations they are necessary.

It would be a simple task to put the words, actions and interests of Christ into one column and into another the words, actions and interests of the Catholic Church. They would coincide exactly. For the whole life of Christ is "re-presented" in the life of His Mystical Body, the Church.

If you would find there His birth in poverty and loneliness, surrounded by the poorest of His creatures, consider the beginnings of the Church, when her first members were the slaves and the fishermen, the women and the little children, the publicans and the sinners; if you would find there the passionate love of the Magi and the bitter hatred of Herod, the slaughter of the Holy Innocents and the exile into Egypt, consider that the first appearance of the Church was the signal for the most passionate love and bitterest hatred. Persecution drove Her into the exile of the catacombs, while the Faithful gave their lives for Her, just as the Innocents did for Christ. If you would find in the Church the Hidden Life of Christ, look at the monks and nuns who give up the world entirely to devote themselves to the cultivation of the spiritual life. If you search for the Public Life of Christ, you see it present in every detail of her long, stormy history. Like Christ Himself, She is surrounded by most intense love and relentless hatred; like Christ, She attracts men of every rank and condition of society, the most brilliant, the most illiterate, the soldier and the civilian, the rich and the poor, the king and the subject. Like Christ, She has throughout her history been consumed with a burning zeal for souls, seeking always new members of the flock in the far mission fields and watching with jealous care the weak and ailing ones within.

There are still those who say the days of the Church are numbered, that we must tear ourselves away from the old order of the past to build a new society on new foundations. But like Christ, the Church defies Calvary. Again and again, She has risen triumphant after crucifixion to live on, while her enemies staggered toward the darkness of the tomb. Just as the raging tempests of the Sea of Galilee failed to sink the bark of Peter, so will the accumulated hatred and venom of twenty centuries fail to destroy the One True Church of Christ.

Obligations

As for ourselves, we must always remember that **we are the Church**. We are cells in the Mystical Body of Christ. The cells should be images of the Head. Hence, St. Paul's exhortation: "Yours is to be the same mind which Christ Jesus showed. My little children, I am in travail over you afresh, until I can see Christ's image formed in you." (*Phil.* 2:5; *Gal.* 4:19). One of the greatest—if not the greatest—arguments against the Catholic Church is that those looking at Her superficially do not see the resplendent image of Christ. As they say of the Eucharist, "It is not Christ because it looks like bread," so they say of the Church, "She is not Christ because She looks like man." Of course, just as the Son of God took human body and left intact its free human will, so He has taken a Mystical Body, replete with all the limitations, weaknesses and deficiencies of the society of human beings which it is. Nevertheless, these last have a twofold obligation—themselves to grow in likeness to their Head, and to help the Body extend until it embraces every human soul on the earth. The former they do through making use of the appointed channels of grace, the Sacraments, which we are soon to consider in our instructions, the latter through sharing in the Church's apostolate, especially through membership in approved organizations of the laity, and by prayer and good works.

We are all members of Christ, each with his part to play, to enable the Church to fit into and guide and correct the spirit of each age. No one who truly understands the nature of the Mystical Body can hesitate about offering himself to be an agent of the Holy Spirit, who is the Soul of the Church, in the task of sanctifying and saving the souls of men. Christ, living in His Church, has no other hands with which to feed the poor than our hands; He has no other feet with which to visit the sick than our feet; He has no other lips with which to speak the truth than our lips. He is, therefore, incomplete without us, for we are, in the term of St. Paul, His fullness. Apostolic action by the laity is, then, an obvious consequence of the doctrine of the Mystical Body. Equally, a full understanding of the same doctrine will bring with it condemnation of that religious individualism which has been killing spiritual charity ever since the Protestant Reformation of the 16th century. Such reasoning as: "My religion is my own private concern"; "His soul's salvation is no business of mine"; "Let him go to Hell if he wants to"; and similar, often-heard reasons for inaction stand condemned by the doctrine which asserts that we are all cells of the same living organism, the Mystical Christ.

Who are members of the Mystical Body of Christ? Pope Pius XII answered this important question in his 1943 encyclical, *Mystici Corporis Christi*, "On the Mystical Body of Christ":

"We must confess that grave errors with regard to this doctrine are being spread among those outside the True Church, and that among the faithful, also, inaccurate or thoroughly false ideas are being disseminated which turn minds aside from the straight path of truth . . .

"If the Church is a body, it must be an unbroken unity . . . it must also be something definite and perceptible to the senses, as Our predecessor of happy memory, Leo XIII, in his Encyclical *Satis Cognitum* asserts: 'the Church is visible because she is a body.' Hence, they err in a matter of divine truth who imagine the Church to be invisible, intangible, a something merely 'pneumatological,' as they say, by which many Christian communities, though they differ from each other in their profession of faith, are united by an invisible bond . . .

"Actually, only those are to be included as members of the Church who have been baptized and profess the True Faith, and who have not been so unfortunate as to separate themselves from the unity of the Body, or been excluded by legitimate authority for grave faults committed . . . It follows that those who are divided in faith or government cannot be living in the unity of such a Body, nor can they be living the life of its one Divine Spirit . . .

"They, therefore, walk in the path of dangerous error who believe that they can accept Christ as the Head of the Church, while not adhering loyally to His Vicar on earth. They have taken away the visible head, broken the visible bonds of unity, and left the Mystical Body of the Redeemer so obscured and maimed, that those who are seeking the haven of eternal salvation can neither see it nor find it . . .

"For this reason we deplore and condemn the pernicious error of those who dream of an imaginary Church, a kind of society that finds its origin and growth in charity, to which, somewhat contemptuously, they oppose another, which they call juridical . . . There can be, then, no real opposition or conflict between the invisible mission of the Holy Spirit and the juridical commission of Ruler and Teacher received from Christ, since they mutually complement and perfect each other—as do the body and soul in man—and proceed from our one Redeemer, who not only said as He breathed on the Apostles 'Receive ye the Holy Spirit' (*John* 20:22), but also clearly commanded: 'As the Father hath sent me, I also send you' (*John* 20:21); and again: 'He that heareth you heareth me.' (*Luke* 10:16).

"And if at times there appears in the Church something that indicates the weakness of our human nature, it should not be attributed to her juridical constitution, but rather to that regrettable inclination to evil found in each individual, which its Divine Founder permits even at times in the most exalted members of His Mystical Body, for the purpose of testing the virtue of the shepherds no less than of the flocks . . .

"Now since its Founder willed this social body of Christ to be visible, the co-operation of all its members must also be externally manifest through their profession of the same faith and their sharing the same sacred rites, through participation in the same Sacrifice, and the practical observance of the same laws. Above all, it is absolutely necessary that the Supreme Head, that is, the Vicar of Jesus Christ on earth, be visible to the eyes of all, since it is He who gives effective direction to the work which all do in common in a mutually helpful way towards the attainment of the proposed end."

Always love the Church as Christ's other Self. Give Her the loyalty, the obedience, the sacrifice, the service, the trust that you would give to His physical Person, were He still living on in the world.

"What is the Church?" asks St. Augustine. And he replies: "She is the Body of Christ. Join it to the Head and you have one man: the head and the body make up one man. Who is the head? He who was born of the Virgin Mary . . . And what is the body? It is His Spouse, that is, the Church . . . The Father willed that these two, the God Christ and the Church, should be one man.

"All men are one man in Christ, and the unity of Christians constitutes but one man.

"Let us rejoice and give thanks. Not only are we become Christians, but we are become Christ . . . Wonder, rejoice, for we are Christ! If He is the Head and we are the members, then together He and we are the whole man." (Quoted in Mersch, *The Whole Christ*, page 414).

Chapter 22

The Sacramental System

What is a Sacrament? *A Sacrament is an outward sign of inward grace, ordained by Jesus Christ, by which grace is given to our souls.*

Do the Sacraments always give grace? *The Sacraments always give grace to those who receive them worthily.*

Whence have the Sacraments the power of giving grace? *The Sacraments have the power of giving grace from the merits of Christ's Precious Blood, which they apply to our souls.*

Should we have a great desire to receive the Sacraments? *We should have a great desire to receive the Sacraments because they are the chief means of our salvation.*

Is a character given to the soul by any of the Sacraments? *A character is given to the soul by the Sacraments of Baptism, Confirmation and Holy Orders.*

What is a character? *A character is a mark or seal on the soul which cannot be effaced, and therefore the Sacrament conferring it may not be repeated.*

How many Sacraments are there? *There are seven Sacraments: Baptism, Confirmation, Holy Eucharist, Penance, Extreme Unction, Holy Orders and Matrimony.*

Channels of spiritual life

IN our last instruction we mentioned that the Sacraments are the "veins," so to speak, of the Mystical Body of Christ; that is, they are the channels through which the cells receive that wonderful life which makes them sharers in the nature and life of God. We must now discuss these "veins" more fully because, obviously, as the official channels of supernatural life, they are a most important means of our salvation.

The word "sacrament" in its widest sense means simply a sign of something sacred and hidden. The whole world can thus be said to be sacramental because material things are to men signs of spiritual and sacred things. St. Paul emphasized that idea: "For the invisible things of him, from the creation of the world, are clearly seen, being understood by the things that are made; his eternal power also, and divinity." (*Rom.* 1:20). "The heavens show forth the glory of God, and the firmament declareth the work of his hands." (*Ps.* 18:2).

As we have already seen, man is a creature consisting of body and soul. He is not a disembodied spirit nor is he wholly material. We have seen, too, how religion binds him to God and urges him to seek God. But he must seek God according to his own nature, that is by outward expression of his sentiments and aspirations. He does this in the other affairs of his life: if he loves a girl, he feels impelled to show his love by kissing her; if he is angry, he strikes his fist on the table or stamps his foot to demonstrate his anger; if he is pleased he smiles; and so on. Therefore, in his relationship with God, in the practice of religion, he will act also according to his nature, as a being composed of both body and soul.

God, of course, recognizes this. He could give His grace to men in a purely spiritual way—and, of course, He often does. But much of what we have already said in these instructions shows how God has, so to speak, bent Himself to the level of the nature of man. Our Redemption was accomplished in a visible manner, through a living Person whom people could see, touch and hear, Jesus Christ, God and Man. Throughout His life, the Incarnate God constantly used visible and material things to signify what he was doing. He put clay on the eyes to which He restored sight; He touched with His fingers the ears whose deafness was to be cured and the tongue to which the power of speech was to return. Moreover, the Church established by Him was a visible organization, as well as a spiritual organism.

When He had ascended into Heaven, He left His Church to be the channel of grace to men. The fruits of His death had to be applied to souls. As we saw in the last instruction, men had to attain the fullness of Christ. All this could, of course, have been done in a purely spiritual way, but that would not have been in accordance either with man's nature or with God's traditional method of dealing with man. Therefore, God decreed that certain signs—perceptible by men's senses, and signifying grace—should actually be the means by which the soul would receive grace through the Church. These certain signs are seven in number and are called, in a special way, the Sacraments.

What makes a Sacrament

The *Catechism of the Council of Trent* defines a Sacrament as something perceptible by the senses which possess by divine institution the power not only of signifying, but also of accomplishing holiness and righteousness.

In every Sacrament there are three elements: the outward sign, the inward grace and the institution by Christ.

a) **The outward sign.** Some things are of their very nature signs. Smoke is always the sign of a fire. Other signs are conventional, instituted by men. The red and white pole is the sign of a barber's shop; various trumpet tunes have special military significance. But there are some signs specially appointed by God. In the Old Testament, for instance, there was unleavened bread; in the New Testament there are the Sacraments. **These differ from other signs especially in that they have in themselves the power of producing the sacred effects of which they are the signs**. Thus, a crucifix, although it is the sign of our Redemption, is not a Sacrament.

b) **The inward or interior grace.** We shall have more to say about this when we come to consider each of the Sacraments separately. For the present we must point out that the Sacraments give grace *independently of anything human*, automatically and solely by God's will, as expressed by Christ's institution and promise. Technically, this is expressed by a Latin phrase for which there is no English equivalent, *ex opere operato*. It is contrasted with *ex opere operantis*—which would mean that the efficacy or lack of efficacy of a Sacrament would depend on the worthiness of the minister or of the recipient, which is not true. It is not that we believe that no dispositions are required on the part of the recipient of the Sacraments or that the Sacraments work like infallible charms. What the Church teaches is that there must be no **obstacle** to grace on the part of the recipient, who must receive the Sacraments worthily and rightly. **Dispositions are required as conditions for the conferring of grace, but not as causes of the grace conferred.**

The *Catechism of the Council of Trent* explains this rather difficult point as follows: "Since the ministers of the Sacraments represent in the discharge of their sacred functions, not their own but the person of Christ, be they good or bad, they validly perform and confer the Sacraments, provided they make use of the matter and form always observed in the Catholic Church according to the institution of Christ, and provided they do what the Church does in their administration. Hence, **unless the recipients wish to deprive themselves of so great a good and resist the Holy Ghost, nothing can prevent them from receiving (through the Sacraments) the fruit of grace**."

Just as a closed tap is an obstacle to the flow of gas or water from a pipe, or oil on paper is an obstacle to the flow of ink from a pen, so mortal sin, unrepented of, is an obstacle to the flow of grace from the "Sacraments of the Living." Just as in each of these cases it is not the gas or the water or the ink that prevents the required effect, but an obstacle outside of them, so it is not in the Sacraments that the reason for their possible inefficacy is to be found, but in an obstacle in the recipient.

This doctrine is even to be found still stated clearly in the 27th of the Thirty-nine Articles of the Anglican Faith (1571), showing that as of that time the Anglicans still retained a clear idea of the efficacy of Baptism: "Baptism is not only a sign of profession and a mark of difference, whereby christened men are discerned from those that be not christened, but [it] is also a sign of regeneration or New Birth; thereby as by an instrument they that receive Baptism rightly are grafted into the Church."

c) **Institution by Christ.** The Council of Trent defined that the Seven Sacraments of the New Law were instituted by Jesus Christ. Such an infallible decision settles the matter as far as Catholics are concerned, but in this as in other cases, they know that the defined doctrine is supported by weighty arguments from Scripture, Tradition and right reason. If the Sacraments are the signs of grace, and if grace is a sharing in the divine nature, then obviously the Sacraments come from God. That is the way Catholics have regarded the matter for almost twenty centuries. "The Sacraments give grace," they said. "But grace is only given by God through the merits of Jesus Christ. Therefore, if the gift of grace is so annexed to the Sacraments as to make them its principal and even only (as in the case of Baptism) channels, they must have been instituted by God. But everything essential to the Church was given her by Christ during His life on earth; therefore, He, the God-Man, made the Sacraments." This does not mean that Christ gave the Apostles every detail about the method of administering the Sacraments. He determined what special graces were to be conferred through external rites; the latter He defined specifically in the case of some of the Sacraments, but in others He determined it only in a general way.

"The power has ever been in the Church," said the Council of Trent, "that, in the dispensation of the Sacraments, their *substance* being untouched, it may ordain what things soever it may judge most expedient for the profit of those who receive or for the veneration of the said Sacraments."

How many Sacraments are there? It has already been stated that the Council of Trent has defined that there are seven Sacraments, neither more, nor less. The reason is that Christ instituted seven, neither more nor less.

They are:

1. **Baptism,** by which the soul receives supernatural life;
2. **Confirmation,** by which that life is strengthened as growth brings it added difficulties and responsibilities;
3. **Holy Eucharist,** by which the life is nourished;
4. **Penance** or **Confession,** which destroys the disease of sin;
5. **Extreme Unction,** which gives consolation and courage at the approach of death;
6. **Matrimony,** which sanctifies marriage relationships;
7. **Holy Orders,** which confers the priesthood of Christ and enables the Church to carry on His work in the world.

When we come to consider each Sacrament in turn, we shall

show that each was instituted by Christ. For the moment we shall concentrate on the number **seven**.

Christ instituted the Seven Sacraments

There is no list of the seven Sacraments in the New Testament; it is not necessary that there should be. Nor do we find the early Christian writers making lists of seven Sacraments. In fact, the first statement that we have record of that there are seven was probably not made until the twelfth century, but that does not mean that the Church had not always professed her belief in the Seven Sacraments by using them. It is not until the twentieth century that medical experts have established many conclusions about food values, vitamins, calories, balanced diet and the rest, but that does not mean that these things were not understood and used in a general way throughout much of the history of the human race. So, for centuries the Church used the Sacraments, but it was only at the beginning of the era of the great scholastic philosophers that a scientific study of them developed.

But the really important fact is that until the Protestant Reformation (16th century) when the fact that there were always **seven** Sacraments was first challenged, all Christians everywhere in the world believed that there are **seven** Sacraments. In the sixteenth century the fact of **seven** Sacraments was believed, not only in the Roman Church but also by the schismatical Greeks and the Nestorians and the Monophysites. Remember that there had never been any love for Rome among these Greek bodies, which entered into a series of schisms starting in the fourth century, which culminated in the final break called the Great Eastern Schism in 1472. And you must readily admit that the Greek schismatics certainly never adopted their doctrine of **seven** Sacraments merely from Rome. Moreover, the other two heretical sects, the Nestorians and the Monophysites, left the Church about the fifth century. Hence it is clear that at **that** time the whole Church accepted the fact of **seven** Sacraments. It is universally agreed also that the Bishops in the early Church were extremely conservative in regard to the introduction of innovations. It would have been impossible for any one, or for any group of them, to have introduced a new Sacrament without a protest from the rest. But there is not the slightest shred of evidence that the universal Christian Tradition which was in the possession of the Catholic Church in the sixteenth century did not come from Christ Himself. Those who now disagree with that Tradition have the duty to produce positive proof of their views. This they cannot do.

Why seven?

But **why** did Christ institute just **seven** Sacraments? Because seven were necessary to provide for the perfection of the individual Christian and for the government and multiplication of the Church.

Through His death on the Cross, Christ made it possible for each individual to receive a marvelous supernatural life, which would enable him to share in the life of God Himself. This life is conferred in **Baptism**. It would grow and need strengthening, and that is the purpose of **Confirmation**. The regular nourishment of this supernatural life is the **Holy Eucharist**. From time to time, this supernatural life may become weakened through sin—or even driven from the soul if the sin is mortal; it is then cured or restored to the soul through **Penance**. When death draws near, this supernatural life is in need of special strengthening, which it receives from **Extreme Unction**. But man is not only an individual; he also lives in society. As a being with supernatural life, he belongs to a supernatural society, the Church. Therefore, for the government of the Church, Christ instituted the Sacrament of **Holy Orders**. The Church would grow through marriage, and it is the Sacrament of **Matrimony** which sanctifies the union of husband and wife in marriage.

Matter and form

Catholics speak of **matter** and **form** of the Sacraments. This is because a Sacrament is a **sign**, an external rite. This rite consists of the performing of an action and the saying of words. The action is called the **matter** of the Sacrament, the words the **form**. Thus, in Baptism the water and the action of pouring it make up the **matter**; the words said while that is being done are the **form**.

Character

Three of the Sacraments are said to confer a **character** on the soul, and our Catechism defines this character as "a mark or seal on the soul which cannot be effaced." One may think of it as a real quality which perfects and adorns the soul, giving it a new dignity. Thus,

> **Baptism** confers the character of a Christian, a child of God;
> **Confirmation** confers the character of a soldier of Christ;
> **Holy Orders** confers the character of a priest of God.

Once conferred on the soul, these characters remain forever, and therefore these three Sacraments may not be received more than once.

Sacraments of the Living and the Dead

Two of the Sacraments, **Baptism** and **Penance** (**Confession**) are called "Sacraments of the Dead" because they may be received by those who are spiritually dead because of sin. Baptism gives the life of grace to those who have not yet received it; Penance restores the life of grace to those who have lost it by mortal sin.

By contrast, the other five Sacraments are called "Sacraments of the Living" because they can only be received by people who are in the state of grace, "living" the life of grace.

The Sacraments are the official channels of grace to the souls of men. We should therefore be very grateful to God who has given them to us through His love, and we should prove our gratitude by making use of them. The supernatural life is our most precious treasure. Every time we receive a Sacrament, we nourish that life. In addition, each of the Sacraments confers its own grace, in accordance with its purpose. It would be wicked pride to say that we do not need these graces; it is criminal carelessness to try to live without them; it is black ingratitude to refuse to use these priceless gifts from the burning Heart of Christ.

Chapter 23

Baptism

What is Baptism? *Baptism is a Sacrament which cleanses us from Original Sin, makes us Christians, children of God, members of the Church and heirs of Heaven.*

Does Baptism also forgive actual sins? *Baptism also forgives actual sins, plus all punishment due to them, when it is received in the proper disposition by those who have been guilty of actual sin.*

Who is the ordinary minister of Baptism? *The ordinary minister of Baptism is a priest, but anyone may baptize in case of necessity, when a priest cannot come.*

How is Baptism given? *Baptism is given by pouring water on the head of the person to be baptized, saying at the same time these words: "I baptize thee in the name of the Father, and of the Son, and of the Holy Ghost."*

What do we promise in Baptism? *In Baptism we promise to renounce the devil and all his works and all his pomps.*

Is Baptism necessary for salvation? *Baptism is necessary for salvation, because Christ has said, "Unless a man be born again of water and the Holy Ghost, he cannot enter into the kingdom of God." (John 3:5).*

IN the instruction on sin, we saw that by Original Sin, Adam lost for us the state of grace. All human beings, apart from the Blessed Virgin Mary, have inherited this deprivation of grace. They are conceived in Original Sin.

Men are destined to be sons of God

But when we were considering the Blessed Trinity, we remarked that it was the privilege of baptized souls to become sharers in the Divine Nature, and we described at some length the meaning of this glorious privilege. We become indeed sons of God and temples of the Holy Ghost.

At the very beginning of his Gospel, St. John insists on this truth: "But as many as received him, he gave them power to be made the sons of God, to them that believe in his name. Who are born, not of blood, nor of the will of the flesh, nor of the will of man, but of God." (*John* 1:12-13).

St. Paul tells us that God "hath predestinated us unto the adoption of children through Jesus Christ unto himself: according to the purpose of his will." (*Eph.* 1:5). To prove that we are sons, "God hath sent the Spirit of his Son into your hearts, crying: Abba, Father." (*Gal.* 4:6). "For the Spirit himself giveth testimony to our spirit, that we are the sons of God. And if sons, heirs also; heirs indeed of God, and joint heirs with Christ: yet so, if we suffer with him, that we may be also glorified with him." (*Rom.* 8:16-17).

St. Peter speaks of the **new birth** to this divine sonship as "being born again, not of corruptible seed, but incorruptible, by the word of God who liveth and remaineth for ever." (*1 Peter* 1:23).

The very purpose of the Incarnation was to confer this divine sonship on men: "But when the fullness of the time was come, God sent his Son, made of a woman, made under the law: that he might redeem them who were under the law: that we might receive the adoption of sons." (*Gal.* 4:4-5).

Other expressions of this same truth are to be found in the doctrine so stressed by St. John that the purpose of Our Lord's coming was that men might have **life**. "I am come that they may have life, and may have it more abundantly." (*John* 10:10). "I am the resurrection and the life: he that believeth in me, although he be dead, shall live: and every one that liveth, and believeth in me, shall not die for ever." (*John* 11:25-26). And the main narrative of St. John's Gospel closes with these words: "But these are written, that you may believe that Jesus is the Christ, the Son of God: and that believing, you may have life in his name." (*John* 20:31).

Sanctifying grace, a new life

It is clear that in all these passages, the Holy Ghost is speaking of an endowment which those who believe in Christ will possess here on earth, of a life purchased for us by Christ at the price of His Passion and Death, which makes us God's real children. Catholic theology speaks of this life as **sanctifying grace,** and the rebirth or the regeneration to this life takes place at Baptism.

This new life which Christ gives us is absolutely distinct from the natural life we receive by birth from our parents. It is not just the ennobling of the latter by the adoption of Christian rules of conduct. **We actually receive a new principle of life which changes our very nature and raises us to a supernatural level of existence.**

To understand the true significance of a "supernatural level of existence," suppose a horse suddenly found itself in possession of the nature of man, so that it could talk with men, perform real human actions in a human way and experience life on the human plane. The animal could truly be said to have been raised to a supernatural level of existence, that is, to a level beyond what is proper to it merely as a horse.

In much the same way, **sanctifying grace raises man above the natural human level** because it is a further communication of life, a new principal of life, which raises him up to the divine level, the level of God, so that ultimately, in Heaven, he becomes capable of the Beatific Vision and thus able **to know as God knows** and **to love as God loves,** and **to be happy with God's happiness.**

We have already seen how this life remains in the soul, but that it is killed by grievous sin. Mortal sin is so called (*mors, mortis* in Latin means *death*) precisely because it kills supernatural life. Sanctifying grace is also called "habitual" grace because it remains permanently in the soul as its new life, sanctifying it, making it holy and pleasing to God, unless and until it is driven away by mortal sin.

We have seen in another previous instruction how the Church is the Mystical Body of Christ and how we are all members of Christ, cells of the divine organism which continues the life of Christ among men. We are **incorporated** with Christ, made **one body** with Him (*corpus* means *body*). Just as our birth to the new life of Christ takes place at Baptism, so does our incorporation into Him.

Baptism, birth to a new life

The new life that Christ came to give and the new powers which this life confers obviously require a new birth. In the natural order, when we are born of humanity, we are born into human society. In the supernatural order, when we are born of water and the Holy Ghost, we enter a supernatural society, the Catholic Church. Our birth into it and into the life we receive as members of it are every bit as real as our human birth and human life. These make us sharers in human nature; however, Baptism makes us sharers in the Divine Nature.

The solemn teaching of the Church in regard to Baptism is this:

1. It is a **Sacrament**
2. That imprints a **character** on the soul.
3. **Water** is necessary for its administration.
4. It removes **all stain of Original Sin** and **all Actual Sin**, along with **all temporal punishment due to Actual Sin**.
5. It is **necessary for salvation**.
6. It can be validly received **even by infants**.
7. When they grow up, children are thereafter **not free to reject** the Baptismal promises made for them by their sponsors. [This is not to say that such a person no longer has free will, but rather, that he is not **morally** free to reject truth. Here a simple but crucial distinction must be made: The adult Catholic who was baptized as an infant indeed **has the power** to reject his Baptismal promises—which power is reflected in civil law **as a "civil right"**—but he **does not have a MORAL right** to choose what is false. If he did so choose, he would be abusing his faculty of free will, i.e., he would be guilty of license (i.e., choosing to do evil). For a right is defined as "a claim within the boundaries of justice, or goodness," and therefore no one can say he has a moral right to believe what is false or immoral, going against his own judgment and knowledge of what is true. —Publisher, 2002.]

Baptism is defined as **the Sacrament which cleanses us from Original Sin, makes us Christians, children and temples of God, members of the Catholic Church, and heirs to Heaven.** As the Catechism of the Council of Trent teaches (p. 187): ". . . it should be taught that by virtue of this Sacrament we are not only delivered from what are justly deemed the greatest of all evils, but [we] are also enriched with invaluable goods and blessings. Our souls are replenished with divine grace, by which we are rendered just and children of God and are made heirs to eternal salvation."

Baptism is normally conferred in the Catholic Church by pouring water on the head of the person being baptized, while the person baptizing says these words: "I baptize thee in the name of the Father, and of the Son, and of the Holy Ghost."

When Baptism is administered solemnly, these bare essentials are accompanied by all the ceremonies (exorcisms, anointings, etc.) appointed by the Church.

Institution by Christ

If Baptism is a Sacrament, it must have been **instituted by Christ**. That this is the case is very clear from the New Testament.

"And Jesus coming, spoke to them, saying: All power is given to me in heaven and in earth. Going therefore, teach ye all nations; baptizing them in the name of the Father, and of the Son, and of the Holy Ghost." (*Matt.* 28:18-19). "He that believeth and is baptized, shall be saved: but he that believeth not shall be condemned." (*Mark* 16:16).

From the very day on which the Holy Ghost came down on them, the Apostles administered Baptism. Peter's words stung the consciences of the Jews on that day: "Now when they had heard these things, they had compunction in their heart, and said to Peter, and to the rest of the Apostles: What shall we do, men and brethren? But Peter said to them: Do penance, and be baptized every one of you in the name of Jesus Christ, for the remission of your sins: and you shall receive the gift of the Holy Ghost." (*Acts* 2:37-38). St. Paul was baptized immediately after his miraculous conversion. (*Acts* 9:18).

Peter proceeded to baptize the Gentiles. "Can any man forbid water, that these should not be baptized, who have received the Holy Ghost, as well as we? And he commanded them to be baptized in the name of the Lord Jesus Christ." (*Acts* 10:47-48).

Therefore, Baptism has all the essentials of a Sacrament. It is an **outward sign** (the washing with water accompanied by the words) of **inward grace** (re-birth) **ordained by Jesus Christ**.

Methods of administration

Note that because of the words of Christ to Nicodemus (*John* 3), only true, natural water is the valid matter of Baptism. There must be a real washing. This can be *validly* done by immersion, by pouring **or** by sprinkling. [If Baptism is done by sprinkling, the water must flow on the head of the person baptized. —Publisher 2002]. The law of the Western Patriarchate of the Catholic Church (the Latin Rite) now states that the **one baptizing must pour the water three times on the head of the one being baptized while pronouncing the words "I baptize thee in the name of the Father, and of the Son, and of the Holy Ghost."**

It is true that, for twelve centuries, immersion was a common practice in the Catholic Church. St. Thomas Aquinas, who lived in the thirteenth century, says clearly: "Baptism can be conferred by sprinkling and also by pouring . . . as also the Blessed Lawrence is related to have baptized." He recalls that thousands of people were baptized together by the Apostles and implies that this was done either by pouring the water or by sprinkling it.

Immersion is unnecessary

The tradition of the Church has always held that Baptism can be validly administered by **pouring** the water over the head of the one to be baptized. Tertullian, who was born in the year 160 A.D., describes Baptism as a "sprinkling with any kind of water." (*De Bapt.,* Ch. 6). St. Augustine says that sins are forgiven by Baptism, even though the water "merely sprinkles the child ever so lightly" (in *Joan* ixxx, 3). Eusebius, in his *History of the Church*, written at the beginning of the fourth century, tells how the sick were baptized by the pouring of water. (vi, 43). The *Didache*, or *The Teaching of* *the Twelve Apostles*, a document which dates from the first century, says clearly that the baptismal water may be poured when there is not enough water for immersion. Therefore, it is certain that throughout the history of the Church, Baptism by pouring has been recognized as valid.

Duchesne, one of the greatest authorities on early Christian archaeology, writes: "We constantly see representatives of the celebration of Baptism on monuments . . . But do we ever see total immersion, the neophyte plunged into the water so as to disappear completely? Such a thing is **never** seen. This immersion is never to be met with in the mosaics of ancient churches, in the paintings of the Catacombs, in ordinary pictures, domestic objects, glasses, spoons, etc.; it is never sculptured or engraved on marble. In all such ancient monuments the neophyte appears standing, his feet in the water, but the greater part of his body out of the water, while water is poured on his head with the hand or with a vase. This is Baptism by infusion, not by immersion; it is not a bath taken by plunging into deep water or into a tank; it is more like a douche [shower] taken over a large vase." (*Churches Separated from Rome*, 62).

As St. Thomas implies, it is most improbable that the three thousand converts baptized by St. Peter on the first Pentecost were immersed, if only because there would not be enough water in Jerusalem at the time. Nor is it likely that the Gentiles baptized in the home of Cornelius or the jailer in the prison at Philippi were plunged into water for the purpose.

The administration of Baptism

Is it necessary to use holy water for Baptism? In danger of death it is certainly unnecessary. In **private Baptism** ordinary water may always be used, but it would be more fitting to use baptismal or holy water. In **solemn Baptism** there is a grave obligation to employ baptismal water, i.e., that water which is specially blessed for the purpose on Holy Saturday, or on the Vigil of Pentecost.

Who may baptize? The ordinary minister of solemn Baptism is a priest, but Canon Law prescribes that its administration is **reserved to the parish priest of the person being baptized** or, of course, to a priest having the parish priest's permission.

In case of necessity, anyone with sufficient use of reason may baptize. This is lawful only in danger of death. If possible two witnesses, or at least one, should be present. In this case, the ceremonies should later be supplied in the Church by the priest.

Who may be baptized? 1. The *valid* Baptism of anyone with the use of reason requires the intention of being baptized.

2. *Lawful* Baptism requires also that the person baptized be properly instructed and sorry for his personal sins.

3. Children of Catholic parents should be baptized as soon as possible after birth.

4. Children of non-Catholic parents may be baptized even against the parents' will if it is foreseen that the child will die before reaching the use of reason. Apart from the danger of death, such children may be baptized **if their Catholic education is assured** and the consent of the father or mother, grandfather or grandmother or guardian is obtained, or if there is no one who has or can exercise parental authority over the child. **If the Catholic education of the child is not assured, Baptism is forbidden, even should the parents request it**.

The necessity of Baptism

The Council of Trent has defined that Baptism is a necessary means of salvation. "Amen, amen I say to thee, unless a man be born again of water and the Holy Ghost, he cannot enter into the kingdom of God." (*John* 3:5). Christ makes no exception to this law; it therefore holds for both adults and infants.

The Fathers of the Church have always insisted on the absolute necessity of Baptism. St. Irenaeus wrote: "Christ came to save all who are reborn through Him to God, infants, children and youths." (II, xxii). St. Augustine is perfectly clear: "If you wish to be a Catholic, do not believe, nor say, nor teach, that infants who die before Baptism can obtain the remission of Original Sin." (III, *De Anima*). "Whoever says that even infants are made alive in Christ when they depart this life without the participation of His Sacrament (Baptism), both opposes the Apostolic preaching and condemns the whole Church, which hastens to baptize infants, because it unhesitatingly believes that otherwise they cannot possibly be vivified in Christ." (*Ep.* xxviii, *Ad Hieron*). St. Ambrose, who brought St. Augustine into the Church, says that from the necessity of Baptism no one is excepted, neither the infant nor the one hindered by any need. (II *De Abraham,* c. xi).

Baptism of Desire; Baptism of Blood

This teaching of the Church is not quite so hard as it seems at first sight, because the Church has always held that **when the Sacramental Baptism of water becomes a physical or moral impossibility, the principal effect of this Sacrament—the remission of Original Sin and the reception of Sanctifying Grace— may be obtained by Baptism of Desire or Baptism of Blood.**

a) *Baptism of Desire* **is a perfect contrition of heart, and every act of perfect charity or pure love of God which contains, at least implicitly, a desire of Baptism**.

That Baptism of Desire can supply for Baptism of Water when the latter is impossible, is clear from the words of Our Lord:

"He that hath my commandments, and keepeth them; he it is that loveth me. And he that loveth me, shall be loved of my Father: and I will love him, and will manifest myself to him . . . If any one love me, he will keep my word, and my Father will love him, and we will come to him, and will make our abode with him." (*John* 14:21, 23).

St. Ambrose (340-397 A.D.) in his sermon on the Emperor Valentinian II, who died while he was under instruction and unbaptized, said: "I hear you express grief that he did not receive the Sacrament of Baptism. Tell me, what else is there in us except the will and petition? But he had long desired to be initiated before he came to Italy, and expressed his intention to be baptized by me as soon as possible . . . Has he not, therefore, the grace which he desired? Surely he received it because he asked for it?" (*De Obitu Valent.*, 51).

St. Augustine agrees: "I find that not only suffering for the name of Christ can supply that defect of Baptism, but even faith and conversion of heart, if there be no time for celebrating the Sacrament." (*De Bapt.*, iv, 22).

According to St. Cyprian the catechumens who suffer martyrdom receive "the glorious and most sublime blood-Baptism." (*Fundamentals of Catholic Dogma*, Ludwig Ott, TAN, 1974, p. 357).

The Council of Trent teaches that justification from Original Sin is not possible "without the washing unto regeneration, or the desire for the same." (*Ibid.*, Ott, p. 357—Also *Denziger*, No. 796).

Therefore, the position of adults who die without even hearing of Christ and His Gospel is that they are saved by the merits of Christ if they die in perfect charity or are perfectly contrite for their sins. This includes, as we have said, the implicit desire for Baptism which is a state of mind in which a man would ardently long for Baptism, if he knew it is necessary for salvation.

Children who die without Baptism are deprived of the direct vision of God in Heaven, but of course, they cannot be worthy of Hell, which is a punishment due only to actual sin. As the glory of Heaven is a free gift on God's part, these infants do not suffer any injustice. St. Thomas Aquinas says of them: "They are free from pain and sorrow, and even enjoy a certain inward peace and happiness, so that they attain at least a minimum of that happiness which would have been their natural end if human nature had not been elevated to a supernatural order." (IV *Sent.* II, *dist.* xxx, Q. 2 ad. 5).

b) **Baptism of Blood is martyrdom suffered by one who has not been baptized.** It is defined as **the endurance of death or deadly suffering for the sake of Jesus Christ**. Therefore, the martyr must be **put to death** or endure sufferings that would naturally cause death; the persecutor must inflict death or deadly violence through opposition to the Church, the Catholic Faith, or a Christian virtue. In the case of adults, death or the deadly violence must be endured from a supernatural motive, and there must be no resistance to try to escape death, and the sufferer must have made acts of Faith and Hope and have at least some sorrow for grave sin committed.

That martyrdom is equivalent to Sacramental Baptism is clear from Christ's own words: "He that findeth his life, shall lose it: and he that shall lose his life for me, shall find it." (*Matt.* 10:39). "Every one therefore that shall confess me before men, I will also confess him before my Father who is in heaven." (*Matt.* 10:32).

It is also the undeniable tradition of the Church, which has since the earliest times honored as martyrs, enjoying the happiness of Heaven, many who were never baptized—the Holy Innocents massacred by King Herod, St. Emerentiana (traditional feastday January 23) and others. "He does an injury to a martyr who prays for him," said St. Augustine (*Serm.* clix, i).

Infant Baptism

It is a common contention of the Baptists that the Bible requires faith and repentance before Baptism and that therefore the Sacrament should not be administered to infants. The various texts they quote are quite irrelevant because they refer only to the Baptism of adults desiring to enter the Church. On the contrary, we are told that whole families were baptized by St. Paul. It would be strange if there were not some children among them. (Cf. *Acts* 16:15; *1 Cor.* 1:16). The earliest Christian writers point out that the words of Christ command **all** to be baptized; He makes no exception for infants. The purpose of Baptism is the remission of Original Sin; they have it on their souls, and they are entitled to have it remitted. We have already quoted St. Irenaeus on this point. A contemporary of his, Origen (185-255), says that infant Baptism is an Apostolic institution and necessary to cleanse infants from their Original Sin. (*Epis. ad Rom., Lib.* v, 9; *In Lev.* viii, 3). At the Third Council of Carthage, held in 253 A.D., St. Cyprian and the other bishops present taught that infants should be baptized as soon as possible after birth. In 416 the Council of Milevi insisted on the necessity of infants being baptized, and this teaching has since been repeated by the Fourth Lateran Council and the Councils of Vienne, Florence and Trent. Therefore, we can say with St. Augustine of infant Baptism: "This the Church always had, always held; this she received from the Faith of our ancestors; this she perseveringly guards even to the end." (*Serm.* xi, *De Verb Apost*).

Our instructions will have revealed that Baptism is the most important of all the Sacraments. By it one receives the only thing that really matters, supernatural life. Therefore, we ought to meditate on the significance of Baptism and never cease to thank God for the tremendous favor He has given us in permitting us to be baptized.

Chapter 24

Confirmation

What is Confirmation? *Confirmation is a Sacrament by which we receive the Holy Ghost, in order to make us strong and perfect Christians and soldiers of Jesus Christ.*

Who is the ordinary minister of Confirmation? *The ordinary minister of Confirmation is a bishop.*

How does the bishop administer the Sacrament of Confirmation? *The bishop administers the Sacrament of Confirmation by praying that the Holy Ghost may come down upon those who are to be confirmed, and by laying his hands on them and making the Sign of the Cross with chrism on their foreheads, at the same time pronouncing certain words.*

What are the words used in Confirmation? *The traditional words used in Confirmation are these: "I sign thee with the Sign of the Cross, and I confirm thee with the chrism of salvation, in the name of the Father, and of the Son, and of the Holy Ghost. Amen." In the New Rite (1971) they are: "Be Sealed with the Gift of the Holy Spirit."*

Which are the Seven Gifts of the Holy Ghost? *The Seven Gifts of the Holy Ghost are:*

1. Wisdom   2. Understanding   3. Counsel
4. Fortitude   5. Knowledge   6. Piety
7. The fear of the Lord

Which are the Twelve Fruits of the Holy Ghost? *The twelve fruits of the Holy Ghost are:*

1. Charity   2. Joy   3. Peace
4. Patience   5. Benignity   6. Goodness
7. Longanimity   8. Mildness   9. Faith
10. Modesty   11. Continency   12. Chastity

Purpose and definition of Confirmation

F ROM our consideration of the significance of Baptism, it will be evident that it is the duty of every baptized person to try to live up to his dignity as a sharer in the Divine Nature, a temple of the Holy Ghost, a brother of Christ, a cell of the Mystical Body. Anyone who has tried knows that this is not easy. To live as a real Christian in the modern neo-pagan world, to resist continually every kind of temptation, to maintain always a thoroughly Christ-like outlook is a task which requires special help from God. That help He gives in a special Sacrament called Confirmation.

Confirmation is defined as **a Sacrament by which we receive the Holy Ghost, in order to make us strong and perfect Christians and soldiers of Jesus Christ**.

The minister

The ordinary minister of Confirmation is a bishop, but under certain circumstances, e.g., danger of death when a bishop can only be found with difficulty, a parish priest may administer the Sacrament.

The practice of reserving the administration of Confirmation under normal circumstances to the bishops dates from the *Acts of the Apostles*. As we shall see more fully in a moment, when Philip the Deacon had converted Samaria, he baptized the converts, but it was the Apostles who went specially to confirm them.

The bishop administers the Sacrament of Confirmation by praying that the Holy Ghost may come down upon those who are to be confirmed, while laying his hands on them and making the Sign of the Cross with chrism on their foreheads, saying at the same time: "I sign thee with the Sign of the Cross, and I confirm thee with the chrism of salvation; in the Name of the Father and of the Son and of the Holy Ghost. Amen." In the New Rite (1971), the words used are "Be sealed with the gift of the Holy Spirit," which is an apparent translation of the "form" or wording for Confirmation used in the Greek Church. (Cf. *Handbook of Moral Theology*, Prümmer, Mercier Press, 1956, No. 577.) In Latin the Greek Church wording is *Signaculum doni Spiritus Sancti*, the verb being understood. The

New Latin Rite version adds the verb *accipe*—"receive."

Confirmation can be administered to all baptized persons and only to them. The present discipline of the Church demands that they have the use of reason. [In the Eastern Churches, the infant is traditionally confirmed immediately after Baptism. —Publisher, 2002].

Anointing with Chrism

Chrism, the oil used in Confirmation, is made of oil of olives and balsam, or balm, and is blessed by the Bishop on Maundy Thursday (Holy Thursday). The olive oil comes from the olive tree which, since the dove brought a branch of it back to Noah in the Ark, has been regarded as the emblem of peace and plenty. Olive oil has always been considered as giving strength to those to whom it is applied. It was used for this purpose especially by the Romans before their battles. It saturates and spreads; it softens and soothes; and it is frequently used for burning and illumination; it is therefore a very fitting symbol of the effects of Confirmation, which strengthens the will against spiritual enemies, diffuses the Holy Spirit over the powers of the soul, gives light to the understanding and facilitates the observance of God's Law.

Mixed with the olive oil is balsam, which is a gum derived from the terebinth tree and other plants. It exhales a fragrance and is said to heal and preserve from putrefaction. Therefore, Confirmation enables the soul to manifest the sweet odor of virtue, and it heals the wounds of sin and preserves from its corruption.

That Confirmation is a true Sacrament—an outward sign of inward grace instituted by Christ—is defined by the Council of Trent.

Confirmation in Scripture

It is clear from the New Testament that Christ promised to give His followers the Holy Spirit for the special purpose of strengthening them in the profession of their faith. "And when they shall bring you into the synagogues, and to magistrates and powers, be not solicitous how or what you shall answer, or what you shall say; For the Holy Ghost shall teach you in the same hour what you must say." (*Luke* 12:11-12).

"But you shall receive the power of the Holy Ghost coming upon you, and you shall be witnesses unto me in Jerusalem, and in all Judea, and Samaria, and even to the uttermost part of the earth." (*Acts* 1:8).

"And I will ask the Father, and he shall give you another Para-clete, that he may abide with you for ever. The spirit of truth, whom the world cannot receive, because it seeth him not, nor knoweth him: but you shall know him; because he shall abide with you, and shall be in you." (*John* 14:16-17).

Earlier, St. John himself remarks: "Now this he said of the Spirit which they should receive, who believed in him: for as yet the Spirit was not given, because Jesus was not yet glorified." (*John* 7:39).

The Apostles and Cornelius the centurion received Confirma-tion in extraordinary ways and not through the Sacrament, as we may read in the *Acts of the Apostles*. But St. Peter told the people that the gift of the Holy Ghost was not meant to be extraordinary, but was promised to all the followers of Christ. "Do penance, and be baptized every one of you in the name of Jesus Christ, for the remission of your sins: and you shall receive the gift of the Holy Ghost. For the promise is to you, and to your children, and to all that are far off, whomsoever the Lord our God shall call." (*Acts* 2:38-39).

Clearly, the gift of the Holy Ghost was to be the normal thing in the Church. What is more natural than to suppose that it would be conferred by a Sacrament?

That such was the case is clear from a study of some incidents in the story of the early Church given us by St. Luke in the *Acts of the Apostles*. Philip the Deacon had converted and baptized the Samaritans. After recording this in detail, St. Luke continues: "Now when the Apostles, who were in Jerusalem, had heard that Samaria had received the word of God, they sent unto them Peter and John. Who, when they were come, prayed for them, that they might receive the Holy Ghost. For he was not as yet come upon any of them; but they were only baptized in the name of the Lord Jesus. Then they laid their hands upon them, and they received the Holy Ghost." (*Acts* 8:14-17).

Later, we are told how St. Paul came to Ephesus. "And it came to pass, while Apollo was at Corinth, that Paul having passed through the upper coasts, came to Ephesus, and found certain disciples. And he said to them: Have you received the Holy Ghost since ye believed? But they said to him: We have not so much as heard whether there be a Holy Ghost." Paul, knowing that if they had even been baptized, they would have heard of the Holy Spirit, soon discovered that the only Baptism they had received was that of St. John the Baptist. Therefore, "Having heard these things, they were baptized in the name of the Lord Jesus. And when Paul had imposed his hands on them, the Holy Ghost came upon them, and they spoke with tongues and prophesied." (*Acts* 19:1-6).

These instances give us the full revelation of a Sacrament. We see a divine gift being communicated by man to men, with the divine result following automatically. It is, in fact, clear that there existed in the Church at the time of the Apostles a normal rite for conferring the Holy Spirit that was distinct from Baptism. Now, only God could institute such a sign; hence, Confirmation must have been given to the Apostles by Jesus Christ, the God-Man.

Just as Catholics today use many different words to describe the Sacraments and make many allusions to them which are understood by all, even though they do not define exactly what they are, so in the early Church we find similar allusions. If a priest today urges his people not to delay the spiritual births of their children, everyone knows he is speaking about Baptism. So too, when the early Christians spoke of "the laying on of hands," "receiving the Holy Ghost," "sign," "seal," "chrism," "unction," "Character," "confirmation," they would be understood to refer to the Sacrament of Confirmation. All the words in that list were in common use before the end of the first century, a fact which adds much weight to our conviction that the Holy Ghost was conferred by an external rite in which "signing" and "sealing" were concerned.

Thus, St. Paul could write to the Corinthians: "Now he that confirmeth us with you in Christ, and that hath anointed us, is God: Who also hath sealed us, and given the pledge of the Spirit in our hearts." (*2 Cor.* 1:21-22). Again: "after you had heard the word of truth, (the gospel of your salvation;) in whom also believing, you were signed with the holy Spirit of promise." (*Eph.* 1:13). "And grieve not the holy Spirit of God: whereby you are sealed unto the day of redemption." (*Eph.* 4:30).

The Hebrews are told that they are no longer to be treated as catechumens. The foundations of faith are already laid, and these include instructions about "the doctrine of baptisms, and imposition of hands." (*Heb.* 6:2). St. John refers to the anointing of the Holy Spirit: "But you have the unction from the Holy One, and know all things." (*1 John* 2:20). "Let the unction, which you have received from him, abide in you." (*1 John* 2:27).

Confirmation in Tradition

Turning from Scripture to the writings of the earliest Christians, we find that even in the third century Confirmation was regarded as a normal rite of the Church, the same as that administered by the Apostles to Philip's converts in Samaria. It is a rite distinct from Baptism, consisting of imposition of hands, anointing and accompanying words, by which the Holy Ghost was conferred on those already baptized and a character or seal impressed upon their souls.

Tertullian, that useful witness as friend and critic to Catholic practice and belief at the end of the second century and the beginning of the third, offers strong evidence for the existence and sacramental nature of Confirmation.

"After having come out of the laver (font), we are anointed thoroughly with a blessed unction according to the ancient rule . . . The unction runs bodily over us, but profits spiritually . . . Next to this, the hand is laid upon us through the blessing, calling upon and inviting the Holy Spirit." (*De Bap.* iv). Again: "The flesh is washed, that the soul may be made stainless. The flesh is anointed, that the soul may be consecrated. The flesh is sealed, that the soul may be fortified. The flesh is overshadowed by the imposition of hands, that the soul may be illuminated by the Spirit." (*De resurr. carnis. n.* 8).

St. Cyprian is equally clear: "Two Sacraments preside over the perfect birth of a Christian, the one regenerating the man, which is Baptism, the other communicating to him the Holy Spirit." (*Epist.* lxxii). Referring to the Confirmation of the Samaritans in the *Acts*, Cyprian writes: "It was not fitting that they should be baptized again, but only what was wanting, that was done by Peter and John;

that prayer being made for them and hands imposed, the Holy Ghost should be invoked and poured forth upon them. Which also is now done amongst us; so that they who are baptized in the Church are presented to the bishops of the Church and by our prayer and imposition of hands, they receive the Holy Ghost and are perfected with the seal of the Lord." (*Epist.* lxxiii).

So we could go on quoting Father of the Church after Father of the Church, but to little purpose. The truth is more than clear. Confirmation has existed in the Church with all the essentials of a Sacrament from the time of the Apostles and of Christ.

The effects of Confirmation

The primary effect of Confirmation is a great increase of the divine life of grace in the soul and consequently a closer and more intimate union with God who dwells there.

Secondly, the sacramental grace is strengthening and is substantially the same as that received directly from the Holy Spirit on the first Pentecost Sunday, and it brings with it the Gifts of the Holy Ghost in fuller and more perfect form than that in which they were received at Baptism. Further, it bestows a right or claim to those spiritual helps or actual graces which will enable us to lead a holier life undeterred by human respect or other worldly obstacles.

By Confirmation, then, one receives in a special way the Holy Spirit, who is the Light, the Love and the Strength of God, guiding our path through life, inflaming our hearts and enabling us to overcome all difficulties. He makes us soldiers in Christ's army, ever fighting against the world, the flesh and the devil, and ever ready to profess our Faith, to suffer for it, to persevere in it no matter at what cost, and to radiate it.

Catholics in the modern world must be centers from which the influence of Christ is radiated. Pope Pius XI, writing to Cardinal Cerejeira in 1934, said: "The Sacraments of Baptism and Confirmation impose—among other obligations, this Apostolate of Catholic Action . . . Through Confirmation we become soldiers of Christ. A soldier must toil and fight, not so much for himself as for others." St. Thomas Aquinas elaborated this point nearly seven centuries ago: "In Baptism man receives power to do those things which pertain to his own salvation, in as much as he lives to himself; whereas, in Confirmation he receives power to do those things which pertain to spiritual combat with enemies of the Faith." (*S. T.* III, Q. lxxii, a. 5). If a majority of the confirmed Catholics in the world today were only living up to their obligations as soldiers of Christ, the spread and growth of the Church would be increased a hundredfold, and with knowledge of the Gospel would come to men all the other blessings God has promised to those who "seek first the Kingdom of God." (Cf. *Matt.* 6:33).

The Gifts of the Holy Ghost

The Gifts of the Holy Ghost are imparted in their fullness in Confirmation. They are enumerated by the Prophet Isaias (*Is.* 11:2) as follows: Wisdom, Understanding, Counsel, Fortitude, Knowledge, Piety and the Fear of the Lord.

Wisdom enables us to consider the eternal truths, to judge all things by them, to set a right value on salvation and the means to it and to relish the things of God. It illuminates the intellect, moderates the passions, rectifies the affections and directs the will. To the soul it brings vigor and energy, facility in well-doing, contempt of earthly riches and, most precious of all, union with God.

Understanding is the power of penetrating the hidden meaning of the great spiritual truths. On those who possess it, the Gospels make a deeper impression than on others; they appreciate more deeply the Sacraments and ceremonies of the Church; they love more deeply the lives of the Saints; they show the world due contempt; and they are better able to guide and advise others.

Counsel is the power of deciding prudently about the concerns of God and salvation, a certain readiness of will to do the better thing.

Fortitude brings firmness of soul in bearing difficulties for God, courage to profess the Faith and to do penance, and the energy necessary for perseverance. It makes us patient and steadfast in our trials and temptations.

Knowledge enables us to see and use temporal things in such a way as to help us toward our eternal salvation.

Piety is the disposition to serve God with tenderness and devotion, and it helps us to practice what religion teaches us, especially about the loving fatherhood of God, the motherhood of Mary and the Church, the spiritual brotherhood of all the members of Christ, and our duty to our relatives and fellow countrymen.

The Fear of the Lord is filial and reverential fear of the majesty, power and justice of God and of the ease with which one can offend Him by sin; this gift of the Holy Ghost is always united with the love of God.

These Seven gifts are necessary for salvation. The virtues of themselves are not sufficient to raise man to the perfection to which he is called. Their incapacity is remedied by these Gifts of the Holy Ghost. They enable us to act correctly in a superhuman way, in order to bring our actions into line with God's own standards of conduct. They enable us to live our human lives as God would live a human life.

The Fruits of the Holy Ghost

The Fruits of the virtues and Gifts infused into our souls by the Holy Ghost are also enumerated by St. Paul. They are Charity, Joy, Peace, Patience, Benignity, Goodness, Longanimity, Mildness, Faith, Modesty, Continency and Chastity. This list is not exhaustive, for every good, supernatural act that is accomplished with ease and delight merits the name of a "fruit of the Holy Ghost."

For the sake of completeness a few brief notes are added on each of the Twelve Fruits of the Holy Ghost:

1. **Charity**—the perfection of God-like love, as displayed in the lives of the Saints, which consists of deeds, not words.
2. **Joy**—happiness resulting from a life of goodness and a clear conscience, pleasure in doing good, consolation in God's service.
3. **Peace**—the state of a soul that is at rest with God, with others and with oneself.
4. **Patience**—the ability to bear with others without resentment or irritation; resignation amid trials.

5. **Benignity**—sweetness of disposition, gentleness, compassion.
6. **Goodness**—willingness to serve and oblige; causes one to try to avoid hurting others.
7. **Longanimity**—calmness in prolonged trial; perseverance in well-doing; indifference to ingratitude or failure.
8. **Mildness**—gentleness, forbearance, meekness.
9. **Faith**—not the theological virtue, but truthfulness, trustworthiness, candor, openness, simplicity, fidelity to promises.
10. **Modesty**—external moderation in speech, in dress, and in manner; reserve; an unassuming disposition.
11. **Continency**—the repression of anger, impatience and sensuality.
12. **Chastity**—purity of body, mind, heart and soul.

We must take care that Confirmation is for us no longer the forgotten Sacrament. If we have not already received it, we must arrange to do so at the earliest possible moment, and to do so worthily after due preparation. We cannot afford to go through life without all the wonderful graces it bestows. For the Church, it is the perpetuation of Pentecost, the means by which she keeps alive the power of the Spirit within her members. [St. Vincent Ferrer (1350-1419) predicted that toward the End of Time Confirmation would fall into disuse and that those who were not confirmed would succumb to believing in and obeying the Antichrist. —Publisher, 2002].

"O Sacred Treasury in which the Holy Ghost is communicated to us, the thought of Pentecost is established in our hearts, we remain for life temples of His Divine Presence, and we are given full possession of a pledge of everlasting glory." (Kolbe, *The Sacrament of Confirmation*).

Chapter 25

The Holy Eucharist (1)

What is the Sacrament of the Holy Eucharist? *The Sacrament of the Holy Eucharist is the true Body and Blood of Jesus Christ, together with His Soul and Divinity, under the appearances of bread and wine.*

How are the bread and wine changed into the Body and Blood of Christ? *The bread and wine are changed into the Body and Blood of Christ by the power of God, to whom nothing is impossible or difficult.*

When are the bread and wine changed into the Body and Blood of Christ? *The bread and wine are changed into the Body and Blood of Christ when the words of Consecration, ordained by Jesus Christ, are pronounced by the priest in Holy Mass.*

D URING the course of these instructions, we have several times alluded to the divine life of grace which is received at Baptism and which makes us sharers in the nature of God. That life, born in the soul at Baptism, strengthened by Confirmation, has for its ordinary nourishment and growth the Holy Eucharist.

The sixth chapter of St. John

Let us look immediately at the Gospel story. St. John *(John 6:25-35)* tells us how Our Lord had just worked two spectacular miracles: He had fed a great multitude containing five thousand men, and He had walked on the water of the Sea of Galilee. Having returned to Capharnaum, He was sought out by the Jews, who immediately asked, "Rabbi, when camest thou hither?" Our Lord, fully aware of their insincerity, replied: "Amen, amen I say to you,

you seek me, not because you have seen miracles, but because you did eat of the loaves, and were filled." And He went on to demand their faith: "This is the work of God, that you believe in him whom he hath sent." They reply by demanding a sign. Moses had given manna in the desert; could Jesus do something comparable to assert His superiority? "Then Jesus said to them: Amen, amen I say to you; Moses gave you not bread from heaven, but my Father giveth you the true bread from heaven. And Jesus said to them: I am the bread of life: he that cometh to me shall not hunger: and he that believeth in me shall never thirst." (*Jn.* 6:25-26, 29, 32, 35). After this they parted, but there must have been a great deal of discussion in the city about what Jesus had said.

Desirous of hearing Him further, they invited Him to explain His teaching in the synagogue. There He expounded His teaching in a manner which left no doubt as to His meaning: "Amen, amen I say unto you: He that believeth in me, hath everlasting life. I am the bread of life. Your fathers did eat manna in the desert, and are dead. This is the bread which cometh down from heaven; that if any man eat of it, he may not die. I am the living bread which came down from Heaven. If any man eat of this bread, he shall live for ever; and the bread that I will give is my flesh, for the life of the world."

Immediately there was uproar. The Jews realized that this at least was incapable of a metaphorical explanation and so, with perfect logic, they asked: "How can this man give us his flesh to eat?" Jesus answered clearly and emphatically: "Amen, amen I say unto you: Except you eat the flesh of the Son of man, and drink his blood, you shall not have life in you. He that eateth my flesh, and drinketh my blood, hath everlasting life: and I will raise him up in the last day. For my flesh is meat indeed: and my blood is drink indeed. He that eateth my flesh, and drinketh my blood, abideth in me, and I in him. As the living Father hath sent me, and I live by the Father, so he that eateth me, the same also shall live by me. This is the bread that came down from heaven. Not as your fathers did eat manna, and are dead. He that eateth this bread, shall live for ever." (*John* 6:47-59).

Christ's promise must be accepted literally

That was more than enough for the Jews. Jesus had answered their challenge by repeating what He had said in such a fashion that there was not the slightest doubt left that He meant them to take Him literally. He begins by an emphatic statement: "Amen, amen I say unto you." Six times in as many verses, He repeats His statement, positively and negatively, adding all the time emphatic words to bring out His true meaning: "For my flesh is meat indeed: and my blood is drink indeed." He is careful to distinguish between eating His Body and drinking His Blood, which distinction would have been without purpose if He was only speaking metaphorically. In any case, there is no possible metaphorical meaning that would fit in with the context. The only figurative meaning of eating another's flesh and drinking his blood in the language used in Our Lord's time was to hate or injure another.

On other occasions, as with Nicodemus, when Jesus had been using metaphors, He had quickly explained His true meaning, but on this occasion there was no metaphor to explain away. "This saying is hard," the Jews said, "and who can hear it? . . . After this many of his disciples went back; and walked no more with him." Jesus let them go. If any mitigation of His teaching had been possible, He was surely bound, in the interests of truth, to call them back and explain their error. Instead He turns to the Apostles, "Will you also go away?" He asks. "And Simon Peter answered him: Lord, to whom shall we go? thou hast the words of eternal life. And we have believed and have known, that thou art the Christ, the Son of God." (*John* 6:56-70).

The Last Supper

The promise made that day in the synagogue at Capharnaum was fulfilled on the night before Jesus died. It was at the Last Supper, of which there are four distinct accounts. Here is one of them, St. Paul's: "For I have received of the Lord that which also I delivered unto you, that the Lord Jesus, the same night in which he was betrayed, took bread. And giving thanks, broke, and said: Take ye, and eat: this is my body, which shall be delivered for you: this do for the commemoration of me. In like manner also the chalice, after he had supped, saying: This chalice is the new testament in my blood: this do ye, as often as you shall drink, for the commemoration of me." (*1 Cor.* 11:23-25). The words given by the other writers are as follows:

St. Matthew: "Take ye, and eat. This is my body. And taking the chalice, he gave thanks, and gave to them, saying: Drink ye all of this. For this is my blood of the new testament, which shall be shed for many unto remission of sins." (*Matt.* 26:26-28).

St. Mark: "Take ye. This is my body. And having taken the chalice, giving thanks, he gave it to them. And they all drank of it. And he said to them: This is my blood of the new testament, which shall be shed for many." (*Mark* 14:22-24).

St. Luke: "This is my body, which is given for you. Do this for a commemoration of me. In like manner the chalice also, after he had supped, saying: This is the chalice, the new testament in my blood, which shall be shed for you." (*Luke* 22:19-20).

The meaning of the words of institution

There is not the slightest ground anywhere in these four accounts of the institution of the Holy Eucharist to justify our accepting any but a literal interpretation of the words of Christ. They could not be simpler. Any fair-minded person must admit that, had Our Lord wished to implement the promise we have been considering above, He could not have used any words more effective or less liable to be misunderstood. No explanation can make them simpler. In fact, once the literal meaning was questioned, the words became perfectly meaningless—so much so that in 1577 Christopher Rasperger was able to write a book on some two hundred different interpretations of them.

If Our Lord had intended a metaphor, He could easily have used one. There are over forty different words He could have used. He spoke in Aramaic, and if the word He used had meant "signify" or something similar, surely one of the accounts that have come down to us would contain some hint of it. Protestants have tried to gather texts against the literal interpretation of these words, but in every case the real meaning is evident from the nature of things, or from the manner of speaking, or from some previous warning.

Further, Christ was not speaking to modern Rationalists. Those who heard Him were ordinary men of the people, not given to analyzing obscure and mysterious phraseology. He was giving them His last will, speaking as a dying father to the children He was about to leave. They were hanging on His words, ready to accept whatever He should tell them. What absolute cruelty it would have been for Christ, the omniscient God, to whose gaze the future was ever present, to use on such an occasion a metaphor that would for centuries plunge the whole Christian world into stupid idolatry.

It is a universal principle of law that the words of a will must be taken in their natural, literal sense, because it is to be presumed that every sane testator is deeply concerned to draw up his will in clear language, without meaningless metaphors. Was the will of the God-Man to be an exception? He—who knew that for centuries the Eucharist would be the very center of all Christian worship and that for the Eucharist thousands would suffer and die—certainly instituted it in the plainest, most unmistakable language possible.

Moreover, St. Paul himself accepted the literal interpretation. After relating his account of the Last Supper, he goes on: "For as often as you shall eat this bread and drink the chalice, you shall show the death of the Lord, until he come. Therefore whosoever shall eat this bread or drink the chalice of the Lord unworthily, shall be guilty of the body and of the blood of the Lord. But let a man prove himself: and so let him eat of that bread, and drink of the chalice. For he that eateth and drinketh unworthily, eateth and drinketh judgment to himself, not discerning the body of the Lord." (*1 Cor.* 11:26-29). This is vigorous language, and the only possible explanation of it is that St. Paul was convinced that in the Holy Eucharist Christ is really and truly present.

And that is the only conclusion we can draw from the Scriptural quotations we have been considering. In the Blessed Eucharist, Christ left Himself, really, truly and substantially present. That dogma, defined by the Council of Trent, is the result of an unprejudiced examination of the Scriptural narrative.

The Real Presence has always been believed

For nearly two thousand years, the Catholic Church has consistently drawn the same inference. The Real Presence has always been the center of her worship. Fortunately, we possess abundant evidence of this from the very earliest times.

In 1873, Bryennios, the Greek Orthodox Metropolitan of Nicomedia, discovered the complete text of a little book of religious instruction probably written before the year 90 A.D. For centuries the book had been alluded to, but its exact nature was not known. It is called the *Didache* or the *Teaching of the Twelve Apostles,* and it is a summary of the moral, individual and social obligations of the first Christians. It is clear from Chapters 14 and 15 of this work that its compiler believed in the Real Presence, Holy Communion and the sacrificial nature of the Mass.

One of the greatest witnesses is St. Ignatius, the illustrious Bishop of Antioch, who was martyred in the year 107 A.D. On his way to Rome, where he was to be thrown to the wild beasts, he wrote letters to the Christian communities in various places. Their evidence is particularly valuable in view of the fact that they were composed only about ten years after St. John wrote his Gospel. To the Ephesians he wrote: "That you may obey the bishop and the priesthood with inseparable intention, breaking one Bread, which is the medicine of immortality, the antidote against death, giving life forever in Jesus Christ." (*Cap.* xx). To Smyrna he wrote of certain heretics: "They abstain from Eucharist and prayer, because they do not acknowledge the Eucharist to be the flesh of our Lord Jesus Christ, which suffered for our sins, which the Father raised up again by His loving-kindness. They, therefore, speaking against the gift of God, die in their dissension." (*Cap.* vii). It would be hard to find anywhere a more explicit statement than this.

St. Justin

Our next witness is St. Justin. He was born of pagan colonial parents in Palestine about the year 100. Having studied philosophy in various schools, he eventually became a Christian and a great defender of the Faith, for which he was martyred about 165 A.D.

Some thirteen years earlier, he had written to the Emperor, Antoninus Pius a plea in favor of the Christians, and a couple of years later he published an account of a *Dialogue with Tryphon,* a Jew he had met at Ephesus. His last work was another letter of protest to the Roman rulers and the Senate against the cruel injustices being perpetrated against the Christians. Describing to Antoninus Pius just what took place when the Christians met together for worship, St. Justin wrote: "We do not receive these as ordinary food or ordinary drink; but as by the Word of God, Jesus our Saviour was made flesh, and had both flesh and blood for our salvation, so also the food over which thanks have been given by the word of prayer instituted by Him . . . is, we are taught, both the flesh and blood of that Jesus incarnate." And he goes on to quote the words of institution in support. There is nothing here to indicate that the early Christians accepted anything less than the true, real and substantial presence of Christ in the Blessed Eucharist. St. Justin was explaining his and our doctrine to the pagans, and consequently he would be particularly careful about accuracy.

Other evidence of the Real Presence

St. Irenaeus—whom we have already met as a valuable witness to the early Church's belief in Papal Supremacy—has many passages which show belief in the Real Presence. In fact, he uses the known fact of Christ's Eucharistic Presence as an argument in favor of His divinity: "How shall they feel assured that the bread over which thanksgiving has been made is the Body of their Lord, and the chalice of His Blood, if they do not declare Him the Son of the world's Creator." (*Adv. Haer.* iv., 18). Several other passages in the same sense could be quoted, but to no purpose. The doctrine of the martyr is clarity itself.

It is, of course, possible to continue our quotations from the earliest writers of the Church on through the centuries. Those we have given, however, are sufficient to convince the enquirer that the doctrine of the Holy Eucharist as defined by the Council of Trent was accepted in even the first three centuries. In fact, to this day the Nestorian and Monophysite Churches—which (on account of their failure to accept the orthodox belief in the Hypostatic Union—the union of the two distinct natures, of God and man, in the one Person of Jesus Christ) broke away in the fifth century—believe in the Real Presence. It must, therefore, have been firmly believed by the whole Church at the time of their separation.

That this is so is proved, not only from the writings we have quoted, but also from an examination of the ancient liturgies, the Roman Catacombs and the inscription of Abercius, which we have already considered when speaking about the Pope. All conspire to clarify the sublime truth that the Blessed Sacrament is God Himself.

That is our Catholic Faith.

The significance of the Real Presence

Jesus Christ is really present as Man and as God in the Holy Eucharist, consecrated during every Mass and reserved in the tabernacles of Catholic Churches. His Body is there, His Blood is there, His Soul is there, His Godhead is there—the God who lived in endless ages alone before any creature was made, the God who created the Angels, men and all the material universe, the God who permeates the sun, the moon and the stars and every fraction of space with His presence. He, that same God, is present with His human nature, really, truly and substantially under the appearances of bread and wine.

The Child who lay on Mary's breast at Bethlehem, the Boy who played in the fields of Nazareth, the Youth who stood by Joseph to learn His trade, the Working Man who supported His Mother by His daily toil, the Preacher and the Wonder-Worker of Galilee and Judea, the Redeemer who suffered and died for us, He is the Holy Eucharist, the Sacrament of Sacraments, the very heart of Catholicism.

How dreadful is the loss of those who do not accept the Real Presence? If they seek Christ, they must draw Him out of the dim past of History; they must use their imagination to create a vivid image of Him engaged in His works of love. If only they could understand the wonder of the Eucharist, which brings Jesus as He is, whole and entire, human and divine, into the sphere of their present lives. If only they could realize that by this means they could touch Him, talk to Him, contemplate Him, or busy themselves about Him more closely, more intimately by far than did His dear friends at Bethany! Just as really as the Jews of Nazareth nearly two thousand years ago, men today are living in Jesus' town. He is in our midst as He was in the midst of those who conversed with Him in the flesh and beheld the sweet gentleness of His countenance. We are no less fortunate than those who knelt beside His crib at Bethlehem or heard His youthful voice at Nazareth or accompanied Him on the weary journeys of His Public Life. He is here, with us, just as He was there, with them.

"O Jesus! my Lord, my God, and my all! I believe that Thou in Thy living manhood art as truly present in the Blessed Sacrament as when Thou didst walk amidst men and converse with them. Relying on Thy word, which shall not pass away, I believe that Thou art here, ever living to make intercession for us. Here is Thy sacred Body, which hung upon the Cross; here is Thy soul, which was sorrowful unto death and agonized in the Garden of Olives on account of my sins; here are those sacred wounds made by the nails and spear; here are those eyes which looked with pity and love on the penitent Peter; here are those ears which heard the cruel cry of the Jews, 'Crucify Him' (*Mark* 15:13) and which listened so compassionately to all the ills of men. 'I do believe, Lord: help my unbelief.'" (*Mark* 9:23).

The Blessed Sacrament is God

Throughout the centuries sacred writers have vied with one another in describing the marvel of the Real Presence. It has been called the greatest work of God, the mirror of the divine perfections, the reflection of the wisdom, the immensity and the eternity of God, a type of all the operations of God, the teacher of the unity of God. It has been described as the continuation and the parallel of the Incarnation and the sum of its wonders, as the mirror of the life of Christ, as the triumph of the Church and even as its very life, as the explanation of the phenomena of the Church, as the compendium of all miracles, as the example of every virtue, as the fountain of all grace, as the magnet of souls. Yet, strive as they may, no writers, no poets, no Saints can say anything more outstanding than this truth— **The Blessed Sacrament is God**.

Chapter 26

The Holy Eucharist (2)

Why has Christ given Himself to us in the Holy Eucharist? *Christ has given Himself to us in the Holy Eucharist to be the life and the food of our souls. "He that eateth me, the same also shall live by me." "He that eateth this bread shall live for ever." (John 6:58, 59).*

Is Christ received whole and entire under either the species of bread or the species of wine alone? *Christ is received whole and entire under either the species of bread or the species of wine alone.*

In order to receive the Blessed Sacrament worthily what is required? *In order to receive the Blessed Sacrament worthily it is required that we be in the state of grace and fasting for one hour before receiving Holy Communion.*

What does it mean to be in the state of grace? *To be in the state of grace is to be free from mortal sin, and pleasing to God.*

Is it a mortal sin to receive Holy Communion in the state of mortal sin? *It is a mortal sin of sacrilege to receive Holy Communion in the state of mortal sin, "For he that eateth and drinketh unworthily, eateth and drinketh judgment to himself." (1 Cor. 11:29).*

Christ is really present

IN our last instruction we saw how Jesus Christ, who is God, has given us in the Blessed Eucharist His own Body and Blood. He becomes really present, under the appearances of bread and wine, when the words He said at the Last Supper are repeated by validly ordained priests during the Holy Sacrifice of Mass. In virtue of these words, the true Body and Blood of Christ become present—

for that is signified by the words. But, as Christ is now living gloriously in Heaven, One Person, at the same time God and Man, He must Himself be present, whole and entire, Godhead and Manhood, wherever either His Body or His Blood are present. Where a person's body and blood are, there he himself is, in person. In Christ there is no *human* person, as we have already seen (pages 122-123). Hence, when by the power of the words of Consecration, His Body and Blood become present under the appearances of bread and wine, He Himself, the Second Person of the Blessed Trinity, becomes present also. Thus, we understand the doctrine defined by the Council of Trent: "**If anyone shall deny that the Sacrament of the Blessed Eucharist contains truly, really and substantially the body and blood, together with the soul and divinity of Our Lord Jesus Christ, and consequently Christ whole and entire . . . let him be anathema**." (Chapter viii, Can. 1).

Wherever Christ's Body is present since His Ascension into Heaven, His Blood must be too, for they are inseparable in the living Christ. St. Paul already understood this: "Therefore whosoever shall eat this bread, or drink the chalice of the Lord unworthily, shall be guilty of the body and of the blood of the Lord." (*1 Cor.* 11:27). Therefore, Christ is whole and entire under the appearance of bread and whole and entire under the appearance of wine.

Similarly, Christ is present under each separate portion when the sacramental species are divided or broken. It is clear that at the Last Supper Christ consecrated only one piece of bread and then broke it, giving a piece to each of the Apostles, and one chalice of wine, from which they all took a sip. This truth is expressed by St. Thomas Aquinas in the verses of his lovely hymn, *Lauda Sion Salvatorem*: "He who partakes of Him neither severs, nor breaks, nor divides Him; he receives Him entire. Whether one or a thousand receive Him, one receives as much as a thousand do; and when received, He is not diminished."

Substance and accidents

We have spoken several times already about the **appearances** of bread and wine. We must explain this a little more in order to bring out a certain truth about the manner of Christ's Eucharistic presence. Consider any object you like—a loaf of bread, for instance. It can be of almost any shape, color, size or weight, so that it is obvious that none of these things is the bread itself. In fact, none of the things we can see or feel or establish any kind of contact with through our senses is the actual bread. The bread **has** these things, but it is not they. They are **appearances;** philosophers call them **"accidents." The thing itself, in its essential nature,** is called the **"substance."** Our senses make no contact with the actual substance. Therefore, the substance could change, and we would not *know* it had changed, unless the appearances changed as well.

Transubstantiation

We have seen that Christ at the Last Supper took a piece of bread into His hands and said over it, "This is My body." The Apostles saw no change, but it is of our Faith that at that moment the **substance** of bread gave way to the **substance** of Christ's Body, while the **appearances** of bread still remained. There was a change-over of substance—a **trans-substantiation**. We know it happened because Christ, who is Truth Itself, said so.

The words Our Lord used were, **"This is My body."** "This," the object in His hand, He declared to be identical with His Body—a fact which could not possibly be true unless a change of substance took place. As the *Catechism of the Council of Trent* puts it: "When instituting this Sacrament, Our Lord Himself said: *'This is my body.'* The word *this* expresses the entire substance of the thing present; and therefore, if the substance of bread remained, Our Lord could not have truly said: *'This is my body.'*"

That such has always been the teaching of the Catholic Church is clear from the following short quotations from St. Ambrose and St. Augustine: "You see how efficacious are the words of Christ. If the word of the Lord Jesus is so powerful as to summon into existence that which did not exist, namely, the world, how much more powerful is His word to change into something else that which already has existence?" (St. Ambrose, *De Sacr.* lib, iv, c. 4). "Before the Consecration, it is bread, but no sooner are the words of Consecration pronounced, than from bread it becomes the flesh of Christ." (*Ibid.*) "Although the species of bread and wine are visible, yet we must believe that after Consecration, the body and blood of Christ alone are there." (St. Ambrose, quoted in Gratian, p. 3, dist. ii, 74). "We faithfully confess that before Consecration it is bread and wine, the product of nature; but after Consecration, it is the Body and Blood of Christ, consecrated by the blessing." (St. Augustine, *ibid.* 41).

The *Catechism of the Council of Trent* goes on to point out that since Christ is present **substantially**, He is not in the Holy Eucharist as in a place. The entire nature of water is present in a drop of it just as much as it is present in a lake. So the whole nature of Christ is present under the appearances of bread in the tiniest consecrated Host. While He remains unchanged in Heaven, the substance of His Body becomes present in the Eucharist. As this is a unique manner of presence revealed to us by God, for which we have no parallel in worldly experience, we cannot hope to elucidate it perfectly. We should be content to admire God's wisdom in coming to us under the appearances of bread and wine—the ordinary food of man—in a manner impervious to the senses.

How Christ is present

Perhaps the manner of Christ's Eucharistic presence will be more clearly understood by the consideration of the following questions and answers:

a) What happens to the substance of the bread and wine at the moment of consecration? Is it annihilated? Does it return to the elements of which it is composed?

The Body and Blood of Christ become present by way of change, not by pushing the substance of bread and wine into smaller space. There is neither annihilation nor a return to constituent elements nor compression. There is simply change. Our Lord said: "**This** is my Body," not, "**here** is my Body."

b) How can the substance of bread be changed into the substance of Christ?

God's power brings about a change of substance. Is there any other way in which Christ could become really present? Yet, God does not leave Heaven that He may reside in the Host; nor is the Body of Christ everywhere. It becomes present under the appearances of bread and wine by the power of God. By experiment we can prove that the appearances of bread and wine remain; we have God's word for it that the substance of bread and wine is no longer there. Consequently, the appearances of bread and wine are not supported by their own proper substance, but by the power of God. You cannot transfer a grin from the face of a cheshire cat to the stone walls of Chester Castle; in the same way, the appearances of bread and wine are not transferred from bread and wine to Jesus Christ. It is not that He begins to look like bread and wine. The appearances of bread and wine remain; but, retaining all their natural characteristics of color, taste and so on, they are miraculously maintained by the direct operation of God.

c) Is the whole Christ present in this Sacrament?

Yes, in the same way as the whole substance of bread is contained in every crumb of the bread.

d) Is the whole Christ present in every particle of the Host?

Yes, in the same way as the whole substance of bread is contained in every crumb, however small.

(e) Is it not ridiculous to think of a perfect man compressed within a wafer?

There is no question of compression or of shrinking. The *substance* of Christ's Body is present by the power of the words of Consecration; everything else is present in the way substance is present: intangible, invisible, indifferent to the limitations of space. In this way, in the way of substance, the whole of Christ's physical Body is present, with all its dimensions—but you cannot see or touch it, simply because you cannot see or touch substance. The whole of the substance of wine is present in the tiniest drop or in a cask. When you pour out a glass you do not injure the substance in any way, even though a separation takes place in the appearances. Similarly, when you break the consecrated Host, you do not break the substance of Christ.

When bread corrupts, it eventually ceases to be bread; the substance changes into something else. When a consecrated Host corrupts, the Body of Christ does not corrupt; it remains so long as the appearances of bread remain, so long as the *accidents* react as bread would react under chemical tests; but when the corruption has progressed to such an extent that those accidents are no longer the accidents of bread, the presence of Christ is withdrawn, and the new accidents are then supported in the natural way by their own proper substance. There are two miracles in this Sacrament; the first in the changing of the substance of bread and wine into the substance of Christ, and the second is the maintenance of the accidents of bread and wine by the direct operation of God.

Why Christ is present

The Catholic Catechism drawn up by Cardinal Gasparri (1852-1943) tells us that Christ instituted the Sacrament of the Holy Eucharist: 1) that out of His deep love for us He might ever remain present in our midst and thus induce us to love and worship Him; and 2) that He might be united to us in Holy Communion, might be the heavenly food of our souls, and thus enable us to safeguard and preserve our spiritual life, and finally be our Viaticum for our journey to eternity at the close of our lives.

Food for our souls

Our Lord has urged us, as we have seen, to eat His Flesh and drink His Blood. Those who refuse to do so are threatened with damnation, but those who respond to His invitation are promised eternal life.

The Blessed Eucharist is, let it be repeated, Christ Himself, the source of all graces. From Him all the other Sacraments derive any goodness they possess. Hence the pre-eminence of this, the Blessed Sacrament. St. Augustine expresses well the fundamental truth: "I am the food of the grown. Grow and thou shalt eat Me; nor shalt thou change Me into thee, as thy bodily food, but thou shalt be changed into Me." (*Confess.* vii, c. 18).

Union with Christ

"He that eateth my flesh and drinketh my blood, abideth in me, and I in him." (*John* 6:57). Those words alone should be sufficient incentive to us greatly to desire Holy Communion, for no other Sacrament can confer grace in such abundance as this, which confers the Source of all grace. In fact, the special, the primary effect of Holy Communion is union with Christ and the members of His Mystical Body by charity. What other interpretation can be put on the words of Christ? He, and they who receive Him, live by one another, remain in one another, and other than that, there could be no closer union or more intimate friendship.

Not only is union with Christ promoted by Holy Communion, but so also is union with one another. "For we, being many, are one bread, one body, all that partake of one bread." (*1 Cor.* 10:17). And St. John Chrysostom comments: "For what is the bread? The Body of Christ. And what do we become who partake of it? The Body of Christ, not many bodies, but one body. For as the bread consisting of many grains is made one, so that the grains nowhere appear—they exist, indeed, but their difference is not seen by reason of their conjunction—so we are conjoined both with each other and with Christ; there not being one body for thee and thy neighbor to be nourished by, but the very same for all." (*Hom.* xxiv, *1 Cor.*).

In the other Sacraments we are sanctified by some element—water, oil; or by some action—the laying on of hands. But in this Sacrament, He comes to us Himself under the sacramental signs of the appearances of bread and wine. "It is called Communion and truly is so, because by it we communicate with Christ," says St. John Damascene. Hence, **the purpose of Holy Communion is to incorporate us more completely into the Mystical Body of Christ**.

St. Cyril of Alexandria compares the union between Christ and the soul in Holy Communion to that which takes place between two pieces of melting wax. "He has kneaded Himself up with us and fashioned us into one complete body, that we may be one as a body joined to the head," adds St. John Chrysostom. **Thus does Holy Communion transform us into Christ**; we pass in some mysterious way into Him, not that we become one nature or one person with Him, but in such a way that He possesses Himself of our souls and bodies. He pervades the soul through and through in all its powers, makes it His own and molds and shapes it to His Divine wishes and instincts, so that we can say with St. Paul: "And I live, now not I; but Christ liveth in me." (*Gal.* 2:20).

Further effects of Holy Communion

Holy Communion actually pours charity into the soul when it is received with attention and devotion. Just as natural food not only supports the body but actually increases it, so Holy Communion invigorates and refreshes the soul, stirring up charity within it.

Moreover, this holy Sacrament forgives "lesser faults," repairing the life of the soul in much the same way as natural food restores and repairs the daily waste of bodily life. "The daily bread is taken as a remedy for daily infirmity," says St. Ambrose. (*De Sacr.*, lib. iv. c. 6). Hence, so long as no affection is retained for venial sins, they will be forgiven by Holy Communion.

Nor is that all. Holy Communion preserves those who receive It from sin in the future. Mortal sin is death to the soul; Holy Communion is life. The devil can scarcely retain much power over souls sprinkled with the Precious Blood of Christ. Therefore, whereas it does not remove temptation, Holy Communion certainly gives grace to resist it. Just as a well-nourished body will not fall prey to all the germs it inhales, so will a soul regularly nourished with the Body and Blood of Christ be able to repel temptations from the world, the flesh and the devil.

Holy Communion also remits the temporal punishment due to sin, in virtue of the fact that it excites charity within the soul, an act of which satisfies for sin and remits part or all of the temporal punishment due to it, according to the fervor with which the act is made.

Lastly, Holy Communion is a pledge of future glory and confers a title to a glorious resurrection. "He that eateth my flesh, and drinketh my blood, hath everlasting life: and I will raise him up in the last day." (*John* 6:55). All the Sacraments, of course, confer Sanctifying Grace, which is the seed of glory, but the Holy Eucharist confers a right to a glorious resurrection, due to the union of the communicant with Christ. Our bodies are, so to speak, consecrated, made holy, by the contact with Christ; a special affinity and kinship is set up between them and Christ, so that He links our flesh to His own glorified flesh and gives us most powerful help against temptation. During His earthly life, He raised to life bodies by His mere touch or word; how much more will He raise up our bodies which have been so closely united with His own sacred Flesh?

Frequent Communion is desirable

In view of all this, it is only too clear that we ought to desire to receive Holy Communion as frequently as possible. Here is the voice of the Church: "Frequent and daily Communion, as a thing most ardently desired by Christ Our Lord and by the Catholic Church, should be open to all the Faithful, of whatever rank and condition of life, so that no one who is in the state of grace, and who approaches the Holy Table with a right intention, can lawfully be hindered therefrom.

"A right intention consists in approaching the Holy Table not through routine, vainglory or human respect, but for the purpose of pleasing God, of becoming more closely united to Him, and of seeking a medicine for human infirmities.

"Although it is most desirable that frequent and daily communicants should be free even from venial sin, yet it is sufficient that they be free from mortal sin and have a purpose of sinning no more." (*Decree* of 1905).

Therefore, for those who are not in the state of mortal sin to refrain from receiving Holy Communion merely because they are afraid of receiving unworthily, or because of violent temptations, or because of fear of past sins, or because they have not been to weekly Confession is clearly against the mind of the Church. In fact, these things, which are so easily made excuses, are the very reasons why Holy Communion should be received frequently. The perfect need it to keep them perfect; the imperfect to make them perfect; the strong to keep them strong; the weak to make them strong. Frequent Confession and Communion and the advice of one's confessor or spiritual director are of immense benefit to those who suffer such doubts and fears. If a person with a correct and tender conscience thinks that he **did** commit a mortal sin since his last worthy Confession, **he should always refrain from Communion**, make a sincere Confession, and receive Communion later. Thus, he knows he has received worthily. But those who have scruples or who tend to that problem, should obey the advice of a good confessor (the priest in Confession).

Preparation and thanksgiving

More abundant fruit will be received from Holy Communion if a serious preparation is made before and a suitable thanksgiving after receiving It. But if circumstances make these impossible, it is better to receive without profound recollection than not to receive at all. "Place in the balance all the good works of the world against one well-made Holy Communion. It will be like weighing a grain of dust against a mountain," said the holy Cure D'Ars. "If it is your daily bread," asks St. Augustine, "why do you only receive it yearly?"

Prudence demands that over such a grave matter the advice of one's confessor should be sought from time to time, but he will not discourage from frequent Holy Communion one who is in the state of grace and approaches with a right intention.

Further practical points

The following are further practical points taken from the Gasparri *Catechism* in regard to reception of Holy Communion. They should be studied carefully.

1. In order to receive the Holy Eucharist worthily, in addition to being baptized (for Baptism is requisite for the reception of any other Sacrament) and in the state of grace (which is requisite for the reception of all the Sacraments of the Living), we must also under pain of grave sin, keep the natural fast.

2. A person who, when about to receive Holy Communion, discovers that he is in the state of mortal sin, should, even though he feels he is truly contrite, go to Confession first. "Now, ecclesiastical usage declares that such an examination is necessary in order that no one conscious to himself of mortal sin, however contrite he may feel, ought to receive the Sacred Eucharist without previous Sacramental Confession. This the holy Council has decreed to be invariably observed by all Christians . . ." (Council of Trent, Session XIII Chapter 7.)

3. The natural fast means that for one hour before the time of receiving Holy Communion we may take nothing by way of food, drink or alcoholic beverage. Water and medicine may be taken, even

right up to the time of receiving Holy Communion. (Cf. Canon 919, the 1983 *Code of Canon Law.*)

4. If we receive Holy Communion not fasting, we commit a grave sin of sacrilege.

5. Holy Communion is allowed without fasting when there is danger of death, or when it is necessary in order to prevent some irreverence to the Blessed Sacrament.

6. Invalids who have been ill in bed for a month and have no certain hope of quick recovery are allowed, with the prudent advice of their confessor, to receive Holy Communion once or twice a week, even though they have taken medicine or something to drink beforehand.

7. Preparation for Holy Communion consists in meditating attentively and devoutly for a while on what we are about to receive and in making diligent acts of faith, hope, charity and contrition.

8. Thanksgiving after Holy Communion consists in meditating attentively and devoutly for a while on what we have received and in making acts of faith, hope and charity, with good resolutions, acts of gratitude and petitions.

9. After Holy Communion, we should particularly ask Our Lord for the graces necessary for our own and our neighbor's eternal salvation, more especially the grace of final perseverance; also for the Church, that she may prevail against her enemies, and for the souls of the faithful departed who may be in Purgatory.

10. Besides the precept of Easter Communion, there is an obligation to receive it when in danger of death—from whatever cause it may arise.

11. When a person has already received Communion, he can receive it again on the same day as Viaticum (Holy Communion received when in danger of death) or when it may be necessary to prevent some irreverence toward the Blessed Sacrament. (The new norms allow Holy Communion to be received a second time on the same day when received the second time in conjunction with participation at a Mass. Viaticum may still be received when danger of death exists, even if the person has already received twice that day. Cf. Canons 917 and 921, pars. 1 and 2, *Code of Canon Law*, 1983. —Publisher, 2002.)

In conclusion, we must show in practical ways, our belief in and love of God-made-Man ever present in the Blessed Sacrament, not only by receiving Him frequently in Holy Communion, but by visiting Him often during His lonely sojourn in the tabernacle on the altar, where He is reserved for our adoration; by taking part in the public acts of faith, which are part of the liturgy of the Church—the Forty Hours Devotion, processions, etc.; by watching during Exposition, when He is solemnly enthroned to receive our homage; by contributing to the building and adornment of His earthly dwelling-places, our Catholic Churches; in short, by making the Eucharistic Lord the very center of our lives.

"O sacred banquet, in which Christ is received, the memory of His Passion is renewed, the mind is filled with grace, and a pledge of future glory is given to us.

> Thou didst give them bread from heaven:
> Containing in itself all sweetness.

Let Us Pray.

"O God, who under a wonderful Sacrament hast left us a memorial of Thy Passion, grant us, we beseech Thee, so to venerate the sacred Mysteries of Thy Body and Blood as ever to feel within ourselves the fruit of Thy redemption: Who livest and reignest for ever and ever, Amen." (Part of the liturgy for the Benediction of the Blessed Sacrament.)

Chapter 27

Holy Mass— The Eucharistic Sacrifice

Is the Blessed Eucharist a Sacrament only? *The Blessed Eucharist is not a Sacrament only; it is also a sacrifice.*

What is a sacrifice? *A sacrifice is the offering of a victim by a priest to God alone, in testimony of His being the Sovereign Lord of all things.*

What is the Sacrifice of the New Law? *The Sacrifice of the New Law is the Holy Mass.*

What is the Holy Mass? *The Holy Mass is the Sacrifice of the Body and Blood of Jesus Christ, really present on the altar under the appearances of bread and wine, and offered to God for the living and the dead.*

Is the Holy Mass one and the same Sacrifice with that of the Cross? *The Holy Mass is one and the same Sacrifice with that of the Cross, inasmuch as Christ, who offered Himself, a bleeding victim, on the Cross to His Heavenly Father, continues to offer Himself in an unbloody manner on the altar, through the ministry of His priests.*

For what ends is the Sacrifice of the Mass offered? *The Sacrifice of the Mass is offered for four ends: first, to give supreme honor and glory to God; second, to thank Him for all His benefits; third, to satisfy God for our sins and to obtain grace of repentance; and fourth, to obtain all other graces and blessings through Jesus Christ.*

Is the Mass also a memorial of the Passion and Death of Our Lord? *The Mass is also a memorial of the Passion and Death of Our Lord, for Christ at His Last Supper said, "Do this for a commemoration of Me." (Luke 22:19).*

Sacrifice

W E often use the word *sacrifice* in everyday speech. It means giving something up for a higher purpose. Thus a young man sacrifices his life for his country in war; a girl sacrifices her opportunity of marriage to care for her sick mother; a student sacrifices his leisure time in the pursuit of learning.

In Scripture, however, *sacrifice* has a special technical meaning: **It is the offering to God of some sanctified object, made by a legitimate priest, who destroys or otherwise changes that object in acknowledgement of God's supreme dominion over man**.

The history of sacrifice in the Bible shows that **every true sacrifice has six distinguishing marks:**

1. **An external, visible sign united to internal devotion**. In the Old Testament these were lambs, goats, doves, oil, bread, salt, wine and other things.

2. It must be **offered to God alone.**

3. It must be **offered in acknowledgement that God is the highest authority, and in profession of our complete submission to Him.**

4. It must be **offered by a priest and presented by him to God** for and in the name of the people. Even peoples who had only natural religions had a priesthood, consisting essentially of people in authority who alone were empowered to offer sacrifice.

5. **The purification of the victim** through prescribed external ceremonies as a preparation before the offering.

6. **The victim must be partially or totally destroyed.**

The pages of the Old Testament are full of references to sacrifices as prescribed by God Himself. The most important of them was the Jewish Pasch, a sacrifice in memory of the deliverance of the Israelite people from the slavery of Egypt.

Yet, not only the Jewish, but practically **every religion has had a system of sacrifice**; therefore, **sacrifice is an essential feature of man's relation with his Creator**. Men want to express their sentiments toward God, and history has proved that they have universally found that sacrifice is the best way to do it. It is a tangible expression of adoration and devotion; it expresses thanksgiving, too, and sorrow for offenses against God; it is also an act of supplication or intercession. These four motives are to be found more or less completely in all sacrifices.

In our last instructions we considered the Holy Eucharist, the Sacrament of the true Body and Blood of Christ really present under the appearances of bread and wine. We shall see in a few moments how it is also a sacrifice.

The Christian Sacrifice

Sacrifice is natural to man; it has been an essential element in all religions. Is it not to be expected, then, that in the religion of Jesus Christ, which we have seen is universal and intended for all men, there should be a sacrifice? Was the New Testament to lack what the Old Testament possessed? If so, how could the New be said to be the fulfillment and completion of the Old? If the Christian religion were to lack sacrifice, what adequate method of worshipping God would it possess? The New Testament is founded on the sacrifice of the Cross (cf. page 125f), from which it receives its life and meaning. Is it not to be expected that this supreme sacrifice would in some way be perpetuated in Christianity?

Melchisedech and Malachias

In *Psalm 109* King David prophesied of Christ: "Thou art a priest for ever according to the order of Melchisedech," and his words were applied to Christ specifically by the author of the Epistle to the Hebrews (*Heb.* 5: 6). Now Melchisedech, high priest and King of Salem, offered a sacrifice of bread and wine in thanksgiving for Abraham's victory. Therefore, **the priesthood of Christ must be like that of Melchisedech**; His sacrifice must be of bread and wine.

Malachias, the last of the Old Testament Prophets, speaks thus of the sacrifice of the New Law: "I have no pleasure in you [priests of Jewry], saith the Lord of hosts: and I will not receive a gift of your hand. For from the rising of the sun even to the going down, my name is great among the Gentiles, and in every place there is sacrifice, and there is offered to my name a clean oblation." (*Mal.* 1:10-11). Clearly and definitely the sacrifice of the Old Law is rejected, and its place is to be taken by a clean (unbloody) sacrifice offered universally (from the rising of the sun to its going down) by the Gentiles.

Put together these two prophecies, and you find that the Sacrifice of the New Law is to consist in an unbloody offering under a rite of bread and wine by the Gentiles [non-Jews] all over the world.

The Last Supper

Now turn to the Last Supper in Sacred Scriptures, bearing in mind what we have already said about the institution there of the Holy Eucharist. Recall the words of Christ again. Why does He say: "This is my body, **which is given for you**" and "This is the chalice, the new testament in my blood, **which shall be shed for you?**" (*Luke* 22:19-20). The meaning of Christ—particularly clear from the use of the present participle passive in the Greek text—was that His Body and Blood were "here and now" being offered for sacrifice eucharistically, as on the next day they would be physically. Note that He said that His Body and Blood were being given not **to** you, but **for** you, indicating that the Eucharist is a sacrificial offering to God for the remission of our sins. Then He told his Apostles to repeat His sacrifice for the Church, which He knew was to go on until the End of Time: "Do this for a commemoration of me."

According to St. Matthew, Our Lord at the Last Supper called His blood **"of the New Testament, which shall be shed for many unto the remission of sins."** (*Matt.* 26:28). Moses, sprinkling the people with blood after the re-establishment of the covenant of the Old Law, said: "This is the blood of the covenant which the Lord hath made with you." (*Exodus* 24:8). It was the blood of sacrifice. Our Lord definitely connects His Blood, the Blood of the New Testament, with the sacrificial blood of the Old. It has the same character as the others; it is the blood of sacrifice, sealing a new relationship between God and man. Thus, the Last Supper included the real sacrifice of Christ's Body and Blood in an unbloody manner, which was sealed by the Blood of Christ on the Cross the next day. Holy Mass is the unbloody, clean Sacrifice of Jesus Christ on

Calvary, re-enacted under the appearances of bread and wine, as instituted by Christ at the Last Supper and repeated or continued right up to and including our time. The Mass, too, is therefore also a sacrifice.

St. Paul

In the passage we have already considered from his first letter to the Corinthians, St. Paul contrasts the Christian Eucharist with the sacrifices of the pagans: "But the things which the heathens sacrifice, they sacrifice to devils, and not to God . . . You cannot drink the chalice of the Lord, and the chalice of the devils: you cannot be partakers of the table of the Lord, and of the table of devils." (*1 Cor.* 10:20-21). The comparison would be meaningless if the Eucharist were not a true and real sacrifice.

The Epistle to the Hebrews again refers to the essentials of sacrifice: "We have an altar, whereof they have no power to eat who serve the tabernacle." (*Heb.* 13:10). St. Paul is trying here to console the Jewish Christians in case any of them should regret being cut off from their ancestral worship, and his clear meaning is that our religion has a sacrifice just as the religion of the Old Testament had sacrifices. But the two are distinct.

Tradition

Turning once more to the Tradition of the Church, we find that from the earliest times Christian writers, including the "Fathers of the Church," use such expressions as "sacrifice," "oblation," "host," "offering," "victim," "altar" and "priest" in reference to the Holy Eucharist.

St. Cyprian says quite definitely: "Because he offered bread and wine and blessed Abraham, Melchisedech was a priest of the Most High God. But who is a greater priest than Our Lord Jesus Christ, who offered not only the bread and wine of Melchisedech, but His own Body and Blood?" (*Lib.* 2, *epist.* 3).

St. Hippolytus, who lived at the beginning of the third century, wrote a treatise in which he puts into the mouth of Christ at the Last Judgment these words: "Come forth, ye bishops and priests, ye who have daily offered My Body and My Precious Blood." (*Lib. de Antichristo*).

Just as in the case of the Real Presence, there is valuable evidence of the belief of the early Church regarding the sacrificial nature of the Mass to be found in the Catacombs beneath Rome. There one sees the Eucharistic symbols of bread and wine, the fish (the accepted symbol of Christ) and, side by side with them, pictures of the sacrifice of Abraham and of a priest offering sacrifice at the altar.

Holy Mass, Calvary re-enacted

The only conclusion from all these considerations is that the Holy Eucharist is not only a Sacrament, but the One Sacrifice of the New Law, and **as a sacrifice, we call it the Holy Mass**.

But how is Holy Mass related to the Sacrifice of Christ on Calvary? Catholic belief is that **the Mass is simply Calvary re-enacted**—though in a sacramental, symbolic, but nonetheless **real** manner. Let us consider the following.

Already we have shown at considerable length that Jesus Christ is the High Priest of the New Law, in virtue of His sacrificial death on the Cross (Page 125f). Our observations about the eucharistic sacrifice according to the rite of Melchisedech, that fulfilled the prophecy of Malachias, that was instituted by Christ at the Last Supper and referred to by St. Paul—make it clear that He (Christ) is also the Eucharistic Priest. On Calvary, He made once and for all the necessary sacrifice of reparation, **but He is a Priest forever. Priests of this earth are merely his agents, offering sacrifice in His name.**

There is no doubt that Christ was the Victim of the Cross. He, too, is the Victim of the Mass. Having ascended into Heaven, He retains the marks of victimhood: the wounds in His hands, feet and side. Consequently, in the Holy Eucharist, He is still a Victim, manifesting His victim state through His abasement in assuming the appearances of bread and wine and through the mystic separation of His Body from His Blood, signified by the separate Consecration of the bread and wine and by the two species (bread and wine).

Thus, the Sacrifice of the Cross and the Sacrifice of the Mass have each the same Priest and each the same Victim, Jesus Christ. And both are offered by means of the same Body and Blood, visible on the Cross, but hidden on the altar.

Therefore, Calvary and the Mass are essentially one and the same sacrifice.

Recall the six essentials for a true sacrifice and you will see how they are present in the sacrifice of Christ. 1) There is a true Victim, external, visible and certainly animated by internal devotion. 2) He is offered to God alone, atoning for the sins of man. "For God sent not his Son into the world, to judge the world, but that the world may be saved by him." (*John* 3:17). 3) He is offered as an acknowledgement of God's supreme authority, 4) by a Priest, Christ Himself. 5) In this case there was no need for the victim to be purified (although in the traditional Offertory of the Mass there is a "purification of the host before it is consecrated); 6) all that was necessary was that He be destroyed, and this certainly took place through the death of Christ on the Cross, a death attributed to His one divine personality.

The objects for which Mass is offered

The four objects of all sacrifice are found in a super-eminent way in the Sacrifice of the Mass. It is offered:

1. **To honor and glorify God**, and what could do this more effectively than the offering to God of an Infinite Victim by an Infinite Priest—both being His own Son? All the prayers of all the Saints are as nothing compared with one such sacrifice.

2. **To thank God for His goodness**. The very word "eucharist" means "thanksgiving." God has made it possible for us to repay His infinite kindness by offering to Him an infinite gift in Holy Mass.

3. **To make atonement**. Just as Calvary reconciled all the world to God, so the special effect of the Mass is to operate our reconciliation with Him. God will certainly be appeased by the offering of such a Priceless Gift as His own beloved Son—not that Mass directly cancels sin, for in itself Mass is not a Sacrament; but it has the power to propitiate for sin by giving the graces needed to make us seek forgiveness.

Mass has also the power to cancel the temporal punishment

(spiritual debt) due to sin. This must be paid by the sinner either on earth or in Purgatory. It is our debt to God. Our Lord at the Last Supper said expressly that His Blood was being shed "unto the remission of sins." (*Matt.* 26:28). Hence it has been the tradition of the Church to offer up Mass especially in propitiation for sins and for the relief of the Poor Souls still suffering in Purgatory from the temporal punishment due to their sins. When St. Monica, St. Augustine's mother, was dying, she had no other request to make of him and his companions than that "everywhere, wherever they might be, they would remember her at the altar," and her son states that after death, prayers and the Sacrifice of Redemption were offered for her.

4. **In supplication**, for in the Mass we unite ourselves with Christ, the divine Mediator who prays with us and for us, offering for us His own adorable Body and Blood. The Mass is surely, then, the most powerful means at our disposal of attaining all the graces and blessings we need. Temporal blessings, too, will also flow from the riches of the Mass, but only in so far as our requests are in accordance with God's holy will.

In a previous instruction we considered the wonderful doctrine of the Mystical Body of Christ. We saw how every baptized Christian is a cell of Christ's spiritual organism, the Church. All the cells gain or lose by the action of the other cells. Now, from this Mystical Body, the Mass—the infinite sacrifice of the Body and Blood of Christ—is rising to Heaven from morning to night somewhere in the world. Hence, the whole Church—the Church Triumphant, the Church Militant and the Church Suffering—benefits by the continuous offering of this Sacrifice. Even the Saints in Heaven are rejoiced by the ceaseless stream of honor and glory rising in their honor before the eternal throne of God.

When Mass is offered for individuals, they certainly benefit, but God has kept hidden the secret of the extent to which each soul will benefit. We know that one Mass could pay the debt of all the souls in Purgatory and of all the Faithful on earth because it is infinite, but God's justice and His positive will in the matter have to be taken into account as well.

It is not possible for us here to describe in detail all the beautiful ceremonies of the Mass. Those who love the Mass as they ought will obtain some of the many pamphlets and books which explain the significance of everything connected with it.* For us a very brief summary must suffice.

Vestments

To celebrate Mass, the priest uses *special vestments*. This shows that he is set apart specially from the rest of men for the purpose of offering the Infinite Sacrifice. The vestments worn by the Catholic priests to offer Mass have come down to us from antiquity. Early on, special garments were set aside for those who offered the Holy Sacrifice. The Church, always conservative, still retains the traditional vestments of the priest for Mass. They are themselves an excellent witness of the continuity of the Church. In the course of time, they have been modified and embellished somewhat, but essentially they have remained the same.

Some of the vestments used are in different colors because each day in the year is set aside as the celebration of a particular feast in honor of which the Mass is offered. The colors have been adopted to remind us of the significance of these feasts—white, for Our Lord, Our Lady and Saints who were not martyrs; red, for Masses of the Holy Ghost (the Flame of God's Love), the Precious Blood and martyrs; purple for Masses of penance and supplication; black for Masses of the dead; and green when there is no special feast apart from the ordinary Sunday.

The actual ceremonies of the Mass are very ancient. In fact, in the works of St. Justin mentioned in a previous instruction, we find descriptions of Mass in the Catacombs in the second century which would fit Mass as we know it today in all its essentials.

---

*The very finest book for popular reading about the Mass that we know of is Ven. Martin von Cochem's *The Incredible Catholic Mass*, TAN, Rockford, Illinois. 1997. This book will inspire both priests and people alike. —Publisher, 2002).

The ceremonies of Holy Mass

Here is a very brief view of the traditional Mass:

A. **Prologue:**
1. Prayers at the foot of the altar, originally the priest's private preparation.
2. The *Introit* said at the right-hand side of the altar (i.e., the people's right). Originally it was a psalm sung by the choir as the priest moved to the altar in procession.

B. **Prayers and instructions:**
1. The *Kyrie,* a preliminary litany, in Greek, 5th century.
2. The *Gloria in Excelsis* in joyful Masses. Drawn from ancient documents and introduced into Sunday Masses about 500 A.D.
3. Prayers or *Collects*, sound the *motif* of the feast or occasion. On special days the Romans assembled in one church (*Collects*) before marching to another for Mass. Before setting out, a prayer was said, *Oratio ad Collectam.*
4. The *Epistle,* or Lesson, from Scripture, adapting the Jewish custom of a Scriptural reading.
5. The *Gradual, Alleluia Chant or Tract*, a portion of a psalm; so-called because it was originally led by the chanter standing on a step (*gradus*).
6. The *Gospel*, the life and words of Christ, during the reading of which all stand.
7. The *Creed*, said in certain Masses. Found in the Mass since the 5th century.

C. **The offering of gifts:**
1. The *Offertory Antiphon*, now said by the priest, was once chanted by the choir. Originally sung while the people brought their offerings in procession to the altar.
2. The *Offering of the bread*. God is asked to accept the unspotted Host to be offered by an unworthy servant.
3. *Wine and water are mixed*—only a drop of water or so, to signify the union of the members of the Mystical Body with their Head, also symbolizing the major role played by Christ

and the minor role played by man in man's salvation.

4. The *Offering of the chalice,* that, when consecrated, it may be accepted by God "as a sweet odor for our salvation."

5. The *Offering of ourselves* for the sacrifice offered externally; signifies the internal surrender of the soul to God. (In High Mass incense is blessed and used.)

6. The priest *washes his hands,* saying the psalm *Lavabo.* Originally a necessity after handling the gifts of the people.

7. The *Orate Fratres.* Turning to the people, the priest asks them to pray that his sacrifice *and theirs* will be acceptable to God.

8. The *Secret* or silent prayer, the oldest Offertory prayer, the purpose of which is for the priest and people to express their spirit of priesthood and victimhood, of offering and being offered.

D. **The Canon** (First part). Canon means fixed rule, and is that part which does not change.

1. A *dialogue* between priest and people said to date to Apostolic times.

2. The *Preface*—a solemn address before (*prae-fatio*) God. The word originally applied to the whole Canon.

3. The *Sanctus*, a hymn of praise from Scripture.

E. **The Canon** (Second part).

"Of all holy things this Sacrifice is the most holy; to the end that it might be worthily and reverently offered and received, the Catholic Church instituted, many years ago, the sacred Canon, so pure from every error, that nothing is contained therein which does not in the highest degree savor of a certain holiness and piety, and raise up into God the minds of those that offer the Mass. For it is composed out of the very words of the Lord, the traditions of the Apostles, and the pious institutions also of holy Pontiffs." (Council of Trent, Sess. XXII).

1. Prayer for God's acceptance of the sacrifice and for the Church Militant, mentioning the Pope, the local Bishop and some of the faithful by name. Called the *Commemoration of the Living*.

2. *Commemoration of the Church Triumphant*, begging the intercession of the Apostles, early Popes and Roman martyrs.
3. *Immediate preparation for the Consecration*.
4. **The Consecration (and major Elevation immediately after the Consecration)** when Transubstantiation takes place as the priest pronounces the words of institution used by Christ at the Last Supper, and then raises the Consecrated Host and Chalice for the veneration of the people.
5. The *Victim is offered to God*, while the priest recalls the principal events in Christ's life and the sacrifices of the Old Testament.
6. The *Commemoration of the Dead*, some of whom are mentioned by name.
7. Second *commemoration of the Church Militant and the Church Triumphant*—"us sinners . . . Thy holy Apostles and Martyrs."
8. *Conclusion* of the Canon when the priest raises the Consecrated Species to God with these words: "By Him, and with Him, and in Him, is to Thee, God the Father Almighty in the unity of the Holy Ghost, all honor and glory for ever and ever. Amen." Thus is summed up the first object of the Sacrifice.

F. **The Sacrificial Banquet**.
1. The *Lord's Prayer*, in the Mass since the 6th century.
2. The *Breaking of the Host*, as Christ did at the Last Supper. One piece is placed in the Chalice on top of the Precious Blood.
3. The *Agnus Dei*, the words of St. John the Baptist hailing Christ as the Lamb of God, recalling the sacrificial lamb of the Jewish pasch.
4. *Preparation for Holy Communion* (In High Mass, the Kiss of Peace). Three prayers.
5. The *Priest's Communion* and, usually, the *Communion of the people*.

G. **Thanksgiving**.
1. The *Communion antiphon* (formerly sung during the distribution of Holy Communion to the people).
2. The *Postcommunion prayers*. Thanksgiving.
3. The *Ite Missa Est* or solemn dismissal.

4. The *Blessing* of the priest.
5. The *Last Gospel*, so often recited as a thanksgiving after Mass that it was added to the Mass in the 16th century. Usually, the beginning of St. John's Gospel.

How to assist at Mass

"The best way of assisting at Mass is for the Faithful who are present to join with the priest in offering the Divine Victim to God, calling to mind the Sacrifice of the Cross and uniting themselves to Jesus Christ by Sacramental or at least Spiritual Communion." (The Gasparri *Catechism*).

While it is recommended to use a Missal at Mass and to join with the priest in the actual words he is saying, it should always be remembered that this is a means to an end, and not an end in itself. There are good souls who can derive more fruit from following the Mass without a Missal.*

At all events, let us remember that the Mass is the greatest action we have on this earth. It is not only a prayer, but an action, and the self-same action as that performed by Christ on Calvary, re-enacted by Him once more, each time Mass is offered. By His loving omnipotence God has made it possible for us to stand beneath His Son's Cross with Mary, St. John and St. Mary Magdalen on the first Good Friday. Every Mass lost is a Calvary lost, and the loss of one Calvary is an infinite, irreparable loss. May God give us faith to understand and realize this sublime truth.

---

*In fact, St. Leonard of Port Maurice (1676-1751) says this is the best way to offer Mass—for those able to do it. (Cf. *The Hidden Treasure—Holy Mass*. TAN, Rockford, Illinois 1971. —Publisher, 2002.)

Chapter 28

The Sacrament of Penance (1)

What is the Sacrament of Penance? *Penance is a Sacrament whereby the sins, whether mortal or venial, which we have committed after Baptism are forgiven by the absolution of a priest in Confession.*

Does the Sacrament of Penance increase the grace of God in the soul? *The Sacrament of Penance increases the grace of God in the soul, besides forgiving sin; we should, therefore, go often to Confession.*

When did our Lord institute the Sacrament of Penance? *Our Lord instituted the Sacrament of Penance when He breathed on His Apostles and gave them power to forgive sins, saying, "Whose sins you shall forgive, they are forgiven."*

How does the priest forgive sins? *The priest forgives sins by the power of God, when he pronounces the words of absolution.*

What are the words of absolution? *The words of absolution are: "I absolve thee from thy sins, in the name of the Father, and of the Son, and of the Holy Ghost."*

Are any conditions for forgiveness required on the part of the penitent? *Three conditions for forgiveness are required on the part of the penitent—Contrition, Confession and Satisfaction.*

What is Contrition? *Contrition is a hearty sorrow for our sins, either because by them we have offended so good a God, or because we are afraid of being punished for them, together with a firm purpose of amendment.*

What is a firm purpose of amendment? *A firm purpose of amend-*

ment is a resolution to avoid, by the grace of God, not only sin, but also the dangerous occasions of sin.

How may we obtain a hearty sorrow for our sins? *We may obtain a hearty sorrow for our sins by earnestly praying for it and by meditating on such considerations as may lead us to it.*

What consideration concerning God will lead us to sorrow for our sins? *This consideration concerning God will lead us to sorrow for our sins: that by our sins we have offended God, who is infinitely good in Himself and infinitely good to us.*

What consideration concerning our Saviour will lead us to sorrow for our sins? *This consideration concerning our Saviour will lead us to sorrow for our sins: that our Saviour died for our sins, and that those who sin grievously are "crucifying again to themselves the Son of God, and making Him a mockery." (Heb. 6:6).*

When we go to Confession, is that sorrow for our sins sufficient which is caused only by the knowledge that by them we have lost Heaven and deserved Hell? *When we go to Confession, that sorrow for our sins is sufficient that is caused only by the knowledge that we have lost Heaven and deserved Hell.*

What is perfect contrition? *Perfect contrition is sorrow for sin arising purely from the love of God, that we have offended the Infinite, Supreme Being, whom we love.*

What special value does perfect contrition have? *Perfect contrition has this special value: that by it our sins are forgiven immediately, even before we confess them. Nevertheless, if they are mortal, we are strictly bound to confess them afterwards before we receive Holy Communion; otherwise, we commit a mortal sin of sacrilege.*

What is Confession? *Confession is a Sacrament of the Church, otherwise called Penance, whereby we accuse ourselves of our sins to a priest who is approved by the Bishop for this function.*

What if a person willfully conceals a mortal sin in Confession? *If a person willfully conceals a mortal sin in Confession, he is guilty of a great sacrilege, by telling a lie to the Holy Ghost in making a bad Confession.*

How many things have we to do in order to prepare for Confession? *We have four things to do in order to prepare for Confession: first, we must pray heartily for the grace to make a good Confession; second, we must carefully examine our conscience to determine what sins we have committed since our last good Confession; third, we must take time and care to make a good act of contrition; and fourth, we must resolve by the help of God to renounce our sins and to begin a new life for the future.*

What is Satisfaction? *Satisfaction is doing the penance given us by the priest.*

Does the penance given by the priest always make full satisfaction for our sins? *The penance given by the priest does not always make full satisfaction for our sins. We should therefore add to it other good works and penances and try to gain indulgences.*

WE have been studying how God became Man to redeem the human race from sin and to save human beings from Hell. He came to conquer sin, and He conquered it finally on the Cross. But the merits of Christ's death must be **applied to our souls**; hence, Our Lord Jesus Christ instituted Seven Sacraments to act as the official channels of grace from Him to us. Through Baptism His conquest of Original Sin becomes, so to speak, our conquest. But **Baptism would be of little use if there were not some similar means by which actual sins could be forgiven which are committed after Baptism has been received.** God, with His infinite knowledge, knows that a large number of men, perhaps even the majority, offend Him, even seriously at least once in a lifetime. For all of them Baptism would be unavailing for salvation unless He also instituted another *Sacrament* for the forgiveness of sins committed **after** Baptism. We say another *Sacrament* because the Sacraments are the normal channels of grace to the soul. Moreover, grace is itself so vitally important and the loss of it so immeasurably serious, that it would seem to be very much in accordance with God's infinite goodness to give us some sign of forgiveness perceptible to the senses.

Catholic doctrine

The Church has, in fact, defined that such a Sacrament does exist, and it is called the Sacrament of Penance, or more popularly called "Confession." (It is now also popularly called the Rite of Reconciliation.) Here are the clear words of the Council of Trent: "As a means of regaining grace and justice, penance was at all times necessary for those who had defiled their souls with any mortal sin . . . Before the coming of Christ, penance was not a Sacrament, nor is it since His coming a Sacrament for those who are not baptized. But *the Lord then principally instituted the Sacrament of Penance, when, after His Resurrection from the dead, He breathed upon His disciples saying: 'Receive ye the Holy Ghost. Whose sins you shall forgive, they are forgiven them; and whose sins you shall retain, they are retained.' (John* 20:22-23). By which action so signal and words so clear the consent of all the Fathers has understood that the power of forgiving and retaining sins was communicated to the Apostles and to their lawful successors, for the reconciling of the Faithful who have fallen after Baptism. Moreover, Christ left priests, His own vicars, as judges, unto whom all the *mortal* sins into which the faithful may have fallen should be revealed in order that, in accordance with the power of the keys, they may pronounce the sentence of forgiveness or retention of sins." (Sess. XIV, cc. i & v.).

Christ passed on the power to forgive sin— The evidence of Scripture

There is, of course, no question that *Christ* has the power to forgive sins because *He is God*. He exercised that power continually during His life on earth. Moreover, **He passed it on to the Apostles**. First to Peter, and then to all the Apostles, He said: "And I will give to thee the keys of the kingdom of heaven. And whatsoever thou shalt bind upon earth, it shall be bound also in heaven: and whatsoever thou shalt loose upon earth, it shall be loosed also in heaven." (*Matt.* 16:19). Consideration of this text reveals that the spiritual power promised by Christ is *unlimited*, save by what is known to be

God's law, that it is *judicial* and that it will be *ratified in Heaven*. It is *judicial* because it embraces both *binding* and *loosing*.

Yet the Council of Trent refers us to an event that took place after Our Lord's Resurrection for the principal words of institution of the Sacrament of Penance. "Now when it was late that same day, the first of the week, and the doors were shut, where the disciples were gathered together, for fear of the Jews, Jesus came and stood in the midst, and said to them: Peace be to you. And when he had said this, he showed them his hands and his side. The disciples therefore were glad, when they saw the Lord. He said therefore to them again: Peace be to you. As the Father hath sent me, I also send you. When he had said this, he breathed on them; and he said to them: Receive ye the Holy Ghost. Whose sins you shall forgive, they are forgiven them; and whose sins you shall retain, they are retained." (*John* 20:19-23).

What a solemn scene is described in those words! Remember, it was after the Resurrection. Jesus Christ visited the upper room on a special mission. This is indicated by the fact that He breathed on His Apostles. Why is that recorded by St. John? Surely, all the circumstances suggest that an event of unique importance was taking place. Christ was giving His Spirit to the Twelve and to their successors; He was telling them that their mission was similar to that which He had received from His Father. Therefore, when He told them to forgive sins, they received the power He possessed. The words themselves are incapable of any other interpretation. To say that this incident merely gives the Apostles the power either 1) to preach the Gospel of repentance, or 2) to declare that God has forgiven sins or 3) to say He has given the Apostles power to take away only the penalty due to the sins is to do violence to both the text and the context. The special mission of the Apostles is actually to forgive sins, and they are to exercise that power in a judicial way. Just as the general power of binding and loosing is promised in judicial language, so is this more particular power conferred. The obvious meaning of the words is that forgiveness is not to be granted or withheld indiscriminately, but as the sinner deserves. The power is unrestricted, applying to all sins. And what the Apostles decide is God's decision.

The power here conferred was obviously not to cease with the death of the Apostles. It was being given to them **in their offi-**

cial capacity as priests of the Church to be handed on to their successors in office. Whatever powers are needed for the Church's work, even though the words conferring them were necessarily spoken to the Apostles alone, are also given to their successors, since *His Mystical Body, the Church, is to continue forever Christ's work*, and a chief part of that work is undoubtedly the forgiving of sins. Without power to do this in God's name, the Church could scarcely be said to be the continuation of Christ's life among men. A glance at the tradition of the Church in the matter ought to convince any fair-minded enquirer that such has been the continuous belief and practice of the Church throughout the centuries.

The evidence of Tradition

Starting with the fifth century, we find the Bishop, St. Augustine, warning the faithful: "Let us not listen to those who deny that the Church of God has power to forgive all sins." (*De agon. Christ,* iii). St. Ambrose makes the same point in several places. For example: "Christ granted this [power to forgive sins] to the Apostles, and from the Apostles it has been transmitted to the office of priests." (*De poenit.* II, ii, 12).

In the fourth century, St. Pacian, Bishop of Barcelona, wrote: "This [forgiving sins], you say, only God can do. Quite true; but what He does through His priests is the doing of His own power." (*Ep.* I *ad Sympron*, 6).

In the East, St. Athanasius, who died in 375 A.D., is particularly clear: "As the man whom the priest baptizes is enlightened by the grace of the Holy Ghost, so does he who in penance confesses his sins receive through the priest forgiveness in virtue of the grace of Christ." (*Frag. contra Novat*).

Note that Fathers in both East and West appeal all the time to the words of Christ, which they interpret in exactly the same way as the Council of Trent interpreted them eleven hundred years later.

From the third century comes the voice of another bishop, St. Cyprian: "Let each confess his sin while he is still in this world, while his confession can be received, while satisfaction and the forgiveness granted by the priests is acceptable to God." (*De Lapsis* c. xxix).

During the second century, a controversy arose between the Church and the Montanist heretics, who maintained that some sins could be forgiven while others could not. **The very existence of such a controversy is testimony to the general belief that the Church has the power to forgive sins.** Against their false ideas, Pope Callistus (218-222) published a famous edict in which he declared: "I forgive the sins both of adultery and of fornication to those who have done penance." Tertullian then left the Church as a protest against the doctrine that the Church can forgive **all** sins. Therefore, the fact that the Church can forgive all sins was the orthodox teaching received at the end of the second century. In fact, Tertullian refers to a more ancient work, *The Pastor*, written by one Hermas as early as 140, saying that this book is wrong because it favors the pardoning even of adultery.

Denis of Corinth, who died about 170 A.D., taught that Christ left the power to forgive sins to the Church and that it was all-embracing. Our authority for this fact is Eusebius in his *History* (IV, xxiii).

Going back still further, we come to that work we have already found so useful, the *Didache*. It has two references to Confession, the second of which exhorts: "On the Lord's day, come together and break bread . . . having confessed your transgressions that your sacrifice may be pure." (XIV, i). St. Clement, who died in 99 A.D., in his famous letter to Corinth, begs the "seditious to submit themselves to the presbyters [priests] and receive correction so as to repent." (c. lvii).

The first essential of a Sacrament is institution by Christ. In regard to the forgiveness of sin, that essential is certainly present. The constant practice of the Church shows that the other essentials are there, too: the outward sign—consisting of actions and words—produces an inward grace.

According to St. Thomas Aquinas, the proximate **matter** of the Sacrament of Penance is the acts of the penitent—contrition, confession and satisfaction—but because these differ from the matter of, say, Baptism, in which some material thing is employed externally, later theologians prefer, with the Council of Trent, to speak of them as *quasi*-matter. The **form** of the Sacrament is defined by Trent as the actual words of absolution pronounced by the priest: "I absolve thee from thy sins, in the name of the Father, and of the Son, and of the Holy Ghost."

Effects of the Sacrament

The teaching of the Church in regard to the *effects* of this Sacrament may be summed up under two headings:

A. If the penitent confesses *mortal* sins not previously forgiven:
   a) The sins with their *eternal* punishment are remitted, and the remaining debt of *temporal* punishment is partially remitted;
   b) His merits, which were cancelled by his mortal sins, revive and regain their previous efficacy;
   c) A special grace is given for avoiding sin in the future.

B. If the penitent has to confess only *venial* sins, or mortal sins that were previously forgiven:
   a) The venial sins are forgiven;
   b) Sanctifying grace is increased;
   c) Grace is given to avoid sin in the future;
   d) The debt of temporal punishment is decreased.

Jurisdiction or "Faculties"

Because Our Lord conferred the power to remit sins only on the Apostles and not on all the Faithful, it is and always has been the teaching of the Catholic Church that bishops and priests *alone* have this power. In order to use it, they need not only the *power* of the Sacrament of Holy Orders, but also the *authority of jurisdiction*. They receive the *power* at ordination; the *authority of jurisdiction* is conferred by the proper ecclesiastical authority, the local bishop. Catholics usually speak of the *authority of jurisdiction* by saying that a priest has "*faculties*" to hear Confessions. Thus, according to traditional practice in the Church, a priest visiting a diocese other than his own could not hear Confessions there without the permission of the bishop. A Liverpool priest could not hear Confessions, for instance, in Birkenhead across the Mersey without the permission of the Bishop of Shrewsbury, in which diocese Birkenhead is situated. A New York priest could not hear Confessions in Brooklyn, another diocese, without receiving faculties from the Bishop of Brooklyn. But according to Canon 967.2 of the 1983 *Code of Canon Law*: "Those who enjoy the faculty of hearing confessions habitually, whether in virtue of office [because they are the Pope, a Cardinal or a Bishop] or by grant from the ordinary [e.g., the bishop] of the place [diocese] of incardination [the official inscription of a priest to work under the jurisdiction of a diocesan bishop, etc.], or in the place where they have a domicile, can exercise the same faculty everywhere, unless the local ordinary [the bishop] denies it in a particular case, with due regard for the prescriptions of Canon 974.2 and .3." Every priest can, however, absolve anyone who is at the point of death because, under such circumstances, the Church automatically gives all her priests jurisdiction for such emergencies.

Contrition and purpose of amendment

The part of the penitent in this Sacrament is summed up under the threefold heading: **contrition, confession** and **satisfaction**.

Contrition is defined as **heartfelt sorrow for sins we have committed, with hatred of them and a firm purpose of amendment to commit them no more**. And a **firm purpose of amendment is a resolution not to commit sin again and to avoid as far as possible the proximate or near occasions of it**. It is obvious that **there can be no true contrition without a firm purpose of amendment**. In fact the latter is the best test of the worth of one's contrition. Note that "a firm purpose of amendment" is a **resolution**, that is, a **determination** not to sin again, and not a mere wish or desire. In making this resolution, we rely on God's grace, rather than on our own strength. This resolution must apply not only to the sins themselves, but it must include also the determination to avoid any person, place or thing which, from experience, we know will lead us into sin, and also the determination to make use of any means necessary to help us overcome the sin in the future.

Contrition for sin should be

    a) **Inward**—not only on the lips, but coming from the heart;

b) **Supernatural**—from more than merely natural motives, and prompted also by the truths of our Faith;

c) **Profound**—so that sin is hated above every other evil;

d) **Universal**—including all mortal sins committed since Baptism and not already forgiven by this Sacrament.

If a penitent has no mortal sins, but only venial sins to confess, he must make an act of sorrow for some of the venial sins, or at least one of them, and that is sufficient for the effect of the Sacrament of Penance to occur.

Perfect and imperfect contrition

There are two kinds of contrition, **perfect contrition** and **imperfect contrition** (sometimes referred to as attrition).

Perfect contrition is a sorrow and hatred for sin, springing from a motive of supernatural charity, because we love God and inasmuch as sin is an offense against God, who is supremely good and worthy to be loved above all things. It washes away sin immediately, even apart from the Sacrament of Penance, but it obviously implies the desire to receive the Sacrament of Penance as soon as possible, **and it is definitely NOT sufficient by itself to permit the penitent to receive Holy Communion without Confession first—otherwise, the person would commit a mortal sin of sacrilege.**

Why is this so? The reason is twofold: The first is that a human being never knows for certain if he is in the state of grace (i.e., has Sanctifying Grace in his soul). Scripture says: "And yet man knoweth not whether he be worthy of love or hatred" (*Ecclesiastes* 9:1), that is, whether he is at enmity with God or not because of his sins. When combined with Confession, the level of our contrition need only be "imperfect," which is sorrow for sin out of fear of the punishment we will receive (Hell, for being guilty of unforgiven mortal sin at the time of our death). It is not at all difficult to have imperfect contrition, for we all fear punishment.

And the second flows out of the first—that Christ instituted the Sacrament of Penance precisely to help us overcome our sins—even if our contrition is "imperfect." For the grace of this Sacrament is very powerful to help us achieve forgiveness. **And it is out of obedience to Christ and His Holy Catholic Church that we must**

refrain from receiving Communion after we have committed a mortal sin, until we can make a worthy Confession. The certitude of forgiveness in Confession, versus the certitude of forgiveness from perfect contrition, is due to our confessing to a priest (who is a trained moral theologian, our judge and is an *alter Christus*— "another Christ") and the all-inclusiveness of our contrition, ideally to cover all our sins, but of necessity at least all our mortal sins, plus the need for only imperfect contrition (sorrow because of fear of punishment) for forgiveness within the Sacrament of Penance. If all we had to do after committing mortal sin is make an act of perfect contrition to be forgiven for certain, then Christ's instituting the Sacrament of Penance would be useless for those able to make an act of perfect contrition. He would therefore have acted in vain, as far as they are concerned. But we know this cannot be so. Our Lord did nothing in vain.

All Christians, nonetheless, should form the habit of constantly making acts of perfect contrition, since perfect contrition may well be the means of the soul's salvation, should one commit a mortal sin and then die or be killed before being able to go to Confession. In this way the good one may have done in life will not be rendered void for eternity, nor need a person who has committed a mortal sin be so afraid of sudden death as he would be if he had not made an act of perfect contrition.

Imperfect contrition is that **supernatural** sorrow and hatred for sin which is aroused either by reflection on the baseness of sin or by the fear of Hell and its torments. Imperfect contrition is sufficient for the valid reception of the Sacrament of Penance, but we should, of course, always strive after perfect contrition, for the perfection of our soul and the reason given immediately above.

Contrition is not "feeling." It is an act of the intellect and will, not of the senses. Consequently, no one ought to be perturbed by not being able to **"feel"** sorry when going to Confession, so long as the proper disposition of the will exists. Feelings can be most misleading in this matter.

Without sorrow for sin there is no forgiveness. In fact, a person who goes to Confession knowing that he has no real sorrow for his sins, **not only does not obtain forgiveness** for his sins, but **he also commits a grave sin of sacrilege**.

Confession was imposed by Christ

Confession **is that Sacrament of the Church whereby one accuses himself of his sins to a priest who is lawfully authorized by his bishop to hear Confessions in order to obtain sacramental absolution.**

When we are thinking about the words by which Our Lord conferred on His Church the power to forgive sins, we saw that this power is twofold—**to forgive sins or to retain them. The exercise of such a judicial power would be quite impossible unless the sinner made known his sins to the person with the power to forgive. Equally, it would have been absolutely useless for Christ to confer such a power on His Apostles and their successors if people could still have their sins forgiven by telling them in their hearts to God. Thus, there is implied in Our Lord's words to the Apostles a divine mandate to all of His followers to confess their sins to the priests.**

The words of Christ show that the power given to His priests is all-embracing. **But how can priests make a judgment—as they are clearly told to do—without hearing the evidence?** And who can give the evidence but the sinner himself? **Hence, the inspired words of Scripture imply the necessity of Confession.**

Confession in the Christian Tradition

If Christ did not impose the obligation of Confession, who did? All the Eastern Churches retain Confession as a divine institution, even those which split off from Rome—with the series of schisms starting in the fourth century and continuing through the ninth (867) to the eleventh century (1053) and culminating finally in the fifteenth (1472). They certainly never adopted Confession from the Western Church, and the Western Church certainly never adopted it from the Eastern Church. The Eastern Church, moreover, never once accused the Western Church of "inventing" Confession. Therefore, the belief must have been firmly rooted in Christendom from the fourth through the fifteenth centuries. Now, if it had been introduced only sometime **during** the first eight or nine centuries, there ought certainly to be some evidence of what would be so striking an innovation. But there is none. Also, in view of the conservative nature of the early Church, there would surely have been some protest against such a hard practice being suddenly imposed on the whole Church. But there is no evidence of either sort. On the contrary, the only evidence we have is that the practice of Confession was accepted as a divine institution by the whole Church throughout the first nine centuries, that is, through the schism of Photius (867), Partriarch-Archbishop of Constantinople—and beyond that, into the modern era.

Here is a very clear quotation from Pope St. Leo the Great, who died in the year 461: "God, in His abundant mercy, has provided two main remedies for the sins of men, that they may gain eternal life by the grace of Baptism, and also by the remedy of Penance. Those who have violated the vows of their Baptism may obtain the remission of their sins by condemning themselves; the divine goodness has so decreed that the pardon of God can only be obtained by sinners through the power Jesus Christ Himself has conferred upon the rulers of the Church, the power of imposing canonical penance upon sinners who confess their sins, and of allowing them to receive the Sacraments of Christ after they have purified their souls by a salutary satisfaction . . . Every Christian, therefore, must examine his conscience and cease putting off the hour of his conversion from day to day; he ought not to expect to satisfy God's justice on his death-bed. It is dangerous for a weak and ignorant man to put off his conversion to the last uncertain days of his life, when he may be unable to confess and obtain priestly absolution; he ought, when he can, to merit pardon by a full satisfaction for his sins." (*Epist.* cviii).

St. Pacian, whom we met already, urged the sinner to confess in spite of his shame: "I appeal to you, my brethren, you who are not ashamed to sin and yet are ashamed to confess . . . I beseech you, cease to hide your wounded conscience. Sick people who are prudent do not fear the physician, though he cut and burn even the secret parts of the body." (*Paraenesis ad poenit.*, n. 6, 8).

St. John Chrysostom, who died in 347, is particularly eloquent on this subject: "Be not ashamed to approach [the priest] because you have sinned; nay, rather, approach him for that very reason. No one says: because I have an ulcer, I will not go near the doctor or take medicine; on the contrary, it is just this that makes it needful to call in physicians and apply remedies. We [priests] know well how to pardon because we ourselves are liable to sin. This is why God did not give us Angels to be our doctors, nor send down Gabriel to rule the flock, but from the fold itself He chooses the shepherds, from among the sheep He appoints the leader, in order that he [the leader] may be inclined to pardon his followers and, keeping in mind his own frailty, may not set himself in hardness against the members of the flock." (*P.G.*, LXIII, 463).

Nearly a century earlier, St. Cyprian tells how "to those who implore the mercy of God, peace can be granted through his priests . . . And because in Hell there is no Confession . . . they who repent with their whole heart and ask for it, should be received into the Church and therein saved unto the Lord." (*Ep.* lv, n. 29).

About the same time, Origen plainly speaks of secret Confession: "When you have eaten some indigestible food, and your stomach is filled with an excessive quantity of humor, you will suffer until you have gotten rid of it. So in like manner, sinners who hide and retain their sins within their breasts become sick therefrom almost to death. If, however, they accuse themselves, confess their sins and vomit forth their iniquity, they will certainly drive from their souls the principle of evil. Consider carefully whom you choose to listen to your sins. Know well the character of the physician to whom you intend to relate the nature of your sickness . . . If he gives you advice, follow it; if he judges that your sickness is of such a nature that it should be revealed publicly in church for the edification of the brethren and your own more effective cure, do not hesitate to do what he tells you." (*On Ps.* xxvii).

St. Iranaeus contrasts private and public Confession (*Adv. Haer.* I, xiii, 7), and St. Clement, contemporary of St. John the Evangelist, wrote to the Corinthians: "It is better for a man to confess his sins than to harden his heart." (li, 1).

This outline of the teaching of the earliest Christian writers shows the following:

1. That the telling of one's sins was considered necessary for regaining God's friendship.
2. That it was done by Confession, not to a layman, but to a priest.

3. That priests, as the representatives of Christ, exercise the power of absolving.
4. That the sinner must overcome his shame and his repugnance to Confession if he is to be saved.

This teaching, be it noted, goes back to the first century. Rightly, then, does Pope St. Leo the Great (d. 461) appeal to the rule of the Apostles, which made Confession in secret to a priest sufficient without a public declaration being necessary.

Confession has, in fact, been such an outstanding characteristic of the Church since Apostolic times that the presence or absence of it might well be used as one of the criteria by which the authenticity or lack of authenticity of any Christian body might be established. A denomination without sacramental Confession cannot be part of the One True Church of Christ. At the beginning of the fourth century, the following remarkable words were written by Lactantius: **"That is the true Church in which there is Confession and Penance,** which applies a wholesome remedy to the sins and wounds whereunto the weakness of the flesh is subject." (*Div. Inst.,* IV, 30).

Chapter 29

The Sacrament of Penance (2)

FOLLOWING are some practical points about **what** sins are to be confessed.

For the valid reception of the Sacrament of Penance, confession must be **vocal** (or at least the equivalent of vocal) and **integral** or **complete.** A reasonable cause excuses from an oral accusation of oneself in the Sacrament of Penance. But the communication with the priest would then have to be in the form of sign language or writing.

Integrity

A confession is "integral" or "complete" when the penitent confesses ALL the mortal sins which have not already been confessed—of which, after careful examination, he is conscious—along with their number and their character, plus the circumstances that alter their character.

If a person cannot recall exactly the number of his mortal sins, he should state their probable number and add "about." It is not sufficient to say merely "a few times," or "many times."

One who, through no fault of his own, omits a mortal sin from his Confession receives the Sacrament validly, and the forgotten sin is still forgiven; but when he remembers it, he is bound in conscience to accuse himself of it at his next Confession.

A person who, through his own fault, deliberately omits a mortal sin in Confession not only gains nothing by the Confession, but he commits a mortal sin of sacrilege as well. If he has been guilty of doing this, or if he feels that he has invalidated his Confession through lack of true sorrow for his sins, he should go to Confession again as soon as possible and tell the priest how many bad Confessions he has made and how many sacrilegious Holy Communions he has received, together with all the mortal sins told in the bad Confessions and/or that he has committed since.

Confession should always be **humble** and **devout.** The penitent should tell his sins briefly, clearly and modestly, without embellishments, useless words or excuses.

Examination of conscience

From all that has been said above, it is obvious that before Confession the penitent must **examine his conscience**. That means that he must recall as carefully as possible the sins committed since his last good Confession. After asking God's help, he should mentally go through the Commandments of God and of the Church, finding out if he has sinned against any of them, remembering all the time that he is only **bound** to confess mortal sins. The number of the mortal sins committed should be decided upon, together with their character and any circumstances that may alter their character.

Circumstances that alter the character of our sins and therefore must be included in the Confession are such as turn a venial sin into a mortal sin (e.g. when a lie gravely harms another's character) or when a mortal sin is made graver still by circumstances (e.g., a theft that is committed from a sacred place).

One who has not been guilty of mortal sin may still, of course, receive the graces bestowed by the Sacrament of Penance by confessing with sorrow his venial sins committed since his last Confession, or even mortal or venial sins from the past which have already been confessed and forgiven in the Sacrament. This is often called a devotional Confession.

The reasons to confess venial sins in Confession are as follows:

1. They provide matter for the Confession (for the Sacrament to be administered, there have to be sins confessed).
2. Confession helps us to overcome all our sins, but especially those which are confessed; and as we are enjoined by Our Lord to be perfect ("Be you therefore perfect, as also your heavenly Father is perfect"—*Matt.* 5:48), confessing venial sins helps toward that objective.

3. Confessing our venial sins makes us more aware of *all* our venial offenses against God's law, opening our consciences to recognize those venial sins that—before adopting this practice—we may not have been aware that we were committing.
4. Adopting the practice of confessing venial sins leads to confessing *all* our faults, even the most minor (called peccadillos and imperfections), so that soon we may well find ourselves confessing even our temptations, which Confession also helps overcome.
5. Confessing venial sins heightens one's awareness of the seriousness of sin—of even venial sin, which willingly entered into, can easily lead one to commit mortal sin.
6. The Sacrament of Penance removes part of the temporal punishment due to our sins, so that our stay in Purgatory (if we should go there after death) would be shortened.
7. Confessing our venial sins—and confessing often—lessens our inclination to all sin.

All should remember that a person does not stand still in the spiritual life: He will either get better or worse. If he were to overcome even all his venial sins and then stop his practice of frequent Confession, for example, he would run the risk of sliding backward into sin; hence, the need to continue in this practice of frequent Confession, no matter how good he may become and no matter how slight the sins he has to confess.

Frequent Confession is recommended

How often should we go to Confession? Church law lays down the minimum of once a year for the laity. Those who have committed mortal sin are well advised to go to Confession as soon as possible afterwards, although they would not add to their mortal sins by postponing their Confession, so long as they have the intention to go when God's law requires it or when the Church commands it.

"Confessions of devotion," those made by people in the state of grace, are highly recommended by the Church and are a great means of perfection, because they increase Sanctifying Grace in the soul and they obtain for the person the special graces of this Sacrament. In her Canon Law, for example, Holy Mother Church lays down the following: "The faithful who are in the habit of going to Confession **once a fortnight** [every two weeks] unless legitimately impeded . . . can gain all indulgences without actual Confession, for which otherwise Confession would be a necessary condition. The indulgences of an ordinary or extraordinary jubilee, and those granted in the form of a jubilee, are excepted from this concession." (*Canon* 931 [of the old Codex, i.e., of 1917. vs. 1983]). **Hence, a good practical rule is: To go to Confession at least once every fortnight** [every two weeks].

The method of Confession

There is no obligatory formula for the telling of one's sins. Just as one is at liberty to choose one's own confessor, so one is at liberty to use any approved form for confessing his sins. Most Catholic prayer books contain one. The following is as simple as any: "Father, my last Confession was (two weeks, a month) ago. I have . . . (here tell your sins: e.g., missed Mass on Sunday once through my own fault, taken pleasure in impure thoughts six times, for which I am sorry, told lies of excuse two times and injured a person's character by uncharitable talk once). I include from my past life the sin of (e.g. missing Mass . . .) which I confessed before. I am sorry for all my sins." The priest will then impose a penance and may give some advice, after which he will ask the penitent to recite the Act of Contrition prayer as an indication of sorrow for his sins, and he will then begin to say the words of absolution, during which the penitent should listen attentively. When both penitent and priest have finished, the penitent returns to the Church, renews his sorrow for his sins, thanks God for forgiveness, and says his penance (although the only obligation is to say it before one's next Confession).

General Confession

A General Confession is the confession of all the mortal sins of one's past life, or in the case of its not being one's first General Confession, then of all the mortal sins of one's life since his *last* General Confession. In making a General Confession, it is also good to mention one's habitual venial sins and his bad habits, omissions and failings, so that the confessor can form a good idea of the overall direction of one's spiritual life. General Confessions should be made by appointment with the Confessor, so that he can budget the extra time required to hear it and not be inconveniencing others by the wait. According to St. Alphonsus Liguori, a doctor of the Church, it is *not necessary* to make a General Confession so long as a person believes that his confessions have been sincere, complete and contrite.

A "General Confession" is made for one of three reasons: 1) if there is serious doubt about the validity of former Confessions, 2) before a person enters upon a change of state in life or assumes a major new office, and 3) as a pious act aimed at his spiritual improvement.

In the **first instance**, i.e., **where there is a doubt about the validity of former confessions**, General Confession is **necessary** only when there is real ground for thinking that one's previous Confessions have been invalid; it is **advisable** if there is really great doubt about their validity; it is **permissible** if it seems probable that the penitent will derive profit from it. In cases of scrupulosity (where a penitent confuses non-sins for sins and venial sins for mortal sins, or where he doubts unduly that he has been forgiven), the confessor should be the judge if a General Confession is called for.

In the **second instance**, it is an excellent practice to make a General Confession **before one enters upon a new state of life**, such as the priesthood, the religious life or marriage, **or before one assumes a major new office**, especially within the Church, such as becoming a seminary rector, an abbot, a mother superior, a bishop, a cardinal or the Pope. For General Confession, among other benefits, helps the penitent to see his life in the perspective of eternity; also, he sees more clearly the overall spiritual progress that he is making, (or absence thereof), and the growth in moral perfection of his life. It also helps him toward a firm purpose of amendment, plus it gives him a clean slate, so to speak, as he starts into the new state or office. Finally, it strengthens him to avoid past sins and imperfections and to enter the new state or office better prepared to meet its particular challenges.

In the **third instance**, General Confession is **a powerful pious act**. Periodically, it is a good idea for all to make a General Confession. The Society of Jesus (the Jesuits) particularly have been enthusiastic advocates of General Confession, especially after a person completes one of their long "Ignatian Retreats." They have found that this practice is very beneficial to one's sanctification—for all the reasons given in the paragraph above.

Satisfaction

Satisfaction **is the penance imposed on the penitent by the confessor for the sins made known to him in Confession; this penance has, by Christ's merits applied through the Sacrament, special value for the payment of the debt of temporal punishment due to sin!** The penance is imposed by the priest prudently, having regard to the nature of the sins confessed and the disposition of the penitent, not only as a help to the latter in leading a new life and as a remedy for his weakness, but also as a penalty and a correction for past sins now forgiven. If a penitent finds himself for some reason unable to perform the penance imposed, he should make this fact known to the confessor, with all due deference, and ask him to change it. The Sacramental penance should be supplemented by other prayers, good works and penances.

Absolution

The act by which the confessor in the name of Christ remits sins in the Sacrament of Penance is called **absolution**. The words of absolution are the "form" of the Sacrament. Sometimes the priest may be bound to refuse absolution, e.g., when he prudently decides that the penitent has not the dispositions requisite to receive it. For a good reason he may defer absolution for a time, especially if the penitent agrees to that course with a view to bettering himself.

The *Roman Ritual* says: "Those are incapable of receiving absolution who give no sign of sorrow for their sins, who refuse to lay aside some hatred or enmity, to restore when they can someone else's property, to avoid some proximate occasion of sin, or who are unwilling to give up their sinful lives and amend them; those again who have given public scandal but refuse to make public reparation and remove the scandal. Finally, a confessor should refuse to absolve sins that are by Church law specifically reserved to a higher authority, namely the local bishop or the Pope."

The seal of Confession

The priest is bound to inviolable secrecy in regard to the sins revealed to him in Sacramental Confession. Even to save his own life or his good name, or to save the life or good name of another, he cannot be excused from this obligation. No law and no oath can force him to break the seal of Confession, either directly or indirectly. Only permission freely and formally given by the penitent can release a priest from his obligation to the strictest secrecy about sins he has heard in Confession. History is full of instances of priests suffering imprisonment, torture and death rather than reveal in any way what they had heard in the confessional.

In 1605, Fr. Garnett, S.J., went to his death on the gallows for refusing to reveal knowledge of the famous Gunpowder Plot obtained from one of the conspirators in the confessional. In 1863, a Fr. McLaughlin went to prison for contempt of court rather than betray the confidence of a thief. In 1802, Fr. Kelly, and in 1860, Fr. Gahan suffered imprisonment for the same reason. In 1911, the Abbe Bruneau was beheaded in France for murder rather than tell the name of the real criminal, his housekeeper, who revealed the fact on her deathbed seven years later. The most famous case is that of St. John Nepomucene, who was drowned in the river Moldau by King Wenceslaus of Bohemia in 1393 for refusing to reveal to him the Queen's confession. The body was recovered and buried. Three hundred twenty-six years later, during the process of his beatification, the martyr's skull was placed on a table, at which time the tongue fell out. It was seen to be red and fresh. (Cf. *American Ecclesiastical Review*, Jan., 1926).

The unanimity with which Catholic priests everywhere have for nineteen centuries preserved the confessional seal is surely a miracle, accounted for only by the fact that they are God's instruments in forgiving sins through the Sacrament of Penance.

Confession, a great gift of God

What a wonderful manifestation of God's mercy Confession is. Here is a sinner, a grave sinner, one who has violated the most essential and important of the Commandments of God—a murderer maybe, or a man sunk deep in the slime of lust, a man who has frittered away the years of his life in deliberate disobedience to the known will of his God, a man who has again and again rejected grace, a man who has repeatedly despised the goodness of God, a man on whom the Precious Blood of Jesus has been wasted. If such a man had violated the laws of the world as he has violated the laws of God, what would be his fate? He would be dragged from his house, publicly perhaps, by the rough officers of justice; he would be flung into a comfortless prison. After days and days of waiting and anxiety, he would be brought into the open court. The story of his crimes would be flashed across the headlines of every newspaper. It would be retold on the radio and TV at the fireside of every home in the land. Nothing at all would be done to spare him; he would have to bear it all in expiation for his crime. And at the end, a judge in solemn dignity would tell him that his life is to be forfeited and that he must suffer a death of public infamy and ignominy to expiate his crime. Thus does the world deal with its criminals.

But what if that same wretched sinner appears before the tribunal of God in Confession? Christ takes him by the hand, wards off the crowd and brings him to a secret tribunal. No witnesses are called against him; no finger of scorn is pointed at him. A word into the ear of the priest enters the priest's mind, and in a moment it has passed away. Just as a little child on a calm summer evening might take a pebble and fling it into the bosom of a deep, still, placid lake: for an instant there is a ripple on the face of the water; there is a little circlet of waves. Presently these die away; the waters close and the pebble is lost. So also, for an instant the sound of the sinner's voice makes but a ripple on the ear of the priest, thrills for a second on the delicate tympanum of his ear and passes from that into the unfathomable ocean of the merciful Heart of Jesus. The waters of Christ's mercy close over it, and that sin is gone. (See the author's complete explanation on pages 411-413.)

What a great grace Confession is, and at how small a price!

Surely no sacrifice ought to be too great for the assurance of the forgiveness of the Heart of Jesus. Yet, full of love, full of commiseration, He alone comes to us with mercy, sparing every feeling of the sinner, making every difficult thing smooth and trying to anticipate by the sweetness of His mercy all the humiliation and all the pain. It is the only tribunal where, when a man is found guilty, the only sentence pronounced on him is one of acquittal. How wrong it is, how superficial, how ignorant to suggest that Confession is an intolerable burden. He alone who is offended by sin has the right to declare the terms on which the sin will be forgiven. Christ has done that by instituting the Sacrament of Penance, a most powerful invention of the love and mercy of His Sacred Heart. Its very existence makes one ever grateful for the privilege of membership in the Church which offers such a treasure to her children.

Chapter 30

The Catholic Priesthood

What is the Sacrament of Holy Orders? *Holy Orders is the Sacrament by which bishops, priests and other ministers of the Church are ordained and receive the power and the grace to perform their sacred duties.*

W E have already studied the priesthood of Jesus Christ and the perpetuation of His supreme Sacrifice in the Holy Mass. Because the Church possesses the Mass, she necessarily possesses a priesthood, which must be a continuation of Christ's priesthood in the same way as the Mass is a continuation of His Sacrifice. We would naturally expect to find the priesthood conferred by some outward and significant rite, and this we do find.

Holy Orders defined

The Sacrament of Holy Orders was instituted by Jesus Christ to provide the Church with bishops, priests and other ministers, each receiving power and grace for the due fulfillment of the sacred duties belonging to the degree of priesthood conferred on him. It is a dogma, defined by the Council of Trent, that Holy Orders is one of the seven Sacraments instituted by Christ.

Christ founded a visible, perpetual priesthood

Holy Scripture tells us that Christ instituted a **visible priesthood,** which belongs only to those who are properly chosen and ordained.

a) **The Apostles were specially chosen by God.** "And Jesus said to them: Come after me, and I will make you to become fish-ers of men." (*Mark* 1:17). "You have not chosen me: but I have chosen you; and have appointed you. . . ." (*John* 15:16).

They were ordained by a special rite and given special offices. To them alone was given the power of consecrating the Body and Blood of Christ: "Do this for a commemoration of me." (*Luke* 22:19). These words made them priests because they gave the power to offer sacrifice to God. Later they received the power to forgive sins, as we saw in the last instruction.

b) **The priesthood of the New Law had to be perpetual because the Sacrifice was to be perpetual.** Therefore, the Apostles ordained other ministers by an external and visible rite, namely, the "imposition of hands."

The 6th Chapter of the *Acts of the Apostles* describes the choosing of seven deacons by the general body of the disciples of Christ. "These they set before the apostles; and they praying, imposed hands upon them." (*Acts* 6:6).

Before St. Barnabas and St. Paul went forth on their missionary journeys, they were ordained as priests. "And as they were ministering to the Lord, and fasting, the Holy Ghost said to them: Separate me Saul and Barnabas for the work whereunto I have taken them. Then they, fasting and praying, and imposing their hands upon them, sent them away." (*Acts* 13:2-3). "And when they had ordained to them priests in every church, and had prayed with fasting, they commended them to the Lord, in whom they believed." (*Acts* 14:22).

To St. Timothy, St. Paul wrote: "Neglect not the grace that is in thee, which was given thee by prophecy, with imposition of the hands of the priesthood." (*1 Tim.* 4:14). "I admonish thee, that thou stir up the grace of God which is in thee, by the imposition of my hands." (*2 Tim.* 1:6).

Through the imposition of hands, then, the clergy were distinguished from the rest of the Faithful. To them alone belonged the office of ruling the Church, of dispensing the Sacraments and of offering the Holy Sacrifice.

"Take heed to yourselves, and to the whole flock, wherein the Holy Ghost hath placed you bishops, to rule the church of God, which he hath purchased with his own blood." (St. Paul speaking to the meeting of the bishops at Ephesus, *Acts* 20:28).

"Let a man so account of us as of the ministers of Christ, and the dispensers of the mysteries of God." (*1 Cor.* 4:1).

"For every high priest taken from among men, is ordained for men in the things that appertain to God, that he may offer up gifts and sacrifices for sins." (*Heb.* 5:1).

The priestly power is conferred by a Sacramental rite

c) **The rite by which priestly power was conferred was a real and true Sacrament**. The imposition of hands, which St. Paul says was only given to a few carefully chosen men, is certainly a sign perceptible to the senses and productive of grace. We have already quoted St. Paul telling St. Timothy that a special grace has been entrusted to him, enkindled in him by God, through the imposition of hands.

Moreover, it was instituted by Christ. He alone could attach grace to an external sign, and He instituted the priesthood, as we have seen. Unless Christ really instituted the rite of the laying on of hands, it is very difficult to explain how the Apostles all came to use it with such constant unanimity.

It is clear that in the generation immediately succeeding the Apostles, the hierarchy of bishops, priests and deacons was everywhere established. Here are a few quotations from St. Ignatius of Antioch (d. 107):

"Your commendable presbyterate, worthy of God, is united with the bishop as the strings of the lyre." (*Eph.* 4:1). "The bishop is in the place of God; the priests are the senate of the Apostles, and the deacons are the ministers of Jesus Christ." (*Magn.* vi). "I salute the Church of Philadelphia . . . especially if they are united with the bishop and his priests and deacons, who have been appointed according to the will of Christ." (*Phil.* 7:2).

Only an Apostolic and divine origin can explain the existence of a hierarchy such as St. Ignatius describes. **The mere fifty years that had passed since Christ's death were not enough to explain the spontaneous evolution of such an elaborate organization.** Even the Rationalists now admit this fact. Writing to St. Polycarp (c.69-c.155), St. Ignatius declares that the bishop must watch over both spiritual and temporal things, allowing nothing to be done without his permission; that he must stand fast before the attacks of heretics 'like the anvil beneath the hammer'; that he must be mild and gentle, testing each wound as its nature demands; and that he must allow no one to be overlooked, widows, slaves, husbands and wives.

Major and Minor Orders

In English, it is usual to speak of Holy Orders in the plural. The reason for this is that besides the priesthood and episcopate, there are other "Orders" or steps leading up to the priesthood. The first step, not an Order, but an introduction to them, is the Tonsure, which makes a man a cleric and a candidate for the Orders. Then come the first four steps, the "Minor Orders": porter, lector, exorcist and acolyte. In modern times, those in Minor Orders have no duties which may not be fulfilled by ordinary layfolk, and the exorcist is expressly forbidden to attempt to exercise the function indicated by the name (casting out devils). After the four Minor Orders come the three Major Orders: subdeacon, deacon and priest. In the Western Church all three carry with them the obligation of celibacy and also of reciting daily the Divine Office. As it seems most probable that all the Orders below the diaconate were not instituted by Christ, they cannot be sacramental in their nature.

"These minor orders [porter, lector, exorcist and acolyte], with the subdeacon, are not of divine origin and so are not sacramental." (Donald Attwater, *A Catholic Dictionary*, Macmillan, 1958 Edition, p. 323). "The present ministries of acolyte and reader or lector . . . for centuries had been called minor orders. They were never considered part of the sacrament of orders and in 1973 were all reduced to Church ministries to which men can be appointed in a special liturgical ceremony presided over by a bishop or, for religious, a major superior." (Fr. John Hardon, S.J., *Modern Catholic Dictionary*, Doubleday, 1980 Edition, p. 352.) The office of porter was abolished in 1972 by Pope Paul VI, but it too can be conferred as a special ministry with permission from the Holy See (Hardon, p. 428), the office of exorcist was also abolished in the same year, "but episcopal conferences may petition the Holy See to confer the ministry of exorcist if this would be useful or necessary for their territory." (Hardon, p. 202).

The episcopate is the fullness of the priesthood and is possessed by bishops. While a simple priest can do all that is essential to the priesthood—namely, offer the Holy Sacrifice of the Mass and administer the Sacraments of Penance, Holy Eucharist, and Extreme Unction, and in case of necessity, Confirmation also, plus, be the *official* minister of Baptism and the *official* Church witness of Matrimony—he cannot transmit his power to others, i.e., administer Holy Orders. Only a bishop can do that. Without bishops, therefore, the priesthood would die out.

It was remarked in an earlier instruction that the Sacrament of Holy Orders confers a character on the soul of the recipient, marking him forever as a priest of God. "The Lord hath sworn, and he will not repent: Thou art a priest for ever according to the order of Melchisedech." (*Psalm* 109:4, and *Hebrews* 5:6).

Celibacy

"Why do Catholic priests not marry?" is still one of the questions frequently asked by those outside the Church. The answer is that clerical celibacy is neither a divine law nor a dogma of the Church. It is simply a disciplinary law of the Western Church imposed with a view to the dignity and duties of the priesthood.

Our Lord praises most highly the state of virginity. "His disciples say unto him: If the case of a man with his wife be so, it is not expedient to marry." (*Matt.* 19:10). That conclusion, He said, cannot be taken in by everybody, but only by those who have the gift. "For there are eunuchs, who were born so from their mother's womb: and there are eunuchs who were made so by men: and there are eunuchs who have made themselves eunuchs for the kingdom of heaven. He that can take, let him take it." (*Matt.* 19:12). According to the teaching of Jesus on this occasion, the prohibition of divorce is a divine precept binding all Christians, but the practice of celibacy is a divine counsel for the elite few.

Similarly, St. Paul led a life of celibacy and recommended it to all who felt called to that life. "For I would that all men were even as myself: but every one hath his proper gift from God; one after this manner, and another after that. But I say to the unmarried, and to the widows: It is good for them if they so continue, even as I." (*1 Cor.* 7:7-8). Later, he makes it perfectly clear that there is no command of the Lord either to marry or to lead a life of celibacy (*1 Cor.* 7:25-28). Nevertheless: "But I would have you to be without solicitude. He that is without a wife, is solicitous for the things that belong to the Lord, how he may please God. But he that is with a wife, is solicitous for the things of the world, how he may please his wife: and he is divided. And the unmarried woman and the virgin thinketh on the things of the Lord, that she may be holy both in body and in spirit. But she that is married thinketh on the things of the world, how she may please her husband." (*1 Cor.* 32-34).

St. John in the *Apocalypse* speaks of those who have preserved their virginity as the special associates of the Immaculate Lamb of God: "These follow the Lamb whithersoever he goeth. These were purchased from among men, the firstfruits to God and to the Lamb." (*Apoc.* 14:4).

From the earliest times virginity has been practiced in the Church by those who wished to dedicate themselves to God. St. Ignatius of Antioch, St. Justin and other early writers all refer to the great number of Christians who were, as Tatian (120-200, a Syrian Christian apologist and missionary of the second century) said, living "a celibate life for the sole purpose of uniting themselves more intimately with God."

If so many of these early Christians were practicing celibacy in imitation of Christ and His Mother, was it not imperative that their leaders, the bishops, priests and deacons, should give an example of perfect Christian asceticism?

Nevertheless, as far as we have a record of it, the earliest *law* enforcing celibacy was not passed until about the year 300 by the Council of Elvira in Spain. By the time of St. Leo the Great (440-461), the law of clerical celibacy was obligatory throughout the Western Church.

No one is forced to be a priest, and the young man who is called to the priesthood knows quite well that he must freely bind himself to the obligation of celibacy. To do so is one of his greatest joys. He knows that God will bless his work in return for such a great sacrifice. He knows that he will be free to do his priestly work for God unencumbered by having to provide and care for a wife and family. He knows, too, that God gives His grace to His priests in a special way to keep them chaste. Every day he will consecrate at Mass and call down upon the altar the King of Virgins and receive Him in Holy Communion; every day he will recite the Divine Office, an hour of obligatory prayer; he will meditate frequently on the divine truths, and throughout his priestly life he will receive every help to preserve intact the chastity he has chosen for himself. Far from finding it a burden, he will consider it a great privilege to be called to be one of the special friends of the Lamb of God. Those who say priestly chastity is impossible utter a wicked libel, not only against the Catholic priesthood, but against all moral, unmarried people living in the world.

Anglican Orders

Are Anglican ministers real priests? On September 13th, 1896, Pope Leo XIII answered that question in a solemn document called *Apostalicae Curae* (from its first two Latin words of the text). **"Ordinations carried out according to the Anglican rite have been and are absolutely null and utterly void,"** he says. This condemnation is based on theological and not historical grounds. Let us glance at the reason the Pope gives.

He writes: "The words which until recently were commonly held by Anglicans to constitute the proper form [the essential words of the Sacrament] of priestly ordination—namely, 'Receive the Holy Ghost'—certainly do not in the least definitely express the sacred Order of Priesthood, or its grace and power, which is chiefly the power of offering the Sacrifice of the Mass.

"This form had indeed afterwards added to it (in 1662) the words 'for the office and work of a priest,' etc.; **but this rather shows that the Anglicans themselves perceived that the first form** (1552) **was defective and inadequate**. But even if this addition could give the form its due signification, it was introduced too late, as a century had already elapsed since the adoption of the Edwardine Ordinal, for as the hierarchy had become extinct, there remained no power of ordaining." He goes on to point out that from the prayers of the Ordinal "has been deliberately removed whatever sets forth the dignity and office the priesthood in the Catholic rite. **That form** [the essential words of the Sacrament], **therefore, cannot be considered apt or sufficient for the Sacrament which omits what it ought essentially to signify**." (Emphasis added).

The same is true of the consecration of bishops. Even when, in 1662, the words "for the office and work of a bishop" were added to the form used since the time of Edward VI in 1552, they could only be understood in a sense alien to the true Catholic tradition. Thus, the form [essential words of the Sacrament] "approved" by Edward VI, even when amended, was powerless to confer the fullness of the priesthood. Therefore, no bishop could be validly consecrated so long as this form was employed, that is, in the Anglican Church since 1552. And if those who were "consecrated" by this form ordained priests, they were trying to do the impossible. Priests can only be ordained by bishops, and once the truly Catholic hierarchy had become extinct among the Anglicans, there were no other bishops who could ordain more priests.

Nor is that all. With regard to the defect of intention, Pope Leo XIII continues: "The Church does not judge about the mind and intention, in so far as it is something by its nature internal; but in so far as it is clearly manifested externally, she is bound to judge according to it. When anyone has rightly and seriously made use of the due form and the matter requisite for effecting and conferring a Sacrament, he is considered by the very fact to do what the Church does. On this principle rests the doctrine that a Sacrament is truly conferred by the ministry of one who is a heretic or unbaptized, provided the Catholic rite is employed [and provided he is normally empowered to be the minister of that Sacrament]. On the other hand, **if the rite be changed, with the obvious intention of introducing another rite not approved by the Church, and rejecting what the Church does, and what by the institution of Christ belongs to the nature of the Sacrament, then it is clear that not only is the necessary intention wanting to the Sacrament, but that the intention is adverse and destructive of the Sacrament**." (Emphasis added.)

That is what happened in the Anglican Church. The traditional rite of ordination was changed, and another substituted in its place, precisely because the Reformers rejected belief in the Sacrifice of the Mass and **did not intend to ordain "Massing," or sacrificing priests**.

Writing in the *National Review* for September, 1925, the Anglican Bishop Knox stated: "The Pope refused absolutely to recognize our Anglican Orders on the ground that our Church does not ordain priests to offer the Sacrifice of the Mass. In spite of attempts made by our Archbishop to conceal this defect, **the Pope from his point of view was unquestionably right**. It is true that certain priests of the Church of England offer so-called Masses, but as they were not ordained by the Church with the intention that they should offer the Body and Blood of Christ to the Father, the Sacrament of their Ordination is **for this purpose a failure**.

"The Prayer Book and Ordinal [containing the rite, or ceremony, including the words] are simply un-Catholic, since they show no sign of fulfilling the most important of all Catholic functions.

"If the Sacrament of Orders is administered without the intention of ordaining priests to offer sacrifices, **the persons ordained are not priests at all**. We have here not a question of some imperfectly instructed bishop. **We are concerned with the purpose and the object of a church**.

"No one reading the Roman Ordinal can doubt that it is full of the intention of ordaining sacrificing priests. No one reading the English Ordinal can suspect that it has such an object. It [i.e., the English Ordinal] clearly expresses some power of absolution, it definitely expresses administration of a sacrament. **But of sacrifice there is not a single word from first to last, nor is there in the consecration of a bishop a hint that bishops are to ordain sacrificing priests**." (Emphases added).

To summarize: In the Bull *Apostolicae Curae* (1896), the Pope (Leo XIII) decided irrevocably:

1. That the Christian priesthood is essentially a sacrificing priesthood;
2. That Cranmer and the framers of the Edwardine Ordinal for the Anglican Church expressly rejected that concept of the priesthood;
3. That they chose that particular form and ceremony for the

administration of Holy Orders **for the express purpose** of incorporating their repudiation of a sacrificing priesthood;

4. That they did effectively repudiate a sacrificing priesthood;
5. That therefore they rendered the meaning of the rite and ceremony indeterminate by cutting out an essential element of it;
6. That those who used the new form made by Cranmer must be presumed to have intended to confer through it what it was intended to confer, a non-sacrificing priesthood;
7. That a non-sacrificing minister is **not a Catholic priest**;
8. That therefore those ordained by the Edwardine Ordinal are not Catholic priests, deacons, or bishops, and as the Catholic priesthood is the only true Christian priesthood, Anglican ministers are, in fact—truth and reality—mere laymen, incapable of administering any of the Sacraments which require a priest for their minister.

Thus, in the Anglican Church there is no Real Presence, no True Sacrifice, no valid Confirmation, no sacramental absolution from sin and no effective Last Anointing. How wrong it is that the movement which brought with it the deprivation of the priesthood and the Sacraments which depend on it should be called the "Reformation!"

The world's debt

No human language can describe the spiritual benefits given by the Catholic priesthood to mankind, but even in the temporal sphere, the Catholic priesthood has been the greatest civilizing influence ever found throughout the whole course of history. Christianity is the source, the measure and the nursery of all true civilization, and Christianity has always been what its priesthood has made it. In every department of culture, pioneer work has been done by the Church in every century; through her priesthood she has carried the light of the Faith and the blessings of Christian morality and education to every country in the world. It was the Catholic priesthood which from the end of the fourth century converted the German hordes and so made possible the great work of Charlemagne in founding the Holy Roman Empire four hundred years later. When

Europe was largely Christian, it was the Catholic priesthood which carried the Gospel to pagan lands. China was covered with missionary stations even in the fourteenth century. From that day to this, the work of preaching the Gospel has gone on all over the world. The famous Reductions of Paraguay—the communal mission villages for the Indians established in the 17th century—were but one example of the beneficial results of an activity that is as universal as it is untiring in its efforts, even for the material well-being of men. Bancroft, an American historian, declared that in the French colonies in America, no notable city was founded, no river explored, no cape circumnavigated, without a Jesuit showing the way.

Morality is the inseparable companion of religion, and the two combined are indispensable for the growth of culture. For nearly twenty centuries the Catholic priesthood has never ceased to inculcate the practice of the Ten Commandments by preaching the love of God and of all men for His sake, by preaching purity in the relations of men and women with one another, and by holding up the example of Christ as the ideal of perfection. It has thus been the greatest cultural force in the history of our race.

In regard to strictly social work, it was the Catholic priesthood— from St. Paul to Cardinal Lavigerie, who died in 1892—that was principally responsible for the abolition of slavery and the slave-trade. The first medical faculty in Europe, the famous School of Salerno, was, like all the great Universities, established by Catholic priests. In 1340, for example, the University of Oxford had about 30,000 students. It was due "entirely to the clergy of the Church of Rome" wrote Hume, that the precious literature of antiquity was preserved from extinction. The idea of scientific progress is of purely Catholic origin, while the slogan "Education for All" was first uttered by a Pope—Innocent III in the thirteenth century. Long before any university was founded, cathedral schools and other renowned scientific institutions, directed by Catholic priests, worked in the interests of secular knowledge. Wherever there was an elementary school, it was conducted by priests. Immediately after the invention of printing, it was the demand and taste of the clergy that created a market for books. Erasmus complained: "The booksellers declare that before the outbreak of the Reform they disposed of 3,000 volumes more quickly than they now sell 600."

Early Humanism was supported by famous clerics like Erasmus and Petrarch; the greatest Spanish writers of the seventeenth century were priests: Cervantes (author of *Don Quixote*), Lope de Vega (who dominated the Golden Age of drama), Calderon (writer of *The Purgatory of St. Patrick*) and others.

Turning to the world of science, St. Albert the Great was far in advance of his time as a student of natural science and even compiled an encyclopedia. Roger Bacon, a Franciscan Monk of the thirteenth century, is rightly called the Father of Experimental Science. The following are but a few of the more outstanding names of famous scientists numbered among the priests and Religious of the Catholic Church:

Jose Algue (born 1856), a Jesuit, who invented the barocyclonometer, used to detect the approach of cyclones;

Bartholomeus Anglicus (13th cent.), a Franciscan who wrote the first great medieval encyclopedia of science;

Joseph Bayma (d. 1892), an Italian Jesuit, author of *Molecular Mechanics*,

Ruggiero Boscovich (d. 1787), a Jesuit astronomer, famous engineer and inventor of a micrometer which required no artificial illumination of the field of the telescope. He was a Fellow of the Royal Society of London;

Louis Bourheois (d. 1878), one of the first to present and develop the problem of the eoliths [chipped flints];

Paul Camboue (d. 1929), a Jesuit missionary and geologist, made valuable investigations on the large spiders of Madagascar, discovered the silk thread spun by them, and advanced the art of spinning and weaving;

George Camel (d. 1706), a Jesuit botanist, after whom the evergreen shrub *Camellia* is named, made valuable investigation of the plants and natural history of the Philippines;

Jean Baptiste Carnoy (d. 1899), founder of the science of cytology [development of cells];

Bonaventure Cavaliere (d. 1647), popularized the use of logarithms in Italy and was renowned for his "Method of Indivisibles," a forerunner of integral calculus;

Christopher Clavius (d. 1612), a Jesuit, the "Euclid of the 16th century," Vernier's precursor and architect of the Gregorian Calendar reform;

Nicolaus Copernicus (d. 1543), a Canon of Frauenburg, certainly a cleric and a member of the Third Order of St. Dominic, founder of modern astronomy;

Procopius Divisch (d. 1765), made instruments necessary for his outstanding experiments in hydraulics and electricity; one of the first to apply electricity to the cure of disease; erected a lightning conductor before Franklin's suggestions were known;

Joseph Eckhel (d. 1798), founder of the scientific study of the coins of classical antiquity;

Charles Michel de l'Epee (d. 1789), inventor of the sign alphabet for the deaf and dumb;

Pierre Gassendi (d. 1655), the "Bacon of France," first to observe the transit of Mercury across the sun's disc;

Andrew Gordon (d. 1751), first used a cylinder of glass to produce frictional electricity; invented electrical chimes;

Francesco Grimaldi (d. 1663), discovered the diffraction, interference and dispersion of light passing through a prism;

Rene Just Hauy (d. 1822), pioneer in pyro-electricity and father of crystallography;

Lawrence Hengler (d. 1858), invented the horizontal pendulum used in seismographs;

Pierre Heude (d. 1902), zoologist, author of the standard work on the land molluscs of China;

Athanasius Kircher (d. 1680), inventor of the magic lantern; authority on volcanoes; deciphered hieroglyphics; perfected the speaking tube and the aeolian harp; first definitely stated the germ theory of disease;

Thomas Linacre (d. 1524), founder of the Royal College of Physicians, London;

Edme Mariotte (d. 1684), established the law of gases that bears his name;

Gregory Mendel (d. 1884), author of Mendel's Law of Heredity;

Giuseppe Piazzi (d. 1826), discovered the first planetoid, Ceres, January 1st, 1801;

Jean Picard (d. 1682), first accurately measured a degree of the meridian;

Jean Pitra (d. 1889), Cardinal, archeologist, discovered the "Inscription of Autun";

Giovanni Battista Riccioli (d. 1671), introduced the lunar nomenclature still in use;

Bernardino de Sahagun (d. 1590), Aztec archeologist, compiled Aztec history, grammar and dictionary;

Christopher Scheiner (d. 1650), invented the pantograph and a telescope which made possible the first systematic investigation of sun spots;

Berthold Schwarz (13th century), inventor of firearms;

Angelo Secchi (d. 1878), inventor of the meteorograph, laid foundations of the unique "Sun Records," discovered the "flash spectrum," discovered the five Secchi types of stars;

Lazzaro Spallanzani (d. 1799), first to explain correctly the nature of the spermatazoa and the physiologic process of digestion. Proved regeneration of matter and the falsity of spontaneous generation;

Niels Steensen (d. 1686), bishop, "father of geology," discovered the excretory duct of the parotid glands;

Basil Valentine (14th century), founder of analytical chemistry, "the last alchemist and the first chemist;"

Francesco de Vico (d. 1848), discovered six comets.

For the first geographical chart or map, we are indebted to Fra Mauro of Venice (d. 1459); the father of comparative philology is Hervas y Panduro (d. 1809); the first Sanskrit grammar was written by Paolino di san Bartolomeo in 1790. Cardinal Baronius (1538-1607) and other Catholic scholars are the founders of historical criticism. In the sphere of art, one can trace the influence of the Catholic priesthood from the days of the Catacombs to Fra Angelico and to the Beuron school of the present day.

Agriculture, mining and the handicrafts owe an enormous debt to the priesthood. It was, indeed, Catholic bishops and priests who laid the basis of the science of national economy and so enabled the economic life of nations to be placed on a scientific foundation.

To say that the Church is the enemy of progress, culture or civilization is a most wicked calumny. The Catholic priesthood is the greatest civilizing agency in the history of mankind. The few names mentioned above are some little indication of the scope and work of the clergy in every branch of human achievement. But add to that list the names of all those who have been taught by the Catholic priesthood and you will have a majority of the great names of the Christian era.

The Church and science

The Church teaches all her children to love nature because of its beauty, in which she sees the vestiges of the Almighty. Catholic theologians are not afraid of scientific research; they welcome it and keep abreast of it. As the Bible is the writing of God's Holy Spirit, so Nature is the work of His hands; they cannot contradict one another. But, rightly, the theologians ask for facts, and not mere theories. The latter are proved false if they contradict what is known to be God's truth. Too much modern scientific theory is accepted as fact, especially by those who are always ready to decry religion. Science and religion come from the one source, God, eternal Truth; therefore there can be no real antagonism between them. That is why the Catholic Church, largely through its priesthood, has always been and always will be science's **greatest friend**.

Respect for priests

Catholics have the greatest respect and reverence for their priests. They address them as "Father," because the priest does for the life of the soul what parents do for the life of the body. From the Baptismal font to deathbed, Catholics are dependent on their priests for their soul-life; priests, in their turn, realize that their devotion to their people must be absolutely limitless and completely selfless. Of course, priests are human. St. Peter, Christ's first Vicar, described himself as a sinner, and Christ even called him "Satan." (*Matt.* 16:23). And it was Peter who denied Christ. Yet, in spite of it, Christ made him a priest and the first Pope. This choice by Christ made no automatic change in his character, as we can see from the story of the *Acts of the Apostles,* when he had to be rebuked by St. Paul. The facts are that Christ wishes to use human acts as His instruments, and man alone can provide human acts with a right intention. No amount of weakness, or even badness, in Peter could interfere with the official work done through him by Christ, so long as he himself contributed his act for Christ's work. So it is in the priesthood; Christ operates through the actions of His priests. They are and always will be human beings, with their faults and failings, their ways and their mannerisms. But the **office** of the priesthood demands reverence, no matter how poorly some exceptional individual priest *personally* merits it. It will be found that the vast majority of Catholic priests have not disappointed the hopes centered in them by God, who called them to their state of life, and by the Catholics who so depend on them. As Christ founded and protects His Church, so He founded and protects His priests, upon whom the Church depends.

"If I saw a priest and an angel, I would bend my knee first to the priest and then to the angel." (St. Francis of Assisi).

Chapter 31

Extreme Unction and Indulgences

What is the Sacrament of Extreme Unction? *The Sacrament of Extreme Unction is the anointing of the sick with holy oil, accompanied with prayer.*

When is Extreme Unction given? *Extreme Unction is given when we are in danger of death by sickness.*

What are the effects of the Sacrament of Extreme Unction? *The effects of the Sacrament of Extreme Unction are to comfort and strengthen the soul, to remit sin and even to restore health, when God sees it to be expedient.*

What authority is there in Scripture for the Sacrament of Extreme Unction? *The authority in Scripture for the Sacrament of Extreme Unction is in the 5th Chapter of St. James, where it is said: "Is any one sick among you? Let him bring in the priests of the Church; and let them pray over him, anointing him with oil in the name of the Lord. And the prayer of faith shall save the sick man; and the Lord shall raise him up; and if he be in sins they shall be forgiven him." (James 5:14-15).*

What is an Indulgence? *An Indulgence is a remission, granted by the Church, of the temporal punishment (spiritual debt) which often remains due to sin after its guilt has been forgiven.*

The Sacrament of Extreme Unction defined

IT has already been mentioned that Christ, in His infinite goodness, instituted a special Sacrament to confer the graces required during life's last struggle. It is called Extreme Unction, Last Anointing and Anointing of the Sick. It is defined as **a Sacrament instituted by Jesus Christ whereby spiritual assistance is bestowed**

on people who have come to the age of reason, who are sick and in grave danger of death. This assistance is most profitable when death is imminent, and even sometimes affords relief from bodily ailments.

The Council of Trent has defined that "this sacred Anointing of the Sick was instituted by Christ Our Lord as a true and proper Sacrament of the New Dispensation, was insinuated in St. Mark's Gospel, but commended to the faithful and promulgated by St. James the Apostle."

Extreme Unction in Scripture

The words in St. Mark are: "And they cast out many devils, and anointed with oil many that were sick, and healed them." (*Mark* 6:13). Is this a reference to the Sacrament of Extreme Unction or not? Most medieval writers seem to have thought it was, but modern commentators ask how the Apostles could administer a Sacrament when they were not yet ordained and how the sick could receive it without being baptized. Consequently, the Council of Trent says that the Sacrament is at most "insinuated" here.

The classic text is in the Epistle of St. James: "Is any man sick among you? Let him bring in the priests of the church, and let them pray over him, anointing him with oil in the name of the Lord. And the prayer of faith shall save the sick man: and the Lord shall raise him up: and if he be in sins, they shall be forgiven him." (*James* 5:14-15).

The Greek word used by St. James and translated as "sick" really means "seriously ill." That is its meaning in other places of Scripture, e.g., *John* 4:46; *John* 11:1, 3, 6; *Acts* 9:37; *Phil.* 2:27.

"In the Lord's name" obviously means by the Lord's command or authority.

"Prayer offered in faith" seems to indicate the acceptance of a truth on the authority of God, i.e., that this particular sacramental prayer is known to have some special effect in virtue of God's word.

"Will restore the sick man" seems to refer principally to spiritual healing, for that is the sense in which the words are used throughout this Epistle.

"The Lord will give him relief" refers most probably to both spiritual and physical relief, for they cannot be entirely separated.

It is clear from this text that Extreme Unction is a true Sacrament. It is certainly an outward sign (the anointing with oil) of inward grace (strengthening of the soul and the remission of sin) instituted by Christ ("in the name of the Lord"—*James* 5:14).

The evidence of Tradition

As in the case of the other Sacraments, we naturally look to the tradition of the Church for evidence that Extreme Unction has always been regarded as a Sacrament. It must be admitted that among the very early Fathers there is a scarcity of testimony on the point. For this there are many reasons, the principal being that this was never a publicly administered Sacrament with which the external discipline of the Church was concerned and about which it was necessary to write a great deal. Again, we would naturally expect to find most evidence in the commentaries of the Fathers on the Epistle of St. James, but unfortunately, the earliest such commentary we possess belongs to the 8th century and is by the Venerable Bede. Nevertheless, evidence is not entirely lacking.

Origen quotes the passage from *James* 5:14-15, adding another phrase, "Let them lay hands on him." This proves, of course, that the passage was known and acted upon in the third century, but commentators on Origen prove that he was really referring to a Sacramental rite supplementary to but distinct from Penance.

There are more or less obscure references in Tertullian, Aphraates (4th century), St. Ephrem and St. Augustine. In the life of St. Hypatius, who died before 450, we are told that when he was infirmarian in his monastery and not yet a priest, he reported to the Abbot, who was a priest, any case of serious sickness, so that the invalid might be anointed. "It often happened," the author adds, "that in a few days, God co-operating in his efforts, he sent the man home restored to health." (Bollandist, *Acta Sanctorum,* June 17th).

St. John Chrysostom has a particularly interesting reference when he compares parents with priests, saying that both beget to life. But parents, he says, cannot ward off death; whereas, priests can ward off spiritual death through forgiving sins, and he immediately quotes the text of St. James. If he were thinking of Penance, he would certainly have quoted St. John. (*On the Priesthood,* III, vi).

In the 5th century, Victor of Antioch seems to anticipate the definition of the Sacrament. "Oil both cures pains and is a source of light and refreshment. The oil, then, used in anointing signifies the mercy of God, and the cure of the disease, and the enlightenment of the heart. For it is manifest to all that the prayer effected all this; but the oil, as I think, was the symbol of these things." (Cramer, *Cat. Graec. Patrum.* I, p. 324). Note the distinction between signification and causality.

Passing over passages in St. Ambrose and St. Cyril of Alexandria, we find that in 416, Pope Innocent I wrote to Decentius, Bishop of Eugubium, about the ministry of Extreme Unction. His letter was later incorporated in various early collections of Canon Law. From it we gather that Extreme Unction was regarded as a Sacrament on a par with Penance and the Eucharist, that it can be administered by priests or bishops, although the oil used can be blessed by a bishop only, and that it remits sin. (*Denzinger,* 99).

St. Bede refers to the letter of Pope Innocent, repeating his injunctions and adding that the oil is to be consecrated in the name of the Lord and that when priests anoint the sick, they should do so invoking the name of the Lord. He concludes: "If the sick be in sins and shall have confessed them to the priests of the Church, and have striven with a good heart to abandon them and to amend, they shall be forgiven." *(P.L.,* xciii, 39). Amalarius of Metz, writing a century later, understood St. Bede to teach that Extreme Unction certainly forgives sin.

Many of the ancient liturgical books of the Church, as well as the decrees of various Councils from the 9th century onwards, refer to the "Anointing of the Sick."

The really significant fact is that, in the 9th century, Extreme Unction was regarded as a true Sacrament all over the Christian world. Even the earliest schismatics and smallest eastern sects had this belief. The unanimous agreement of the whole Church is surely an infallible criterion of truth.

Matter, form, effects, minister

The matter of the Sacrament is the anointing with oil of olives, specially blessed by the bishop. This blessing is necessary for validity. At least one of the senses or the forehead must be anointed.

The form is the prayer prescribed in the liturgical books of the particular rite to which the priest belongs. In the West, the following prayer is used: "Through this holy anointing and His most tender mercy, may the Lord pardon thee whatever faults thou hast committed by sight. Amen." (This prayer is repeated for the ears, nose, mouth, hands and feet.) In the new Roman Rite (1972) it reads: "Through this holy anointing and His most loving mercy, may the Lord assist you by the grace of the Holy Spirit, so that when you have been freed from your sins, He may save you and in His goodness raise you up."

The effects of Extreme Unction are:
1) An increase of grace;
2) Relief of mind and help to meet the temptations of one's last agony;
3) Removal of the vestiges of sin, remission of venial sins and even of mortal sins when the sick person is not conscious of them and has at least attrition (imperfect contrition) for them and is unable to make his Confession;
4) Sometimes, the cure of sickness—when God sees that such a cure is for the good of a person's soul.

The ordinary minister of Extreme Unction is the parish priest of the place where the person is living; but in case of necessity, or when leave to do so can be reasonably expected from the parish priest or the bishop of the diocese, any priest can administer the Sacrament.

Who may be anointed?

The Sacrament is administered to any member of the Church who, having come to the use of reason, is in **danger of death through sickness or old age.** It can be given **only once** during the same period of danger of death; but if the danger passes away and then recurs, the Sacrament can be repeated.

If a person is not in possession of his senses, he may be given Extreme Unction if, when he was conscious, he asked for it, at least implicitly, or would have asked for it, even though he afterwards loses the use of his senses, or even of his reason.

Before being anointed, the sick person should go to Confession, if he can, or at least make an act of contrition, and also make acts of faith, hope, charity and submission to God's will.

The necessity of Extreme Unction

Extreme Unction is not absolutely necessary for salvation, but it is wrong to neglect it. **Relatives and friends have a grave duty (under pain of mortal sin) to see that the priest is called to those who are seriously ill, and/or in danger of death** (the frailty of old age may constitute a danger of death); they should not wait until there is extreme danger of death. We should all be anxious to show Our Lord how we appreciate this wonderful Sacrament by willingly receiving it as soon as we fall dangerously ill and by calling the priest to others at the earliest possible moment after it is known that an illness or an accident might prove fatal. Even when a person is apparently dead, he may be anointed for some considerable time after death seems to have taken place (up to and even beyond several hours, based on the priest's judgment in the particular case), for according to medical science, *apparent* death often precedes *actual* death.

All should pray that they will not die without receiving this "Last Sacrament." The idea that the sick are disturbed by the priest's being called in to anoint them is often a temptation of the devil. Experience shows that the Sacred Anointing brings with it great consolation and peace of soul. In any case, it is better to risk disturbing the invalid rather than to risk his eternal salvation.

Indulgences

One of the effects of Extreme Unction is to remove the "vestiges" or "lingering traces" of sin, the scar left by the wound of sin. This embraces the mental obscurity, the frailty, the lack of vigor in resisting further evil, which are the result of sin. Extreme Unction restores the person to complete spiritual health.

Further, it has been the constant teaching of Catholic theologians that this Sacrament also removes the temporal punishment (spiritual debt) due to sin, but **depending upon the dispositions of the recipient.** Extreme Unction is not an automatic means of escaping Purgatory; temporal punishment is remitted entirely only when the dispositions of the recipient are perfect.

Guilt and satisfaction

When considering certain of the Commandments, we saw that before certain sins can be forgiven, the injury done by them must be repaired. Restitution must be made for theft, for example. *But all sins carry with them a duty of making reparation to God.* Even though they are forgiven in the Sacrament of Penance, God requires expiation for them.

The prophet Nathan told King David: "The Lord also hath taken away thy sin: thou shalt not die. Nevertheless, because thou has given occasion to the enemies of the Lord to blaspheme, for this thing, the child that is born to thee, shall surely die." (*2 Kings* 12:13-14).

The coming of Christ did not change this law. **He bore the penalty for sin to give value to our expiations, not to dispense us from them.** St. Paul told the Colossians: "Who now rejoice in my sufferings for you, and fill up those things that are wanting of the sufferings of Christ, in my flesh, for his body, which is the church." (*Col.* 1:24). The metaphor used is that of a poor man trying to contribute toward a sum which a richer man has paid in advance. Christ's sufferings are more than sufficient in themselves to make atonement for all possible sin, but God requires that, as members of Christ's Mystical Body, we should add our prayers, works and sufferings to those of Calvary in expiation for our sins.

St. Augustine wrote long ago: "Man is forced to suffer even after his sins have been forgiven, though it was sin that caused him to fall back into such misery. For the punishment outlasts the guilt, lest the guilt should be accounted slight, if with its forgiveness, the penalty also came to an end." (*In Joan.* cxxi. v., 5).

The Treasury of the Church

It follows from the doctrine of the Mystical Body that the merits of one member can be made available to another. That is the whole basis of our Redemption. Christ's merits belong to the Body of which He is Head. So do all the merits of all the Saints and the holy souls who have been members of the Church from the beginning. Hence, the Church has at her disposal an infinite treasury of merits.

The Church can remit satisfaction

Christ gave the Church complete power of binding and loosing (cf. page 283f). She has the right, therefore, to loose or remit some of the expiation due to God by a sinner after the guilt of his sin has been forgiven. St. Paul did this in the case of a sinful man in Corinth. He first ordered him to be excommunicated, but after he had shown his sorrow, the Apostle pardoned him and remitted his punishment. "To him who is such a one, this rebuke is sufficient, which is given by many: So that on the contrary, you should rather forgive him and comfort him, lest perhaps such a one be swallowed up with overmuch sorrow . . . For, what I have pardoned, if I have pardoned any thing, for your sakes have I done it in the person of Christ." (*2 Cor.* 2:6-7,10).

It was the custom in the early Church for sinners to receive severe penances for their sins. These lasted for a considerable time, even for years. But often the penitents went to those about to be martyred, who gave them letters interceding with the bishop for a remission of the penance which had been imposed in consideration of the sufferings the martyr was to endure. When the persecutions ceased, the bishops still continued to remit the canonical penances, as we know from many writings and from the decrees of several Councils. The ancient penitentials of England and Ireland provide for relaxation in certain cases. From the 8th century onwards the severe penances of the early Church were changed into prayers, fastings, scourgings, pilgrimages, almsgiving and such like. Thus the Penitential of Egbert, Archbishop of York, says: "For him who can comply with what the penitential prescribes, well and good; for him who cannot, we give counsel of God's mercy. Instead of one year on bread and water, give twenty-six solidi in alms, fast till None* on one day of each week and till Vespers* on another, and in the three Lents bestow in alms half of what he receives."

Indulgence defined

All this leads us to the definition of an **Indulgence,** which is **the remission by God of the temporal punishment (spiritual debt) due to sins whose guilt has already been forgiven,** a remission which the Church grants apart from the Sacrament of Penance.

The Council of Trent issued this decree about Indulgences: "Since the power of conferring Indulgences has been granted by Christ to His Church, and the Church has from the very earliest times made use of this power divinely bestowed upon her, this Holy Synod teaches and orders that the use of Indulgences, which are most salutary for Christians and approved by the authority of Sacred Councils, is to be retained in the Church." (Chapt. xxi, par. 3).

By means of Indulgences, the Church remits **the temporal punishment** due to sin by applying to the living, by way of absolution, and to the dead, by way of suffrages ("Masses, prayers, or acts of piety offered for the repose of the souls of the faithful departed"— Fr. John Hardon, S.J., *Modern Cath. Dict.*), the infinite satisfaction paid by Jesus Christ as well as the superabundant satisfaction wrought by the Blessed Virgin Mary and the Saints.

It is true that there were abuses in regard to Indulgences in the Middle Ages, but some of the notions still current about the nature of Indulgences are very far removed from the truth. **An indulgence is not** a *pardon* for sin, *permission* to commit sin, *exemption* from any law or duty, nor the *purchase* of the release of a soul from Pur-

---

*None (from *nona hora*, "the ninth hour") is that part of the official Divine Office of prayers and hymns which is sung in cathedrals and religious orders between noon and 3:00 p.m., commemorating the death of Our Lord, which took place at 3:00 p.m., "the ninth hour" of the ancient Jewish reckoning of the day. Vespers (from the Latin *vesper*, "eveningtide") are the evening hour prayers and hymns of the Divine Office sung daily in cathedrals and religious communities in the evening, usually between 3:00 p.m. and 6:00 p.m. —Publisher, 2002.

gatory. For the Church has never given her authority to the proposition that an Indulgence can be applied to any given soul with unfailing effect. In fact, Pope Sixtus IV in 1477 taught expressly that Indulgences for the dead are applied "by way of suffrage" i.e., by way of petition or recommendation to God and depending on His acceptance for the specifically intended Poor Soul. The intercession of the living for the souls in Purgatory is very effective, but it is entirely up to God as to *what* Poor Soul will benefit by a person's prayers and indulgences offered for a particular individual thought to be in Purgatory.

Plenary and Partial Indulgences

There are two kinds of Indulgences:

1. **Plenary,** whereby the **entire debt** of temporal punishment is remitted;
2. **Partial,** whereby only a **portion** of the debt is remitted.

A Plenary Indulgence is said to be granted **only in the sense** that a person has fulfilled all the basic outward requirements of the Church for gaining one. If a person cannot gain the indulgence in full or plenary fashion, he can yet gain it partially, according to his dispositions.

The conditions for gaining an indulgence are:

1. The person must be baptized and not excommunicated;
2. He must have at least the general intention of gaining indulgences;
3. He must duly perform the good work required;
4. He must be in the state of grace, at least when he finishes the work prescribed.
5. The person gaining the indulgence must be a subject of the grantor of the indulgence.

And if it is question of gaining a Plenary Indulgence, he must also:

a) Not have his affection set on any venial sin. (There is a theological opinion that it is sufficient only to desire earnestly to be free from attachment to sin in order to fulfill this requirement.)

b) Receive Communion on the day he gains the Plenary Indulgence.

c) Go to Confession seven days before or after the day he gains the Plenary Indulgence.

d) Say some prayers for the intentions of the Pope. (An "Our Father" and "Hail Mary" suffice.)

When an indulgence of, say, 100 days is attached to a certain prayer, it does not mean that the one who recites the prayer will be relieved of 100 days' punishment in Purgatory. The Church has never really defined what is meant by an indulgence of so many days or years. Historically speaking, we know that the traditional terminology arose from the remissions of the canonical penalties, as we have described above. But it is by no means certain that 100 days' indulgence will benefit a soul as much as 100 days' canonical penance. There is no evidence that the old canonical penance can be taken as an absolute and constant standard. [Since 1967, the terminology of so many days' indulgence has been dropped, and indulgences are spoken of merely as **"partial"** or **"plenary."** —Publisher, 2002.]

Unless the contrary is stated, we can apply the indulgences we gain to the souls detained in Purgatory, when such indulgences have been granted by the Pope; but no indulgence can be applied by us to persons still living.

Acts carrying a Plenary Indulgence

According to the New Norms (as of 1967) for gaining indulgences, a person can gain only one Plenary Indulgence on one and the same day; there is only one exception to this rule, and that is when a person has already gained one for that day and then on the same day is in danger of death, when he can also gain the Plenary Indulgence connected to the apostolic blessing usually imparted with the Last Sacraments.

   The following is only a partial listing of acts that carry a Plenary Indulgence, according to the *Handbook of Indulgences*, issued by the Holy See in 1967. The following list is exerpted from the general listing for use of the Faithful and does not include those Plenary Indulgences granted to particular institutes:

1. For a visit of adoration to the Blessed Sacrament for at least half an hour.
2. For receiving the Pope's blessing when given to the city and to the world, even over the radio.
3. For the hour of death when a priest cannot be present to give the Sacraments and apostolic blessing with plenary indulgence, provided that during life one habitually said some prayers. . . . (The condition "provided that during life one habitually said some prayers" in this case supplies for the three usual conditions for gaining a plenary indulgence. And this plenary indulgence can be gained even if the person had already gained a plenary indulgence for some other good work on that same day.)
4. For the receiving of one's first Holy Communion or for being devoutly present at the ceremonies of first Holy Communion.
5. For the priest who celebrates his first Mass with some solemnity and also for the faithful who devoutly assist at that Mass.
6. For saying the Rosary in a church or public oratory, or in the family, or in a religious community, or in a Pious Association. (By the Rosary is here meant at least five decades. For the gaining of the plenary indulgence, the Rosary must be said continuously, without interruption; to the vocal prayer there must be added devout meditation on the mysteries; in public recitation, the mysteries must be announced according to approved custom; but in private recitation, it suffices that one simply add meditation on the Mysteries to the vocal prayer.)
7. For reading Sacred Scripture for at least half an hour, as spiritual reading, with the reverence due to the Divine Word.
8. For making the Way of the Cross. (Where the stations are properly erected, all that is required is devout meditation on the Passion and Death of Christ [not necessarily on that phase represented by the respective station] and movement from one

station to another. However, when there is such a number of people that movement from station to station cannot be made without disturbance, it is sufficient if the one who leads the stations moves from one to the other, the rest remaining in their places. Those "impeded" from making the Stations can gain the same plenary indulgence by devout reading and meditation on the Passion and Death of Christ for at least half an hour.)

9. For visiting the parish church on the feast of the titular (the Saint for whom it is named) and on the second day of August (Portiuncula). (When visits to a church are prescribed, the prayers for the Pope's intentions are one Our Father and one Creed).

10. For devoutly visiting the church or oratory of Religious on the feast day of their sainted Founder.

11. For renewing one's baptismal vows by using any customary formula during the celebration of the Easter Vigil or on the anniversary of one's baptism.

(For a complete listing of general acts carrying a Plenary Indulgence, see the *New Regulations on Indulgences*, TAN, 1970, pages 27-32.)

Acts carrying a Partial Indulgence

According to the New Norms for gaining indulgences (as of 1967), a Partial Indulgence can be gained by any of the following prayers or acts.

The following enumeration contains the more common prayers and good works enriched with partial indulgences, as listed in the *Handbook of Indulgences* issued by the Holy See June 29, 1968. The Prayers not given in full here can easily be found in the prayerbooks normally used by the faithful:

1. "Direct, we beseech Thee, O Lord, our actions by Thy holy inspirations and carry them on by Thy gracious assistance, so that every prayer and work of ours may always begin from Thee and through Thee be happily ended. Amen."

2. The acts of Faith, Hope, Charity, and Contrition using any good formula. (Each act is indulgenced.)
3. A visit of adoration to the Blessed Sacrament.
4. The hymn *Adoro Te Devote*—"Devoutly I adore Thee."
5. The prayer "To Thee, O Blessed Joseph" (Usually said during the month of October.)
6. "We give Thee thanks, Almighty God, for all Thy benefits, Who lives and reigns forever and ever. Amen."
7. "Angel of God, my guardian dear, to whom His love commits me here, ever this day be at my side, to light and guard, to rule and guide."
8. The *Angelus* and in the Paschal Time the *Regina Coeli*.
9. The *Anima Christi*—"Soul of Christ."
10. A visit to a cemetery and prayer for the Poor Souls.
11. Spiritual Communion. (Any devout formula will suffice.)
12. The devout recitation of the Apostles Creed or the Nicene Creed.
13. Recitation of Lauds or Vespers of the office of the Dead.
14. Recitation of *De profundis* (*Ps.* 129).
15. For teaching or studying Christian Doctrine.
16. For saying the prayer, "Behold, O kind and Most Sweet Jesus" before an image of the Crucified after Communion.
17. "Hear us, O Lord, Holy Father, Almighty and Eternal God, and graciously send Thy holy Angel from Heaven to watch over, to cherish, to protect, to abide with, and to defend all who dwell in this house, through Christ our Lord. Amen."
18. The Act of Reparation to the Sacred Heart ("Most sweet Jesus . . .").
19. The Act of Dedication of the Human Race to Christ the King.
20. For each of the official litanies: The Most Holy Name of Jesus, the Sacred Heart of Jesus, the Most Precious Blood of Our Lord Jesus Christ, the Blessed Virgin Mary, St. Joseph and All Saints.
21. For the *Magnificat*.
22. For the *Memorare*.
23. For the *Miserere*.
24. For devoutly taking part in a public novena before the feasts of Christmas, Pentecost, the Immaculate Conception.

25. For devoutly making use of an object of piety (crucifix, cross, rosary, scapular, medal) properly blessed by any priest.

26. For the recitation of the Little Office of the Passion of Christ, of the Sacred Heart of Jesus, of the Blessed Virgin, of the Immaculate Conception, or of St. Joseph.

27. Any approved prayer for priestly or religious vocations.

28. For spending some time in devout mental prayer.

29. "Let us pray for our Pope . . . The Lord preserve him, and give him life, and make him to be blessed upon the earth, and deliver him not up to the will of his enemies."

30. "O sacred banquet, in which Christ is received, the memory of His Passion is renewed, the mind is filled with grace, and there is given to us a pledge of future glory."

31. For devoutly and attentively being present at a sermon.

32. For participating in a monthly recollection.

33. "Eternal rest grant unto them, O Lord, and let perpetual light shine upon them. May they rest in peace."

34. "O Lord, reward with eternal life all those who do us good for Thy name's sake."

35. For saying the Rosary privately. (For this private recitation outside a church the decades may be separated. Though one does not need to mention the Mystery, one should add meditation to the vocal prayer.)

36. For reading Sacred Scripture as spiritual reading with the veneration and devotion due to the word of God.

37. For the *Salve, Regina*—"Hail, Holy Queen."

38. "Holy Mary, help those in misery, strengthen the fainthearted, comfort the sorrowful, pray for the people, mediate for the clergy, intercede for all devout women; may all experience thy help who celebrate thy holy festival."

39. For saying the prayer in the missal in honor of the Saint whose feast is being celebrated, or any approved prayer.

40. For devoutly making the Sign of the Cross, saying the words: "In the name of the Father and of the Son and of the Holy Spirit. Amen."

41. "We fly to thy protection, O holy Mother of God. Despise not our petitions in our necessities, but deliver us always from all dangers, O glorious and blessed Virgin."

42. For the devout recitation of the *Tantum ergo*.
43. For reciting the hymn *Te Deum* in thanksgiving.
44. For reciting the hymn *Veni Creator*, and also for saying: "Come, Holy Ghost, fill the hearts of Thy faithful and enkindle in them the fire of Thy love. Send forth Thy Spirit and they shall be created, and Thou shalt renew the face of the earth."
45. For renewing one's Baptismal vows, using any customary formula.
46. "Visit this house, we beseech Thee, O Lord, and drive far from it all snares of the enemy. Let Thy holy angels dwell herein, who may keep us in peace, and let your blessing be always upon us, through Christ our Lord. Amen."

(The preceding list of acts and prayers enriched with partial indulgences is taken from *New Regulations on Indulgences*, TAN, Rockford, IL 61105, 1970, pp. 33-38.)

The value of Indulgences

There can be no doubt that indulgences are a great stimulus to the growth of holiness within the Church. St. Alphonsus Liguori (1696-1787) says that, to become a Saint, nothing more is needed than to gain all the indulgences we can. Fr. Faber lists what he calls the Eight Beatitudes of Indulgences:

1. They keep us among the thoughts of the purgative way;
2. They have an unworldly effect on us;
3. They keep the doctrine of Purgatory before us;
4. They are an exercise of charity to the faithful departed;
5. They are a means of promoting God's glory;
6. They honor the satisfactions of Jesus, Mary and the Saints;
7. They deepen our views of sin and give us a greater horror of it;
8. They keep us in harmony with the spirit of the Church.

We may add that indulgences also develop the sense of solidarity among Catholics by reminding us of the Communion of Saints, the doctrine of the Mystical Body, and the infinite merits of Christ's

Redemption, which make indulgences possible. They obviously encourage prayer, fasting and almsgiving, and they incite us to receive the Sacraments of Penance and Holy Communion more frequently.

Chapter 32

Marriage (1)

What is the Sacrament of Matrimony? *Matrimony is the Sacrament which sanctifies the contract of a Christian marriage and gives a special grace to those who receive it worthily.*

What special grace does the Sacrament of Matrimony give to those who receive it worthily? *The Sacrament of Matrimony gives to those who receive it worthily a special grace to enable them to bear the difficulties of their state, to love and be faithful to one another, and to bring up their children in the fear of God.*

Is it a sacrilege to contract marriage in mortal sin or in disobedience to the laws of the Church? *It is a sacrilege to contract marriage in mortal sin or in disobedience to the laws of the Church; instead of a blessing, the guilty parties thereby draw upon themselves the anger of God.*

What is a "mixed marriage"? *A "mixed marriage" is a marriage between a Catholic and one who, even though baptized, does not profess the Catholic Faith.*

Has the Church always forbidden mixed marriages? *The Church has always forbidden mixed marriages and considered them unlawful and pernicious.*

Does the Church sometimes permit mixed marriages? *The Church sometimes permits mixed marriages by granting a dispensation for very grave reasons and under special conditions.*

Can any human power dissolve the bond of marriage? *No human power can dissolve the bond of marriage because Christ has said, "What therefore God hath joined together let no man put asunder."* (*Matt.* 19:6).

Marriage made and ruled by God

M ARRIAGE was made by God Himself when He created Adam and Eve. "A man shall leave father and mother, and shall cleave to his wife; and they shall be two in one flesh." (*Gen.* 2:24).

Matrimony comes from two Latin words, *matris* and *munus,* meaning the **duty of motherhood.** The very name indicates God's purpose in instituting marriage.

That is the first thing we must remember about marriage—that God made it. What God made, God governs. Therefore, the laws made by God in regard to marriage cannot be wrong, unreasonable or too difficult. He, the infinitely wise and good God, made marriage for the good of the man, the woman and the children, and for the happiness of the family, the good of the State and the well-being of the human race. Thus, to violate God's laws in marriage can only result in injury to all those whom God intended to benefit by His laws.

At the same time, men are free to marry or not to marry; they are free in choosing their partner in marriage. But once the marriage contract has been freely entered into, the parties to it are subject to the laws of God governing marriage.

Christian Marriage is a Sacrament

Having studied the nature of the Sacraments and their purpose, one would expect that Christ would institute a special Sacrament to confer the graces necessary to enable members of His Church to attain His ideal of marriage. And thus the Council of Trent has defined: "If any one shall say that Matrimony is not truly and properly one of the Seven Sacraments of the Evangelical Law, instituted by Christ our Lord, but was invented in the Church by men, and does not confer grace, let him be anathema." (*Session* XXIV). But long before that, Pope Innocent IV, in the profession of Faith prescribed for the Waldensian heretics in 1208, included Marriage among the Sacraments.

St. Paul's allusion

St. Paul speaks of marriage in such a way that its sacramental nature can be deduced from his words. "The husband is the head of the wife, as Christ is the head of the church. He is the saviour of his body. Therefore as the church is subject to Christ, so also let the wives be to their husbands in all things. Husbands, love your wives, as Christ also loved the church, and delivered himself up for it: That he might sanctify it, cleansing it by the laver of water in the word of life. . . For this cause shall a man leave his father and mother, and shall cleave to his wife, and they shall be two in one flesh. This is a great sacrament; but I speak in Christ and in the church." (*Eph.* 5:23-26, 31-32).

Here the union of man and wife in marriage is compared to the union between Christ and His Church, which we have already considered in the instruction on the Mystical Body. There we saw that with His Church, Christ forms one mystical personality, to such an extent that He imprints His image to an extraordinary degree on His Church. In marriage, husband and wife form one principle, so that the joys and sorrows of one are the joys and sorrows of the other. As the union between Christ and His Church is absolutely indissoluble, so is Christian marriage. More—the union between Christ and the Church comes about through the grace which flows from the Head to all the members. Therefore, it can be inferred that a power of bestowing grace belongs to Christian marriage. Otherwise, the comparison used by St. Paul would lose much of its significance, and his statement that "This is a great sacrament" would be almost meaningless.

So St. Paul attributes to Christian marriage the three necessities of a Sacrament. As it is a contract, it is certainly an outward rite. It is said to signify the union between Christ and His Church, which is a union of grace. Moreover, it is a sign which produces the grace which it signifies, because it is clearly regarded as a supernatural and permanent union (like that of Christ and the Church). But the union between husband and wife cannot be permanently supernatural without Sanctifying Grace, to which actual graces are joined. Only Christ can attach such grace to an outward sign. Therefore, Christian marriage must be an outward sign of inward grace instituted by Christ, and therefore a Sacrament.

As we shall see later, Christ demanded two properties of every Christian marriage—unity and indissolubility. Even the Apostles expressed amazement at the difficulty of this doctrine. Therefore, we are justified in thinking that Our Lord could never make such a demand unless He knew He was going to give the necessary graces to the partners in marriage. The usual way for Him to do that would be through a Sacrament.

However, all this is rather incidental to the main argument. Even the Council of Trent does not claim that Scripture clearly teaches that marriage is a Sacrament instituted by Christ; it only declares that St. Paul "alludes" to it. The main argument that it is a Sacrament is from the constant teaching and practice of the Church.

The evidence of Tradition

No one will deny that in the twelfth century marriage was regarded as a Sacrament by both the Western and Eastern Churches, and even by schismatical and heretical sects. In 1181 the Council of Verona proclaimed that marriage is a Sacrament. If marriage was regarded as a Sacrament **after** the Great Eastern Schism, which divided East and West, it must have been regarded as a Sacrament before the Schism. [Photius, the usurping Patriarch of Constantinople, broke from Rome in 867, and Cerularius (a Patriarch of the same city) in 1053. The final break came in 1472.] For there never was an argument about this matter connected with the East-West split. The Western Church certainly never got the idea from the Eastern, and the Eastern Church certainly did not copy it from the Western. The only other alternative is that each side adopted the idea independently, which would be absurd, because, if either of them had done so, it would have been exposed to the severest criticisms from the other side. Hence, if the notion that marriage is a Sacrament was adopted by the Church, it must have been before the earliest of the schismatic churches detached itself from Rome. But there is not the slightest evidence of such a change taking place. The early Church was most conservative, and if any individual, or party, or diocese, or community had tried to introduce a new Sacrament, there would certainly have been a protest, of which we would surely find some evidence today.

On the contrary, all the evidence we have is that the early Church always regarded marriage as a Sacrament. St. Augustine called it a Sacrament in many a passage. "It is certain," he says, "that a Sacrament is recommended to believers in wedlock when the Apostle says, 'You who are husbands must show love to your wives, as Christ showed love to the Church.' Of this Sacrament the substance undoubtedly is that the man and the woman who are joined together in wedlock, should remain inseparable as long as they live." (*De Nupt. et Concup.,* i, 10). "The excellence of marriage is threefold: faithfulness, offspring, Sacrament." (*De Gen. ad Lit.* ix, 7).

St. Ambrose wrote: "We also do not deny that marriage was sanctified by Christ." (*Epist.* xix, 7). Elsewhere he calls it a "heavenly sacrament." (*De Abraham,* I, vii).

Tertullian, while still a Catholic, wrote that marriage "enjoys the protection of divine grace." (*Ad Uxorem,* II, vii). A little further on he speaks of marriage as being ratified by the Church and sealed with a blessing.

Of even greater weight than these testimonies of the Fathers is the evidence of the most ancient liturgical books. From these it can be gathered that since earliest times prayers were used at the marriage ceremony that referred to the special graces granted to the newly married persons.

The contract

The external sign which constitutes the Sacrament of Matrimony is simply the valid **contract** made by a man and woman to live together as husband and wife. **Whenever a contract or agreement to live as husband and wife is validly made by Christians, it is a Sacrament and causes grace.** If there is no valid contract, there is no Sacrament. Thus, the external consent, usually expressed in words, to the mutual agreement to live as husband and wife, is both the **matter** and the **form** of the Sacrament. In every Sacrament it is the minister who uses the matter and form, which together make up the outward sign. In marriage, the outward sign is made by the contracting parties themselves; therefore **they are the ministers of the Sacrament.** From this it follows that, in certain exceptional cases provided for in Church Law, marriage can be contracted and the Sacrament received without the presence of a priest. Moreover, non-Catholics, provided they are validly baptized and have no diriment impediments to the marriage, normally receive the Sacrament validly, for they are definitely excluded from the Canon Law which requires the presence of a parish priest at their wedding.

The graces of Christian marriage

The special graces given to worthy recipients of the Sacrament of Matrimony enable them to bear the difficulties of their state, to love and be faithful to one another, and to bring up their children in the fear of God. What these three headings cover is a matter of common experience—differences of temper and disposition, poverty and want of work, bad habits, ill-health, difficulties in the characters of the children, jealousies, etc. What a pity, then, that marriage can rightly be called the "forgotten Sacrament," because so many of those who receive it scarcely think of it afterwards and very often fail to ask God to bestow the very graces through it that they need.

Marriage ruled by the Church

If marriage is a Sacrament, it must be directly under the power of the Church. Of course, marriage has certain purely civil aspects, which do not touch its essence, e.g., the amount of the dowry, rights of succession to property, etc. With these the Church has no wish to interfere. But, apart from these, **everything pertaining to marriage must be regulated by the Church.** It is a right that has always been claimed and used by ecclesiastical authority, which has often insisted on enforcing legislation completely at variance with the civil laws.

"To decree and ordain concerning the Sacrament is, by the will of Christ Himself, so much a part of the power and duty of the Church, that it is plainly absurd to maintain that even the smallest fraction of such power has been transferred to the civil ruler. . . . Among Christians, every true marriage is, in itself and by itself, a Sacrament, and nothing can be further from the truth than to say that the Sacrament is an added ornament, or outward endowment, which can be separated and torn away

from the contract at the caprice of man." (Pope Leo XIII, Encyclical *Arcanum*).

Thus, divorce laws, which interfere with the substance and essential properties of marriage, are regarded by the Church as an unwarranted interference with her rights.

The primary object of Marriage

The primary object of all marriage is the procreation and education of children. If the sexes did not exist, marriage could not exist. It is evident that sexual faculties have been given to individuals, not for their own particular purposes, but for the preservation of the race. The union of the sexes has no real justification, except to serve the ends of the species. As the pleasure attached to eating cannot be the purpose for which one eats, so too it is in the case of marriage. The pleasure attached to the use of the sexual faculty is bestowed for a definite purpose by the Creator, and that purpose is primarily the begetting of children.

Inseparably united with the conception and birth of children is their future education. Throughout the whole of nature, the young are cared for by their parents until they can look after themselves. So it is with the human race. **Parents have the right and the duty of supervising everything connected with the education of their children.** That right and duty are part of the primary object of marriage.

Unity of marriage

From this primary object spring two properties of marriage—unity and indissolubility. Even though the ease of obtaining a divorce is increasing with alarming rapidity, Western Civilization still regards the principle, "one man, one wife," as essential for the welfare of society. Once that principle goes, there would be no provision for the education of the children, for it would be impossible to state definitely who were their parents. The possession by one husband of more than one wife, called polygamy, is also against the Natural Law, because, although it does not necessarily *prevent* the primary objects of marriage being achieved under certain circumstances, it certainly renders them more difficult. The presence of several wives in the same family circle could hardly be thought to be conducive to the education of their respective children.

Divorce forbidden

A marriage between baptized persons, which has been consummated, can be dissolved by no human authority whatsoever. In that case **divorce is absolutely impossible.** But the prohibition of divorce is not a specifically Catholic or even a specifically Christian doctrine. It rests primarily on the Natural Law, which binds the whole of humanity. Everything which tends to frustrate the primary end of marriage is obviously unnatural. A state of affairs in which married people could separate and remarry at will or by caprice would obviously militate strongly against the proper education of the offspring of the broken marriages. The present-day prevalence of divorce has reduced marriage almost to such a state. Laws have become lenient, collusion is prevalent, and the very number of divorce cases before the courts makes a proper consideration of them impossible.

But, even though the granting of divorce were restricted to the narrowest limits, it would still be against the Natural Law because the very fact of the existence of the possibility of the dissolution of a marriage tends to deflect the care of parents from their children, to encourage the parents to practice birth prevention and to be less careful in regard to conduct liable to cause friction between them. If the conviction is always there that, whatever happens, divorce is impossible, differences will be glossed over and forbearance and patience encouraged. Moreover, if it is known that the possibility for divorce exists, even in a very limited way, young people contemplating marriage will be less careful in the choice of a partner than in the case where they know there is no escape from a contract once it is ratified and consummated. If divorce were allowed for misconduct, it would be practically an encouragement to commit adultery. It is true that there had been some relaxation of the law among the Jews before the time of Christ, but He restored the primitive ideal: "Moses by reason of the hardness of your heart permitted you to put away your wives: but from the beginning it was not so." (*Matt.* 19:8).

Turning from the Natural Law to the teaching of Christ, the following passages of Scripture must be considered in regard to divorce.

"And it hath been said, Whosoever shall put away his wife, let him give her a bill of divorce. But I say to you, that whosoever shall put away his wife, excepting for the cause of fornication, maketh her to commit adultery: and he that shall marry her that is put away, committeth adultery." (*Matt.* 5:31-32). "What therefore God hath joined together, let no man put asunder." (*Matt.* 19:6).

"He saith to them: Because Moses by reason of the hardness of your heart permitted you to put away your wives: but from the beginning it was not so. And I say to you, that whosoever shall put away his wife, except it be for fornication, and shall marry another, committeth adultery: and he that shall marry her that is put away, committeth adultery. His disciples say unto him: If the case of a man with his wife be so, it is not expedient to marry." (*Matt.* 19:8-10).

"And he saith to them: Whosoever shall put away his wife and marry another, committeth adultery against her. And if the wife shall put away her husband, and be married to another, she committeth adultery." (*Mark* 10:11-12).

"Every one that putteth away his wife, and marrieth another, committeth adultery: and he that marrieth her that is put away from her husband, committeth adultery." (*Luke* 16:18).

"Whilst her husband liveth, she [a married woman] shall be called an adulteress, if she be with another man: but if her husband be dead, she is delivered from the law of her husband; so that she is not an adulteress, if she be with another man." (*Rom.* 7:3).

"To them that are married, not I but the Lord commandeth, that the wife depart not from her husband. And if she depart, that she remain unmarried, or be reconciled to her husband. And let not the husband put away his wife." (*1 Cor.* 7: 10-11).

The meaning of all these texts taken together is perfectly obvious: divorce is forbidden. In other translations, the phrase "except it be for fornication" appears in the texts from St. Matthew. In regard to the first of these, there is no difficulty because Our Lord was speaking only of the right of separation. But the supporters of divorce—even Anglican bishops—quote the second text in their favor. Mgr. Knox's translation renders the passage this way: "But I tell you that the man who puts away his wife (setting aside the matter of unfaithfulness) makes an adulteress of her, and whoever marries her after she has been put away, commits adultery." (*Matt.* 5:31-32). This is a perfectly legitimate translation and disposes of the difficulty. But, even apart from this clarification, if it is taught that Our Lord here permits divorce because of fornication or adultery, the whole context of this passage suffers violence, and the meaning of all the texts we have quoted is destroyed. The main point is that Our Lord was obviously contrasting His new law with the state of affairs existing previously. There would have been no contrast, and certainly no reason for the Apostles' obvious surprise, if He had been permitting divorce because of infidelity.

For Catholics, of course, the teaching of the Church is the surest guide. The Council of Trent declares: "If anyone saith that the Church has erred in that she hath taught, and doth teach, that . . . the bond of matrimony cannot be dissolved on account of the adultery of one of the parties . . . . let him be anathema." (*Sess.* xxiv, 7).

The Pauline Privilege

The marriage to each other of two unbaptized persons establishes a *natural* marital bond only—as opposed to a *supernatural* bond, which occurs in a marriage between two baptized people. But if one of the unbaptized parties gets baptized, and the other (who is also opposed to Christianity), either departs or refuses to live with him (or her) in peace and without serious danger of grave sin against the faith or morals of the Christian party, the natural marriage bond is dissolved in favor of the supernatural marital bond, at the moment when a sacramental marriage would afterwards be contracted. **The natural marriage is dissolved by the baptized party's marrying a Catholic partner**. This privilege comes from the authority of St. Paul. "If the unbeliever depart, let him depart." (*1 Cor.* 7:15). This is therefore called the **Pauline Privilege.** If it is used, it is not the Baptism of the Christian party, but the subsequent Christian marriage that dissolves the previous *natural* marriage bond. Before the dissolution can take place, however, certain "interpellations" or official questions by the Church must be put to the departing unbaptized person and these answered in the negative. There are two basic questions: 1) "whether he or she wishes to receive Baptism," and 2) "whether he or she at least wishes to cohabit in peace with the baptized party" without interfering with the religious obligations of the convert. (Canon 1144, par. 1, *Code of Canon Law*, 1983).

It was stated above that a marriage between baptized persons which has been consummated, can never be dissolved. For centuries, however, the Popes have exercised the right to dissolve non-consummated marriages, for the two persons are not yet "one flesh." (*Matt.* 19:5). The contract has not, so to speak, been absolutely completed, for marriage consists of 1) the **oral contract** between the marrying couple (in Latin called *ratum*, "the rite" or public ceremony of the vows), and 2) the **consummation** of the marriage by natural sexual union (in Latin, *consummatum*). However, for a decree of nullity of the non-Catholic's Baptism to be issued by the Catholic Church, there has to be an invalidating factor in the administering of the Sacrament of Baptism to the non-Catholic, e.g., the use of the wrong sacramental words, or the pouring of a liquid other than water.

Decrees of nullity

Divorce must not be confused with **decrees of nullity.** We have seen that marriage is essentially a contract. It may be found, after the "marriage" has taken place, that for one reason or another, the contract was invalid right from the start. Possibly it did not constitute a **free agreement** on the part of both parties to the marriage, or there was a diriment impediment present (e.g., one of the parties was already married). The declaration that the "marriage" has never been a valid contract and therefore never a valid marriage is called a **decree of nullity.** This is vastly different from a divorce, which attempts to break the bond of a ratified and consummated marriage. The decree of nullity is simply a declaration that the bond of marriage never existed; obviously what never existed cannot be broken. There is a huge difference between tearing up a genuine British pound note (comparable to divorce) and declaring that another British pound note is a counterfeit (comparable to annulment).

There are, of course, always some who are only too ready to calumniate the Church in this matter of divorce. An unbiased examination will reveal that she has always been scrupulously fair and just in deciding the matrimonial cases presented to her. She has never dissolved the bond of a ratified, consummated marriage and never will do so; nor has she ever granted an annulment without most careful consideration of the case.

Chapter 33

Marriage (2)

The importance of matrimonial consent

T HE marriage contract and the Sacrament of Matrimony are constituted by the **consent** of the parties. Therefore, this consent
is vitally important. If it is not there, there is no marriage.

**Matrimonial consent is defined as an act of the will by
which each party gives and accepts the perpetual and exclusive
right to actions, which are in themselves fitted for the generation of children.**

**The marriage consent agreement must be manifested exter-
nally, must be mutual and simultaneous, and must be free and
deliberate.** It presupposes certain knowledge, just as the consent to
any other contract does. Therefore, ignorance or error may, in very
exceptional cases, invalidate the consent and therefore the marriage.
Moreover, there are other conditions attached to the consent which
may invalidate the contract. In these days of divorce and birth prevention, there is a danger that these other conditions are being
attached more frequently. But, in regard to any particular marriage,
only ecclesiastical authority is competent to decide on the validity
or invalidity of the marriage contract. If the suspicion should arise
that there was defect in the consent of the parties to a Catholic marriage, the matter must be referred to the competent authority within
the Church, usually through one's parish priest.

Formalities demanded by the Church

Because **consent** is so important, the Church demands that it be
given publicly and with certain legal formalities. Just as the State
regulates civil contracts, so the Church regulates spiritual contracts,
one of which is marriage. The law of the Council of Trent is that

Catholics must marry before the parish priest, or some other priest delegated by him, and two witnesses. In virtue of the *Ne Temere* decree which came into force at Easter, 1908, that law of the Council of Trent, which had not been observed in England, owing to the peculiar circumstances of the Catholics after the Reformation, became obligatory, and it now applies throughout the whole Church. Baptized non-Catholics contracting marriages among themselves are exempt from the law. **The practical result of the decree of 1908 is that Catholics married in registry offices or Protestant churches are not married in the sight of the Church or in the sight of God, and therefore not at all. To live as man and wife after attempting such a "marriage" is to live in a state of grave sin.** The penalty of excommunication which was traditionally imposed for this sin and was covered in the 1917 *Code of Canon Law* was lifted in the 1983 *Code*.

Since Vatican II (1962-1965), however, the Catholic Church has allowed Catholics to marry non-Catholics in a Protestant church so long as a duly authorized Catholic priest is present as an official witness for the Church and to confirm publicly that the Catholic Church approves of and sanctions this particular marriage because all Church requirements for a valid and licit ("legal" by Church law) marriage have been met. This allowance by the Church is a public recognition that it is the two parties to the marriage who confer the Sacrament of Matrimony on one another. The normal requirement for Catholics to be married before a priest and two witnesses is to allow the Church the opportunity to insure that the marrying couple understand the nature and obligations of marriage, plus the rights of the partners thereto; that no impediments to the marriage contract exist; that a valid, licit marriage takes place; and that the marrying couple receive the official blessing of the Church from the priest.

Impediments: diriment and impeding

In order to safeguard the sacred contract of the Sacrament of Matrimony, the Church includes in her law a list of the impediments to marriage. By an impediment we mean anything that makes the celebration of a marriage either unlawful (termed an "impeding" impediment) or invalid (termed a "diriment" impediment). Some of the impediments result from the Natural Law; others merely from ecclesiastical law.

It is beyond the scope of these instructions to provide details of the theology concerned with matrimonial impediments. We must content ourselves with the list as given by Cardinal Gasparri in his *Catechism*. Those who are interested may obtain further details from any manual of moral theology or canon law.

The **diriment (invalidating) impediments,** which render a marriage null, are: age; impotence that is antecedent to the marriage and perpetual; a bond arising from an already existing marriage; diversity of religion, when one of the parties is not baptized; Holy Orders; solemn profession in a religious Order; abduction; crime; consanguinity (being close relatives); affinity (relation by marriage); public decency—(e.g., an invalid marriage or a public or notorious cohabitation); spiritual relationship arising from Baptism; and legal relationship, due to adoption (in countries, that is, where the civil law regards this as a diriment impediment to marriage).

The **impeding impediments** which render a marriage unlawful, though still valid, are: a simple vow, either of virginity, or of perpetual chastity, or not to marry, or of receiving Holy Orders, or of embracing the religious life; difference of religion in the parties concerned, both of whom are baptized; legal kinship arising from adoption (in those countries, that is, where the civil law regards this as an impediment to marriage).

Mixed marriages

Canon law states that "the Church most severely forbids everywhere marriages between two baptized persons one of whom is a Catholic, the other a member of a heretical or schismatic sect; if there is danger of perversion for the Catholic spouse and the offspring, the marriage is also forbidden by divine law." [1917 *Code of Canon Law*]. The use of the superlative, *"most* severely,"—rare in Canon Law—emphasizes the severity of this prohibition. The Church is concerned with one thing above all others—the good of souls. She is a Mother with two thousand years of experience in the ways of man. Her laws are drawn up for the good of everybody and as the result of many years of bitter experience. She is bound to oppose ruthlessly anything that will imperil the salvation of one single soul. She knows that mixed marriages are a danger to souls and that in the majority of cases they turn out to be spiritual catastrophes. The faith of the Catholic party is practically always weakened, but even more serious is the weakening of the faith of the children. If the Catholic party dies young, what is to happen to the faith of the little children left to the Protestant parent?

The Church traditionally has traditionally shown her horror and detestation of mixed marriages by her law forbidding any solemnity, any music and any blessings at their celebration—even after a dispensation has been granted. In many places, such marriages were not even allowed to take place in the church.

Traditionally, only for very grave reasons and under special conditions would the Church grant her children dispensations to contract mixed marriages. Even then she would demand from the parties a solemn guarantee that the children would all be brought up as Catholics and that the faith of the Catholic party would not be menaced.

That the Church law against mixed marriages is of long standing is exemplified by the following quote: "The prohibition of mixed marriages is already found in Canon XVI of the Synod of Elvira (306), which rules that if heretics do not want to join the Catholic Church, no Catholic girl should be given them in marriage. Later, this prohibition recurs frequently in other early Councils of the Church." (Waywod, *A Practical Commentary on the Code of Canon Law* (for 1917), 1962, Vol. 1, page 613.)

Since mixed marriages are gravely forbidden, it is evident that a Catholic who is keeping company with a Protestant with a view to marriage—with no certainty that the non-Catholic will enter the Church or that a grave cause exists for the granting of a dispensation—is committing sin and should mention it in Confession. All should remember that laws are made to be observed and not to be dispensed. The seeking of dispensations often indicates weakness of faith.

No non-Catholic who understands the situation correctly can be critical of the stand taken by the Church in regard to mixed marriages. The reasons are perfectly obvious and absolutely logical. She is strictly bound to do everything possible to safeguard the faith of her children and to ward off evil from them. She would be failing lamentably in her duty if she did not prohibit mixed marriages and try by every means in her power to dissuade her children from contracting them.

The New *Code of Canon Law* of 1983 states the case somewhat differently:

Canon 1125—The local ordinary [bishop] can grant this permission [a dispensation for a mixed marriage] if there is a just and reasonable cause; he is not to grant it unless the following conditions have been fulfilled:

1° the Catholic party declares that he or she is prepared to remove dangers of falling away from the faith and makes a sincere promise to do all in his or her power to have all the children baptized and brought up in the Catholic Church;

2° the other party is to be informed at an appropriate time of these promises which the Catholic party has to make, so that it is clear that the other party is truly aware of the promise and obligation of the Catholic party;

3° both parties are to be instructed on the essential ends and properties of marriage, which are not to be excluded by either party. (*Code of Canon Law*—Latin-English Edition, Canon Law Society of Amer., 1983,m p. 409).

Courtship

Courtship is the natural preparation for marriage, and it is on the courting that the happiness of a marriage may depend. As marriage is a holy, a sacramental state, the preparation for it ought to be holy also. Young people should remember that the marriage agreement is to be made for life. There is no escape from it. Hence, the time of preparation should be one of *thought* and *prayer.* Marriages built only on sentiment and mere physical attraction have but a weak foundation and may not last. The modern romanticism about "love at first sight" should not mislead sensible young people. The ordinary rules of prudence must be observed. Parents should be consulted, and as a rule, their consent should be obtained. There are exceptional cases, of course.

The fact that two people are engaged to be married gives them no right whatsoever to stimulate mutual sex feelings and appetites. The ultra-modern idea that "sex compatibility" must be determined before marriage to save future disasters is completely wrong. Evil means may not be used to attain any object, no matter how good; and sexual intercourse outside of marriage is in itself evil. It is an assault on the institution of marriage; when engaged in, it will kill family life; it glorifies self-gratification; it brutalizes woman and it degrades man. "Take heed to keep thyself, my son, from all fornication, and beside thy wife never endure to know a crime." (*Tobias* 4:13). "You have heard that it was said to them of old: Thou shalt not commit adultery. But I say to you, that whosoever shall look on a woman to lust after her, hath already committed adultery with her in his heart." (*Matt.* 5:27-28). Courtship must not be reduced into a merely carnal engagement, nor must it be based on the idea that married happiness is founded more on physical facts than on spiritual. Love cannot be decided by such experimentation. In fact, this and similar modern ideas are simply the acceptance of the standards of the farmyard and the brute in place of the high ideals of Christ and His Church. God intends the intimacies of love for the married only, and those who are only engaged have no right to such liberties.

Most people today have lost the horror of sin that should attend and is the natural consequence of practicing true Catholic virtue. The result is that people fall into sexual immorality little by little, and thereby they become blind to its evil results. Those tempted to sexual immorality should reflect upon St. Paul's warning: "Be not deceived, God is not mocked." (*Gal.* 6:7). For everyone who commits sin is in effect trying to mock God and is saying to himself, "I can violate Your law and do so without consequences." These people should reflect upon Solomon's wisdom: "By what things a man sinneth, by the same also he is tormented." (*Wisdom* 11:17). Sexual immorality by couples before marriage tends 1) to fracture mutual trust, 2) to lead to other bad habits, 3) to promote selfishness, 4) to cause the loss of God's special blessings reserved to the virtuous, 5) to inculcate a callous attitude toward sin, 6) to tarnish and sully the beauty of their relationship and 7) to lead to a high incidence of divorce. Those courting should realize that the powerful attraction of two people in love was created by God, but to mar it by sin is to invite unhappiness into their lives.

Rights of husband and wife

Matrimony is a bilateral contract, the primary purpose of which is, as we have seen, the begetting of children. Therefore, each of the contracting persons has equal rights in everything relating to this object, and each has the duty of respecting the rights of the other. In the use of marriage, husband and wife are absolutely equal; if one desires the debt to be paid the other is bound in justice to render it. That is the general principle—which does, however, admit of a few exceptions. "Let the husband render the debt to his wife and the wife also in like manner to the husband. The wife hath not power of her own body, but the husband. And in like manner the husband also hath not power of his own body, but the wife. Defraud not one another, except, perhaps, by consent, for a time, that you may give yourselves to prayer; and return together again, lest Satan tempt you for your incontinency." (*1 Cor.* 7:3-6). If husband and wife, by mutual consent, agree not to exercise their rights, they are quite entitled not to do so. If ever it appears necessary to render the debt in order to forestall the danger of unchastity, it is obligatory to pay it. If, however, the purpose of the request of husband or wife is some vicious or unnatural act, against the primary object of marriage, it may be the duty of the other to refuse. So long as the purpose of marriage is not frustrated, sexual intercourse in marriage is good and holy; at the worst, there might occur some venial sin of excess. **But if marital relations are so exercised that the primary object of the act is frustrated, by being performed in an unnatural manner, there is certainly grave sin.**

Birth prevention

Artificial or unnatural birth-prevention, often wrongly called "birth control," is **wrong in itself**—and it is not wrong "just because the Church forbids it." To employ a human faculty in an unnatural manner, perverting its natural object, is to disobey the Natural Law, which, after all, is but the law of God implanted by Him in His creation. Birth prevention is immoral because it consists in the gratifying of sexual pleasure while frustrating the object of the act and the very reason for pleasure being attached to the act by Almighty God.

It is simply mutual masturbation, which reduces the purpose of marriage to mere pleasure and nothing more. In the Old Testament, God struck Onan dead for practicing a primitive form of "birth control." (Cf. *Gen.* 38:1-10).

It would be remiss not to mention at this juncture that modern "low-dose" birth control pills (by far the most commonly used) **very often do not actually prevent a conception from occurring, but are really abortifacient**, that is to say, they allow a conception to occur, but often prevent the embryo's implantation in the womb (or uterus) of the mother. In this case, the newly conceived child is denied by the chemistry of the birth-control pill a healthy, normal home in the uterus of the mother, and subsequently it is expelled. The net effect of low-dose birth control pills is that they often abort the new baby by denying it the natural means of life. In effect, they kill it by causing an abortion.

A word also needs to be mentioned about Natural Family Planning and periodic continence. Each method of limiting the birth of children relies on the use of the reproductive faculty only during the woman's infertile periods, thus avoiding pregnancy. The use of the term "Natural Family Planning" has come under sharp attack from traditional Catholic writers in recent years because it implies the right of the couple to "plan" their family; whereas the Catholic norm is to let God plan one's family and to accept the children when (and if) God gives them—as a blessing from Him on the marital union and on society. Except for the use of NFP for fertility reasons, i.e., to aid in a legitimate way in conceiving a child (as opposed, e.g., to *in vitro* fertilization), the **planning** aspect NFP would appear to reflect acceptance of the neo-pagan practice of "family planning"—albeit using "natural" as opposed to artificial means. **Proponents of NFP, it would seem, are confusing a *legitimate means* during an emergency situation or for a "serious reason" with an *illegitimate end* in the case of no family emergency or "no serious reason," and presume then to conclude that NFP is morally acceptable as a way of life.** The *end* or purpose of NFP—that is, "planning" one's family—*is not acceptable* in principle, being against Natural Law and the teachings of the Church. A couple does not have the right to "plan their family," even though the means used are those of NFP and do not violate the Church's proscriptions against artificial birth control. As Cardinal Ottaviani, former head of the Holy Office (Sacred Congregation for the Doctrine of the Faith), declared before the assembled bishops at Vatican Council II, "I am not pleased with the statement in the [draft] text that married couples may determine the number of children they are to have. **Never has this been heard of in the Church.**"* This is the 2,000-year tradition of the Church, supported by Sacred Scripture (cf. *Genesis* 38:1-10, *et al.*) and reiterated by the Popes in the Ordinary Teaching Magisterium of the Church (e.g., *Casti Connubii*—"On Marriage," Pius XI, 1930; *Address to Midwives,* Pius XII, 1951; *Humanae Vitae*—"On Human Life," Paul VI, 1968, No. 10). Also, it should be noted that the *Catechism of the Catholic Church* (2nd Ed., 1997) does not use the term "Natural Family Planning." Rather, it uses the term "periodic continence" (*CCC*, No. 2370), that is, the practice of continence, or abstinence from sexual union, during the woman's fertile time each month.

On the other hand, periodic continence, i.e., refraining from use of the marital act during the woman's fertile time each month, as a "safety net" for a serious reason (cf. *Humanae Vitae*, No. 10), is completely legitimate, **but only under certain very specific conditions**. And they are the following:**

1. That there be **a serious reason** to practice periodic continence.
2. That it be with the **mutual consent** of the marriage partners.
3. That this continence **not be the near occasion of mortal sin** for either party.
4. That the periodic continence last **only so long as the serious reason lasts**.
5. It is recommended that the situation be **reviewed by one's confessor** to insure that all the requisite conditions are present.

The Rhine Flows into the Tiber—A History of Vatican II, Fr. Ralph M. Wiltgen, S.V.D. (Hawthorne Books, N.Y., 1967; reprint, Rockford, Illinois: TAN, 1985), p. 269, emphasis added.

**Cf. *Moral Theology*, Rev. Heribert Jone, O.F.M. Cap., J.C.D. (Westminster: Newman Press, 1962; reprint, Rockford, Illinois: TAN, 1993), No. 760, p. 542.

In his 1951 Address to the Italian Catholic Union of Midwives Pope Pius XII said the following: "From the obligation of making this positive contribution [the generation and rearing of children], it is possible to be exempt, for a long time **and even for the whole duration of married life**, if there are serious reasons, such as those often provided in the so-called 'indications' of the **medical, eugenical, economic** and **social order**. It therefore follows that the observance of the infertile period may be licit from the moral point of view; and under the conditions mentioned, it is so in fact." (Emphasis added.) Thus, the Church is not asking married couples to do the impossible.

It should be stated here, however, that couples may practice **complete abstinence** from marital relations, for good reason, with the mutual consent of both partners and so long as there is no danger of sin to either. This can be for the lifetime of the marriage partners, in which case it is called a Josephite Marriage, called such after St. Joseph, who lived a celibate marriage with the Blessed Virgin Mary; or it could be for a time only.

Lest there be any misunderstanding about the meaning of Pope Pius XII's use of the terms "**medical, eugenical, economic** and **social order**," some further explanation follows:

"Medical" refers to the physical (or even psychological) health of one or both of the marriage partners, usually the woman. If there is serious risk, for example, to her life or health, this could constitute a "medical" reason. A woman who has had a number of children, for example, and is approaching the end of her childbearing years may develop serious physical complications that would pose serious risk to her or to her unborn child in a new pregnancy. This could constitute a serious reason in the medical sphere.

"Eugenic" refers to the couple's not being genetically able to produce normal offspring. Perhaps the couple's children are all being born with Down's Syndrome or are deficient in some other serious way.

"Economic" refers to *true financial hardship* brought about despite the couple's best efforts to support their family, all the while not wasting their means on luxuries and non-essentials. Perhaps their country is very poor; perhaps good economic opportunity just does not exist for them. When severe financial hardship exists, there can be sufficient reason to practice periodic continence. But the economic "serious reason" would be the easiest to misinterpret or abuse when deciding in favor of periodic continence—this because of poor stewardship by the parents, or an improper set of values that puts materialism before one's primary responsiblity in marriage. The key to a right decision is honesty—with God, with oneself, with one's spouse and with one's confessor.

"Social Order" refers to unusual interruptions in the social sphere that disrupt one's normal life—due, for example, to a catastrophic flood, earthquake, volcanic eruption, hurricane, tornado, war, fire, etc.—and which impinge immediately upon the family's ability to function well.

In all these cases, a couple **may** resort to periodic continence, yet they are not obliged to do so. Traditionally the Church has never criticized married couples for simply accepting the children God sends. Overall, it should be noted, as a classic Catholic marriage manual states: "The control of births, therefore, should always be the exceptional situation in marriage, never the normal." Further, "The modern Catholic couple must be reminded that parenthood is the business of marriage. This is their vocation. The Catholic husband and wife should do this work with wisdom and prudence, and, where there is good cause, may consider family limitation. But family limitation does not *have* to be considered. Most of you will find that the best evidence of a lifetime of worthwhile work will be your children. You should want children; and parenthood, God willing, should be more than an incidental experience in your married lives. If you have a truly Catholic conscience and a love of children, you will find that alleged obstacles can be overcome. Far from losing happiness, you will gain great long-range satisfaction."*

Married couples tempted to birth prevention should contemplate long and hard on the fact that the Almighty and All-Knowing God has created human nature as it is **and that it is He who has built into the nature of man and woman His own form of birth regu-**

---

*Rev. George A. Kelly, *The Catholic Marriage Manual* (New York: Random House, 1958), p. 46 and pp. 45-46.

lation. When a mother nurses her babies, they will usually be spaced about 18 to 24 months apart. A woman who marries during her twenties, if she and her spouse be healthy, will tend to have from four to twelve children. **This is God's plan for the control of births!** This is the size of family He wants!

The Almighty, All-knowing and All-provident God created human beings without man's advice and obviously in the way He intended. In His own plan, He provides for the new children born into this world. None of us knows for certain if he or she will live out the next half-hour—or even the next few minutes—in this uncertain world of ours. Therefore, everything we plan or do requires of us at least an implicit act of confidence in God's all-provident care. What married couple, as they begin their lives together, can ever imagine the future for their family? It is really all in God's hands. Couples with large families marvel at the uncanny providence that seems to care for their needs, often in strange ways. A college professor and a father of 14 once commented: "All I can say is that God gives large families special help." He was mystified but awed at God's providence in the case of his own family. And this experience of God's unusual providence for families is confirmed again and again by married couples who live according to God's law.

Obviously, parents of minor children have to shepherd their means and use them carefully. They must avoid spending on non-essentials, for the most part, unless they have been blessed with means over and above their needs. They have to avoid, of course, squandering their money on excessive drink, on illegal drugs, on gambling, on expensive non-essentials, etc. And above all they must avoid all immorality—mortal sins of every kind; otherwise, they cannot expect God to bless them and their family or to hear their prayers for material help as He otherwise would. "Now we know that God doth not hear sinners; but if a man be a server of God, and doth his will, him he heareth." (*John* 9:31). (Of course God hears and answers the prayers of sinners who repent—or want to—and are trying to overcome their sins, but not the prayers of mortal sinners who are unrepentant and determined to continue in their sin.) "And whosoever shall keep the whole law, but offend **in one point**, is become guilty of all." (*James* 2:10, emphasis added).

For a couple to practice "birth control" or "family planning" (as opposed to periodic continence under the legitimate circumstances stated above) is really a form of blasphemy (an insult) against God. It is tantamount to telling the Infinite, All-knowing God that He did not know what He was doing when He created us as we are, or that He cannot provide for children born to large families. On the contrary, there is a divine wisdom to the reproductive arrangement which He has created: by the time a woman is in her sixties, normally all of her children will be grown and able to function on their own. And when the mother and father are in their senior years and need extra assistance in their lives, usually at least one of their children is able to help the parents in their old age.

But, if in the process of raising a family that, by today's standards, would be considered large, a couple has financial or other troubles, they may rightly address Almighty God and pray with confidence and humility in the following manner: "We have obeyed Thy command and Thy law, O Lord, in bringing these children into the world. Now we are in great need by reason of *(here mention the specific need)*, and we therefore humbly ask Thy help in this grave necessity—Thou who hast said, 'Cast thy care upon the Lord, and he shall sustain thee: he shall not suffer the just to waver for ever.' " (*Psalms* 54:23). Married couples should always realize that God holds the whole world, and each one of us, "in His hand," so to speak, and He will take care of us all . . . as He has so capably been doing since the dawn of creation. It may not be in the manner that we would like it to be, or even that we anticipate. In answering our prayers, He often acts in ways that tend to humble us and to keep us constantly aware of our dependence on Him. Better this mode of married life, however, than our becoming proud and losing our souls.

Writing about **"birth control,"** Pope Pius XI says: "Some justify this criminal abuse on the ground that they are weary of children and wish to gratify their desires without their consequent burden. Others say that they cannot on the one hand remain continent nor on the other can they have children because of the difficulties, whether on the part of the mother or on the part of family circumstances.

"But no reason, however grave, may be put forward by which anything intrinsically against nature may become conformable

to nature and morally good. Since, therefore, the conjugal act is destined primarily for the begetting of children, those who in exercising it deliberately frustrate its natural power and purpose sin against nature and commit a deed which is shameful and intrinsically vicious . . . Any use whatsoever of matrimony exercised in such a way that the act is deliberately frustrated in its natural power to generate life is an offense against the law of God and of nature, and those who indulge in such are branded with the guilt of grave sin . . . . No difficulty can arise that justifies the putting aside of the law of God which forbids all acts intrinsically evil. There is no possible circumstance in which husband and wife cannot, strengthened by the grace of God, fulfill faithfully their duties and preserve in wedlock their chastity unspotted . . . . Let no one be so rash as to assert that which the Fathers of the Council [of Trent] have placed under anathema, namely, that there are precepts of God impossible for the just to observe. God does not ask the impossible, but by His commands, instructs you to do what you are able, to pray for what you are not able, that He may help you." (Encyclical Letter, *Casti Connubii,* "On Marriage," 1930, emphasis added).

Here, in a few sentences, the Holy Father debunks once and for all the specious arguments to be found in that great volume of literature which has been poured forth by the modern votaries of immoral birth prevention. All their reasons put together, he says in effect, cannot justify a practice which is evil in itself. Indulgence in such a thing is bound to bring with it evils far greater than its advocates vainly hope to remedy. In fact, the prevalence of birth prevention is probably the greatest social evil in the world today because it directly attacks the family, which is the parent cell of society—and thereby it attacks society itself. And, as many writers have pointed out, the modern evil of abortion is ultimately really only a form of "birth control."

One who thinks seriously about the Catholic attitude toward birth prevention must soon become convinced of its unanswerable rightness. To the modern world it seems austere, even impossible, but the modern world forgets that Marriage is a Sacrament, which confers all the graces needed by those who have received it to meet and overcome the difficulties of their state. Is the Church wrong in expecting to find in husbands and wives good-will, self-control, character, virtue and docility? Is she out-of-date in supposing that one marries for reasons other than mere pleasure, more pleasure and the most possible pleasure? Is she mistaken in making a clear distinction between love and sexuality and insisting that sex and its allurements have a spiritual side and must be controlled on spiritual principles? Is she to be blamed for harping on the fact that one ought to marry only after a solid apprenticeship of will-training, self-control and sacrifice? Is she out of touch with reality when she tells her children to rely on God's grace for the strength, courage and fortitude to fulfill their obligations? Is she completely impractical when she suggests that the True Religion offers **helps**—as well as prohibitions—and when she therefore urges married people to pray regularly, to practice special devotion to the Immaculate Mother of God, to receive daily if possible the "Bread of Angels" in the Eucharist, and to cultivate a thoroughly Catholic mind and heart in regard to the glorious vocation of marriage?

Chapter 34

Devotion to Mary and the Saints

Why does the Catholic Church show great devotion to the Blessed Virgin? *The Catholic Church shows great devotion to the Blessed Virgin because she is the Immaculate Mother of God.*

How is the Blessed Virgin the Mother of God? *The Blessed Virgin is the Mother of God because Jesus Christ, her Son, who was born of her as man, is not only man, but is also truly God.*

Is the Blessed Virgin our Mother also? *The Blessed Virgin is our Mother also because, being the brethren of Jesus, we are the children of Mary.*

Have all mankind contracted the guilt and stain of Original Sin? *All mankind have contracted the guilt and stain of Original Sin, except the Blessed Virgin Mary, who, through the merits of her Divine Son, was conceived without the least guilt or stain of Original Sin.*

What is this privilege of the Blessed Virgin called? *This privilege of the Blessed Virgin is called the Immaculate Conception.*

Is it forbidden to give divine honor or worship to the Angels and Saints? *It is forbidden to give divine honor or worship to the Angels and Saints, for this belongs to God alone.*

What kind of honor or veneration should we pay to the Angels and Saints? *We should pay to the Angels and Saints an inferior honor or veneration than that which we pay to God, for this is due to them as the servants and special friends of God.*

How are we in communion with the Saints in Heaven? *We are in communion with the Saints in Heaven by honoring them as the glorified members of the Church, and also by our praying to them, and by their praying for us.*

GOD'S First Commandment is that He alone shall receive divine honor or worship. Every Catholic accepts that as one of the basic truths of his religion. But nowhere does God state that those of His creatures who are nearest and dearest to Him shall not be proportionately honored for His sake. In fact, devotion to them—His own Mother, the Angels and the Saints—is one of the most ancient practices of Christianity. No one can fully understand Catholicism unless he appreciates the reasons why the Church has always been faithful to this practice.

Mary, Mother of God

The **Third General Council** of the Church, held at Ephesus [in present Western Turkey] in the year 431, solemnly defined that the Blessed Virgin Mary is the Mother of God. That this is so follows from the truth already explained, that there is only one Person in Jesus Christ, God the Son (cf. page 122). Mary is the Mother of that one Divine Person. Otherwise, of whom was she the Mother? There is no human person in Christ, and she certainly could not be the Mother of a mere human nature, independent from a person.

The Scripture story

Consider the Scripture story. "And in the sixth month, the angel Gabriel was sent from God into a city of Galilee, called Nazareth, to a virgin espoused to a man whose name was Joseph, of the house of David; and the virgin's name was Mary. And the angel being come in, said unto her: Hail, full of grace, the Lord is with thee: blessed art thou among women. Who having heard, was troubled at his saying, and thought with herself what manner of salutation this should be. And the angel said to her: Fear not, Mary, for thou hast found grace with God. Behold thou shalt conceive in thy womb, and shalt bring forth a son; and thou shalt call his name Jesus. He shall be great, and shall be called the Son of the most High; and the Lord God shall give unto him the throne of David his father; and he shall reign in the house of Jacob for ever. And of his kingdom there shall be no end.

"And Mary said to the angel: How shall this be done, because I know not man? And the angel answering, said to her: The Holy Ghost shall come upon thee, and the power of the most High shall overshadow thee. And therefore also the Holy which shall be born of thee shall be called the Son of God. And behold thy cousin Elizabeth, she also hath conceived a son in her old age; and this is the sixth month with her that is called barren: Because no word shall be impossible with God. And Mary said: Behold the handmaid of the Lord; be it done to me according to thy word. And the angel departed from her.

"And Mary rising up in those days, went into the hill country with haste into a city of Juda. And she entered into the house of Zachary, and saluted Elizabeth. And it came to pass, that when Elizabeth heard the salutation of Mary, the infant leaped in her womb. And Elizabeth was filled with the Holy Ghost: And she cried out with a loud voice, and said: Blessed art thou among women, and blessed is the fruit of thy womb. And whence is this to me, that the mother of my Lord should come to me?" (*Luke* 1:26-43).

"Now the generation of Christ was in this wise. When as his mother Mary was espoused to Joseph, before they came together, she was found with child, of the Holy Ghost. Whereupon Joseph her husband, being a just man, and not willing publicly to expose her, was minded to put her away privately. But while he thought on these things, behold the angel of the Lord appeared to him in his sleep, saying: Joseph, son of David, fear not to take unto thee Mary thy wife, for that which is conceived in her is of the Holy Ghost. And she shall bring forth a son: and thou shalt call his name JESUS. For he shall save his people from their sins. Now all this was done that it might be fulfilled which the Lord spoke by the prophet [*Isaias* 7:14], saying: Behold a virgin shall be with child, and bring forth a son, and they shall call his name Emmanuel, which being interpreted is, God with us. And Joseph rising up from sleep, did as the angel of the Lord had commanded him, and took unto him his wife. And he knew her not till she brought forth her firstborn son: and he called his name JESUS." *(Matt.* 1:18-25).

There is little need to quote the evidence of the early Christian writers on behalf of a dogma defined early in the 5th century.

Mary is to be honored

More important is the obvious conclusion that God's Mother is worthy of honor. "Immediately next to being God is being the Mother of God," says St. Albert the Great. (Quoted in *Mary,* Canice, p. 36). "The humanity of Christ, from the fact that it is united to the Godhead; and created happiness, from the fact that it is the fruition of God; **and the Blessed Virgin, from the fact that she is the Mother of God; have all a certain infinite dignity from the Infinite Good, which is God.** And on this account there cannot be anything better than these; just as there cannot be anything better than God," writes St. Thomas Aquinas in the 13th century. (Pt. 1, Q. 25, Art. 6, Reply to Obj. 4, emphasis added). Indeed, the great writers of the Church have from earliest times vied with one another in hailing the dignity of Mary. All agree that even God Almighty could not bestow on Mary a more glorious state, a higher dignity than the state and dignity of His own Mother. The state of the Motherhood of God is the supreme state that can be given to a mere creature.

Because of the inexpressible dignity that is hers, the Catholic Church has from the beginning given Mary the highest form of honor below that reserved for God alone. The Church's practice has always reflected her belief that, provided Mary is not "adored" (which is the unique honor given to God alone), she cannot be honored to excess.

The Immaculate Conception

From Mary's divine Motherhood, all her other dignities flow. The first of these is her **Immaculate Conception.** On December 8th, 1854, Pope Pius IX defined infallibly that "the doctrine which declares that the most Blessed Virgin Mary, in the first instant of her conception, by a singular grace and privilege of Almighty God, in view of the merits of Jesus Christ, the Saviour of the human race, was preserved exempt from all stain of Original Sin, is a doctrine revealed by God, and therefore must be believed firmly and constantly by all the faithful." That is what the doctrine of the Immaculate Conception means. It does not refer to the conception of Christ within Mary, but to Mary's own conception within the womb of her mother, St. Anne. This took place in the natural way, but from the first moment in which she existed as a human being, she was free from every stain of Original Sin. (See page 53).

In Scripture

That doctrine is nowhere expressly taught in Scripture, but it is to be found in the traditional interpretation of certain passages of the Bible: "I will put enmities between thee and the woman, and thy seed and her seed; she shall crush thy head, and thou shalt lie in wait for her heel." (*Gen.* 3:15). Thus God spoke to the Serpent in Eden.* God says that He is going to put enmity between Christ's Mother and Satan. That would not be unless Mary were to be completely and absolutely free from sin from the first moment of her conception.

Thus the announcing angel saluted Mary as "full of grace," thereby indicating a unique freedom from sin within her soul.

In Tradition

Two points find particular emphasis in the writings of the early Fathers—Mary's unique sinlessness and her position as "the second Eve." Here are just a few quotations. Mary is called "the tabernacle exempt from defilement and corruption" by St. Hippolytus in the 3rd century. (*Bibl. patrum,* II, 496). Origen hails her as "worthy of God, immaculate of the immaculate, most complete sanctity, perfect justice, neither deceived by the persuasion of the serpent, nor infected with his poisonous breathings." St. Ambrose described her as "a virgin immune through grace from every stain of sin." (*Sermo*

---

*Another translation of the second phrase, which some Church Fathers have adopted, is, *"He* shall crush thy head and thou shalt lie in wait for *His* heel." Who is the man referred to who shall crush Satan and be attacked by him? Only Christ, surely. He is the Child of the woman referred to by God. Between Him and Satan there is obviously absolute, complete enmity. [The Catholic Church has traditionally translated *Genesis* 3:15 as "She shall crush thy head, and thou shalt lie in wait for her heel," referring to the Blessed Mother of God. —Publisher, 2002.]

xxii in *Ps.* cxviii). Maximus of Turin called her "a dwelling fit for Christ . . . because of original grace."

Here is the beautiful prayer of St. Ephraim (306-373, a Doctor of the Church): "Most holy Lady, Mother of God, alone most pure in soul and body, alone exceeding all perfection of purity . . . . alone made in thy entirety the home of all the graces of the Most Holy Spirit, and hence exceeding beyond all compare even the angelic virtues in purity and sanctity of soul and body . . . . my Lady most holy, all-pure, all-immaculate, all-stainless, all-undefiled, all-incorrupt, all-inviolate . . . . spotless robe of Him who clothes Himself with light as with a garment . . . flower unfading, purple woven by God, alone most immaculate." (*Opp. Grae. Lat.,* III, 524-537). Again he says Mary was as innocent as Eve before her fall.

The Immaculate Conception is reasonable

Surely the doctrine of the Immaculate Conception is strictly in accordance with what right reasoning would lead us to expect. God became man to conquer sin. Was the very flesh from which His human body was formed to have been once stained by the very thing He came to conquer? Was it not fitting from every point of view that God should be born of a sinless creature? He could bring this about, and therefore He did so. Was there to be no case at all in which Christ, the perfect Mediator, had not succeeded completely in His task, not one person in whose regard the wrath of God was anticipated rather than appeased?

Of course, Mary, being a human creature, needed to be redeemed. The doctrine of the Immaculate Conception means that God gave her the unique privilege of being redeemed by **prevention** rather than by **cure.**

The feast of the Immaculate Conception has been celebrated in the Greek Church since the 7th century and in the West since the 9th, when it was first kept in Ireland.

Mary's sinlessness

It is also Catholic teaching that Our Blessed Lady was always absolutely sinless. The Council of Trent defined: "If anyone says that man once justified can during his whole life avoid all sins, even venial sins, as the Church holds that the Blessed Virgin did by special privilege of God, let him be anathema." (*Sess.* vi., *cent.* 23). St. Augustine had proclaimed a thousand years earlier: "Except, therefore, the Holy Virgin Mary, about whom, on account of the honor of Our Lord, I will not allow the question to be entertained, when sins are under discussion—for how do we know what increase of grace was bestowed on her, to enable her to overcome sin in every way." (*De Natura et Gratia,* 36).

Certain it is, too, that Mary not only never sinned but was actually made incapable of sinning by an exceptional privilege of grace. "The divine influence, safeguarding her against all sin . . . . rested on the very singular and personal relation of Mary to God which makes her the bride and vesture of God. Because of this relation, God owed it to His own dignity and holiness to safeguard Mary against sin, lest her sin should be imputed to Him, or lest it should appear that He had a share in it. Because of this relation also, all graces necessary to preclude sin are virtually ensured and guaranteed to Mary in and through the principle of this grace." (*Scheeben, Mariology,* II, 135). Mary was physically capable of sin, in the sense that her free will remained, but because of the overwhelming grace of God with which she freely co-operated, she became morally incapable of any offense.

Mary assumed into Heaven

On November 1st, 1950, Pope Pius XII defined as a truth revealed by God that, when the course of her life on earth was finished, Our Lady was taken up body and soul into Heaven. The Feast of the Assumption has been celebrated since the 5th century according to the records we have, and countless Saints, Doctors of the Church and theologians have proclaimed their belief in the doctrine, basing their arguments on Holy Scripture, which presents to us the Mother of God as always closely united with her Divine Son and as always sharing His lot, particularly in that struggle against Satan, which, as was foretold in *Genesis,* was to lead to a complete victory over sin and death—two words always joined in the writings of St. Paul.

Mary's virginity

That Our Lord was born of a virgin is a dogma defined as an article of Faith by the 5th General Council in 553 and again by the Lateran Council of 640. It was foretold clearly by the Prophet Isaias and it is taught explicitly in the New Testament in the passages already quoted at length. "Behold a **virgin** shall conceive," said Isaias, "and bear a son, and his name shall be called Emmanuel." (*Is.* 7:14). No text in Scripture contradicts these clear testimonies. The fact that Jesus is described as Mary's "first-born" Son by no means implies that she had other sons, any more than the phrase, "they had not yet come together," implies that they had sexual intercourse at any subsequent time. The "brethren of Jesus" mentioned in the Gospels are not other sons of Mary, but merely the relatives of Jesus. She remained a virgin until the end of her life. St. Ambrose called the denial of this a sacrilege.

Mary, Mother of All Men

When she accepted the privilege of the Divine Maternity, Mary gave us Christ. To her absolutely free consent at that moment we owe not only the physical Christ, but the mystical Christ also. Indeed, we owe to her all we owe to Christ, because the Incarnation of the Second Person of the Blessed Trinity took place dependent upon her consent. That consent was ratified as she stood beneath the Cross. For the Sacrifice offered on Calvary, she provided the Priest and the Victim, and with His intentions and desires she was most perfectly confirmed and in agreement. As He offered Himself for the redemption of men, so did she offer Him and herself as well. Consequently, every member of the Church owes the very life of his soul, the Sanctifying Grace won for him by the Sacrifice of Jesus Christ on Calvary, to Mary also. She is, in other words, the spiritual mother of all men.

Mary, the Channel of Grace

Further, it is the teaching of the Catholic Church that every grace given to men comes to them through Mary—Sanctifying

Grace, actual graces, the virtues, Gifts of the Holy Ghost, even temporal blessings. Very many of the writings of the Saints could be quoted in support of this belief, but we must content ourselves with the authoritative words of the successors of St. Peter.

"She is like a heavenly river upon whose flood all graces and gifts are borne to us unhappy mortals." (Benedict XIV—1740-1758—Bull: *Gloriosae Dominae*).

"Every grace which is given to this world passes through a threefold process. It is dispensed in most perfect order, from God to Christ, from Christ to the Blessed Virgin, and from the Blessed Virgin to us." (Leo XIII—1878-1903—quoting St. Bernardine, *Jucunda semper*).

"By reason of this communion of sorrow and purpose between Mary and Christ, she merited to be called most rightly the Restorer of a lost world and therefore the Almoner of all the gifts which Jesus earned for us by His death and by His Blood . . . She administers the treasures of His merits as by a mother's right." (Pius X—1903-1914—*Ad diem illum*).

The great theologian, Fr. Hugon, O.P., sums up this aspect of Catholic teaching in the following words: "The Blessed Virgin is so associated with Christ in all things relating to salvation, that she is the mother of His Mystical Body by grace, as she was the mother of His natural Body by generation . . . . Hence, it can be safely laid down that she is the secondary cause wherever Christ is the principal cause . . . . Christ in glory is the primary, universal intercessory cause, through whom all the benefits of salvation come to us; Mary is the secondary, universal intercessory cause, so that **no grace descends to men except through the hands, that is the intercession of Mary.**"

Sanctifying Grace is the life of the soul. That life comes to all men from God, through Christ and Mary. Just as we derive the natural lives of our bodies from God through our physical parents, so we derive the life of our souls from God, through our spiritual parents. Mary is, therefore, really and truly the spiritual mother of all men. As cells of the Mystical Christ, they are dependent on her for life; they are really and truly related to her in the spiritual order, just as they are related to their earthly mothers in the natural order.

Is it any wonder, then, that since the earliest times, the Catholic

Church has been proud to pay special honor to the Blessed Virgin Mary? The paintings in the catacombs show the exceptional position she occupied in the minds of the Faithful, even during the era of the Roman persecutions. Devotion to Her was placed on a firm foundation by the writings of the learned and devout Fathers of the Church. During the Middle Ages, that devotion grew; Mary's feasts were established, churches were built in her honor, and she was given a place in the Christian liturgy corresponding to her position as God's holy Mother and the channel of all graces to men. In modern times she has herself helped to promote the love of men for her by many startling visions—to St. Catherine Labouré, to whom she revealed the Miraculous Medal in 1830, again to St. Bernadette Soubirous at Lourdes in 1858 and to the three children—Lucia, Jacinta and Francisco—in 1917 at Fatima, to mention only a few.

Devotion to Mary is an integral part of Catholicism

Devotion to Mary, therefore, is and always has been an integral part of Catholicism. By practicing it, the Church simply follows the example of God Himself—who chose her from among all the women of all time to be His Mother—and of Christ, who worked His first miracle at Cana at her request and who from the Cross commended all men into her keeping. "To Jesus through Mary" is a thoroughly Christian sentiment, as well as a most useful criterion for the development of the love of God in the soul. The King of Heaven and earth will certainly not close His ears to the requests of His Queen and Mother, and the Mother of all Men will certainly not fail to harken to the prayers of her children and form them to the perfect image of her Son.

Devotion to the Saints—a Catholic teaching

The Council of Trent (1545-1563) has defined the Catholic teaching in regard to the invocation of the Saints as follows: "The Saints, who reign together with Christ, offer up their own prayers to God for men. It is good and useful suppliantly to invoke them and to have recourse to their prayers, aid and help for obtaining benefits from God, through His Son Jesus Christ, who alone is our Redeemer and Saviour. Those persons think impiously who deny that the Saints, who enjoy eternal happiness in Heaven, are to be invoked; who assert that they do not pray for men; who declare that asking them to pray for each of us in particular is idolatry, repugnant to the word of God, and opposed to the honor of the One Mediator of God and men, Christ Jesus." (*Sess.* xxv).

Devotion to the Saints—a reasonable doctrine

Throughout the Bible the practice of asking the prayers of others is recommended. "Pray one for another, that you may be saved," urged St. James. (*James* 5:16). Long before, God Himself had ordered Abimelech to ask Abraham's prayers: "He shall pray for thee, and thou shalt live." (*Gen.* 20:7). Moses had interceded for the Israelites in the desert, and the prayer of Job for his friends was heard. St. Paul repeatedly asked for the prayers of his brethren: "I beseech you therefore, brethren, through our Lord Jesus Christ, and by the charity of the Holy Ghost, that you help me in your prayers for me to God." (*Rom.* 15:30).

Remembering that the Church is Christ's Mystical Body and that the Saints are the glorified members of it (the triumphant cells of the organism), how can it be maintained that they do not pray for men, or that those who are still the militant members of that Body should not ask them to intercede for them? St. Jerome (a Father and Doctor of the Church) stated this truth nearly sixteen hundred years ago: "If apostles and martyrs, while still in the flesh and still needing to care for themselves, can pray for others, how much more will they pray for others after they have won their crowns, their victories, their triumphs? Moses, one man, obtains God's pardon for six hundred thousand armed men, and Stephen prays for his persecutors. When they are with Christ, will they be less powerful? St. Paul says that two hundred and seventy-six souls were granted to his prayers, while they were in the ship with him. Shall he close his lips after death and not utter a syllable for those who throughout the world have believed in his gospel?" (*Adv. Vigil,* 6).

With regard to the Angels, it is clear from Scripture that they intercede for men: "And the angel of the Lord answered, and said: O Lord of hosts, how long wilt thou not have mercy on Jerusalem, and on the cities of Juda, with which thou hast been angry?" (*Zach.* 1:12). The Angel Raphael told Tobias: "When thou didst pray with tears . . . . I offered thy prayer to the Lord." (*Tob.* 12:12).

Christ Himself tells us that the Angels have an interest in what passes on earth: "So I say to you, there shall be joy before the angels of God upon one sinner doing penance." *(Luke* 15:10). Elsewhere, He warns us against scandalizing little children: "See that you despise not one of these little ones: for I say to you, that their angels in heaven always see the face of my Father who is in heaven." *(Matt.* 18:10).

If the Angels pray for us, it is certain that the Saints, their companions in Heaven, who are united to us by grace in the supernatural organism of the Body of Christ, also do so.

The Saints are filled with intense love of their fellow men for Christ's sake. They also have great power with God, because they have passed through their time of trial and are wholly pleasing to Him. Is it not reasonable, therefore, that the Church Militant should from the beginning have begged the intercession of the Saints?

Beneficial results of honoring the Saints

Catholic devotion to Mary and the Saints has been more than justified by results. Through this devotion the true practice of religion has been fostered, in that more prayers have been offered to God than would otherwise have been. **The knowledge of the intercession of Mary and the Saints has encouraged Catholics of all ages to pray through them to God.** In those Protestant churches which rejected the principle of the intercession of the Saints at the time of the Reformation, fewer prayers than ever were offered to God alone, than were offered before the Reformation.

Devotion to the Saints has kept the family spirit alive in the Church. The bond of the common life of the Mystical Body has been fostered and strengthened. Catholics are able to pray now, here on earth, to those whom they know will be their companions and friends for all eternity in Heaven.

The practice of the Church in canonizing certain of her departed children has succeeded in keeping before the Faithful the highest ideals of the following of Christ. The canonized Saints are the inspiration of Catholics, and those who are intent on advancing in the love of God delight in reading the lives of the Saints for their encouragement and imitation.

Moreover, the history of the Church is full of instances in which Our Lady and the Saints have responded to prayers offered through their intercession. Almost every Catholic can relate such an instance as the result of his own personal experience. **From the experience of those who pray, it has been proved beyond doubt that it is far better to have the Angels and Saints praying with us and for us than for us to be praying alone directly to God**.

Mary's unique position

There is, however, a difference between true devotion to Mary and devotion to the Saints, in that Mary is the Mother of Jesus and the spiritual Mother of all mankind. Acknowledgment of her Motherhood should be at the basis of all devotion to her. That implies consecration to her as her little children or her "slaves," and an attempt to live in the spirit of such a consecration. In that way, one will give full scope to Mary to accomplish her motherly work within his soul. As St. Augustine says, we are all, so to speak, hidden within her until the day she will bring us forth to eternal glory. The degree of our glory will be proportionate to the perfection with which we mirror Christ. And the motherly work of Mary is precisely to form us to the image of the Son who was formed in her. By giving her everything we are and have, we can be sure that she will dispose of all according to God's holy will, to which hers is perfectly conformed.

Chapter 35

What Happens After Death? (1)

How is your soul like to God? *My soul is like to God because it is a spirit and it is immortal.*

What do you mean when you say that your soul is immortal? *When I say my soul is immortal, I mean that my soul can never die.*

Of which must you take more care, of your body or of your soul? *I must take more care of my soul, for Christ has said, "What doth it profit a man if he gain the whole world, and suffer the loss of his own soul?" (Matt. 16:26).*

When will Christ come again? *Christ will come again from Heaven on the Last Day to judge all mankind.*

What are the things Christ will judge? *Christ will judge our thoughts, words, deeds and omissions.*

What will Christ say to the wicked? *Christ will say to the wicked, "Depart from Me, you cursed, into everlasting fire, which was prepared for the devil and his angels." (Matt. 25:41).*

What will Christ say to the just? *Christ will say to the just, "Come, ye blessed of My Father, possess you the kingdom prepared for you." (Matt. 25:34).*

Will everyone be judged at death, as well as on the Last Day? *Everyone will be judged at death, as well as on the Last Day: ". . . it is appointed unto men once to die, and after this the judgment . . ." (Heb. 9:27).*

What does "Life everlasting" mean? *"Life everlasting" means that the good shall live forever in the glory and happiness of Heaven.*

What is the "glory and happiness of Heaven?" *The "glory and happiness of Heaven" is to see, love and enjoy God forever.*

What does Scripture say of the happiness of Heaven? *Scripture says of the happiness of Heaven, "That eye hath not seen, nor ear heard, neither hath it entered into the heart of man, what things God hath prepared for them that love Him." (1 Cor. 2:9).*

Shall not the wicked also live forever? *The wicked also shall live forever and be punished forever in the fire of Hell.*

What do you mean by Limbo? *By Limbo I mean a place of rest, where the souls of the just who died before Christ were detained.*

Why were the souls of the just detained in Limbo? *The souls of the just were detained in Limbo because they could not go up to the Kingdom of Heaven until Christ had opened it for them by His atoning death on the Cross.*

What are the four last things to be ever remembered by all people? *The four last things to be ever remembered by all people are: Death, Judgment, Hell and Heaven.*

D EATH is the dissolution of the union between the soul and the body which must happen to every human being at the end of his life. "And . . . it is appointed unto men once to die, and after this the judgment," says St. Paul. (*Heb.* 9:27).

The very **certainty of death** never allows men to forget it. Moreover, each succeeding generation has pondered the question, "What then? What happens after death?" Reason tells us that the soul is immortal, as we have already seen. Therefore, the soul is certain to live on after its separation from the body. What is to become of it? The soul will still be its conscious self, able to experience happiness or misery under the new conditions to which it has gone. What will those conditions be? Those who have never died obviously have to rely on Revelation to answer this question. God alone knows what confronts men after death, and He alone can tell us about it. This He has done, and His Revelation is contained in the definite teaching of the Catholic Church.

In regard to death itself we should remember that it is:

a) **A punishment for sin:** God said to Adam and Eve: "Of the tree of knowledge of good and evil, thou shalt not eat. But in what day soever thou shalt eat of it, thou shalt die the death." (*Gen.* 2:17).

After their sin, He solemnly pronounced the sentence: "In the sweat of thy face shalt thou eat bread till thou return to the earth, out of which thou wast taken; for dust thou art, and into dust thou shalt return." (*Gen.* 3:19). "Wherefore as by one man sin entered into this world, and by sin death; and so death passed upon all men, in whom all have sinned." (*Rom.* 5:12) . . . "For the wages of sin is death." (*Rom.* 6:23).

b) **The moment on which our eternity depends:** For after death there is no more time for repentance or merit. "I must work the works of him that sent me, whilst it is day: the night cometh, when no man can work." (*John* 9:4).

c) **Uncertain as to its time and circumstances:** "Be you then also ready: for at what hour you think not, the Son of man will come." (*Luke* 12:40).

The Particular Judgment

Immediately after death the soul stands before the tribunal of Christ to face *the Particular Judgment.* As soon as the soul is separated from the body, its fate is decided by God. There is no formal definition of the Church on this point, but it is clear from the Union Decree of Pope Eugene IV in 1439, the profession of faith of Michael Palaeologus in 1274, the Bull *Benedictus Deus* of Benedict XII in 1336 and the professions of faith of Gregory XIII (1572-1585) and Benedict XIV (1740-1758). The Vatican Council [Vatican I—1869-1870] intended to define this doctrine, but was prorogued [postponed] before it had time to do so.

There are no texts of Scripture which clearly and directly teach that **immediately** after death the eternal destiny of each separated soul is decided by the just judgment of God, but that truth is implied in many passages. The parable of the rich man and Lazarus is one: "And it came to pass, that the beggar died, and was carried by the angels into Abraham's bosom. And the rich man also died: and he was buried in hell." (*Luke* 16:22). To the penitent thief Christ said from His Cross: "Amen I say to thee, **this day** thou shalt be with me in paradise." (*Luke* 23:43, emphasis added). St. Paul longed to be free from his body so that, through death, he might enjoy his eternal reward: "For we know, if our earthly house of this habitation be dissolved, that we have a building of God, a house not made with hands, eternal in heaven. For in this also we groan, desiring to be clothed upon with our habitation that is from heaven . . . And therefore we labor, whether absent or present, to please him. For we must all be manifested before the judgment seat of Christ, that every one may receive the proper things of the body, according as he hath done, whether it be good or evil . . . But I am straitened between two: having a desire to be dissolved and to be with Christ, a thing by far the better. But to abide still in the flesh, is needful for you." (*2 Cor.* 5:1-10; *Phil.* 1:23-24). "For I am even now ready to be sacrificed: and the time of my dissolution is at hand. I have fought a good fight, I have finished my course, I have kept the faith. As to the rest, there is laid up for me a crown of justice, which the Lord, the just judge, will render to me in that day: and not only to me, but to them also that love his coming. Make haste to come to me quickly." (*2 Tim.* 4:6-8). In the *Acts of the Apostles*, St. Peter showed that he believed that Judas was already consigned to Hell: "Judas hath by transgression fallen, that he might go to his own place." (*Acts* 1:25).

That the early Church certainly believed in the fact of the Particular Judgment is clearly and emphatically stated by St. Augustine: "Souls are judged when they depart from the body, before they come to that Judgment (i.e., the General Judgment) which must be passed on them when reunited to the body, and are tormented or glorified in that same flesh which they here inhabited." (*De Anima et ejus Origine,* ii, 8). In support, he quotes the parable of the Rich Man and Lazarus.

St. Gregory the Great stated his belief that, "Just as happiness rejoices the elect, so it must be believed that from the day of their death, fire burns the reprobate." (*Dial.,* lv, 28).

When, where?

Of course, there was a good deal of controversy throughout the first centuries as to the details and circumstances of the Particular Judgment, but the Second Council of Lyons, in 1274, decreed that souls free from sin are at once received into Heaven, and half a century later, Pope Benedict XII defined that "the souls of those who depart this life in the state of mortal sin descend into Hell immediately after death and are there subject to infernal torments," and those who die in the state of grace "behold the Divine Essence intuitively and face to face."

The common opinion of theologians is that the Particular Judgment will take place where death occurs and that it will be instantaneous. At the moment of death the soul will be internally illuminated as to its own innocence or guilt and will immediately, on its own initiative, make its way to Heaven, to Hell or to Purgatory.

All, of course, are meant to attain a destiny of eternal happiness. Those who are quite unfit for it, as a result of their death in deliberate mortal sin, will go to Hell; those who are not quite fit, owing to the presence of venial sin or some spiritual debt still due to the justice of God, will go to Purgatory; those who are quite fit will be admitted at once to Heaven.

Hell: A Catholic teaching

The word "Hell" is derived from the Anglo-Saxon *helan,* meaning "to hide." "Hel" in ancient Norse mythology was the goddess of the underworld. But in relation to Catholic doctrine, Hell means a place of punishment after death.

The Catholic Faith is stated in the ancient Athanasian Creed: "They that have done what is good shall go into life everlasting, and they that have done evil into everlasting fire." The Church has repeatedly defined the same truth, e.g., at the Council of Florence: "The souls of those who depart in mortal sin, or only in Original Sin, go down immediately into Hell to be visited, however, with unequal punishments." In 1336 Pope Benedict XII made the following definition: "We also define that, according to God's general ordinance, the souls of those who depart this life in actual mortal sin descend straightway after death into Hell, where they suffer its torments; yet nonetheless, in the day of Judgment all will appear before the tribunal of Christ, there to render an account of their actions."

Hell in Scripture

On almost every page, the New Testament clearly teaches the doctrine of Hell. St. John the Baptist proclaimed his belief in it: "Every tree therefore that doth not yield good fruit, shall be cut down, and cast into the fire . . . he will thoroughly cleanse his floor and gather his wheat into the barn; but the chaff he will burn with unquenchable fire." *(Matt.* 3:10-12).

Our Lord continually warns His followers and others that, unless they obey His teaching, they may die in their sins and so merit eternal punishment. Thus, "whosoever shall speak a word against the Son of man, it shall be forgiven him: but he that shall speak against the Holy Ghost, it shall not be forgiven him, neither in this world, nor in the world to come." *(Matt.* 12:32). "And if thy hand, or thy foot scandalize thee, cut it off, and cast it from thee. It is better for thee to go into life maimed or lame, than having two hands or two feet, to be cast into everlasting fire." *(Matt.* 18:8). The punishment for adultery is to be "cast into hell." (Cf. *Matt.* 5:28-29).

Several of the parables end with the condemnation of the wicked to Hell. Thus: "In the time of the harvest I will say to the reapers: Gather up first the cockle, and bind it into bundles to burn." *(Matt.* 13:30). "So shall it be at the end of the world. The angels shall go out, and shall separate the wicked from among the just. And shall cast them into the furnace of fire: there shall be weeping and gnashing of teeth." *(Matt.* 13:49-50). "Bind his hands and feet, and cast him into the exterior darkness: there shall be weeping and gnashing of teeth." *(Matt.* 22:13). "And the unprofitable servant cast ye out into the exterior darkness. There shall be weeping and gnashing of teeth." *(Matt.* 25:30). Describing the Last Judgment, Christ could not be clearer: "Then he shall say to them also that shall be on his left hand: Depart from me, you cursed, into everlasting fire which was prepared for the devil and his angels." *(Matt.* 25:41).

Throughout St. John's Gospel runs the theme that those who accept Christ shall enjoy eternal life; whereas those who reject Him will be lost forever. In almost every chapter he speaks of the life that is to come, stressing that because it is more to his purpose: "But these are written, that you may believe that Jesus is the Christ, the Son of God: and that believing, you may have life in his name."

(John 20:31). It is very obvious that if the reward for acceptance of Christ and all His teaching is to be eternal life, those who deliberately reject Him will be deprived of life and therefore will suffer eternal death.

Practically the whole of the second chapter of St. Peter's second Epistle is devoted to the theme that wrongdoers will receive eternal punishment in Hell. The Prince of the Apostles says that, "There were also false prophets among the people, even as there shall be among you lying teachers, who shall bring in sects of perdition, and deny the Lord who bought them: bringing upon themselves swift destruction. . . God spared not the angels that sinned, but delivered them, drawn down by infernal ropes to the lower hell, unto torments, to be reserved unto judgment. . . The Lord knoweth how to deliver the godly from temptation, but to reserve the unjust unto the day of judgment to be tormented. And especially them who walk after the flesh in the lust of uncleanness, and despise government, audacious, self-willed, they fear not to bring in sects, blaspheming. Whereas angels who are greater in strength and power, bring not against themselves a railing judgment. But these men, as irrational beasts, naturally tending to the snare and to destruction, blaspheming those things which they know not, shall perish in their corruption, receiving the reward of their injustice." *(2 Peter* 2:1-13).

St. Jude is even more emphatic. He speaks of the godless men, who, like the fallen angels and the people of Sodom and Gomorrha, "having given themselves to fornication, and going after other flesh, [homosexuality and beastiality], were made an example, suffering the punishment of eternal fire. . . to whom the storm of darkness is reserved for ever." *(Jude* 1:7,13).

Writing to the Thessalonians, St. Paul is particularly clear: "It is a just thing with God to repay tribulation to them that trouble you. . . In a flame of fire, giving vengeance to them who know not God, and who obey not the gospel of our Lord Jesus Christ. Who shall suffer eternal punishment in destruction." *(2 Thess.* 1:6-9). Elsewhere, he says on several occasions that "the unjust shall not possess the kingdom of God." *(1 Cor.* 6:9; *Gal.* 5:20, 21; *Eph.* 5:5).

Eternal punishment

It will have been noticed that throughout these Scriptural references to Hell the note of **eternal** punishment is always present. During the first three centuries, this was taken for granted. The acts of the early martyrs state again and again that they delighted to suffer temporary pains for Christ in order to avoid eternal damnation. St. Ignatius of Antioch, for example, spoke of those who corrupt the True Faith going into fire that can never be extinguished; whereas, the martyrs always had the thought of that punishment before their eyes. *(Ad. Ephes.* XVI, 1; *Epist. de martyrio S. Polycarpi,* 113). It is true that Origen advanced his famous *theory* of successive trials and thus denied the eternity of Hell, but the really significant thing is that the Church condemned him for it. A Synod was held at Constantinople in 543 and its decrees, confirmed by Pope Vigilius, condemned all those who deny the eternity of Hell. Ten years later, this condemnation was renewed by the 5th General Council held at Constantinople.

St. Justin, who lived in the first half of the second century, went so far as to teach that if Hell does not exist, "either there is no God, or if there is, He does not concern Himself with men, and virtue and vice have no meaning." *(Apol.* ii, 9).

Again and again, St. Basil the Great (c. 330-c. 379) stressed the fact of the existence of Hell as a place of eternal punishment; St. John Chrysostom answered all the objections of the pagans and heretics against eternal punishment; and St. Augustine proved the Catholic doctrine from Scripture and reason.

Belief in Hell is reasonable

When we turn to the consideration of the doctrine of an eternal Hell from the point of view of pure reason, we see at once that, provided God has appointed a definite time of trial for men, He cannot be so dependent upon them that, because of their malice, He is forced to prolong that time indefinitely. If certain members of our race come to the end of their period of probation still hating God, in spite of all His love for them and the help of His grace, God has surely no obligation to extend their time of trial. The very thought of putting God under such an obligation to the malice of His creatures is unworthy of Him. Therefore, if the dissolution of the union between soul and body marks the end of the time of probation, once that has taken place, there is no further hope of salvation if it has not been achieved by then. It is the belief of all peoples, the universal conviction of mankind, that eternal retribution is dealt out immediately after death.

Again, if men knew that there were to be a further period of trial after death, what would compel them to preserve the moral and social order?

There will always be many things about Hell which the human mind cannot fully understand. The judgments of God are inscrutable, His ways undiscoverable. (Cf. *Rom.* 11:33). Yet we can at least understand that all is one in God. He is Justice, and He is Mercy. The two attributes cannot be at variance with one another. Each finds its infinite perfection in Him "Who will have all men to be saved, and to come to the knowledge of the truth." (*1 Tim.* 2:4). God, because He is Goodness Itself, rewards the good and punishes the evil. St. Thomas Aquinas therefore says that Hell glorifies the justice and goodness of God. He made men free to love Him; He does everything possible to win their love; throughout life He pursues them with His graces; and He only condemns them when they knowingly and willfully turn against Him and die as His enemies. Can we honestly blame Him for that? To maintain that He is always bound to forgive His creatures, no matter how wickedly they turn against Him, is to make God helpless in the face of their sin. If they knew they were always certain of ultimate forgiveness, men who did not love God would have no motive at all to make them leave their evil ways. **As it is, those who go to Hell only do so because they choose to go there. They put themselves in Hell. They have never asked for mercy, and they never will. They are fixed in evil forever.**

The existence of Hell is sure evidence of Christ's complete victory over Satan. If Hell did not exist, the devil could promise eternal happiness to all sinners, and would thus triumph over Christ, who died to conquer sin. In such circumstances, God's law would be quite meaningless.

Where is Hell?

It is certainly a place, and it seems from Sacred Scripture that it is within the earth, though there are many theories on this point. In the *Book of Numbers* Core, Dathan and Abiron—who caused a schism from Moses and Aaron among the Israelites—are described as descending alive into Hell, and the earth is even said to have opened up to receive them. "And immediately as he had made an end of speaking, the earth broke asunder under their feet: And opening her mouth, devoured them with their tents and all their substance. And they went down alive into hell, the ground closing upon them, and they perished from among the people." (*Numbers* 16:31-33). There is no reason why this and similar passages should be considered as metaphors; they should be understood in their most natural sense. Thus, many theologians believe that Hell is really within the earth, although the Church has decided nothing definite on the subject. "We must not ask where Hell is," says St. John Chrysostom, "but how we are to avoid it." *(In Rom. hom.* xxxi).

The pains of Hell

What do the damned suffer in Hell? It is customary to distinguish between the **pain of loss** and the **pain of sense**.

The pain of loss consists in the loss of the direct vision of God and so absolute a separation of all the powers of the soul from God that it can find in Him not even the slightest peace or rest. All God's supernatural gifts are lost; of the Sacraments, only their characters remain as marks of confusion to the damned who were baptized, confirmed or ordained. We cannot imagine the positive pain caused in the damned by the loss of God. They who were created to enjoy infinite Truth and infinite Goodness, now realizing it, they find themselves thwarted forever. They know that they depend absolutely on God, yet He is their eternal enemy. They know that they have sacrificed infinite bliss for passing pleasure, and the remorse caused by such a thought brings with it depression beyond the scope of human imagination. They know, too, that the God whom they hate is infinitely happy, and bitterness consumes them as they strive in vain to injure Him.

The same is true in regard to their fellow creatures who have attained the same eternal reward. The pain of loss is the very core of Hell; compared with it, the sufferings of the senses are almost infinitesimal. Yet it is only the logical consequence of that complete aversion to God, which is the essence of every grave sin. "The fire of hell is unbearable," wrote St. John Chrysostom, "and its torments awful. But if you were to keep together a thousand hell fires, it would be as nothing compared to the punishment of being excluded from the beatific glory of Heaven, hated by Christ and compelled to hear Him say, 'I know you not.'" (*Hom. in Matt.* xxiii, 8).

The pain of sense consists in the torment of fire, so often mentioned in the Bible. Theologians agree that this is a real fire, but the Church has never condemned the opposite opinion. It is also generally held that while the fire of Hell is a physical reality, it is not a material fire like that with which we are familiar in everyday life. Fr. Ott says, "The fire of Hell was conceived by individual Fathers [of the Church], such as Origen and St. Gregory of Nyssa . . .in a metaphorical sense as a symbol for purely spiritual pains, especially for the torments of the gnawing of conscience. This opinion has not been formally condemned by the Church. The majority of the Fathers [the ancient Christian theologians], the Schoolmen [the Middle Age Scholastic theologians] and the majority of modern theologians believe it to be a physical fire, but stress the difference between this fire and ordinary fire." (*Fundamentals of Catholic Dogma*, Ludwig Ott, p. 481. TAN. Rockford, IL 1974). Suffice it to say that the fire of Hell must be such as to cause torment to both body and soul, that it burns without consuming and without needing a continually renewed supply of fuel, and that Our Lord seems to imply that it does not give light. A decree issued by the Holy See in 1890 forbids priests to give sacramental absolution to those who deny the reality of the fire of Hell.

The very essence of the punishment of Hell is to be found in the **"pain of loss"** (*poeni damni* in Latin); this consists in the suffering due to the loss of the "Beatific Vision," i.e., our sight of God in Heaven. Nevertheless, the damned also suffer tremendously in various other ways, e.g., from shame, from regret, from despair, but also from the "pain of sense" (*poena sensus*), "which is caused by outside material things" (Ott), i.e., things outside the person suffering, of which the "fire of Hell" is undoubtedly the principal pain, which is mentioned often in Scripture. (Cf. Ott, *Fundamentals of Catholic Dogma*, pp. 480-481, Section 2). Condemned souls never enjoy the slightest pleasure of any description; they are continually subjected to the gloatings and reproachings of the devils and other lost souls, plus all the hideousness associated with the company of the damned, and they will suffer a special punishment when, after the final Resurrection of the Dead, each soul is reunited with its body, which it directed into sin. Not all the pains of those in Hell are equal. The worse one's earthly life has been, the more acute will be his sufferings in Hell. God "will render to every man according to his works." (*Rom.* 2:6). However, Our Lord makes it clear that condemnation to Hell is the greatest of all misfortunes: "It were better for him, if that man had not been born." (*Matt.* 26:24). The view that time would bring a mitigation of the pains of Hell was condemned by the Congregation of the Holy Office in 1893.

The idea of a Hell of eternal punishment is unpopular in these times. But to deny it is the height of foolishness. God has told us that it exists, and it is to our own advantage not to forget about it. If there were no Hell from which to save us, why did Christ die on the Cross—and undergo thereby an agony and death that was the most painful and humiliating one conceivable? Was it not to teach us the seriousness of life and the terrible personal tragedy of eternal damnation? If Hell were not a grim reality, why did He insist on it again and again in His teaching? For example, in speaking about the Last Judgment Our Lord said: "Then he shall say to them also that shall be on his left hand: Depart from me, you cursed, into everlasting fire, which was prepared for the devil and his angels." (*Matt.* 25:41). To neglect such serious warnings by living as God's enemies is really to make ourselves worthy of God's condemnation. The wise man will repeat to himself again and again those words of Christ: "For what doth it profit a man, if he gain the whole world, and suffer the loss of his own soul? Or what exchange shall a man give for his soul?" (*Matt.* 16:26).

Heaven: A Catholic teaching

Like the word "Hell," "Heaven" is of Anglo-Saxon derivation, meaning probably "the abode of the Godhead." In Scripture it is used in many senses to denote the region of the clouds and of the stars, the dwelling of God, the abode of the Angels and the souls of the just. Thus, Heaven has come to signify both the happiness and the abode of the just in the next life.

It is of Catholic Faith, defined by Pope Benedict XII in 1336, that the souls of the just who die without any stain of sin or debt of punishment due to sin, see God immediately face to face. In the Old Testament this truth is gradually and progressively unfolded, but in the New Testament it is explicitly and clearly taught in very many places.

Heaven in Scripture

In the first three Gospels, called the Synoptics, Our Lord speaks of a future eternal kingdom which the just shall possess and in which they shall see God. For instance, in the Sermon on the Mount, He says: "Blessed are the poor in spirit: for theirs is the kingdom of heaven. . . Blessed are the clean of heart: for they shall see God. . . Blessed are they that suffer persecution for justice' sake: for theirs is the kingdom of heaven. . . Be glad and rejoice, for your reward is very great in heaven." *(Matt.* 5:3-12).

St. Paul is equally explicit: "For we know, if our earthly house of this habitation be dissolved, that we have a building of God, a house not made with hands, eternal in heaven. For in this also we groan, desiring to be clothed upon with our habitation that is from heaven. . .that which is mortal may be swallowed up by life. . .while we are in the body, we are absent from the Lord. (For we walk by faith, and not by sight.) But we are confident, and have a good will to be absent rather from the body, and to be present with the Lord." (2 *Cor.* 5:1-8). "We see now through a glass in a dark manner; but then face to face. Now I know in part; but then I shall know even as I am known." (*1 Cor.* 13:12).

Two chapters of St. John's *Apocalypse* are largely devoted to the description of Heaven. "And night shall be no more: and they shall not need the light of the lamp, nor the light of the sun, because the Lord God shall enlighten them, and they shall reign for ever and ever." *(Apoc.* 22:5). In his first Epistle the Beloved Disciple says that we shall see God as He is (*1 John* 3:2), and in his Gospel he defines eternal life as follows: "Now this is eternal life: That they may know thee, the only true God, and Jesus Christ, whom thou hast sent." *(John* 17:3).

Heaven in Tradition

When we turn to the constant Tradition of the Church, we find that the Fathers of the Church agree that the direct sight of God in Heaven is the reward awaiting those who die in God's favor. Indeed, there is little need to go beyond St. Ignatius of Antioch. In his letter to the Romans, he describes how his body has become irksome to him, for it hinders him from giving himself entirely to his Saviour. "To die," he says, "is to sink from the sight of this world and to rise again in God, to attain Christ, to be reborn to life, to enter into pure light." Although some of the earlier writers seem to have thought that the direct sight of God would not be the lot of the just until after the General Resurrection, it is clear that the majority believed then just what the whole Church believes yet today. St. Augustine speaks for all when he says that Heaven consists before all else in the vision of God and in the full possession of the Truth, of Perfect Truth, known no longer in a concept or image, but in itself, through a direct and immediate vision. The Saints enjoy the Beatific Vision already, the separation of soul and body being no hindrance to it.

Where is Heaven?

The general opinion of theologians is that Heaven is a special and glorious abode in which the Blessed have their specific home and where they dwell. It is a special place with definite limits, outside and beyond the limits of this earth. All further details regarding its locality are quite uncertain. The Church has decreed nothing on this subject.

The happiness of Heaven

Essentially the happiness of Heaven consists in seeing God immediately and directly, clearly and distinctly, face to face, as He is in Himself. This is known as **the Beatific Vision.** It far transcends all the powers of the created natures of men or Angels. We have already seen how, even during this life, the soul that is free from mortal sin possesses the seed of the vision of God, Sanctifying Grace, a new nature, elevating it to the divine order. Still, it is clear from Scripture that our sharing in the divine nature, our adopted sonship of God, cannot attain full perfection until our glorification after death: "And not only it, but ourselves also, who have the first-fruits of the Spirit, even we ourselves groan within ourselves, waiting for the adoption of the sons of God, the redemption of our body." (*Rom.* 8:23). But glory is not merely the reward of grace; it is its development, issuing from grace as the fruit from the seed. Just as the soul in grace is enabled during its earthly sojourn to know God by faith in a manner far surpassing its own nature, so after death, the intellect of the Blessed is supernaturally perfected by the light of glory, which enables it to see God as He is and to possess the fullness of all Being, all Truth, all Goodness and all Beauty. That was defined by the Council of Vienne in 1311.

The primary object of the Beatific Vision is God Himself, as He is. By direct intuition the Blessed see the essence of God and therefore all His perfections and all three Persons of the Blessed Trinity. Created ideas and images will give way to this Great Reality, which contains the knowledge of all else within it.

The secondary object of the Beatific Vision includes everything the Blessed have a reasonable interest in knowing. Thus, those in Heaven understand all the mysteries they believed on earth; they see each other and rejoice in the company of dear ones separated from them by death. They know, too, the honor paid to them by those still on earth.

Although the Blessed **see** God, they cannot **comprehend** Him, for He cannot confer on any created intellect the power of comprehending Him as He comprehends Himself. To do so would be to make the finite infinite, which is contradictory. Incomprehensibility is an attribute of God, as defined by the Fourth Council of the Lateran (1215) and Vatican Council I (1869-1870).

Degrees of happiness in Heaven

The Beatific Vision, like the punishment of Hell, admits of degrees. It is said that a soul in Heaven is perfectly happy, in much the same way as it may be said that a thimble and a barrel are perfectly full of water. The barrel contains many thousand times as much water as the thimble, but each is full to capacity. So it is with the souls in Heaven. During their time of trial here on earth, they obtain for themselves greater or lesser capacity to know and love God supernaturally, according to the strength of the life of grace in their souls. "In my Father's house there are many mansions. If not, I would have told you: because I go to prepare a place for you," said Our Lord (*John* 14:2), and, "The Son of man shall come in the glory of his Father with his angels: and then will he render to every man according to his works." (*Matt.* 16:27). It is evident, therefore, that the Catholic who is so closely in touch with the sources of grace here on earth, will, other things being equal, have a greater capacity for the Beatific Vision than those who on earth have lived their lives "outside" the Church.* A non-Catholic may live according to his conscience, worshipping God and being of service to his fellow man, but because the life of grace in his soul has not during life

---

*Quote marks are used in this paragraph because **everyone** who is saved eternally is a Catholic and a member of Christ's Mystical Body. Protestants who are properly baptized are actually subjects of the Catholic Church, in so far as they have had Original Sin washed away and the indelible mark of Baptism is on their souls. But it is hard to know how even a "good" Protestant can regain the state of grace once lost by mortal sin and/or continue in the state of grace, because of his or her lack of spiritual knowledge that comes with Catholic instruction and because of the absence of the many actual graces that come from the reception of the Catholic Sacraments of Penance and Holy Communion. "Non-Catholics" who were not sacramentally baptized and are saved are saved through Baptism of Desire (which can be described as justification based on the desire to do whatever God wills them to do—though they are unable, through no fault of their own, to profess explicitly and to practice the Catholic Faith—while also being sincerely contrite for all sins committed because they offend God). But it is even harder to know how non-Catholics who are not baptized are saved because they do not have 1) Sacramental Baptism, 2) correct spiritual knowledge, or 3) the use of the Catholic Sacraments. Consider the words of St. Peter in Sacred Scrip-

been nourished through the Sacraments, his soul's capacity for the sight of God will be less than that of a Catholic, who perhaps has made less use of his graces and opportunities, but who has nevertheless nourished his soul-life through regular reception of the Sacraments. And just because eternal happiness is essentially the enjoyment of the direct vision of God, the significance of this difference between Catholic and "non-Catholic" is tremendously important, more important indeed than we can ever conceive.

It is impossible for us to understand the **changelessness** of the happiness of Heaven. It is a final state which will be unaltered for eternity. During life we associate happiness with change: We go for a holiday because we want a change, but this is because nothing created can **completely satisfy** our desires and aspirations. Every pleasure has some limitation, some imperfection. Our minds, too, are always changing, outgrowing the old, craving for the new. But in the face-to-face vision of God, there is no imperfection. He is perfection without limit, filling every desire and aspiration of the soul. Once we see Him as He is, we will be filled to capacity with knowledge and love of Him. For all eternity it will be impossible for us to know or love Him more. Hence, progress towards God is impossi-

---

ture: "And if the just man shall scarcely be saved, where shall the ungodly and the sinner appear?" (*1 Peter* 4:18). But with God, all things are possible. However, both non-Catholics who are not baptized and Protestants need to realize that Jesus Christ said: "He that believes and is baptized shall be saved, and he that believes not shall be condemned." (*Mark* 16:16). Any non-Catholic who even **suspects** he should be a Catholic to fulfill Christ's will that he "believe and be baptized," and yet does not investigate the Catholic religion to ascertain if it is in fact the true "Faith of Christ" (*Gal.* 2:16), as it maintains it is, then such a person would be guilty of any and all of the otherwise "unknown sins" he might commit because he did not know for sure they are sins, nor realize their gravity. For he had the opportunity to become a Catholic, to be properly instructed, and to be assisted by the grace of the Sacraments instituted by Christ Himself for his sanctification. And yet he refused to investigate the True Church of Christ. God would then hold him accountable—depending on the circumstances of his particular case—for all the "unknown" sins he has committed and did not repent of—because he could have known the truth, but refused God's grace and failed through his own fault to inform himself.

ble once we have attained our eternal reward. The grace in the soul at the time of death fixes the degree of our blessedness forever.

Of course, there can be change in regard to the secondary objects of the Beatific Vision, the "accidental" reward which relates to created things, as we have already mentioned.

We have been speaking of the Beatific *Vision.* That is because the essence of eternal happiness is to **see** God with the mind, to know Him, that is, face to face. Such knowledge necessarily gives birth to the most intense love. Once the soul sees God, it will be drawn toward Him by an overwhelming force, an attraction so intense that it cannot be described in human words. It will be bound to God forever in the embrace of unchanging, ceaseless, perfect love, which, obviously, will exclude all possibility of sin, but will fill the soul with indescribable joy. **What a reward! Surely it is worthy of any sacrifice to attain it! For, as Scripture says, "Eye hath not seen, nor ear heard, neither has it entered into the heart of man, what things God has prepared for them that love him." (*1 Cor.* 2:9).**

Chapter 36

What Happens After Death? (2)

What is Purgatory? *Purgatory is a place where souls suffer for a time after death on account of their sins.*

What souls go to Purgatory? *Those souls go to Purgatory that depart this life in venial sin; or that have not fully paid the debt of* temporal *punishment due to those sins of which the guilt has been forgiven.*

What is temporal punishment? *Temporal punishment is punishment for a spiritual debt that is yet unsatisfied, but which will have an end, either in this world, or in the world to come.*

How do you prove that there is a Purgatory? *We prove that there is a Purgatory from the constant teaching of the Church; and also from the doctrine of Holy Scripture, which declares that God will render to every man according to his works; that nothing defiled shall enter Heaven; and that some will be saved, "yet so as by fire."* (*1 Cor.* 3:15).

How are we in communion with the souls in Purgatory? *We are in communion with the souls in Purgatory by helping them with our prayers and good works: "It is therefore a holy and wholesome thought to pray for the dead, that they may be loosed from sins."* (*2 Machabees* 12:46).

Purgatory

THE soul which loves God perfectly at the moment of death goes straight to Heaven. The soul which does not love Him at all goes straight to Hell. Both Heaven and Hell will endure for all eternity. But it is obvious that between these two states, perfect love and no love at all, there can be many intermediate conditions. Love can exist with a certain admixture of self under one form or another.

Purgatory is a place or condition of temporal punishment for those who, departing this life in God's grace, are not entirely free from venial sins, or have not fully paid the satisfaction due to their transgressions.

Purgatory: A Catholic teaching

Several Councils of the Church defined the doctrine of Purgatory (e.g., The Second Council of Lyons, 1274, and Florence, 1439), and their teaching is summarized in this clear statement of the Council of Trent: "Whereas the Catholic Church, instructed by the Holy Ghost, has from the Sacred Scriptures and the ancient tradition of the Fathers taught in Councils and very recently in this General Council that there is a Purgatory, and that the souls therein detained are helped by the suffrages [intercessory prayers] of the Faithful, but principally by the acceptable Sacrifice of the altar; the Holy Synod enjoins on the Bishops that they diligently endeavor to have the sound doctrine of the Fathers in Councils regarding Purgatory everywhere taught and preached, held and believed by the Faithful." (Session 25, Par. 1).

Thus, two truths are articles of Faith: the first, that Purgatory exists; the second, that the souls detained there can be helped by our prayers.

The definition of Purgatory given above refers to *satisfaction* and *venial sin*. There are many instances in the Old Testament of God forgiving sins, yet demanding that reparation be made by those who have offended Him. Thus, although God, as the book of *Wisdom* says, "brought him out of his sin, and gave him power to govern all things" (*Wis.* 10:2), He still condemned him: "In the sweat of thy face shalt thou eat bread till thou return to the earth, out of which thou wast taken: for dust thou art, and into dust thou shalt return." (*Gen.* 3:19). Again, when Moses and Aaron doubted His word, He forgave their sins, but He kept them from the land of promise as a punishment. (*Num.* 20:12). David's sin was forgiven, but the life of the child was declared forfeit because David had made the enemies of God blaspheme. (*2 Kings* 12:13-14).

In the New Testament we are enjoined to "bring forth therefore fruit worthy of penance" (*Matt.* 3:8), as we have already seen (page

193f). The whole penitential system of the Church is clear evidence of the traditional belief in the necessity of self-denial to atone for sins forgiven and also evidence for the conviction that, unless atonement is made during this life, it will have to be made after death. God's justice must be satisfied here or hereafter. The question is, where will it be done?

Further, venial sins unrepented at the moment of death must be expiated in some way. They clearly do not merit Hell. On the other hand, a stained soul cannot be admitted to the Beatific Vision. "Thy eyes are too pure to behold evil, and thou canst not look on iniquity," cried the Prophet Habacuc to God. (*Hab.* 1:13). Where, then, is this satisfaction to be made?

The Church's answer to both of these problems has always been the state of Purgatory.

Purgatory in Scripture

For proof, we turn first to the Old Testament. There we find a revealing episode about Judas Machabeus (d. 160 B.C.), commander of the Israelites' forces: "And making a gathering, he sent twelve thousand drachms of silver to Jerusalem for sacrifice to be offered for the sins of the dead, thinking well and religiously concerning the resurrection, (for if he had not hoped that they that were slain should rise again, it would have seemed superfluous and vain to pray for the dead), and because he considered that they who had fallen asleep with godliness, had great grace laid up for them. It is therefore a holy and wholesome thought to pray for the dead, that they may be loosed from sins." (*2 Machabees* 12:43-46).

It is obvious that belief that the prayers of the living can help the dead implies belief in a place of temporary punishment after death. The damned are beyond help; the Blessed do not need it. So when the great Judas sends an offering that prayers might be said for the dead, he may definitely be said to have believed in Purgatory. And his belief is seconded by the writer, who adds the phrase: "It is therefore a holy and wholesome thought to pray for the dead." So, even those who, quite falsely, refuse to acknowledge that this Second Book of *Machabees* is really part of the inspired Scriptures, have to admit its value as historical testimony to Jewish belief and practice.

Turning to the New Testament, we find these words put into the mouth of Christ by St. Matthew: "And whosoever shall speak a word against the Son of man, it shall be forgiven him: but he that shall speak against the Holy Ghost, it shall not be forgiven him, **neither in this world, nor in the world to come.**" (*Matt.* 12:32, emphasis added). St. Isidore of Seville (560-636, a Doctor of the Church) aptly commented on these words when, about the end of the sixth century, he wrote that they prove that in the next life "some sins will be forgiven and purged away by a certain purifying fire." *(De ord. creatur., xiv, 6). In his famous *City of God,* St. Augustine also argues: "That some sinners are not forgiven either in this world or in the next would not be truly said unless there were others (sinners) who, though not forgiven in this world, **are forgiven in the world to come.**" (*City of God*, XXI, xxiv, emphasis added). Many other early writers give the same interpretation, including St. Gregory the Great, St. Bede and St. Bernard.

From St. Paul, the following text may be quoted as supporting the doctrine of Purgatory: "According to the grace of God that is given to me, as a wise architect, I have laid the foundation; and another buildeth thereon. But let every man take heed how he buildeth thereupon. For other foundation no man can lay, but that which is laid; which is Christ Jesus. Now if any man build upon this foundation, gold, silver, precious stones, wood, hay, stubble: Every man's work shall be manifest; for the day of the Lord shall declare it, because it shall be revealed in fire; and the fire shall try every man's work, of what sort it is. If any man's work abide, which he hath built thereupon, he shall receive a reward. If any man's work burn, he shall suffer loss; but he himself shall be saved, yet so as by fire." (*1 Cor.* 3:10-15).

The traditional interpretation of these words sees in them a reference to Purgatory, but it is not quite so obvious as one might be led to believe. The "fire" in which the "day of the Lord" will reveal itself is the fire of judgment, which accompanies the chariot of the Lord coming to judge the world. "It is," says Prat, "an intelligent fire, which will make clear the contrast between good doctrine, durable like gold, silver and marble; and worthless doctrines, which are as destructible as wood, hay and straw." By this fire, the imprudent architects will find their consciences tried and their due punishment inflicted. But in the last phrase of the quotation, "by passing through fire," the word "fire" has its ordinary sense, for the Apostle is making this comparison: They shall be saved, but not without pain and distress, like people surprised by a sudden conflagration, and saved by rushing through the flames. Hence, the Catholic doctrine of Purgatory finds very solid support here, even if the "fire" mentioned is not the actual fire of Purgatory. In support of this opinion, St. Robert Bellarmine quotes St. Ambrose, St. Jerome, St. Augustine, St. Gregory and Origen.

The Tradition of the Church

When the Tradition of the Church is examined, it is found that all the earliest writers in both East and West mention the custom of praying for the dead. Tertullian, at the beginning of the third century, alludes to anniversary Masses in two different passages: "On one day every year," he says, "we make oblations for the dead, as for their birthdays" (*De Cor. Mil.,* 3), and "The faithful widow prays for her husband's soul, and begs for him in the interim repose, and participation in the first resurrection, and she makes offerings for him on the anniversary of his death." *(De Monog.).* Tertullian charges a widow with infidelity if she fails to pray for the soul of her departed husband.

St. Cyprian, St. Clement of Alexandria and Origen are all perfectly clear in their evidence that it was just taken for granted in their day that the departed Faithful were in a condition in which they could be helped by their brethren still on earth. In fact, the practice of praying for the dead soon passed into the official liturgy of the Church, and it is as clear in the fourth century as it is today in our time.

In a famous passage in his *Confessions,* St. Augustine writes this of his mother, St. Monica: "Lay this body anywhere, she says; let not the care of it in any way disturb you. Only this I ask of you, that you remember me at the altar of the Lord wherever you are." (*Confessions* ix, 27).

St. Cyril of Jerusalem (315-386) wrote: "Then we pray for the Holy Fathers and Bishops that are dead; in short, for all those who have departed this life in our communion; believing that the souls of those for whom prayers are offered receive very great relief, while this holy and tremendous victim lies upon the altar." (*Cath. Myst.,* v. 9).

Many of the ancient liturgies contain formulas of prayers for the dead. Here is one, taken from the *Apostolic Constitution* (about 400 A.D.): "Let us pray for our brethren who sleep in Christ, that God who in His love for men has received the soul of the departed one, may forgive him every fault, and in mercy and clemency receive him into the bosom of Abraham, with those who in this life have pleased God." (viii, 41).

Going back still further, we find that the inscriptions of the Catacombs bear out all that has been said about the faith of the early Christians in the existence of Purgatory. On the tombs of the Faithful, words of hope were inscribed and petitions for peace and for rest; and with each recurring anniversary, the Faithful gathered at the tomb of the departed to pray for the repose of his soul.

"There is not a single liturgy existing," wrote Cardinal Wiseman, "whether we consider the most ancient period of the Church or the most distant part of the world, in which this doctrine (of prayers for the dead) is not laid down. In the Oriental liturgies, we find parts appointed in which the priest or bishop is ordered to pray for the souls of the faithful departed; and tables were anciently kept in the churches, called *Diptychs,* on which the names of the deceased were enrolled, that they might be remembered in the Sacrifice of the Mass and the prayers of the faithful."

Therefore, those who reject belief in Purgatory and prayers for the dead have before them the colossal task of explaining away the constant Tradition of twenty centuries of Christianity. It is so ancient and so well attested that any but the most prejudiced observer is bound to admit that it represents the mind of Christ.

The Doctrine of Purgatory is reasonable

Moreover, such a person is also bound to admit that the Catholic doctrine about Purgatory is most reasonable. For example, how many people do we know who have truly perfected themselves— who have arrived at a point in their lives where they commit at worst only the very smallest sins—and also who have lived a holy, penitential life? Many people die with venial sins still unforgiven or the debt of temporal punishment still unpaid. God's justice demands that this payment be made sometime, and therefore after death is the only time left to do it. **Thus, reason alone demands the existence of a state of temporary purgation**. As someone has well said, "The denial of Purgatory implies a poor idea of God and a very flattering idea of self."

Further, it is surely reasonable to suppose that God in His Providence has appointed some penalties for venial sins in order to encourage men to avoid them; but if there is no Purgatory, where venial sins that are unforgiven at the moment of death can be atoned for, what sanction has God's justice appointed for them?

The pains of Purgatory

It is the doctrine of the Church that the souls detained in Purgatory make atonement through suffering.

They know, however, that their eternal happiness is secured. The Canon of the Mass, indeed, describes them as "resting in Christ" and "sleeping in peace."

Nevertheless, because they are separated from God for a time, these Holy Souls have to endure the pain of loss. In their case, this is most severe, for they desire God with all their being. The greater the good one desires and the more vehemently one desires it, the greater the pain when that desire is frustrated. The souls in Purgatory are free from the temptations of life on earth; they have only one desire, to be with God in Heaven. The temporary frustration of that desire is for them the cause of most intense suffering. Moreover, they know that their separation from Infinite Love has been caused through their own fault, and they understand what increase of bliss they might have enjoyed had they avoided sin or made more satisfaction on earth for the sins they had committed.

On the other hand, the suffering souls have far less to bear than those damned in Hell, for they are conscious that their torment will end in due course, when they will then begin to enjoy the direct vision of God; moreover, they suffer patiently and generously, fully aware that their present sufferings are the necessary prelude to a glorious reward.

It is certain that, in addition to the pain of loss, the souls in Purgatory suffer torment of the senses. It is most probable that this pain is caused by real fire, although there is no dogmatic definition on this subject. St. Augustine says quite definitely that the pain caused by the fire of Purgatory is more severe than anything a man suffers in this life. St. Gregory the Great repeats the same opinion, with which St. Thomas Aquinas and St. Bonaventure agree. (And these four are all Doctors of the Church.) In fact, St. Thomas teaches that it is the same fire as the fire of Hell, though not as to its duration. The pains by which we can make satisfaction in this life are very, very small in comparison to the expiatory sufferings of Purgatory, because this present life is the time of mercy; whereas after death is especially the time of justice.

Still, one must not forget that the detained souls love God most ardently, that they will never cease to love Him, and that this knowledge alone brings them immense consolation.

How true, then, is the following description: "What is Purgatory? A joyous Hell, a sad Heaven. There souls rejoice because they are sure that they will some day enjoy God; but they also suffer because they cannot yet enjoy God. As surely as Heaven is made Heaven by the possession of God, and as surely as Hell is made Hell by the loss of God, so Purgatory is made Purgatory by this transitory character: transition between the future possession of God and the present loss of Him." (Toth: *Life Everlasting,* page 160).

Nothing is known for certain about the **duration** of Purgatory, except that it will be proportionate to the sins and punishment which remain to be expiated. It will begin immediately after death, according to the definitions of Pope Benedict XII (1334-1342) and the Council of Florence (1439), and it will not last beyond the Final Judgment. (Ven. Louis of Granada, O.P., the learned Spanish Dominican spiritual writer, comments that adults who go to Purgatory commonly spend 30 to 50 years there. See *The Sinner's Guide.* TAN, Rockford, IL 1986.—Publisher, 2002.)

Devotion to the souls in Purgatory

Devotion to the "Holy Souls" is as old as the Church itself, in the sense that it means assisting them with our prayers and good works. Already we have examined the constant Tradition of the Church in this respect; we have seen that prayer for the dead goes back even to the pre-Christian era. But, even apart from this, it is clearly reasonable to do all in our power to help these suffering members of the Mystical Body of Christ.

In the first place, helping the Holy Souls promotes the honor and glory of God. He "longs" for them to come to Him; they were made for Him, and it is their destiny to live with Him in infinite bliss forever. Yet, because He is Justice, God cannot release them from their pains; full atonement must be made. Hence, when we—by our Masses, prayers, indulgences and other good works—aid these suffering souls, we enable God to bestow on them sooner the direct sight of Himself; we cause the Cross of Christ to triumph in them, and we multiply the bountiful harvest of the sufferings of Christ. What more glorious mission-field is there for our compassionate charitable prayers and good works than the sweet prison of Purgatory?

Secondly, prayer for the suffering dead is one of the greatest of the spiritual works of mercy. If helping people in their bodily needs is blessed by Christ as an act of charity, how much more pleasing to Him will be the spiritual helping of souls who cannot help themselves? They are still separated from God, yet they long for Him most intensely, without being able to do anything for their own relief. Think of a meteor flying through space, rushing toward the earth at tremendous speed. It meets with no impediment until it comes to the atmosphere of our planet. Then its motion is checked, and intense heat is generated within it by the friction caused by passing through the air. Similarly, when the soul leaves the body, it finds itself within the circle of God's attraction, impelled toward Him with the utmost violence; but if there be even venial faults upon it, they will act like the atmosphere on the meteor, impeding its union with God, till the soul burns with unsatisfied desires, and all trace of sin is at last purged away. In that state, we can help those souls. We can assist those who can do nothing for themselves; we can relieve a fellow creature of most grievous torment and help to clothe him with the garment of glory. Can there be any greater act of charity than this?

Thirdly, every good work done for God earns its own reward.

"And whosoever shall give to drink to one of these little ones a cup of cold water only in the name of a disciple, amen I say to you, he shall not lose his reward." (*Matt.* 10:42). Further, when souls are released from Purgatory through the help of those on earth, they cannot forget the latter before the throne of God. Helping the Holy Souls, therefore, is a sure way of obtaining the special intercession of the Saints. Again, "Blessed are the merciful: for they shall obtain mercy." (*Matt.* 5:7). If we help the Suffering Souls now, God will certainly inspire others to help us when our time of purgation comes.

Therefore, good Catholics try always to help those detained in Purgatory by offering for them the infinite Sacrifice of the Mass, by prayers, by works of self-denial, by the gaining of Indulgences and by other good works. The Church has bestowed a special blessing on the so-called "Heroic Act," in virtue of which a member of the Church Militant offers for the souls in Purgatory all the satisfactory works which he will perform during his lifetime, and also the suffrages which may accrue to him after his death, i.e., the prayers said and/or the good works offered for the repose of his soul, if it is in Purgatory.

Can the souls in Purgatory pray for us? Should we pray to them? St. Alphonsus Liguori, a Doctor of the Church, (d. 1787), wrote the following in one of his many books: "The souls in Purgatory, being beloved by God and confirmed in grace, have absolutely no impediment to prevent them from praying for us. Still, the Church does not invoke them or implore their intercession, because ordinarily they have no knowledge of our prayers. But we may piously believe that God makes our prayers known to them." *(Great Means of Salvation,* Chap. I). That expresses the common opinion of theologians today, and also reflects the faith of the pious laity.

A consoling doctrine

"Sweet is the consolation of the dying man, who, conscious of imperfection, believes that there are others to make intercession for him when his own time for merit has expired; soothing to the afflicted survivors the thought that they possess powerful means of relieving their friend. In the first moments of grief, this sentiment will often overpower religious prejudice, cast down the unbeliever on his knees beside the remains of his friend, and snatch from him an unconscious prayer for [this person's eternal] rest; it is an impulse of nature, which for the moment, aided by the analogies of revealed truth, seizes at once upon this consoling belief. But it is only a flitting and melancholy light [for non-Catholics], while the Catholic feeling, cheering, though with solemn dimness, resembles the unfailing lamp, which the piety of the ancients is said to have hung before the sepulchers of their dead." (Cardinal Wiseman, *Lecture* XI).

Dr. John Brittan Clark, a Protestant minister, wrote in the *Boston Evening Transcript* (April 12th, 1930): "The very early Church Fathers, those nearest to the time of Christ, believed in and taught prayer for the dead . . . The Protestant Church's position on prayer relative to the dead was due, doubtless, to sharp antagonism to the Church of Rome and a strong revolt against the doctrine of Purgatory. Personally, I do not agree with the Protestant churches, which give up prayer for the dead and to the dead. I offer both every day of my life, and to me, this is a source of great comfort and consolation . . . This praying for and to our dear ones in the other life seems to me a most natural, spontaneous impulse of our hearts."

Mallock, another non-Catholic, in his book, *Is Life Worth Living?,* writes the following: "It is becoming fast recognized that it [Purgatory] is the only doctrine that can bring a belief in future rewards and punishments into anything like accordance with our notions of what is just and reasonable. So far from its being a superfluous superstition, it is seen to be just what is demanded at once by reason and morality; and a belief in it is not an intellectual asset only, but a partial harmonizing of the whole moral ideal."

Limbo: The teaching of the Church

We still have to discuss the place in the next world of two classes of people—1) the very young who die without Baptism and 2) the people who died before Christ ascended into Heaven, opening it for the just. The small children in the Christian era who die without Baptism (of water, of desire or of blood) are permanently excluded from Heaven, through no fault of their own, because they have Original Sin on their souls. The people who died before Christ opened the gates of Heaven by His death on the Cross were able to save their souls by leading a morally correct life with the help of God's grace "in anticipation of" Our Lord's Redemption. Some of these people may have completed their purification in Purgatory before Christ's Ascension, or they may have escaped Purgatory altogether. In conjunction with this question of the salvation of those who died before Christ's Redemption, we may also legitimately ask, "Where did the soul of Christ go while His Body remained in the tomb between His death and His glorious Resurrection?"

The *Catechism of the Council of Trent,* commenting on the article of the Apostles' Creed in which we say: "[I believe that] . . . He descended into hell," says: "We profess that, immediately after the death of Christ, His soul descended into hell and dwelt there as long as His body remained in the tomb; and also that the one Person of Christ was at the same time in hell and in the sepulcher. Nor should this excite surprise; for as we have already frequently said, although His soul was separated from His body, His Divinity was never parted from either His soul or His body . . . 'hell' then here signifies those secret abodes in which are detained the souls that have not obtained the happiness of Heaven . . . that into which the souls of the just before the coming of Christ the Lord were received, and where, without experiencing any sort of pain, but supported by the blessed hope of redemption, they enjoyed peaceful repose. To liberate these holy souls . . . Christ the Lord descended into hell." (Pp. 62-63, *Catechism of the Council of Trent*). Catholic tradition has called this happy place of waiting "*Limbo.*"

Therefore, **Limbo** may be defined as a) the temporary place or state of the souls of the just who died before the Redemption, and although purified from sin, were excluded from the Beatific Vision until Christ's triumphant Ascension into Heaven; this is known as "the Limbo of the Fathers." And b) the permanent place or state of those unbaptized children and others who, dying without grievous personal guilt (i.e., without mortal sin committed by themselves), are excluded from the Beatific Vision on account of Original Sin alone; this is known as "the Limbo of Children."

The Limbo of the Fathers

There are several references to the "Limbo of the Fathers" in Scripture. Our Lord refers to it as a banquet, a marriage feast, Abraham's bosom and, even, paradise. (Cf. *Matt.* 8:11; 25:10; *Luke* 13:29; 14:15; 16:22; 23:43). St. Paul refers to Our Lord's descent into Limbo: "Now that he ascended, what is it, but because he also descended first into the lower parts of the earth?" (*Eph.* 4:9). St. Peter is even more explicit. "Because Christ also died once for our sins, the just for the unjust: that he might offer us to God, being put to death indeed in the flesh, but enlivened in the spirit, in which also coming he preached to those spirits that were in prison." (*1 Peter* 3:18-19).

The implication of these texts is that certain souls who died before the Redemption were detained in a place of temporary happiness, awaiting the opening of Heaven by Our Lord. For, as a result of Adam's sin, Heaven was closed against men. Even those already purified from sin could not enjoy the direct sight of God until our Redemption had been completed by Christ's visible Ascension into Heaven. The just who had lived under the Old Law, and who, either at death or after a time in Purgatory, had attained the perfect holiness required for entrance into glory, had to await the coming of God-made-Man and the full accomplishment of His visible mission. In the meantime, they were, as St. Peter says, "in prison"; nevertheless, in His words from the Cross to the penitent thief ("This day thou shalt be with me in paradise"—*Luke* 23:43), Our Lord implied that their condition was a happy one, in spite of the postponement of the higher bliss to which they looked forward.

The Limbo of Children

Turning now to the lot of those who die in Original Sin without being burdened by serious personal guilt (this includes primarily, and possibly *only*, unbaptized children who die before attaining the use of reason, plus mentally handicapped persons who never attained the use of reason), we can find no definite statement of a positive kind in the New Testament. Still, remembering the teaching of the Church on the necessity of Baptism (page 225f), we are forced to the conclusion that those who die without Baptism (of water, blood or desire), yet not having grievous (i.e., mortal) personal sin on their souls, while not meriting eternal damnation, are excluded from eternal bliss in Heaven. **Throughout the centuries, there has been much speculation as to the fate of these souls, since the Church has not settled the question by a dogmatic definition, but many theologians have thought that they will enjoy a state of natural happiness forever in a state and place called "Limbo" (or "the Limbo of Children,"** to distinguish it from "the Limbo of the Fathers," where the just of the Old Testament awaited Redemption). By that we mean a state of such happiness as is due to a human being who has died without having on his soul the guilt of personal mortal sin, yet who has not received the supernatural destiny which comes, as we have seen, only as the flowering of the seed of the life of Sanctifying Grace. It has been well said that the loss of the Beatific Vision fills the souls in Limbo with no more regret than a man experiences because he cannot have a weekend cottage on the moon. However nice a thing may be, if we know that it is beyond our capacity, was never due to us, and is quite impossible of attainment, we do not worry in the least about it. So will it be with the unbaptized child in its state of natural happiness.

Of course, there is no question of injustice in regard to Limbo. Sanctifying Grace (a sharing of the life of God in the soul) is, by definition, something which is not due to us and is a free gift, which God gives to whom He will. Thus, if God gives His grace (a sharing in His life) to one individual, but not to another, the latter suffers no injustice whatsoever.

The End of the World

Holy Scripture tells us clearly that this world will not last forever. When Our Lord was explaining to His disciples the parable of the tares, He said: "And the enemy that sowed them, is the devil. But the harvest is the end of the world. And the reapers are the angels. Even as cockle therefore is gathered up, and burnt with fire: so shall it be at the end of the world." (*Matt.* 13:39-40). Again: "I am with you all days, even to the consummation of the world." (*Matt.* 28:20). The 24th chapter of *Matthew* tells how Our Lord warned His Apostles of the End of the World and described the events that would herald it. St. Peter is most explicit: "Seeing then that all these things are to be dissolved, what manner of people ought you to be in holy conversation and godliness? Looking for and hasting unto the coming of the day of the Lord, by which the heavens being on fire shall be dissolved, and the elements shall melt with the burning heat? But we look for new heavens and a new earth according to his promises, in which justice dwelleth." (*2 Peter* 3:11-13).

How and when will the world end?

As to the *manner* of the world's ending, we gather from Scripture that a) it will be unforeseen, unexpected: "For yourselves know perfectly, that the day of the Lord shall so come, as a thief in the night" (*1 Thess.* 5:2); b) the present world will be purified by fire (cf. the text of St. Peter quoted above); c) the world will not be destroyed but renewed: "But we look for new heavens and a new earth according to his promises, in which justice dwelleth." (*2 Peter* 3:13). "And I saw a new heaven and a new earth. For the first heaven and the first earth were gone, and the sea is now no more." (*Apoc.* 21:1).

The *time* of the End of the World is known to God alone: "But of that day or hour no man knoweth, neither the angels in heaven, nor the Son, but the Father." (*Mark* 13:32). In the Fifth Lateran Council, Pope Leo X forbade anyone to make any definite assertions about the time the world is to end. However, theologians have gathered from the Scriptures certain signs which may help men to foresee the approach of the last day: 1) the Gospel will have been preached throughout the world; 2) the Jews will have been converted, principally through the preaching of the Prophet Elias, who will return toward the End of Time to preach to the Jews, while the Patriarch Henoch preaches to the Gentiles; 3) a great apostasy of the Catholic nations; 4) the coming of Antichrist, who pretends to be the true Messias, and whom the Jews at first accept as such and later reject; 5) great physical and natural disturbances in nature; 6) wars, plagues, etc. These signs of the End of Time will not necessarily occur in the sequence given here.

The Resurrection of the Body—
A Catholic teaching

It is Catholic teaching, defined by the Fourth Lateran Council (1215) and clearly stated in the Catholic Creeds, that "all men shall rise again with their own bodies, which they now bear, to receive according to their works."

Scripture

This truth is to be found in the Old Testament, vaguely at first, but clearly and explicitly in the Second Book of *Machabees:* "The King of the world will raise us up, who die for his laws, in the resurrection of eternal life. . . It is better, being put to death by men, to look for hope from God, to be raised up again by him." (*2 Mach.* 7:9-14).

Martha, sister of Lazarus, expressed the Jewish belief when she said to Jesus of her dead brother: "I know that he shall rise again, in the resurrection at the last day." (*John* 11:24).

Our Lord's following words need little elucidation: "And they that have done good things, shall come forth unto the resurrection of life; but they that have done evil, unto the resurrection of judgment." (*John* 5:29).

"Now this is the will of the Father who sent me: that of all that he hath given me, I should lose nothing; but should raise it up again in the last day. And this is the will of my Father that sent me: that every one who seeth the Son, and believeth in him, may have life everlasting, and I will raise him up in the last day." (*John* 6:39-40).

"And thou shalt be blessed, because they have not wherewith to make thee recompense: for recompense shall be made thee at the resurrection of the just." (*Luke* 14:14).

In fact, we find Our Lord defending the doctrine of the Resurrection against the Sadducees, whom He blames for being ignorant of the Scriptures: "And Jesus answering, said to them: You err, not knowing the Scriptures, nor the power of God. For in the resurrection, they shall neither marry nor be married; but shall be as the angels of God in Heaven . . . Now that the dead rise again, Moses also showed, at the bush, when he called the Lord, the God of Abraham, and the God of Isaac, and the God of Jacob; For he is not the God of the dead, but of the living." (*Matt.* 22:29-30; *Luke* 20:37-38).

For St. Paul, the Resurrection of the Body is one of the fundamental truths of Christianity. "Now if Christ be preached, that he arose again from the dead, how do some among you say, that there is no resurrection of the dead? But if there be no resurrection of the dead, then Christ is not risen again. And if Christ be not risen again, then is our preaching vain, and your faith is also vain." (*1 Cor.* 15:12-14). This doctrine he preached at Athens, at Jerusalem, before Felix and before Agrippa. (*Acts* 17:18-32; 23:6; 24:15; 26:8). Again and again, he mentions it in his Epistles. (*Rom.* 8:11; *1 Cor.* 6:14; *2 Cor.* 4:14; 6:1; *Phil.* 3:21; *1 Thess.* 4:12-15; *2 Tim.* 2:11; *Heb.* 6:2).

Tradition

There is scarcely any doctrine so clearly stated in the writings of the earliest Fathers as that of the Resurrection of the Body. They had to defend it against the pagans, who denied the immortality of the soul, and against the Gnostics, who said that all matter is evil. It is almost superfluous to quote texts, for beginning with the *Didache* (first century), they all repeat the same truth, that every man is destined to rise again with his own body. St. Cyril of Alexandria shows how this is possible because God is all powerful. St. Irenaeus says it is most fitting because our bodies have been the temples of the Holy Ghost and have been nourished with the Body and Blood of Christ. St. Clement, in his famous letter to the Corinthians, says it would be unnatural to deprive the body of its share in the soul's future reward.

It has been already stated that we shall rise again with the *same* bodies. It is of Faith that the risen bodies will be not only *specifically* the same, i.e., real human bodies, but *numerically* the same also. Each person will have, after the final resurrection, substantially the same body which was his during life. Each will be the same human person he was from birth, with the same soul, the same bodily life and probably the same material bodily substance. It is true that during life the substance of one's body is changing continually, but no one would maintain that this process interrupts the vital identity of the body from infancy to old age. One's DNA, for example, always remains the same; moreover, there is very little change in one's bones, brain tissue, and nervous system. The very idea of the Resurrection of the Body would be destroyed if the dead were to rise with bodies not their own.

The endowments of glorified bodies

Just as everything came perfect from the hand of God at the time of the Creation, so everything will be restored to perfection after the Resurrection of the Body. The risen bodies will be invested with immortality. "He shall cast death down headlong forever: and the Lord God shall wipe away tears from every face, and the reproach of his people he shall take away from off the whole earth: for the Lord hath spoken it." (*Is.* 25:8). "I will deliver them out of the hand of death. I will redeem them from death: O death, I will be thy death." (*Osee* 13:14). "For he must reign, until he hath put all his enemies under his feet. And the enemy death shall be destroyed last." (*1 Cor.* 15:25-26).

All the bodies of the risen will be identical with their earthly bodies; they will be entire and they will be immortal. But the bodies of the just will be distinguished by four transcendent endowments, often called qualities—impassibility, brightness, agility and subtility.

a) **Impassibility:** The risen bodies will be beyond the reach of pain or inconvenience. This is the sense of St. Paul when he says, "So also is the resurrection of the dead. It is sown in corruption; it shall rise in incorruption." (*1 Cor.* 15:42). "And God shall wipe away all tears from their eyes: and death shall be no more, nor mourning, nor crying, nor sorrow shall be any more, for the former things are passed away." (*Apoc.* 21:4).

b) **Brightness:** "It is sown in dishonor, it shall rise in glory." (*1 Cor.* 15:43). The risen bodies of the just shall shine like the sun, but their brightness will be of different degree in proportion to their holiness on earth. "Then shall the just shine as the sun, in the kingdom of their Father." (*Matt.* 13:43). But, "One is the glory of the sun, another the glory of the moon, and another the glory of the stars. For star differeth from star in glory. So also is the resurrection of the dead." (*1 Cor.* 15:41-42).

c) **Agility:** The body will be able to move with the utmost ease and speed wherever the soul wishes. "It is sown in weakness, it shall rise in power." (*1 Cor.* 15:43).

d) **Subtility:** The body becomes subject to the absolute dominion of the soul, sharing in the soul's more perfect spiritual life, until it becomes itself like a spirit. "It is sown a natural body, it shall rise a spiritual body." (*1 Cor.* 15:44). Fr. Garrigou-Lagrange says "Subtility renders the body capable of penetrating other bodies without difficulty. Thus, the glorious body of the risen Christ entered the Cenacle, though the doors were closed." (*Life Everlasting*, Garrigou-Lagrange, TAN, Rockford, IL, 1996, p. 254).

The General Judgment

After the Resurrection of the Dead, the General or Final Judgment will take place, when all men will publicly have to render an account of their lives before Christ's tribunal. So state the Creeds, and few things are more clearly proclaimed in the Bible.

Scripture

"And when the Son of man shall come in his majesty, and all the angels with him, then shall he sit upon the seat of his majesty. And all nations shall be gathered together before him, and he shall separate them one from another, as the shepherd separateth the sheep from the goats: And he shall set the sheep on his right hand, but the goats on his left. Then shall the king say to them that shall be on his right hand: Come, ye blessed of my Father, possess you the kingdom prepared for you from the foundation of the world. . . Then he shall say to them also that shall be on his left hand: Depart from me, you cursed, into everlasting fire which was prepared for the devil and his angels." *(Matt.* 25:31-41). (Cf. also *2 Cor.* 5:10; *Joel* 3:2; *Apoc.* 20:12; *Acts* 10:42; 17:31; *Rom.* 2:5-16; 14:10; *1 Cor.* 4:5).

There is no need to quote the Fathers in support, for their unanimous belief in the General Judgment has never been questioned.

The Catechism of the Council of Trent (1566) states: "God

decreed that there should be a General Judgment in addition to the Particular Judgment to show forth His own glory, as well as that of Christ and of the just; also to put the wicked to shame and that man might receive, both in body and soul, sentence of reward or punishment in the presence of all."

Circumstances

With regard to the circumstances of the Final Judgment, much has been vividly described for us in the Gospels by Christ Himself, but much also remains hidden. *When* it will take place is uncertain; therefore, Christ bids us always to be prepared. The day of the Lord will come like a thief, like lightning appearing suddenly, like a trap, like the Deluge. (Cf. *Matt.* 24:27, 37-42; *Luke* 21:34).

Scripture seems to imply that the place of the General Judgment will be on this earth. The prophet Joel appears to say that it will be in the Valley of Josaphat, which some identify with the Valley of Cedron, a ravine situated between Jerusalem and the Mount of Olives and used for centuries as the principal cemetery of the Holy City.

Christ Himself confirms that He will judge the world as Man, and in the 24th, 25th and 26th chapters of St. Matthew's Gospel, He describes His coming. (Cf. *John* 5:26). Cardinal Gasparri (1852-1934, author of a comprehensive, authoritative Catholic Catechism) says: "Although the power to judge all men belongs to all the Three Persons of the Holy Trinity, yet for a special reason it is attributed to Jesus Christ both as God and as Man, because He is 'King of Kings and Lord of Lords,' and among the prerogatives of a king is included the power of judgment, which implies rendering to each reward or punishment in accordance with his merits." *(Catechism,* No. 117). St. Paul tells us that "it is the saints who will pass judgment on the world," meaning that they will aid Christ in a judicial capacity. St. Thomas conjectures that the greater Saints will make known the sentence of Christ to others.

No one will escape this Judgment. Baptized infants will be there to behold the glory of Christ; the unbaptized will realize the justice of their eternal loss of the Beatific Vision. The judgment will embrace all deeds, good or bad, forgiven or unforgiven, every idle word and every secret thought. (Cf. *Matt.* 12:36; *1 Cor.* 4:5). Theologians agree that even the secret sins of the just will be made known so that the justice and mercy of God may be glorified. This manifestation will add to the glory of the just, in the same way as the repentance of St. Mary Magdalen is for her a source of joy and honor.

At the Last Judgment, all the relations of God with His creatures will culminate and find their complete explanation and justification. God's purpose will be accomplished; the human race will attain its final destiny; and the reign of Christ over mankind will commence.

Chapter 37

The Devotional Life of a Catholic (1)

How should you begin the day? *I should begin the day by making the Sign of the Cross as soon as I awake in the morning and by saying some short prayer, such as: "O my God, I offer my heart and soul to Thee."*

How should you rise in the morning? *I should rise in the morning diligently, dress myself modestly, and then kneel down and say my morning prayers.*

Should you also hear Mass if you have time and opportunity? *I should also hear Mass if I have time and opportunity, for hearing Mass is by far the best and most profitable of all devotions.*

Is it useful to make daily meditation? *It is useful to make daily meditation, for such was the practice of all the Saints.*

On what ought we to meditate? *We ought to meditate especially on the "Four Last Things"—Death, Judgment, Heaven and Hell and on the Life and Passion of our Blessed Lord.*

Ought we frequently to read good Catholic books? *We ought frequently to read good Catholic books, such as the Holy Gospels, the lives of the Saints and other spiritual works, which will nourish our faith and piety and will arm us against the false maxims of the world.*

And what should you do with regard to your eating, drinking, sleeping and amusements? *With regard to my eating, drinking, sleeping and amusements, I should use all these things with moderation and with a desire to please God.*

Say the "Grace Before Meals." *"Bless us, O Lord, and these Thy gifts, which we are about to receive from Thy bounty, through Christ our Lord. Amen."*

Say the "Grace After Meals." *"We give Thee thanks, Almighty God, for all Thy benefits, Who lives and reigns forever and ever. Amen. And may the souls of the faithful departed, through the mercy of God, rest in peace. Amen."*

How should you sanctify your ordinary actions and employments of the day? *I should sanctify my ordinary actions and employments of the day by often raising my heart to God while I am engaged in them and by saying some short prayer to Him.*

What should you do when you find yourself tempted to sin? *When I find myself tempted to sin, I should make the Sign of the Cross on my heart and call on God as earnestly as I can, saying, "Lord, save me, or I perish."(Cf. Matt. 8:25).*

If you have fallen into sin, what should you do? *If I have fallen into sin, I should cast myself in spirit at the feet of Christ and humbly beg His pardon by a sincere act of contrition.*

When God sends you any cross or sickness or pain, what should you say? *When God sends me any cross or sickness or pain, I should say, "O Lord, Thy will be done; I offer this to Thee for my sins."*

What little indulgenced prayers would you do well to say often to yourself during the day? *I would do well to say often to myself during the day such little indulgenced prayers as—*

"Glory be to the Father, and to the Son, and to the Holy Ghost; as it was in the beginning, is now and ever shall be, world without end. Amen."

"In all things may the most holy, the most just and the most lovable Will of God be done, praised, and exalted above all forever."

"O Sacrament most holy, O Sacrament divine, all praise and all thanksgiving be every moment thine."

"Praised be Jesus Christ, praised for evermore."

"My Jesus, mercy; Mary, help me."

How should you finish the day? *I should finish the day by kneeling down and saying my night prayers.*

After your night prayers, what should you do? *After my night prayers, I should observe due modesty in going to bed, occupy myself with the thoughts of death, endeavor to compose myself to*

rest at the foot of the Cross and give my last thoughts to my cruci-
fied Saviour.

Does the First Commandment forbid the making of images? *The*
First Commandment does not forbid the making of images, but the
making of idols; that is, it forbids us to make images to be adored
or honored as gods.

What honor should we give to relics, crucifixes and holy pic-
tures? *We should give to relics, crucifixes, and holy pictures a rel-*
ative honor, because and in as much as they relate to Christ and His
Saints and are memorials of them.

Do we pray to relics or images? *We do not pray to relics or images,*
for they can neither see, nor hear, nor help us.

The Rosary

O NE of the most important manifestations of Catholic piety is
the recitation of **the Rosary,** a form of combined vocal and
mental prayer consisting of fifteen decades (sets of ten) of "Hail
Marys," said on beads, each decade being preceded by an "Our
Father" and followed by a "Glory Be to the Father," during the
recitation of which the mind meditates or dwells on the principal
mysteries of the life, death and Resurrection of Our Lord. The set of
beads used in the devotion is itself often called a "rosary."

Take a set of these beads and hold them by the Cross attached to
them. After the Cross will come a large bead, and then three smaller
beads, followed by another single bead. Then you will find five
groups of beads, each consisting of one larger bead and ten smaller
ones. Each of these groups is called a decade.

To "say a Rosary," we begin by reciting the "Apostles' Creed"
while holding the Cross. That is followed by an "Our Father" on the
first large bead and three "Hail Marys," one on each of the three
smaller beads, followed by another single bead. Then we say,
"Glory be to the Father, and to the Son, and to the Holy Ghost, as
it was in the beginning, is now and ever shall be, world without
end. Amen."

These initial prayers are introductory to the Rosary, and they are not usually recited over again when a second and a third set of 5 decades of the Rosary are said.

After the introductory prayers, we then say the five decades, each consisting of one "Our Father," ten "Hail Marys" and one "Glory Be to the Father." (Since the apparition of Our Lady at Fatima, it has become almost universally common in the Catholic Church to add the following short prayer after each "Glory Be": "O my Jesus, forgive us our sins, save us from the fires of Hell, lead all souls to Heaven, especially those who are in most need of thy mercy.") After the last of 5 decades we conclude with the "Hail, Holy Queen." Often people add their own favorite ending prayers after the "Hail, Holy Queen." These can easily be found in any Catholic prayer book.

Mental and vocal prayer

So much for the *external* recitation of the Rosary. Yet, the Rosary is meant to be far more than the mere repetition of a number of vocal prayers. **The essential thing** is to meditate on some special truth or scene from the Gospels, or on some doctrine of our Faith for the length of time it takes to say each decade of the Rosary.

The Fifteen Mysteries

The mysteries upon which we meditate are divided into three groups or classes: Joyful, Sorrowful and Glorious. There are five of each set of mysteries, as follows:

THE JOYFUL MYSTERIES

1. **The Annunciation**: This mystery recalls the visit of the Archangel Gabriel to the Blessed Virgin Mary, offering her the dignity of the motherhood of God, plus Mary's acceptance. Hence the Incarnation and all it has meant to humanity are dependent on her having made a free consent to be the Mother of God. Thus, we owe her everything, as far as our salvation goes.

2. **The Visitation**: This mystery recalls Mary's visit to her relative, St. Elizabeth, the sanctification of St. John the Baptist in her womb through Mary's words, which event prefigures Mary as the

channel of grace from Jesus—in this case to the Precursor, but by implication to us all—and finally the recitation of "*The Magnificat.*"

3. **The Birth of Jesus in the stable at Bethlehem**: This mystery recalls how Mary gave Jesus to us, plus His first adorers (the shepherds and the wisemen). His poverty, hiddenness, love and humility are all manifested. The worldlings did not have any time for the King of kings when He came into their midst.

4. **The Presentation of Jesus in the Temple**: This mystery shows Jesus' perfect obedience to Old Testament "Church" Law (the law of Moses at the time), the story of the aged Simeon and Anna, the prophecy of Simeon, Mary's Sword of Sorrow, Simeon's beautiful prayer *Nunc Dimittis*—"Now dismiss Thy Servant." This mystery shows how even Jesus respected and functioned within the established Church of God, and therefore so should we.

5. **The Finding of Jesus in the Temple** after three days: This mystery recalls how Jesus "lost Himself" as an example for us that we must not lose Him through too much activity—and that we can find Him in the Eucharist, in the Church, and in every soul. Jesus is *still* in the "temple" of our Catholic churches, and it is there we will find Him when we go looking for Him.

THE SORROWFUL MYSTERIES

1. **The Agony of Jesus in the Garden of Gethsemane**: This mystery shows that Our Lord's Passion and Death were caused by sin. It shows also His resignation to God's Will, His appeal to us to "watch one hour" with Him and to pray, lest we fall into temptation and sin. He seems to be asking us for an hour of prayer each day, preferably before the Blessed Sacrament. It displays also the betrayal of Judas and the terrible mental agony of anticipating His bitter Passion, which caused Him to sweat blood.

2. **The Scourging of Our Lord at the Pillar**: This mystery recalls the terrible punishment Our Lord endured, especially for sins of impurity, and the humiliation of it. He is still scourged in His members by uncharitableness. This mystery shows the necessity of mortification of our senses. It was largely because of the scourging that Jesus was wounded so badly that He ultimately bled to death.

3. **The Crowning with Thorns**: Christ is our King, but this mys-

tery reveals that He is still crowned with thorns by our sins, indifference and mockery of His kingly station. The soldiers put a purple garment on Him (the sign of a king) and beat the crown of thorns with a reed. In private revelations He has revealed His Sacred Heart crowned with thorns, but men will still not submit their minds and hearts to His teaching, but they go on "beating Him on the head," so to speak, by their sins and refusal to recognize His true kingship. This mystery also displays the virtues of silence and humility.

4. **Jesus carries the Cross to Calvary**: Among other things, this mystery shows the return which Jesus receives for so much kindness, plus His three falls, the meeting with Mary, Veronica wiping the face of Jesus, how He was helped by Simon of Cyrene, how the women of Jerusalem wept over Jesus, and that we must accept our crosses, unite them with His, and help Him in the work of salvation by assisting Him to carry His Cross—on which all are redeemed.

5. **The Crucifixion**: In this mystery we should imagine to ourselves the anguish of Jesus on the Cross, imagining our hands and feet in place of His, all His pains suffered for us, His three hours of agony, His seven last words, His sacrifice **freely** undertaken for us, His dual role as Priest and Victim, the sorrows of His mother, Mary, her consent to His sacrifice, the thoughts that ran through His mind, especially that many would not accept the graces He had won for them and would be lost eternally.

THE GLORIOUS MYSTERIES

1. **The Resurrection**: In this mystery we should consider the Resurrection as the proof of our faith that Christ returned to earth triumphant over death; His appearance to Mary Magdalene, to the Apostles in the Cenacle, to the disciples on the road to Emmaus; the consolation of His Resurrection when the Church has its Calvary; that we too will rise from the dead and reassume our own bodies.

2. **The Ascension of Our Lord into Heaven**: In this mystery we should consider that Our Divine Lord has ascended into Heaven to prepare a place for us there; that Heaven is our true destiny, our eternal happiness, our reward for having led a good life, and that though Our Lord has ascended into Heaven, He is still intimately concerned for us and with the affairs of this world; that He is just beyond the

"veil" of our consciousness, watching with loving interest all that we do.

3. **The Descent of the Holy Ghost upon the Apostles and Mary**: In this mystery we recall that the coming of the Holy Ghost confirmed the Apostles in grace, enlightened their minds to the truths of Revelation and made them fearless in proclaiming the Gospel; that we too are confirmed with the Sacrament of Confirmation, have the indwelling of the Holy Ghost, the sonship of God, and are soldiers of Christ. Let us act fearlessly in promoting and defending the Faith.

4. **Mary's Assumption into Heaven**: This mystery shows that the assumption of Mary's body into Heaven is a fitting reward for her holiness and fidelity. We should imagine her joy, the welcome given her by Jesus, the angels and the Saints, and that she is there to intercede for us as our Mother and the "Channel of Graces." This mystery reinforces our belief in the Resurrection of the Body.

5. **The Crowning of Mary as Queen of Heaven and Earth**: This mystery should cause us to recall what it means for Mary to be Queen of Heaven and Earth: that she is Queen of the Sacred Heart of Jesus and has the greatest influence with Him, that she is helping to form the members of Christ, that she is the model of the virtues, that she is the best example of the great rewards of sanctity, and that there are many degrees of glory in Heaven.

The history of the Rosary

Traditionally, the Rosary is associated with St. Dominic (1170-1221), to whom Our Lady is said to have appeared, a rosary in hand, asking him to preach its use to the people. Through the Black Death (14th century) and other causes, the use of the Rosary began to decline, but it was established again as a special devotion through the preaching of Blessed Alan de la Roche (d. 1475). It is said that Our Lady appeared to him, promising many favors to those who would honor her by reciting the Rosary. This Tradition has certainly been looked on with favor by the Popes since Leo X (1513-1521). When it was challenged in the 18th century, Prosper Lambertini, later Pope Benedict XIV, replied as follows: "You ask whether St. Dominic was the first institutor of the Rosary, and you show that you yourselves are bewildered and entangled in doubts on the matter? Now, what value do you attach to the testimony of so many Popes, such as Leo X, Pius V, Gregory XIII, Sixtus V, Clement VIII, Alexander VII, Innocent XI, Clement XI, Innocent XIII, and of the others who unanimously attribute the institution of the Rosary to St. Dominic, the founder of the Dominican Order, to an apostolic man—who might be compared to the Apostles themselves and who, undoubtedly due to the inspiration of the Holy Ghost, became the designer, the author, promoter and the most illustrious preacher throughout the world of this admirable and truly heavenly instrument, the Rosary?"

In spite of this strong statement, the question of the origin of the Rosary is still debated at the present day. Fr. Thurston, S.J., wrote a strong article against the Dominican tradition in *The Catholic Encyclopedia* (1909) and again in the revised edition of Butler's *Lives of the Saints* (October 7th). Nevertheless, it would be very rash to reject the usual tradition without exceptionally strong arguments. Moreover, it has never been claimed that the Rosary, the instrument of prayer as we now know it, was necessarily given to St. Dominic in its entirety. "When and where this revelation took place, whether it was made by means of an exterior vision, or by means of an interior manifestation, whether St. Dominic preached the devotion holding in his hands the fifteen decades, or only one decade, or no part of the Rosary at all . . . or merely bade the people, or certain people to recite the mysteries together . . . none of these things matters in the least, for they do not in any way whatever affect the essence of the Tradition." *(American Catholic Quarterly Review,* Vol. 41, Jan., 1916, p. 130).

The Feast of the Holy Rosary originated as a result of the Christian victory over the Turks at Lepanto [a port in Western Greece] on October 7, 1571, which was undoubtedly due to the devotion of the Rosary Confraternities in Rome and throughout all of Europe in reciting the Holy Rosary for a signal victory; Pope St. Pius V had requested everyone throughout Christendom to pray for this intention. After the victory, St. Pius V ordered that a commemoration of the Rosary should be made on that day. In August, 1716, after other victories over the Turks, Pope Clement XI extended the Feast of the Rosary, October 7, to the whole Church.

The importance of the Rosary

The Rosary has received new importance in our own day through the appearances of Our Lady at Lourdes, Fatima and elsewhere. At Fatima in particular, where she appeared in 1917, the Blessed Virgin asked for daily recitation of the Rosary each of the six times she appeared there. Thus, the Blessed Mother of God added her own voice to that of the Saints and the Vicars of her Son.

"After the Divine Office and the Holy Mass, no homage is so agreeable to Jesus and His Divine Mother as the fervent recitation of the Rosary," are words attributed to St. Dominic, and he is said to have worked a miracle to confirm their truth.

St. Louis-Marie de Montfort writes: "It has always been observed that those who bear the mark of reprobation, like the heretics, the proud, the impious, hate or despise the Hail Mary and the Rosary . . . I find nothing more powerful in drawing within us the Kingdom of God, the Eternal Wisdom, than to join vocal to mental prayer by reciting the Holy Rosary and meditating on the fifteen mysteries."

More than fifty Popes have recommended the devotion of the Rosary, but Leo XIII (1878-1903) was outstanding among them. In 1883 he ordered the month of October to be specially dedicated to the Rosary, which was to be said each day during the month publicly in every Catholic Church. Before his death, he issued no less than twelve encyclicals and a large number of decrees and apostolic constitutions recommending the Rosary. Pius XI (1922-1939), in an encyclical of 1937 said: "The Holy Rosary occupies a special and exceptional place among the various public prayers we address to the Virgin Mother of God."

It is not in the least surprising that the Rosary should be thus commended by Our Lady herself, the Saints and a long succession of Popes, for it is of its nature a most excellent form of prayer.

The excellence and value of the Rosary

The Rosary is a blend of vocal and mental prayer—the vocal part consisting of the most beautiful prayers known to man and the mental part consisting of meditation on the life of Christ and His

Mother. It is so easy to say, and it is capable of being said anywhere, in any posture, by anybody, at any time. Repetitive prayer is almost as old as the human race; it is the practice of the Angels in Heaven. In the 135th Psalm the phrase, "For His mercy endureth for ever" is repeated 27 times. Jesus Christ, far from condemning repetitions in prayer, repeated the same prayer thrice during His agony (*Matt.* 26:44) and granted the gift of sight to the repeated prayers of the blind man. (*Matt.* 20:31). The Angels in Heaven never cease to chant before God's throne "day and night . . . . Holy, holy, holy, Lord God Almighty." (*Apoc.* 4:8). St. Paul of Egypt used to say 300 *Our Fathers* every day and he used pebbles to count them. What Our Lord did condemn was the heathen manner of prayer, for as St. Augustine says, they thought more of the perfection and elegance of their elocution and delivery than of cleansing their souls. "And when you are praying, speak not much, as the heathens. For they think that in their much speaking they may be heard." (*Matt.* 6:7).

Rosary beads should always be blessed by a priest before use, for thus special indulgences may be gained.

No one who considers the Rosary objectively can doubt the truth of the words of Pope St. Pius X (1903-1914), nor will he fail to act upon them: "Of all prayers, the Rosary is the most beautiful and the richest in graces; of all, it is the one which is most pleasing to Mary, the Virgin Most Holy. Therefore, love the Rosary and recite it **every day** with devotion; this is the testament which I leave unto you so that you may remember me by it."

The Rosary is not a special devotion; it unites all devotions. It distinguishes no particular order; it is common to all orders. It is to the laity almost what the Divine Office is to the clergy. A truly Catholic mind can hardly now be formed without it. Above all other devotions, it is distinguished by the approbations of the Church, of the Saints, of Mary herself. On earth it possesses special power in forming character and is thus a very touchstone of genuine Catholicism; its influence in Heaven may be gathered from the fact that it is revealed, and its effect on Purgatory from the immensity of its Indulgences. It is the finest profession of Faith, the surest shield against temptation. It teaches the place of Mary and shows us the mysteries of Jesus through her Immaculate Heart; it teaches us how she is the way to Him; it makes us do what she never ceased to do, meditate incessantly upon Him. It shows us, therefore, what she wishes us to do; it is her testament, as the Holy Eucharist is the testament of her Son. It is the truest means of loving her, for love consists in obedience and in imitation. And whoever loves her, she will certainly lead to the Heart of her Son.

Benediction of the Blessed Sacrament

On Sundays and other evenings, the public devotions in Catholic Churches usually conclude with Benediction of the Blessed Sacrament. The celebrating priest usually wears a surplice, a stole and a cope. The consecrated Host is taken from the tabernacle and is placed in a precious ornamental container known as a monstrance (from the Latin, *monstrare,* to show), in which Our Lord in the Eucharist can be seen by the people, and which is placed either on the altar or on a special throne above it. At least twelve candles are lighted on the altar, hymns are sung, the Blessed Sacrament is incensed, and the devotion culminates when the priest removes the monstrance from the throne in order to make the Sign of the Cross over the people with It, as they bow down in reverent adoration.

Pope Pius XII (1939-1958), in the great Encyclical *Mediator Dei,* issued in 1948, has the following to say about Benediction of the Blessed Sacrament: "That custom is particularly to be praised whereby many of the exercises of piety which have become customary among the Christian people conclude with the ceremony of Benediction. For it is an excellent and fruitful thing that the priest, holding the Bread of Angels aloft before the bowed heads of the Christian multitudes, and turning it about duly in the form of a Cross, should pray the Heavenly Father kindly to turn His eyes to His Son, crucified for the love of us, and because of Him and through Him Who willed to be our Redeemer and our Brother, should command supernatural gifts to flow forth to those who have been redeemed by the Immaculate Blood of the Lamb." (*Par.* 157).

The hymns most usually sung at Benediction are the last two verses of two of the hymns composed by St. Thomas Aquinas in the 13th century. The *O Salutaris* is sung first and is followed by the *Tantum Ergo.* Here are prose translations of the Latin:

O Salutaris: O saving Victim, who throwest open the gate of Heaven, the attacks of bitter enemies oppress us; give us strength; bring us aid. Eternal glory be to God, one in three Persons: may He give us life forever in our heavenly home. Amen.

Tantum Ergo: Let us then, in humble prostration, adore so great a Sacrament, and let the ancient forms give way to new rites: let our faith supplement the weakness of our senses. To the Father, and to the Son be praise, songs of joy, salutation, power also and benediction: and to Him who proceeds from both, let equal praise resound. Amen.

After the *Tantum Ergo,* the following are sung by the priest and choir:

V. Thou didst give them bread from Heaven.

R. Containing in itself all sweetness.

Let us pray: O God, Who, under this wonderful Sacrament, has left us a memorial of Thy Passion, grant us, we beseech Thee, so to venerate the sacred mysteries of Thy Body and Blood, that we may ever feel within us the fruit of Thy Redemption. Who livest and reignest, world without end. Amen.

Very often a litany or other motet [hymn] to Our Lady is sung. This fact is interesting because it throws some light on the history of this popular devotion. From the 13th century, it was the custom for the guilds and confraternities to meet in the evening to sing hymns in praise of the Blessed Mother of God. The idea of a popular evening service before a statue of Our Lady soon spread throughout Europe, and it was customary to sing the *Salve Regina* (*Hail, Holy Queen*). In fact, the devotion became known as "the *Salve*" in England or *Salut* in France. *Salut* is to this day the French word for the Benediction service. Thus it seems that to the custom of honoring Mary in the evening was united, in the 16th and 17th centuries, that of exposing the Blessed Sacrament. Exposition itself—consisting of a kind of prolongation of the Elevation of the Host during the Mass, which dates from the 12th century—only became common in the 14th century. Two or three hundred years elapsed before the Exposition and the *Salve* were united to form the present popular evening devotion of the Church. The custom of making the Sign of the Cross over the people with the monstrance containing the Host was added because it was the custom to do this

with the Blessed Sacrament when It was brought back to the tabernacle after being taken to the sick.

The beauty of Benediction

The following is the meditation of an anonymous writer on the
Benediction service: "Yes, great moments of grace are the short
moments of Benediction. The place itself is holy; we are in the presence of God; we kneel at His sacred feet. The Angels of Heaven sur-
round the beautifully decorated and illuminated altar, as on the holy
night they hovered about the manger in the stable of Bethlehem,
chanting the joyful tidings of man's redemption and salvation. The
hour, the flowers, the lighted candles, the scent of incense, the
sweet, mellow tones of the organ, the sacramental hymns—all
attune the heart and excite the mind to pious acts, serious reflec-
tions, consoling thoughts and holy aspirations. Earth vanishes in
these blessed moments; we feel as if transported to Heaven, uniting
our prayers with the supplications of the Saints and our praises with
the music of angelic choirs. Here is found a balm for every wound,
a solace in every sorrow. Here the high and the low, the learned and
the ignorant, the sick and the weary, the anxious and the unhappy,
can find sympathy with Jesus, who opens His heart and His hand,
and cries out to us from His throne of grace: 'Come to me, all you
that labour and are burdened, and I will refresh you.' (*Matt.* 11:28).

"Great and manifold are the graces that come to us from the
hands of our Blessed Saviour at Benediction. The light and warmth
of divine grace flow upon us to illumine the dark spots of our soul,
to strengthen us in our weakness, to enlighten us in our doubts, to
enliven us in our faith, to fill us with consolation in our misfortunes,
to drive away the evil spirits that tempt us and to inspire our
Guardian Angels with the best means for our guidance and protection. At Benediction a peace covers us that is not of earth, a calm
resignation that comes from intimate union with God, who alone is
immutable and without whom all is vanity and affliction of spirit.
We leave the church strong and willing to fight the battle of life; we
leave with an abiding faith and confidence in God; and as the scent
of incense lingers about the sanctuary after Benediction, so do the
graces of this devotion accompany and sweeten our actions long

after we have left the house of God to mingle with the busy throngs and to engage in the distracting scenes of life.

"Oh, let us ponder these things and resolve to take advantage of every opportunity of being blessed by God! For if the blessings of holy people are so fruitful of good, how much more so will be that of Him who is the source of all good—the all-holy and all-powerful God?

"Surely we shall be amply repaid for our efforts when we kneel before the Master's throne and know that besides gaining incalculable good for ourselves, we are giving pleasure to Him whose 'delights were to be with the children of men.'" (*Prov.* 8:31).

Chapter 38

The Devotional Life of a Catholic (2)

Why do we make the Sign of the Cross? *We make the Sign of the Cross, first, to put us in mind of the Blessed Trinity, and secondly, to remind us that God the Son died for us on the Cross.*

In making the Sign of the Cross, how are we reminded of the Blessed Trinity? *In making the Sign of the Cross, we are reminded of the Blessed Trinity by the words, "In the name of the Father, and of the Son, and of the Holy Ghost."*

In making the Sign of the Cross, how are we reminded that Christ died for us on the Cross? *In making the Sign of the Cross, we are reminded that Christ died for us on the Cross by the very form of the Cross which we make upon ourselves.*

The Sacramentals

WE have already studied the Sacraments. They are, you will remember, outward signs of inward grace given us by Jesus Christ. In addition to them, there are in use in the Church lesser signs or visible rites, not as important as the Sacraments, yet based on the same principles and sanctioned by the blessing of the Church. They are called *Sacramentals* and may be defined as **any objects set apart and blessed by the Church to excite good thoughts, to increase devotion and thus to remit venial sin.** They are like the Sacraments because they are means of grace; but they differ from the Sacraments, because they only produce grace indirectly through the suffrage of the Church and by causing devotion in the mind of the user. We can deal here with only a few of the Sacramentals. In all, however, they form six categories.

The Sign of the Cross

The most frequently used sacramental and one of the most important is **the Sign of the Cross.** It takes various forms, all having in common the gesture of tracing two lines intersecting at right-angles to indicate symbolically the figure of Christ's Cross. But, most usually, the Sign of the Cross means the Cross made upon one-self from forehead to breast and shoulder to shoulder while the words "In the Name of the Father and of the Son and of the Holy Ghost, Amen" are said. The **right** hand is raised to touch the fore-head, the breast, the left shoulder and the right shoulder, in turn, while the words are said.

Such a gesture is obviously a profession of Faith. It reminds us of the Blessed Trinity by the words that are used. It reminds us of the death of Christ by the very form that is used. So it indicates belief in the most basic doctrines of Christianity—the Unity and Trinity of God, the Incarnation and the Redemption of mankind by the Eternal Son of God.

The Sign of the Cross dates from Apostolic times. In the second century, Tertullian wrote of it as follows: "In all our travels and movements, in all our comings in and goings out, in putting on our shoes, at the bath, at the table, in lighting our candles, in lying down, in sitting, whatever employment occupies us, we mark our fore-heads with the Sign of the Cross." (*De cor. mil.* iii). Of the Cross as a gesture of blessing, St. Cyril of Jerusalem wrote in the 4th century: "Let us then not be ashamed to confess the Crucified. Be the Cross our seal, made with boldness by our fingers on our brow and in everything; over the bread we eat and the cups we drink, in our comings in and in our goings out; before our sleep, when we lie down and when we awake; when we are travelling and when we are at rest." (*Catech.* xiii, 36).

Today the Sign of the Cross is used continuously in our wor-ship—over 50 times in the Holy Sacrifice of the Mass, 14 times in administering Baptism, regularly in the Divine Office, and as a symbol of blessing. It appears on almost everything used in God's service—altars, linen, churches, books, etc. In our personal devo-tions, we should make it morning and evening, before and after all our prayers, before and after meals, in temptation, in bodily dangers and before every important action or undertaking.

A patriot signifies his loyalty by saluting his country's flag. Catholics manifest their loyalty to Christ by making the Sign of the Cross. It is a sign of faith, as we have seen; it is also a sign of hope, a reminder that all blessings come to us by the Cross; and it is a sign of charity, symbolizing our love for the God who died for us on the Cross.

The Saints have called the Sign of the Cross "a reminder of the price of our redemption," for Christ redeemed us on the Cross; "the book of God's wisdom," because it shows the greatness of His love, the malice of sin, the misery of Hell, and the value of souls before God; and "the mirror of virtues," for through His Cross, Jesus gives us such examples of humility, patience, forgiveness, obedience, courage, generosity, etc.

Therefore, we should never be afraid of making the Sign of the Cross; we should always make it with reverence, devotion and care; we should think often of its meaning; and we should always respect the Cross in any form.

Holy Water

When they enter a church, Catholics first go to a font or basin containing Holy Water, dip their fingers into it and make an ordinary Sign of the Cross on their persons.

This Holy Water is ordinary water to which a little salt has been added and which has been blessed by a priest with a formal and official blessing in the name of the Church, which blessing also includes an exorcism of the devil.

There is abundant evidence that Holy Water has been used in the Church from early times. St. Epiphanius (c. 315-403) records that at Tiberias a man called Joseph poured water on an insane person, having first made the Sign of the Cross and pronounced these words over the water: "In the Name of Jesus Christ of Nazareth, crucified, depart from this unhappy man [*sic*], thou infernal spirit, and let him be healed!" (*Contra haereses,* I). Theodoret relates how Aphraates cured one of the emperor's horses by making it drink water blessed by the Sign of the Cross. (*Hist. eccles.* V).

It is a Catholic custom for Holy Water to be sprinkled over the people before the principal Mass each Sunday. The ceremony is called the *Asperges,* because that is the first verse of the Antiphon usually sung while it is taking place. This practice dates from at least the ninth century, according to the historical records that are available.

Salt is added to the water during the blessing of Holy Water because it is a preservative, and the use of Holy Water will preserve us against the disease of sin. Used entering the church, it reminds us that we need purifying before we enter the presence of Christ in the Blessed Sacrament.

Good Catholics always keep a supply of Holy Water in the home. It is required when the priest brings Holy Communion to the sick, when he administers Extreme Unction, or when he wishes to perform some special blessing. It is customarily used by all practicing Catholics morning and night, after rising and before retiring, and it is usual to keep it in fonts by the doors of the principal rooms for frequent use.

The devout use of Holy Water undoubtedly brings us many blessings from God. It is especially powerful as a safeguard against temptation and as a relief of the Poor Souls in Purgatory when sprinkled on the ground or floor on their behalf, and especially when sprinkled on their graves. (Cf. *Charity for the Suffering Souls.* Fr. John A. Nageleisen. 1895. TAN 1982. Pp. 131-137.)

The great St. Teresa of Avila tells us the following: "I have often found by experience that there is nothing from which the devils fly more quickly and return not again than from Holy Water. They also fly from a Cross, but they return again immediately. Certainly, the power of Holy Water must be great; for my part, my soul feels particular comfort in taking it, and very generally a refreshment and interior delight which I cannot express and which comforts my soul."

Here is one of the prayers used by the priest in blessing water.

"O God, Who for the benefit of mankind hast made use of the element of water to signify so many and so great mysteries, mercifully hear our prayers and impart the power of Thy blessing to this element prepared by manifold purifications, that this Thy creature may receive the effect of Thy divine grace, for the chasing away of devils and the curing of diseases, and that whatsoever shall be sprinkled with this water in the houses and places of the faithful may be freed from all uncleanness and delivered from all evil. Let no pestilential spirit reside therein, no infectious air remain about. Let the snares of the hidden enemy be removed, and may whatever is found to be opposed to the safety or repose of those dwelling therein be banished by the sprinkling of this water, that the welfare we seek by the invocation of Thy Holy Name may be given to us and that we may be protected from all manner of attacks, through our Lord Jesus Christ."

Genuflections

After taking Holy Water from the font near the door of the church, Catholics choose their place, but before entering the bench or pew, they genuflect, or go down on the right knee toward the altar.

This is an act of supreme reverence and adoration to Jesus, who is ever present in the Holy Eucharist, who is reserved in the tabernacle on the altar.

If the Blessed Sacrament is exposed on the altar, as after the Consecration at the Mass or at Benediction, they genuflect on *both* knees and bow profoundly before taking their usual place.

After genuflecting, they enter the bench, kneel, make the Sign of the Cross and begin their prayers. Kneeling, incidentally, is the attitude adopted in prayer from the earliest days of Christianity, following the example of Christ: "And he was withdrawn away from them a stone's cast; and kneeling down, he prayed." (*Luke* 22:41). Describing the martyrdom of St. Stephen, *The Acts of the Apostles* says: "And falling on his knees, he cried with a loud voice, saying: Lord, lay not this sin to their charge." (*Acts* 7:59). Similarly, St. Peter, "kneeling down, prayed" (*Acts* 9:40), and St. Paul: "When he had said these things, kneeling down, he prayed with them all." (*Acts* 20:36). Eusebius, in his *History of the Church,* relates how the knees of St. James the Apostle had become callused like those of a camel through continual kneeling in prayer.

Genuflecting, like all the other outward acts of religion, is a Sacramental with the power to help sanctify us and bring us nearer to God.

Statues

A feature of most Catholic Churches is the presence of statues or images of Our Lord, His holy Mother and the Saints.

Of course, Catholics are not foolish so as to pray to images. Their real attitude is explained in the following quotation from the official decrees of the Council of Trent: "The images of Christ and the Virgin Mother of God and of the other Saints, are to be had and kept, especially in churches, and due honor and veneration are to be given them; not that any divinity or virtue is believed to be in them, on account of which they are to be worshiped, or that anything is to be asked of them, or that trust is to be reposed in images, as was done of old by the Gentiles, who placed their hope in idols; but because the honor which is shown them is referred to those whom the images represent; in such wise that by the images which we kiss, and before which we uncover the head and prostrate ourselves, we adore Christ, and we venerate the Saints whose likeness they bear." (*Sess.* 25).

It is true that the First Commandment of God seems to forbid the Jews to make any image. "Thou shalt not have strange Gods before me. Thou shalt not make to thyself a graven thing, nor the likeness of anything . . . ." But it is clear that the emphasis is in the first and last clauses—"no strange gods," "thou shalt not adore them." Yet, even if the prohibition were absolute, it would not bind Christians, for the positive Jewish law was abrogated by the Gospel. However, it seems that this prohibition to make images was not generally understood in an absolute sense by the Jews themselves, for there were images in the Temple—the brazen serpent, the golden cherubim, the carved garlands of fruit and flowers and trees, the carved lions which supported two basins and the King's throne, etc. Later, Jews appear to have returned to the strictest possible interpretation of the First Commandment, and thus the idea arose that the Jews never had any images. Yet, in addition to those already mentioned in the Temple, they certainly used images in their cemeteries and catacombs.

The first Christians undoubtedly used images. In fact, the Catacombs are the cradle of all Christian art. When the persecutions eased, the art of the Catacombs found its way into the Churches and thus arose the present-day practice of honoring images. It is quite wrong to suggest that the early Church was in the slightest way pre-judiced against the use of images or pictures. They were there and they were taken for granted as being helpful toward spiritual per-fection. On the other hand, it is impossible to believe that the heroic men and women of that time who died amid most terrible tortures rather than indulge in the idolatry of the Romans, practiced idolatry themselves. Pope St. Gregory the Great, writing to an Iconoclast Bishop (i.e., one who wished images to be destroyed), expressed the true Catholic sentiment most admirably: "Not without reason has antiquity allowed the stories of Saints to be painted in holy places. And we indeed entirely praise thee for not allowing them to be adored, but we blame thee for breaking them. For it is one thing to adore an image, it is quite another to learn from the appearance of a picture what we must adore. What books are to those who can read, a picture is to the ignorant who look at it; in a picture, even the unlearned may see what example they should follow; in a picture they who know no letters may yet read. Hence, for barbarians espe-cially, a picture takes the place of a book." (*Ep.* ix. 105).

The statues in Catholic Churches, then, are given a relative honor; that is, they are honored, **not for what they are in them-selves**, but because of whom they represent. A child who kisses her mother's picture is simply showing true affection for her parent; one who bows before the chair of state in the House of Lords is honor-ing the King, not the chair. So too, the Catholic kneeling before the shrine of Our Lady is only honoring the shrine because it represents the Immaculate Queen of Heaven; he adores neither the shrine nor the Blessed Virgin.

Relics

Sometimes, especially after evening devotions, the members of the congregation in a Catholic Church come to the altar for the ven-eration of the relic of a Saint. On Good Friday it is customary to venerate the relic of the True Cross on which Christ died.

The practice of venerating relics can be traced back at least to the second century. After St. Polycarp had been burned at the stake, his disciples "took up his bones, which were more valuable than precious stones and finer than refined gold, and laid them in a suitable place, where the Lord allows us to assemble in gladness and joy to celebrate the birthday of his martyrdom." St. Jerome explained this practice: "We do not worship, we do not adore, we do not bow down before the creature rather than the Creator, but we honor the relics of the martyrs in order the better to adore Him whose martyrs they are." (*Ad Riparium,* ix).

Instances of the same spirit are exceedingly common—a mother fondly treasures a lock of her dead child's hair; nations preserve the pens with which treaties are signed; in fact, museums all over the world offer thousands of examples of a spirit which has always prompted Christian people to venerate whatever belonged to the Saints of God or was closely associated with them.

We must not forget that throughout the history of the Church many wonderful miracles have been wrought through the use of relics, thus proving that their veneration is approved by God. Moreover, images have been made at the express command of God and His Mother. St. Margaret Mary, to whom Jesus revealed His Sacred Heart, told us that He wanted an image of His Heart to be enthroned in every home; Our Lady asked St. Catherine Labouré to have a medal struck according to the design that was revealed to her. This has since been known as "the Miraculous Medal," and through it many wonders have been wrought.

The Way of the Cross

Around the walls of most Catholic Churches will be found fourteen pictures of scenes from the Passion and Death of Christ, each of which is placed above or below a wooden Cross. The crosses are known as the **Stations of the Cross**. The devotion of the Stations, known also as the Way of the Cross, consists in walking around the church and visiting each of these fourteen Stations, meditating for a few moments at each on the events it recalls to our minds. The pictures are there to help us in this meditation.

Of course, the Way of the Cross, like all the lesser devotional practices of Catholics, is quite optional. The greatest possible freedom is allowed where personal and private devotions are concerned. What suits one may not suit another. No one could possibly take up all the particular devotions which different people have found helpful and which are approved by the Church. Devotion (in the singular) is more important than devotions (in the plural); that we be devout and prayerful is more important than that we practice many devotions.

However, the Way of the Cross is particularly recommended, and it usually forms part of the public devotions of the Church during the season of Lent. It brings to our churches the spirit of those who, throughout the ages, have, actually or in desire, visited the Holy Land and the places particularly associated with the sufferings of Christ. As early as the fifth century, we hear of shrines being created in Europe intended to represent the more important shrines of Jerusalem, but it was only after about a thousand years that the practice of the Stations of the Cross became fairly common. Encouraged by the Church, priests began to introduce the Way of the Cross, as we know it, about the end of the 17th century, largely through the inspiration of that great Franciscan preacher, St. Leonard of Port Maurice (1676-1751).

Like most of the popular devotions of the Church, the Way of the Cross is richly indulgenced. "The faithful who with at least a contrite heart, whether singly or in company, perform the pious exercise of the Way of the Cross, when the latter has been legitimately erected according to the prescriptions of the Holy See, may gain a plenary indulgence as often as they perform the same; another plenary indulgence [may be gained], if they receive Holy Communion on the same day, or even within a month after having made the Stations ten times; an indulgence of 10 years may be gained for each Station, if for some reasonable cause they are unable to complete the entire Way of the Cross." (*Raccolta,* 1944).

The method of making the Way of the Cross will usually be found in Catholic prayer books, but there is no need to adhere to any strict formula. All one needs to do is to visit each Station in turn, meditate on it and try to make acts of love and sorrow.

The use of devotions

There are many other devotions which could be described here, but considerations of space make further elaboration impossible.

Experience within the Church will soon reveal the strength and beauty of Catholic devotional life. Nevertheless, first things must come first. Holy Mass and the Sacraments stand apart as the official channels of grace, for which no multiplicity of other devotions can take the place. Frequent, even daily attendance at Mass, with the reception of Holy Communion, ought to be the aim of every devout Catholic. Other devotions will soon find their due place, especially that to the Holy Mother of God, the Channel of all Graces to men and therefore of supernatural life to our souls.

Patience is necessary as one grows in the spirit of Catholic devotional life. Many things which at first seem unattractive may in later years be found to be full of significance and may then make a profound appeal. It is certain that as the years pass by, one's appreciation of the popular devotions of the Church can only grow. Their strong emotional appeal, their simplicity, their associations and their practice by many, together, make them most efficacious means of raising the mind and heart to God.

The Rosary, the Way of the Cross, the use of the Scapulars, the Angelus, Benediction of the Blessed Sacrament, the dedication of each succeeding month, the orderly progress of the Liturgical Year, the veneration of particular shrines—these and many other practices—are all approved by the Church, a loving Mother, with the sole object of bringing her children nearer to God. Their very multiplicity may be a distraction, but there will be little danger if it is always remembered that **devotions are not an end in themselves, but only a means to the end**, which is perfect devotion to God through Jesus Christ, Our Lord, and Mary, His Mother and our Mother.

Chapter 39

The Reformation

How the Reformation began

B Y the Reformation, we mean that particular religious, social and political upheaval which convulsed the world between 1517 and 1648. A more correct term for it would be the Protestant Revolution against authentic apostolic Christianity. Its author was a Roman Catholic Augustinian priest, Martin Luther, who foisted his personal spiritual problems on his nation, and eventually upon millions of people in other countries. He took as his pretext the alleged abuses connected with the preaching of Indulgences. In 1517 a Dominican priest, Johann Tetzel, was preaching to aid the construction of St. Peter's Basilica, Rome, when Luther boldly protested by nailing ninety-five theses to the door of the castle church at Wittenberg. It seemed to be quite true that some of Tetzel's views were not completely orthodox, especially about Indulgences for the dead, and that abuses had arisen in connection with the manner of preaching; nevertheless, it was not only errors and abuses that Luther attacked, but the whole doctrine of Indulgences. "God alone," he said, "independently of human exertion, is all in all in the affair of man's salvation."

Vehement controversy followed Luther's challenge. He was summoned to Rome, but did not go. The Pope sent his representatives to Germany without avail. Luther appealed from the Pope to a General Council, although he subsequently rejected the authority of Councils for that of "The Bible Alone" theory of authority, traditionally called *sola scriptura*—"Scripture alone." Between June 27th and July 15th, 1519, a public disputation was held between Luther and Carlstadt, on the one hand, and John Eck on the other. Luther was hopelessly defeated. But the debate only served to publicize the whole matter. For the first time the press was used as an instrument of popular agitation. The Hussites, heretical followers of John Huss and Wycliffe, and the more secular Humanists joined forces with Luther, who was also backed by some of the German princes, won over especially by Luther's proclamation of their supremacy in religious matters. In 1531 the Smalkaldic League, an offensive and defensive alliance of all Lutherans, was formed, and Luther prepared the people for a possible revolt against the Emperor. In 1530 the Diet of Augsburg recognized for the first time the existence of two denominations in Germany. In 1536 John Calvin had published his "Institutes," the first definite and systematic formulation of Protestantism. Later, he went to Geneva, there to establish a University and to make the city the "Rome of Protestantism."

Its causes

To understand how all these tragedies could come about, one must be familiar with the situation in Europe at the beginning of the 16th century. The authority of the Popes had undoubtedly been weakened through the long residence of the Papacy at Avignon (1309-1377), the dissensions of the Great Western Schism (1378-1417, which developed right after the Avignon residency and consisted in two claimants—then three—being elected Pope) and the worldliness of some of the successors of St. Peter. Too many ecclesiastical appointments had been reserved to Rome. Some Bishops were more temporal rulers than spiritual fathers and showed an independence which brought them into conflict with the Holy See. Many of the lower clergy were poor, ignorant and otherwise unfitted for their sacred calling. Some monasteries had grown extremely wealthy, and there were dissensions among their members. As a body, Christians had grown ignorant, superstitious and indifferent. Civil governments were encroaching on the rights of the Church in ever increasing measure. Social unrest was prevalent, due principally to the disintegration of the feudal system. New geographical discoveries brought about a restlessness and a desire for material gain. The invention of printing made possible the rapid diffusion of subversive views among people unfitted to refute them. In a word, everything seemed to conspire in favor of those who, urged on by selfish and worldly motives, wished to usurp the religious authority of the Pope and confiscate the property of the Church.

The Catholic reaction

When the Revolution broke out, the need for reform within the Church had long been felt. But the "reform" instituted by Luther and those who enlisted under him brought only misery, discord and civil war. Christian unity was destroyed; sects of every description began to arise in ever-increasing numbers. In place of religious liberty and reform came only greater immorality, corruption, dissension and strife. The transfer of property from the Church to the State resulted in an enormous increase in the power of the civil rulers, which in turn could only lead to despotism and tyranny. In the end reform came, but it came from the Catholic Church itself.

Discipline was restored in the older religious orders; new congregations, such as the Society of Jesus, were formed; most of all, the great Council of Trent (1545-1563) re-stated Catholic doctrine on points controverted by the Protestants; it suppressed abuses, prescribed specialized training for the clergy, and in general imposed a thoroughgoing reform.

Henry VIII

In order to appreciate fully the completely irregular position of the Church of England, it is only necessary to survey briefly the story of the coming of Protestantism to these islands. In 1509 King Henry VIII had married Catherine of Aragon, the widow of his brother, Arthur. He had obtained the necessary dispensation from the impediment of affinity (relationship by marriage). When the Lutheran Revolt ravaged Germany, Henry attacked its instigator in a work in defense of the Seven Sacraments, for which Pope Leo X gave him the title "Defender of the Faith." Nevertheless, the King's moral life had been anything but pure. About 1527 he conceived a violent passion for Anne, the sister of Mary Boleyn, with whom he had already had an illicit relationship. Therefore, he petitioned for a decree of nullity in regard to his marriage to Catherine, who had given him a daughter, Mary. This was refused. As a result, Cardinal

Wolsey fell into disgrace and was replaced by Thomas Cranmer.

When he became aware that Anne was to have a child, Henry went through a form of marriage with her in January 1535. In the following May, Cranmer declared the marriage valid and in September the future Queen Elizabeth was born. Meanwhile, Cranmer, in the presence of witnesses, declared that the oath of obedience to the Pope which he had to take was only a matter of form, which would bind him to nothing against the King's interest. Thus began a situation in the life of Henry VIII where divorce followed divorce, while a veritable reign of terror proceeded. Priests and nuns were put to death; over two hundred monasteries and churches were confiscated and plundered; and over eight thousand Religious were expelled from their homes. In 1534 Henry was declared Supreme Head of the Church of England; nevertheless, he always insisted on the recognition of the ancient sacramental system.

Edward VI and Cranmer

Henry VIII died in 1547 and was succeeded by his son by Jane Seymour, Edward VI (1547-1553), who was only nine years old. The poor child was completely dominated by his uncle, the Protector Somerset, and by Archbishop Cranmer. The latter introduced the first and second Books of Common Prayer, replacing the Mass with an English communion service and denying the Real Presence and the sacrificial nature of Holy Mass. Cranmer also legalized the marriage of the clergy. Most important, perhaps, is the fact that he introduced the new form of ordination of the clergy, which by implication denied belief in the Sacrament of Holy Orders and a sacrificing priesthood.

Edward reigned only some six years. Mary Tudor, who succeeded him, and who was the daughter of Henry VIII and his legitimate wife Catherine of Aragon, did her best to restore the ancient Catholic Faith, but with no success. Her marriage to the Spanish King, Phillip II, the loss of Calais and her ruthless measures with the heretics (against the advice of Cardinal Pole) alienated her from the affection of the people. She died after a reign of only five years and Elizabeth, the child of Henry VIII and Anne Boleyn, ascended the throne in 1558.

Queen Elizabeth

This young woman—she was twenty-five—realized at once that, if she declared for Catholicism, she would pronounce her own illegitimacy, thereby acknowledging Mary, Queen of Scots, as the rightful Queen of England. Moreover, the Anglican Church was an easy instrument for her political ends. Therefore, she forthwith annulled Mary Tudor's Catholic religious proclamations and restored the English Church service. In 1559 the Act of Uniformity ordered the use of the Second Prayerbook of Edward VI and made attendance at the new services compulsory. The clergy were forbidden to preach without a royal license. The Act of Supremacy declared the Queen "the supreme governess in all matters spiritual and temporal" and excluded from office in Church and State every Catholic who was not prepared to sacrifice his conscience and his Faith to his temporal interests.

The bishops unanimously opposed all these acts of Elizabeth. In convocation the clergy adopted five articles which affirmed their belief in transubstantiation and other Catholic doctrines, and their acceptance of the supreme authority of the Pope as Vicar of Christ and supreme ruler of the Church. They protested strongly that "the authority in all matters of Faith and discipline belongs, and ought to belong, only to the pastors of the Church and not to laymen." The new acts would never have been passed through Parliament had not three of the Bishops been imprisoned and several new Protestant peers been created specially for the occasion.

Though the Queen and her counselors tried every device to force their consent, the Bishops, with one exception, stood firm; they were deprived of their sees and committed to custody. Two of the fifteen managed to leave the country and died abroad in exile; one, already seriously ill, was allowed to die in his own home. The remaining twelve eventually died in captivity, having resisted the new regime with all the heroism of the greatest of martyrs.

The beginnings of Anglicanism

Elizabeth's next task was to provide a new hierarchy for her establishment. She found herself in a difficulty. The only validly consecrated Catholic diocesan bishop who had submitted to her decrees was Kitchin of Llandaff, and even he refused to take part in the consecration of her nominee to the see of Canterbury, Matthew Parker. This man was very definitely a Protestant and on the occasion of his election, Catholic members absented themselves from the meeting of the Chapter.

Finally, four men consented to officiate at Parker's consecration. They were called Barlow, Scory, Hodgkin and Coverdale. Barlow and Scory were both returned exiles, the former probably and the latter certainly never having been consecrated according to the Catholic rite. Similarly, Coverdale had not received any Catholic consecration. Hodgkin had been appointed a "Suffragan" of Bedford by Henry VIII, but Cardinal Pole had suspended him, so that at the beginning of Elizabeth's reign, he had no right to use his episcopal powers. By these men Matthew Parker was consecrated secretly, between five and six in the morning on December 17th, 1559, the Edwardine Pontifical being used. No contemporary Protestant historian records the fact that this ceremony ever took place, and it was only after more than fifty years that the Protestants claimed to prove that it had taken place by producing the Lambeth Register.

Thus, the Anglican Primate, upon whom all the bishops and ministers of the Anglican Church have ever since depended for their orders, was consecrated by a doubtfully consecrated bishop, Barlow, assisted by a suspended bishop and two who were not bishops at all, using an invalid Pontifical and having no intention whatever to consecrate according to the tradition of the pre-Reformation Church. However, the question of Anglican Orders has already been considered (page 310f).

The next step was the publication in 1562 of the *Thirty-nine Articles* as the official creed of the newly "Established Church." These show that a complete break had been made with the belief of the Catholic Church, for they reject the doctrines of Purgatory and transubstantiation, the veneration of images and relics, and the invocation of the Saints—all as supposedly being repugnant to the word of God. They teach the Lutheran heresy of justification by faith alone and assert that the Bible is the sole rule of Faith. They declare that General Councils may err and that such assemblies cannot meet without the consent of princes; that the Pope has no jurisdiction within the realm of England, but that the English sovereign has supreme authority over all estates, ecclesiastical or temporal, and in all church matters; and that the "Established Church" has power to decree rites and ceremonies and has authority in controversies of Faith.

Thus, the alteration of religion was complete. The Established Church had rejected the Vicar of Christ, the authentic teaching of Christ and the sacrificial worship given us by Christ. Much that was essential in obedience to ecclesiastical authority, in belief and in worship, was cast aside. The break was so thorough and complete that no unprejudiced student of the facts could ever claim that the Elizabethan foundation was the same as that brought to England by St. Augustine in 597 and loved and cherished for a thousand years by all the people of this land.

Continuity?

In 1570 Elizabeth was excommunicated by Pope St. Pius V. The persecution of her Catholic subjects, which had already been severe, was redoubled in intensity. During her reign, 128 priests, 58 laymen and 3 women were executed for the Faith; in addition, 32 Franciscans were starved to death. Thousands suffered fines, imprisonment, confiscations and impoverishment for their adherence to the old and True Church. Between 1535 and 1681, over 600 heroic men and women gave their lives for their beliefs. Could all this have happened if those thousands of persecuted heroes had not been completely and utterly convinced that a new and essentially different religion was being foisted upon them by the civil power? No one who has really studied and understood the history of the English Martyrs can honestly maintain that there is any real continuity of doctrine, worship or discipline between the Elizabethan Church, which is still legally established in England, and the Catholic Church, set up there nearly a thousand years before by St. Augustine of Canterbury (d. 604), who in 597 was sent by Pope St. Gregory the Great to convert England.

As an illustration, let us suppose Mr. A goes to Mr. B's house, batters him on the head, throws him and his family into the street, and establishes himself and his friends on Mr. B's premises. No one would call Mr. A either the same person as or a lineal descendant

of Mr. B, merely because he continues to occupy Mr. B's house—
not even if Mr. A were to go so far as to call himself Mr. B or Mr.
A-B and to wear Mr. B's hat and watch chain. In the same way, you
cannot call the Anglican Church today the same as or a direct
descendant of the Church in pre-Reformation England. The two
have different worship, different faith, and obedience to different
authorities.

Hence, if the Anglican Church is the True Faith, the problem
arises as to where the Church of Christ actually was until 1571,
when the *Thirty-nine Articles* establishing the Anglican Church
became the law in England by an act of Parliament in that year.
Jesus Christ is God; He said He would always be with His Church,
that He would pray for it, and the Holy Spirit would guide it, and
that "the gates of Hell shall not prevail against it." (*Matt.* 16:18).
The Anglican Church was most certainly newly created in the sixteenth century. Where was the true Church of Christ before that
time? If you deny that the Anglican Church was a new creation of
Queen Elizabeth, you have to concede that it was then the same,
essentially, as the pre-Reformation Catholic Church, and you have
to prove that a change in doctrine, worship and jurisdiction is not an
alteration of religion in its essentials. That is manifestly an impossible proposition. The only conclusion we can draw is that Anglican-
ism represents an essential and unlawful change of Christ's religion
for a false one, made by unauthorized persons and imposed by ruthless persecution on the people of that time.

Christ's one, visible, organized Church has existed on earth
since the day He established it. It was in England even in Roman
times; it was re-established there by St. Augustine of Canterbury,
who was sent specifically for that purpose by Pope St. Gregory the
Great in 597, as his official representative and missionary bishop.
For nearly a thousand years the Catholic Church existed in this land,
loyal to the Popes and at one with the universal Church in belief and
worship. The only Christian body now in England that is able to
prove, without a shadow of doubt, that it is one with the pre-Eliza-
bethan English Church—in doctrine, in worship and in obedience to
the same authority—is that Church which is known throughout the
world as the Roman Catholic Church.

Chapter 40

Some Catholic Social Principles

The right to private property

THE right to private property is the right which every human being has from his very nature, that he may own, use and dispose of material and even intellectual things for his own benefit, without interference. John Smith really owns something when it can truly be described as "his," belonging to *him* and to no other person, in such a way that he may sell it, consume it, alter it or exchange it. Others have a duty to respect John's rightful ownership of his property, and they may not interfere with his lawful use or disposal of it.

Comes from the Natural Law

The right to own private property comes from the Natural Law, and it is approved by the positive law of God. By that we mean that man, by reason of the fact that he is endowed with intellect and free will, needs to own in order to be able to live according to his nature and thus attain the object for which God created him. He is not a mere beast, which by means of its senses and physical powers is able to maintain its life. He has been endowed with foresight; he can foresee what he will need in the future and therefore make provision in advance. To do this, he needs to be able to own, not only perishable things, but property which he can call his permanently, such as a plot of land, a house, etc. His natural intelligence urges him to acquire things of this description and to prevent their loss in the future.

Moreover, when a man works, he exchanges his powers, capacity, energies and labor—things which are really part and parcel of himself—for a wage. That wage is really himself under another form. It is indubitably his; so long as he violates no law, he can do what he likes with it. He can invest it, buy land with it, save it up and eventually purchase a business of his own. Whatever he obtains with his wage is still really himself under yet another form. Therefore, if he has the right to exchange his labor for a wage, he certainly has the right to own property, even that type of property which is productive of other goods that can be sold (contrary to what the socialists and communists advocate).

Necessary for the family

Again, the basic unit of society is the family. The head of the family, with the duty of providing for its needs, is the father. In order to provide for his family, as a rational being, he needs to own valuable, even lucrative property which he can pass on to his children. The right of the family in this matter is prior to the right of the State. The State might well cease to exist as such, but the world would still continue to be peopled; the race would still be made up of families, who would depend for their maintenance upon the father, who would, in turn, depend upon his ownership of money, land, a business and other property.

Also for initiative and progress

Private ownership is necessary for the safeguarding of property and initiative and thus for progress. It is a matter of common experience that we are all less careful of what is public property than of what is our own. Nor can it be denied that we will work harder in order to procure something as our own rather than for what is to be common property. To take away the right to private property would mean the destruction of all incentive to hard work, the reduction of all men to the same dead level, the prevention of personal development and the loss of personal contentment.

Scripture

In the Book of *Deuteronomy,* Moses clearly stated the law of private ownership: "Thou shalt not take nor remove thy neighbor's landmark, which thy predecessors have set in thy possession, which the Lord thy God will give thee in the land that thou shalt receive to possess." (*Deut.* 19:14). In *Exodus* we find several of God's commands in this regard: "Thou shalt not covet thy neighbor's house: neither shalt thou desire his wife, nor his servant, nor his handmaid, nor his ox, nor his ass, nor any thing that is his." (*Ex.* 20:17). Jesus Christ repeated and reinforced these commandments of the Old Law. (Cf. *Matt.* 19:18-19; *Mk.* 10:19; *Rom.* 13:9).

A limited right

The right to private ownership is not, however, an absolute and unlimited right. Some things cannot be owned (e.g. daylight) and everything must be used according to its purpose and nature. Moreover, we are social beings, living among others, to whom we have duties in justice and charity. We must not, therefore, use what we own in such a way as to injure others; rather, we have a duty to help them when possible. Our relations with others and our obligations to them limit somewhat our right to use our private property entirely as we may wish (e.g., to build a busy, dirty, noisy, stinky production plant on our private property in the middle of a residential neighborhood; zoning laws would restrict our right to use our property in such a manner, even though *we* might see fit to do so).

Nationalization

Thus, the State has the right—and even the duty—to limit in some respects, and for sufficiently grave reasons, private ownership for the good of all. In some cases, this may be done by merely regulating ownership by, for example, just taxation; that may be necessary, and it may be sufficient. But in other cases, the State may find it necessary to forbid the private ownership of some particular thing or to take over from private owners, after they have been justly compensated. Thus, nationalization of certain industries and enterprises cannot be condemned in principle on grounds of Christian ethics, but State control or ownership may never rightly reach such proportions as to amount to a practical denial of the right to private ownership. The State has no authority to abolish what is natural to man, and we have shown that the right to private property comes from the

Law of Nature itself, i.e., it proceeds from the very being of man, as God created him. Wholesale nationalization, therefore, could never be in the interest of the common good, but would always be against it.

Socialism, Communism and abuses of ownership

Both real Socialism and Communism deny that men have a right to private ownership of productive goods. According to them, all means of production must be owned and managed by the State. With this position they deny the Law of Nature, as we have explained it here. If their doctrine were to be generally accepted, untold misery would result. (And wherever they have seized control of governments, untold misery has resulted.) Those who advocate these dangerous novelties point to the evils which, they allege, have come from the prevalence of the system of private property; but the truth is that these evils have resulted from a flawed money system and often the *abuse* of private property and not from the institution of private ownership itself. And, grave as these evils can be, they are far less serious than those which would undoubtedly result from the complete abolition of private ownership of all the means of production.

No one has condemned the abuses of private property more than the Popes. Again and again, they have pointed out that the goods of the earth, which are meant by God to provide for the needs of all, and the control of them, have passed into the hands of a few, who thus control the entire stream of the life-blood of the human community. This has been allowed to happen because religion and morality have been excluded from all economic affairs, because immoral principles have dominated social life, because wealth has been abused and because the State has failed to take those actions necessary for the common good. Owners of property have in certain cases considered their rights to be absolute and incapable of restriction by any law, human or divine. Greed, avarice and dishonesty of every description have been rampant in financial, industrial and commercial life. Money has often been used as a weapon—without any regard to the needs of society.

But the Church has never ceased to urge that, however grave are the abuses of private property, they can be remedied without confiscation of all private ownership of the means of production, which is the solution of the Communists and true Socialists—and a *wrong* solution indeed. The first step toward reform must be a change in the hearts of men, which will mean a return to the Christian way of life and the application to every department of human life of the Christian principles of social justice and social charity. Politics, international relations, civil life, professional transactions, industry and commerce must be directed according to the moral law, based on God's Natural Law and man's correctly formed conscience, all as taught by Jesus Christ and His Church.

Christ did not hesitate to point out the dangers of wealth. "It is easier for a camel to pass through the eye of a needle, than for a rich man to enter into the Kingdom of Heaven." (*Matt.* 19:24). (The "eye of the needle" was the biblical term for the small door in the walls of an ancient city alongside the city gates, used at night to allow *one individual at a time* to enter; to get a camel through it required divesting him of all his burden, symbolic of the rich man's wealth. Thus the analogy used by Our Lord was perfectly apt.) He insisted, too, that we are only stewards of our possessions, of which an account must eventually be rendered to God. (*Matt.* 25:14-30). The mere fact of possessing riches is not a reason for condemnation by Christ, but neglect of the increased duties and responsibilities, which always accompany the possession of wealth, is certainly a reason for such a condemnation. (*Luke* 16:19-31).

Of course, every man has a right to own and use what is necessary for the present and future needs of himself and those dependent on him; but once those needs have been satisfied, there is a grave obligation in charity to use surplus wealth for the benefit of others, especially the poor. This obligation may be fulfilled in many ways— by giving monetary gifts, by making endowments, by providing opportunities for work and wages, by increasing wages, and so forth. But for all—rich and poor—the selfish and anti-social use of possessions is wrong.

The State obviously has the duty to safeguard the natural rights of its citizens, among which is the right of private ownership. Everything possible should be done to remove abuses and prevent their occurring in the future. Moreover, a sound policy in this matter will include efforts to increase the number of private owners, so that property may be more widely and justly distributed. The first step to be taken toward this objective ought to be the promotion of measures which will bring about a situation where every worker receives a just, living wage and will thus be enabled to acquire a certain moderate ownership of some kind of property.

The right to a living wage

The Church has always held that the system by which a man exchanges his energy or work for a wage on which to live is just in itself, although many grave injustices have arisen in the working out of the system. The contract between employer and worker must, of course, conform to the basic principles of natural justice and human dignity. Wages must be paid justly according to the value of the work done. However, efficient work requires more remuneration than that which is inefficient. Work for which educational preparation or a lengthy apprenticeship is necessary demands higher pay than that which requires no such preparation. The general principle is that equal must be rendered for equal. It must be remembered also that a man's work cannot be made the object of bargaining, like any other commodity or article. He is not mere muscle or physical strength, but a child of God, with a spiritual soul, an intellect and a supernatural destiny.

A right in justice

"That all workers are entitled to a living wage" has been repeated again and again in the social letters of the Popes. But a living wage does not mean merely enough to live on. It must be sufficient to enable a man to support himself, his wife and his family in decency and comfort and to make necessary provision for the future through saving. We add "his wife and his family" because every man has the right to marry and beget children, and thence arises the duty of supporting his wife and children. Wages should be sufficient to enable him to support his family adequately. Special provisions should be made by the Government for the assistance of large families. This can take the form of tax allowances and other forms of assistance, but these aids from the State should never be intended to take the place of just wages.

Normally, the only way in which a man can live is by hiring out his labor. By this means, therefore, he is entitled to obtain all that is necessary to enable him to live decently according to Christian standards and to support his wife and family in the same way. The value of a man's work must equal the cost of a man's living.

The obligations of employers

The duty of paying a living wage falls, in the first place, on the employer. His first duty is the payment of just wages. But the whole community, and therefore in practice, the Government, has the duty of trying to bring about economic conditions which will make it possible for every employer to pay just wages, which most governments in the world today are not doing. Christian moral principles should be sufficient to force the employer to do this, but in an age when these principles are largely ignored, it may be necessary for him to be compelled to do it by law.

There are, unfortunately, cases in which an employer cannot afford to pay a living wage without ruining his business. In this case he is not bound to pay wages which the business cannot afford, nor is he bound to pay full wages to his employees while taking less than just recompense for himself. On the other hand, he has no right to further profit beyond what is necessary and just for himself and his dependents, until he has paid his workers a just, living wage. In such cases, employers and key employees should come together and plan how best to overcome the difficulties which confront them, and they should be aided by the public authority. When even this has failed, the decision must be made as to whether the business can continue or whether some other provision should be made for the workers.

The just minimum

It is clear that wages may vary because the value of work varies. Nevertheless, there is a minimum below which wages may not fall, and that minimum is the amount necessary to support a frugal and well-behaved wage earner, with his dependents. Yet this last is not the only consideration to be taken into account when trying to assess the amount of a just wage. The condition of the particular business or industry must also be considered. Employers should therefore try to estimate wages according to a scale which will allow employees to provide adequately for themselves and their families.

An employer does not satisfy his obligations to his workers merely by paying them a just family wage. He is also bound to provide proper working conditions. Sweat-shop labor was not long ago one of the grave evils of our age. Excessive hours of work, unsanitary conditions, unreasonable demands on human strength, and the unfair employment of cheap female and child labor are examples of the evils which have been fought by associations of workers. Employers are bound to provide sufficient rest, decent hours and proper sanitary conditions for their workers.

Yet the whole community must share responsibility for the evils of sweat-shop labor. The Government which has failed to take steps to remedy bad economic conditions, the consumer who always searches out the cheapest goods, the middleman who seeks to make the maximum possible profit—all bear part of the responsibility for what thereby result in unjust working conditions.

In recent decades, however, workers combined together in unions, which became increasingly more powerful, to secure their rights, and there were many who feared that trade unions would become instruments of party politics in making unjust demands on behalf of the workers—and in many cases this *has* happened!

Nevertheless, the principle that working men have a right to join together to help one another to secure just wages and good working conditions is certainly just. The Church has always defended the right of workers to organize to secure their welfare. On the other hand, she has always insisted that they must not waste their employers' time or property and that they must give a just day's work for a just day's pay.

Strikes and Unions

The principal weapons used by organized labor to secure its rights are the strike and the threat of the strike, and the Church teaches that men are justified in withholding their labor, under certain conditions, when they suffer injustice in the conditions of their work. These "certain conditions" demand very careful consideration. They are as follows:

1) A strike can only be lawfully invoked **when there is a just and grave cause.** The demand made by the strikers must be reasonable, and the advantage to be gained must be proportionate to the harm the strike will cause themselves, their families, their employers, the industry and the country.

2) **There must be some hope of success.** Failure or compromise might leave things worse than they were before.

3) **Other solutions must have been tried and failed.**

4) **Justice and charity must always be preserved.** For example, the worker may be bound by an agreement freely entered into with his employer, which is entirely just and which has been observed by the employer. A sympathy strike by such an employee may easily be rendered unjust because the principle of justice and charity is not being observed by him.

5) **The rights of public duty must be respected.** A strike which violates the rights of a whole community cannot be lawful. Thus, a general sympathy strike, embracing most of the workers of a country, is practically certain to be unjust because the rights of the public are bound to be violated.

Although the Church admits that, in theory, strikes may well be lawful and just, the Popes have always discouraged workers in the use of this weapon. Other less harmful and less dangerous means of settlement should be employed first, with patience, charity and perseverance. It is the duty of the State to try to bring about conciliation in disputes between employers and workers when it is seen that they cannot come to a just agreement unaided. In these times the strike has been used as a political weapon by Communists and other anti-social organizations; **therefore, it is more than ever necessary**

to make sure that all the above conditions are fulfilled before the grave step of calling a strike is taken.

Co-operation between Capital and Labor

In their encyclical letters, the Popes have consistently advocated that the wage system should be modified by a system of profit sharing. It is not within the province of the Church to go into the details as to how this is to be done, but Christian sociologists agree that co-operation, co-partnership and bonus systems are all in keeping with the principle stated by the Church. It has already been stated that the aim of social legislation should be to secure a much wider and equitable distribution of property or ownership. The Church advocates profit-sharing as a means to this end. Through it, workers would be enabled to save, achieve a certain amount of independence, and generally rise above that hand-to-mouth existence which destroys peace and foments discontent.

It ought to be obvious that neither Capital nor Labor has any right to all the fruits of industry. Whatever is produced is the result of the combined efforts of Capital and Labor, and therefore both have a just right to a share of the profits. Neither, however, will secure its rights so long as each is pitted against the other like two armies engaged in war. Capital and Labor should be co-operators in production for their own well-being and for the good of the community at large. Capital cannot do without Labor, nor Labor without Capital; both have identical interests. Common-sense demands that they combine together for the benefit of each and the good of all.

Unfortunately, Capital and Labor have often ceased to represent merely the co-operating factors in industry; they have often become two opposed social classes, pledged to war with one another. Unless this class war—which it has been part of Communist ideology purposely to foment—is brought to an end, there can be no hope of any real solution to the grave social problems of our times.

Vocational organizations

Pope Pius XI in his great encylical letter, *On The Reconstruction of the Social Order*, wrote that the primary duty of the State and of all good citizens is to abolish conflict between the classes and thus to foster and promote harmony between the various ranks of society. Therefore, he went on, the aim of social legislation must be the establishment of vocational groups.

A vocational group may be defined as a public institution intermediate between private industry and the State, which exists for the purpose of promoting the common good of a profession and of those engaged in that profession—a group comparable to the guilds of the Middle Ages.

The prevalent preoccupation of the national legislature of many countries with industrial concerns is regarded by the Popes as offending against the principle that it is unjust for a larger and higher organization to arrogate to itself functions which can be efficiently performed by smaller and lower bodies. The government's duty is to watch, restrain, direct and stimulate, as circumstances suggest or necessity demands. If governments would confine themselves to that duty in regard to industrial life, they would be able to carry out with greater freedom, power and success the tasks that really belong to them, because they alone can effectively accomplish these. It is *society* that should be corporative or vocational, not the *State*. The vocational order should not be something superimposed on society by the State, but rather an organic growth among the subjects of the State. The government should never be regarded as sort of the highest vocational union. It is nothing of the kind.

Functions of vocational groups

Needless to say, there can be no lasting social reform apart from the basic Christian principles of charity and justice. Vocational groups could scarcely come into existence, and they certainly could not achieve their objectives, unless society effectively recognizes the teaching of Christ. Pope Pius XI summed up the matter in the following important passage from his letter on Communism: "It is of the utmost importance to foster in all classes an intensive program of social education adapted to the varying needs of intellectual culture. It is necessary with all care and diligence to procure the widest possible diffusion of the teachings of the Church, even among the working classes . . . . **The reign of justice and charity** in social-economic relations can ONLY be accomplished when professional and inter-professional organizations, based on the solid foundations of Christian teaching, constitute under forms adapted to different places and circumstances, what used to be called guilds." (emphasis added).

Appendix 1

The Church Through the Centuries

The First Century: The foundation of the Church by God the Son, Jesus Christ. The commissioning of the Apostles. Persecution by the Jews. The martyrdom of St. Stephen. The conversion of St. Paul. St. Peter establishes his See at Rome. St. Paul's missionary journeys. The persecution of Nero. The destruction of Jerusalem. The persecution of Domitian. St. John at Patmos.

The Second Century: The infant Church is in conflict with paganism. Continuous persecution by the Roman Emperors and attacks upon Christianity by heathen philosophers. Writings of SS. Ignatius, Papuas, Irenaeus, Polycarp, Justin and others. The Gnostic and Montanist heresies. Controversy about Easter and St. Victor's assertion of Roman Primacy.

The Third Century: Persecution continues. Many saintly martyrs. The early Fathers—SS. Hippolytus, Gregory the Wonder-Worker, Cornelius, Cyprian and others. Also Clement of Alexandria, Origen and Tertullian. The Manichean and Anti-trinitarian heresies and the Novatian schism. Conflict with neo-Platonism. Co-ordination in worship, government and penitential discipline.

The Fourth Century: Christianity spreads; the Roman Empire becomes Christian. The Church is established in Armenia, Iberia and Abyssinia. Constantine is victorious; the Edicts of Toleration are issued. The discovery of the Holy Cross. Renewed persecution in Persia and the short persecution of Julian the Apostate. The beginnings of monastic life under SS. Paul, Pachomius, Anthony of the Desert and others. The first General Council at Nicea (325) and the second at Constantinople (381). The Doctors of the Church: SS. Athanasius, Basil, Cyril of Jerusalem, Gregory Nazianzen, John Chrysostom, Hilary, Ambrose, Ephrem and other writers. The Donatist, Arian and lesser heresies.

The Fifth Century: St. Patrick in Ireland; St. Ninian in Scotland; St. Remigius among the Franks; St. Valentine in the Tyrol and St. Severin in Austria. Terrible persecutions in Persia. Alaric, Attila and Genseric invade Rome. General Councils at Ephesus (431) and Chalcedon (451) define the dogma of the Incarnation. The Doctors of the Church: SS. Cyril of Alexandria, Jerome, Augustine, Peter Chrysologus and Pope Leo I. Pelagian, Nestorian, Monophysite and other heresies.

The Sixth Century: St. Augustine in England. Foundation of the Benedictine Order. Fifth General Council at Constantinople (553). Pope St. Gregory the Great.

The Seventh Century: The Church continues to spread and consolidate in England, Switzerland, Bavaria and other parts of Germany, Belgium and Frisia. The Holy Cross was recovered by Emperor Heraclius. Sixth General Council at Constantinople (680-681). Among the notable Saints are Isidore of Seville, Wilfrid of York, Cuthbert, Benedict Biscop, Columban and Gall.

The Eighth Century: A time of peril. Spain is conquered by Moslem Saracens. The Iconoclast (image-breaking) controversy. After conflict between the Popes and the Emperors, Pope Leo III and Charlemagne undertake to create an Empire in which Church and State can work harmoniously. St. Boniface converts Germany and is martyred. The seventh General Council at Nicea (787) condemns Iconoclasm. Writers include St. Bede and St. John Damascene.

The Ninth Century: The spread of the Church continues in Germany, Denmark, Sweden, Bulgaria. The Holy Roman Empire is established under Charlemagne (800). Eighth General Council at Constantinople (869) condemns Photius, who began the Greek Schism.

The Tenth Century: The Church spreads into Poland, Russia and Hungary. The Benedictine monastery at Cluny is founded. A few of the great Saints include SS. Dunstan and Odo of Canterbury and St. Stephen, king of Hungary.

The Eleventh Century: The renewal of the Greek Schism under Michael Cerularius (1053). Reform of the Church by Pope St. Gregory VII (Hildebrand), who asserts the rights of the Church against the civil authority. Conflict of St. Anselm with William II and Henry I of England. Founding of great contemplative Orders, the Carthusians and Cistercians. The first Crusade (reaches Jerusalem in 1099). Work of St. Peter Damian.

The Twelfth Century: The Church still spreading, especially in Finland. The Crusades preached by St. Bernard. Conflict of Frederick Barbarossa with the Church. Martyrdom of St. Thomas of Canterbury. The third Crusade. Ninth, tenth and eleventh General Councils held at Rome (1123, 1139, 1179). Waldensian heresy. Growth of Christian art. Establishment of many schools.

The Thirteenth Century: The Church in Prussia and China. Attempts to convert the Mohammedans. Conflict of the Church with Frederick II. St. Louis IX in France. Crusades continue. Franciscans, Dominicans, Poor Clares, Carmelites, Servites and other religious orders are founded. Twelfth, thirteenth and fourteenth General Councils held (1215, 1245, 1274). SS. Francis of Assisi, Thomas Aquinas, Bonaventure, Dominic, Albert the Great, Anthony of Padua, Simon Stock, Edmund Rich, Clare, Gertrude and many others. The Holy Land evacuated.

The Fourteenth Century: The century begins with a conflict between Pope Boniface VIII and Philip of France. The Popes move to Avignon. The fifteenth General Council at Vienne (1311-1313). Wycliffe's heresy. The Black Plague (1315-1325). The Great Western Schism (1378-1417, not a schism, but confusion as to who was Pope of two, then three, claimants). St. Catherine of Siena (1347-1380) is the principal Saint. Mysticism was encouraged by writings of Henry Suso, John Ruysbroeck and John Tauler.

The Fifteenth Century: The Great Western Schism continues for seventeen years. St. Joan of Arc burned. Brief reunion with the Greeks. The Turks capture Constantinople (1453). Printing is invented. Spanish Inquisition occurs. America is discovered. Sixteenth and seventeenth General Councils (1414-1418, 1431-1443). SS. Vincent Ferrer, Bernardine of Siena, Lawrence Justinian, John Capistran. Heresy of John Huss. Beginning of Renaissance.

The Sixteenth Century: The Church spreads in India and Japan (St. Francis Xavier), in the Philippines, America, Mexico, Chile, Peru, Paraguay, Brazil. The Protestant Reformation begins (1517). Persecutions occur in Europe. Christendom is divided anew. John Knox in Scotland. The Catholic Counter-Reformation: foundation of the Jesuits, Oratorians, Capuchins, etc. Eighteenth and Nineteenth General Councils held (1512-1517, 1545-1563), the latter being the famous Council of Trent. Many famous Saints: SS. Ignatius Loyola, Francis Xavier, Philip Neri, Teresa of Avila, Pius V, etc.

The Seventeenth Century: Continued expansion of the Church, especially in America. SS. Rose of Lima, Martin de Porres, John Massias, Turibius, Isaac Jogues and companions. Widespread persecution. The Galileo case. Jansenism and Quietism condemned. SS. Robert Bellarmine, Francis de Sales, Vincent de Paul, John Eudes, John Baptist de la Salle, Peter Claver, etc. Apparitions of the Sacred Heart to St. Margaret Mary.

The Eighteenth Century: Missions in China and Korea. Jesuits suppressed (1773-1814). Some relief for English Catholics. French Revolution begins (1789). Growth of skepticism and the decline of faith. The Redemptorists and Passionists founded by SS. Alphonsus and Paul of the Cross respectively. Other Saints include SS. Louis-Marie de Montfort, Benedict Joseph Labre, Leonard of Port Maurice. Bishop Challoner's work for the Catholic revival in England. The Quakers and Methodists founded.

The Nineteenth Century: Conflict between Napoleon and Pope Pius VII (1800-1815). Jesuits reinstated (1814). Persecution at different times in France, Switzerland, Spain, Portugal, Mexico, Prussia, etc. Catholic Emancipation and revival in England, with the restoration of the Hierarchy and conversion of Newman, Manning, Faber and others through the Oxford Movement. Dogmatic definition of the Immaculate Conception (1854). Great progress in America. Pius IX's Syllabus of Errors (1864). The First Vatican Council (1869-1870) and definition of Papal Infallibility. Kulturkampf in Germany (1871-1891). Spoliation of the Papal States (1870). Social Encyclicals of Leo XIII. SS. Catherine Labourè, John Vianney, John Bosco, Gabriel Possenti, Bernadette Soubirous, Therese of Lisieux, etc. Our Lady reveals the Miraculous Medal (1830), and appears at Lourdes to St. Bernadette (1858).

The Twentieth Century: The epic spread of the Church in Africa. Native clergy in the mission fields. St. Pius X (1903-1914) promotes frequent Communion and reforms Church music. Condemnation of Modernism. The World Wars (1914-18; 1939-45). Spread of Communism. Lateran Treaty restores temporal sovereignty of the Popes (1929). Growth of the lay apostolate, Catholic Action. New Code of Canon Law (1918). Persecutions in Russia and Eastern Europe, Spain, Mexico, Northern Ireland, etc. SS. Gemma Galgani, Frances Cabrini, Maria Goretti. Appearances of Our Lady at Fatima (1917) and definition of her Assumption into Heaven (1950). Success of the Communist Revolution in China and Cuba. The Korean War (1950-1953). Second Vatican Council (1962-1965) and a new approach to pastoral affairs. The re-emergence of Modernism. The Vietnam War. The age of the laity. A second New Code of Canon Law (1983). The collapse of the Communist governments in Eastern Europe. The European Union and other international trade arrangements. The melding of the world into more of an economic unity. The beginning collapse of nationalism. The collapse of the Faith in the West and its phenomenal growth in some Third World countries.

Appendix 2

The Principal Heresies

Arianism was the first great heresy which rocked the infant Church. Its founder was Arius (d. 336), who denied that Christ was God, saying He was inferior to the Father. The Church's champion against Arianism was St. Athanasius, and the heresy was condemned at the first General Council of the Church, held at Nicea in 325.

Manicheism was founded by Mani (216-276), a Persian. It taught that in the beginning there existed two opposing principles: one good, the other evil. These two fought for supremacy, and the world was created. Christ had no real body, and He came to teach men the distinction between the kingdoms of light and darkness. To assure the triumph of the kingdom of light, marriage, the use of meat and wine, and ordinary work were forbidden the elect. St. Augustine refuted Manicheism, and it was finally condemned at the Twelfth General Council, the Fourth Council of the Lateran in 1215.

Macedonianism was founded by Macedonius (d. 362). It denied the Godhead of the Holy Ghost and was condemned at the First Council of Constantinople in 381.

Pelagianism was founded by Pelagius, who probably came from Britain. It denied Original Sin and taught that grace, actual or sanctifying, is unnecessary. St. Augustine was the champion of orthodoxy against this heresy, which was condemned at the Council of Carthage in 418, afterwards confirmed by the Pope, and at the General Council of Ephesus, 431.

Nestorianism was founded by Nestorius, Bishop of Constantinople (d. 451). It taught that there are two separate persons in Christ, of one of which Our Lady is the Mother. She is not Mother of God but only of the man, Christ. Nestorianism was condemned at the Council of Ephesus in 431 and at the Council of Chalcedon in 451.

Monophysitism (also called Eutychianism) is named after Eutyches, a monk. It denied that there are two natures in Christ. It was condemned at the Council of Chalcedon in 451.

Semipelagianism was an error of some saintly monks who lived near Marseilles about 428. They said that the beginning of faith and the first desire for goodness arise from man's powers alone, without the help of God's grace. It was condemned at the Second Council of Orange in 529, which was confirmed by Pope Boniface II.

Monothelitism in the 7th century denied the existence of a separate human will in Christ. It was condemned at the Third Council of Constantinople in 680.

Iconoclasm, or image breaking, was originated under the leadership of Leo the Isaurian (d. 741). It rejected all veneration of images. It was refuted by St. John Damascene and condemned at the Second Council of Nice in 787.

The Greek Heresy and Schism was led by Photius, who was intruded into the See of Constantinople in 857. He was deposed and condemned by the Fourth Council of Constantinople in 869, but the Schism was later completed by the Patriarch of Constantinople, Michael Cerularius who, in 1054, rejected the supremacy of the Pope and established the so-called Greek "Orthodox" Church, which is heretical because it teaches that the Holy Ghost proceeds from the Father alone and not from the Father and the Son.

Berengarius (999-1088) was Archdeacon of Angers in France and denied the Real Presence of Jesus Christ in the Eucharist. He was condemned at Rome in 1078 and died reconciled to the Church.

Albigensianism, so-called after the people of Albi in the south of France, was really a revival of Manicheism. It taught that there are two Gods and two Christs; it denied all the Sacraments and the Resurrection of the Body. It recommended suicide and condemned marriage. It was condemned at the Third Lateran Council in 1179 and the Fourth in 1215.

Waldensianism was founded by Waldo, a merchant of Lyons, about 1175. It denied Purgatory, prayer for the dead and indulgences. Claiming to practice Christianity in its pristine purity, it maintained that it is gravely wrong for a judge to pronounce a sentence of death, for anyone to take an oath, or for the clergy to own any, even the smallest property. Waldensianism was condemned at the Third Lateran Council in 1179.

Wycliffe (1324-1384) was probably a Yorkshireman; he claimed that the Bible is the sole rule of Faith, the Pope is not the Head of the Church, the will is not free, and Transubstantiation (the changing of bread and wine at Mass into the Body and Blood of Christ) is untrue; also that man is bound to sin, and God approves of sin. He claimed that Confession is useless, that sinful clergy should be executed, and that mortal sin invalidates the use of ecclesiastical powers. These errors were also taught by John Huss (1369-1415) in Bohemia after Wycliffe's death and were condemned by the Council of Constance in 1414.

Lutheranism was started (1517) by Martin Luther (d. 1546). It is based on the double principle of invincible concupiscence and justification by faith alone. Luther taught the private interpretation of Scripture, denied the Mass, ridiculed indulgences, abolished Confession and mortification, denied Papal Supremacy, and repudiated clerical celibacy. His doctrines were condemned by the Council of Trent, which met from 1545 to 1563.

Calvinism was founded by John Calvin (d. 1648). It is essentially absolute predestinationism. By a direct act of His will, God wills the salvation of some and the damnation of others. Man, vitiated by Original Sin, has no free will. Calvinism is now represented by the Presbyterians. It was condemned at the Council of Trent.

Jansenism was founded by Jansenius (d. 1638), who was the Bishop of Ypres. It taught that men are not completely free from internal forces, some of God's commandments are impossible, good works by unbelievers are sinful, and Christ did not die for the whole race, but only for a few privileged souls. These errors of Jansenius and others of himself and his followers were condemned by Pope Urban VIII in 1642 and by Pope Clement XI in 1705.

Modernism is a heresy that denies all supernatural religion, Divine Revelation, the divinity of Christ and the authority of the Church. It teaches that the religious soul must draw from itself the objects and the motives of its faith and realize the existence of God from the inner conscience and craving after the divine. Modernism was condemned by Pope St. Pius X, who called it "the summation of all error." The French leader of the Modernists was Alfred Loisy (d. 1919). Modernism went quiescent after the condemnation of St.

Pius X (1907), but then re-emerged during and after Vatican Council II (1962-1965) and remained rife through the rest of the 20th Century and into the 21st Century. Many of the laity would even unwittingly utter Modernist beliefs when they would say things like, "The Church doesn't teach that any more," which is an extension of the Modernist error that beliefs change with time and people's perceptions of the truth.

A Testimonial
About The Catholic Church

"WHEN I reflect upon that Church's long, unbroken continuity, extending back to the very days of the Apostles; when I recall her grand, inspiring traditions, her blessed Sacraments, her immemorial language, her changeless creed, her noble ritual, her stately ceremonies, her priceless works of art, her wondrous unity of doctrine, her apostolic authority, her splendid roll of saints and martyrs, reaching up like Jacob's ladder, and uniting Heaven and earth: when I reflect upon the intercession for us of those saints and martyrs, enhanced by the petitions of the Blessed Mother of Our Lord; and last, but not least, when I consider the abiding presence of the Saviour on her altars, I feel that this ONE, HOLY, APOSTOLIC CHURCH has given me certainty for doubt, order for confusion, sunlight for darkness, and substance for shadow. It is the Breath of Life, and the Wine of the Soul, instead of the unsatisfying husks; the father's welcome with the ring and the robe, instead of the weary exile in the wilderness of doubt. It is true that the prodigal must retrace the homeward road, and even enter the doorway of the Mansion on his knees; but within, what a recompense!"

—John L. Stoddard
Rebuilding a Lost Faith

What Should I Do Now?

"Be you therefore perfect, as also your Heavenly Father is perfect." (*Matt.* 5:48). We all have the job of perfecting ourselves, so that when we die, we shall be worthy to enter the presence of God, having no sin on our souls and no spiritual debts left over from whatever sins we may have committed. At the time of our judgment before the Tribunal of God, it will be too late to rectify our lives and make amends to the justice of God for the sins we have committed. Rather, God now gives us *time* in which to work out our salvation. But we should not delay, either in making our conversion to God or in beginning a *serious* effort to become perfect. For nothing imperfect shall be worthy of entering the presence of God. Think of going to the Judgment as preparing for your wedding: You would never think of coming before the altar of God to be married with a spot on your wedding gown or tuxedo. You would want your clothes to be perfect. God has the same attitude about us: "He hath made nothing defective." (*Ecclesiasticus* 42:25). Moral imperfection and disorder have entered the world because of the Original Sin of Adam and Eve, and have been increased by our own personal sins.

But God has taken measures to help man rectify his sinfulness and be worthy to enter His presence when he dies. "For God so loved the world, as to give his only begotten Son, that whosoever believeth in him, may not perish, but have life everlasting. For God sent not his Son into the world, to judge the world, but that the world may be saved by him. He that believeth in him is not judged. But he that doth not believe is already judged: because he believeth not in the name of the only begotten Son of God. And this is the judgment: because the light is come into the world, and men loved darkness rather than light: for their works were evil." (*John* 3:16-19).

In the Book of *Ezechiel*, God inspired the prophet to write at length, twice, on this subject—in Chapters 18 and 33—so there would be no doubt about this issue. Consider these statements: "Is it my will that a sinner should die [i.e., go to Hell for eternity], saith the Lord God, and not that he should be converted from his ways, and live? But if the just man turn himself away from his justice, and do iniquity according to all the abominations which the wicked man useth to work, shall he live? All his justices which he hath done, shall not be remembered: in the prevarication, by which he hath prevaricated, and in his sin, which he hath committed, in them he shall die. And you have said: The way of the Lord is not right. Hear ye, therefore, O house of Israel: Is it my way that is not right, and are not rather your ways perverse? For when the just turneth himself away from his justice, and committeth iniquity, he shall die therein: in the injustice that he hath wrought he shall die. And when the wicked turneth himself away from his wickedness, which he hath wrought, and doeth judgment, and justice: he shall save his soul alive. Because he considereth and turneth away himself from all his iniquities which he hath wrought, he shall surely live, and not die. And the children of Israel say: The way of the Lord is not right. Are not my ways right, O house of Israel, and are not rather your ways perverse? Therefore will I judge every man according to his ways, O house of Israel, saith the Lord God. Be converted, and do penance for all your iniquities: and iniquity shall not be your ruin. Cast away from you all your transgressions, by which you have transgressed, and make to yourselves a new heart, and a new spirit: and why will you die, O house of Israel? **For I desire not the death of him that dieth, saith the Lord God, return ye and live.**" (*Ezechiel* 18:23-32, emphasis added). Much the same is then repeated in Chapter 33, which is summed up when God says: **"As I live, saith the Lord God, I desire not the death of the wicked, but that the wicked turn from his way, and live."** (*Ezechiel* 33:11, emphasis added).

What this means is that God **loves** us and wants us to be saved! But the issue is very clear, we must live a morally good life in order to be saved. And Our Lord made the issue even clearer with regard to *how* to do this: "No man cometh to the Father but by me." (*John* 14:6). "I am the way, the truth and the life." (*John* 14:6). "I am come that they may have life and have it more abundantly." (*John* 10:10). "Except you eat the flesh of the Son of Man, and drink his blood [i.e., receive Holy Communion], you shall not have life in you." (*John* 6:54). "Without me you can do nothing." (*John* 15:5).

"I am the door. By me, if any man enter in, he shall be saved." (*John* 10:9). "Thou art Peter; and upon this rock I will build my church and the gates of hell shall not prevail against it." (*Matt.* 16:18). "He that believeth and is baptized shall be saved: but he that believeth not shall be condemned." (*Mark* 16:16).

In other words, we need Our Lord, we need His Church, in order to be saved, for it is only through Him that we have the "way" to eternal life. And that "way" is Our Lord, who teaches us, through His Church, the certain and true knowledge of what we must do to be saved; plus, He gives us Sanctifying Grace (or a sharing in the life of God, which is imparted to us in Baptism) and the actual graces, or spiritual assistance, to overcome our sins and act morally well.

Quoting Isaias, St. Paul says: " 'In an accepted time I have heard thee; and in the day of salvation, I have helped thee.' [*Isaias* 49:8]. Behold **now is the acceptable time;** behold **now is the day of salvation."** (*2 Cor.* 6:2, emphasis added). What St. Paul is saying is that the matter of salvation is of such importance, that there is **no reason whatsoever to defer making the step of converting and being baptized** . . . and doing so right now, today, so that we can put ourselves on God's side, in His good graces, and begin to work out our salvation, as St. Paul says, "in fear and trembling" (*Philippians* 2:12), lest we fall and go astray and be lost eternally.

"What should I do now?" That, Dear Reader, is *the* question. The answer is fourfold, depending on where you stand spiritually:

1. If you are a non-Catholic, you should approach the Church, begin instruction, become a Catholic, and practice the Faith seriously and faithfully.
2. If you are a fallen-away Catholic, you should return to the Faith, make a sincere Confession, immediately abandon at least all your mortal sins, and resolve to learn the Faith better and to practice it perfectly till death.
3. If you are a tepid or lukewarm Catholic, you should start earnestly to read about the Faith and to begin to practice it more faithfully and more ardently.
4. If you are a dedicated Catholic, you should pick up the pace of your spiritual life, read and pray more, and ask God to help you gain perfection.

We all need to heed those extremely powerful words of Our Lord in the *Apocalypse* (*Revelation*): "Because thou art lukewarm and neither cold, nor hot, I will begin to vomit thee out of my mouth." (*Apoc.* 3:16). Our Lord wants us to be on fire with love of Him and His "Holy Faith"—not lukewarm. "The first commandment of all is . . . thou shalt love the Lord thy God with thy whole heart, and with thy whole soul, and with thy whole mind, and with thy whole strength . . . And the second is like to it: Thou shalt love thy neighbor as thyself. There is no other commandment greater than these." (*Mark* 12:29-30).

And how are we to develop such an ardent love? Can we just "bootstrap" ourselves up to this level of caring in one gigantic step? Obviously not! It is to be achieved by much smaller steps, and relying on the grace of God. Gaining that level of love will require our really learning what Our Lord's Gospel contains, and practicing it. We have to read, and inquire, and let nothing defer or dissuade us in our quest to grow in the knowledge and love of God.

But the reward is great and beyond anything anyone can imagine. St. Paul, who was "caught up to the third heaven" (*2 Cor.* 12:2), describes it thus: "Eye hath not seen, nor ear heard, neither hath it entered into the heart of man what things God hath prepared for them that love him." (*1 Cor.* 2:9). May your quest be a successful one and may we all one day meet in God's holy hill, to rejoice forever in His company and that of all the Saints. May God bless you and direct you.

Publisher
May 13, 2002
St. Robert Bellarmine and
Our Lady of Fatima

About the Author

Fr. Francis Joseph Ripley was a priest of great zeal for souls, with a particular zeal for the reconversion of his native England. Powerful influences on his missionary spirit were his devout Catholic parents—particularly his father—and Mr. Frank Duff, founder of the Legion of Mary, who became a close personal friend.

Francis Ripley was born in 1912 in Windleshaw, St. Helens, Lancashire, England, a region long known for its sterling Catholic Faith dating back to the penal days. When Francis' mother died suddenly in 1916 leaving three little children—Francis being the eldest—the widowed father's two sisters supplied a mother's care, maintaining the home in the same spirit of Catholic fervor. After graduating with honors from the local Catholic grammar school, Francis entered the Jesuit novitiate in London. He was supremely happy there, but persistent ill health indicated that this was not his vocation. Recovering, he entered the Capuchin novitiate and there studied philosophy for three years, but when his superiors decided he was more suited to the secular priesthood, he entered the archdiocesan seminary at Upholland in 1935. There he took first prize in dogmatic theology for three years in a row.

Francis Ripley was ordained in 1939. He was sent to the Gregorian University in Rome for post-graduate study in moral theology and canon law. This was followed by parish work, military service as a chaplain and squadron leader in the Royal Air Force, and frequent speaking on the outdoor platforms of the Catholic Evidence Guild—a work which he had begun as a student. During these early years as a priest, Fr. Ripley wrote a work on the Legion of Mary called *Terrible as an Army*, and, with Frank Duff (under the pen name of F. S. Mitchell), a major work on Catholic Action entitled *Souls at Stake*. Also at this time he penned two small works on marriage called *Letters to Muriel* and *Letters to Molly*. Fr. Ripley's most famous book, *This Is the Faith*, was composed of a series of twice-weekly talks which he had given many times for non-Catholics under the auspices of the Legion of Mary. The first presentation of the talks brought in over 100 converts in three years, with the result that similar ventures were undertaken in many other places, and such inquiry classes became an established method of winning converts. *This Is the Faith* was reprinted many times in England and the United States, with sales soon exceeding 100,000 in North America. The book became a standard textbook in schools and colleges, as well as being used in inquiry classes and for the instruction of converts.

Fr. Ripley joined and eventually would become superior of the Catholic Missionary Society, London, which gave inquiry classes and preached the Faith to non-Catholics. In years to come, Fr. Ripley would also take part in or lead various other initiatives aimed at conversions, including serving as chairman of the Catholic Truth Society and serving as director of the Catholic Information Society in Liverpool from 1962-1970, as well as continually encouraging the work of the Legion of Mary. During his life, Fr. Ripley also edited and/or managed Catholic periodicals including *Flarepath* (Catholic periodical of the Royal Air Force), *Catholic Truth* and *Catholic Gazette*. Fr. Ripley authored many books, booklets, articles and tapes, and he lectured in the United States in 1947, 1973, 1974, 1976 and 1989. He was a canon of the Archdiocese of Liverpool from 1980-1991. Fr. Francis Ripley went to his eternal reward on January 7, 1998.

Books by Fr. Francis Ripley include: *Priest of Christ*; *Your Sunday Gospels*; *A Priest For Ever*; *One Christ, One Church*; *Talks to Legionaries*; *A Basic Guide to Religious Instruction*; *The Apostolate of the Laity*; *Pope Paul Says . . .* (as editor); *The St. Peter Catechism of Catholic Doctrine*; *Frank Duff*; *The Diary of a Small Town Priest*; *The Rosary and the Blessed Virgin in Pre-Reformation England*; *201 New Prayers*; and *Mary, Mother of the Church* (as editor).

The above information was compiled from *Catholic Authors: Contemporary Biographical Sketches*, edited by Matthew Hoehn, O.S.B., B.L.S., St. Mary's Abbey, Newark, 1952; and from *Contemporary Authors* (Gale database).

SAINT BENEDICT✝PRESS

Saint Benedict Press, founded in 2006, is the parent company for a variety of imprints including TAN Books, Catholic Courses, Benedict Bibles, Benedict Books, and Labora Books. The company's name pays homage to the guiding influence of the Rule of Saint Benedict and the Benedictine monks of Belmont Abbey, North Carolina, just a short distance from the company's headquarters in Charlotte, NC.

Saint Benedict Press is now a multi-media company. Its mission is to publish and distribute products reflective of the Catholic intellectual tradition and to present these products in an attractive and accessible manner.

TAN·BOOKS

TAN Books was founded in 1967, in response to the rapid decline of faith and morals in society and the Church. Since its founding, TAN Books has been committed to the preservation and promotion of the spiritual, theological and liturgical traditions of the Catholic Church. In 2008, TAN Books was acquired by Saint Benedict Press. Since then, TAN has experienced positive growth and diversification while fulfilling its mission to a new generation of readers.

TAN Books publishes over 500 titles on Thomistic theology, traditional devotions, Church doctrine, history, lives of the saints, educational resources, and booklets.